STAR WARS ART™

POSTERS

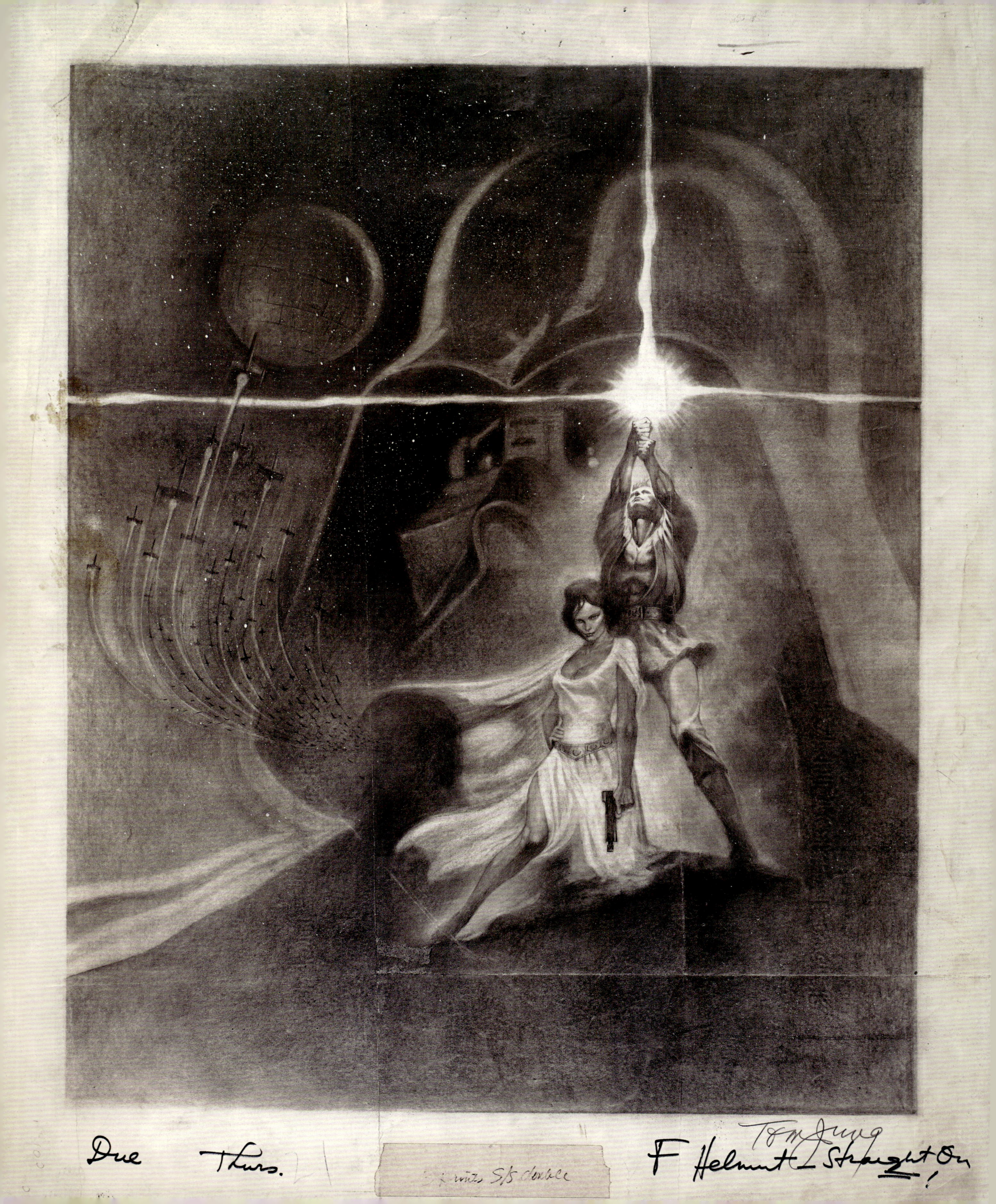
Due Thurs.
Tom Jung
F Helmut – Straight On!

STAR WARS ART™

POSTERS

FOREWORD BY **DREW STRUZAN**
INTRODUCTION BY **ROGER KASTEL**

ABRAMS, NEW YORK

CONTENTS

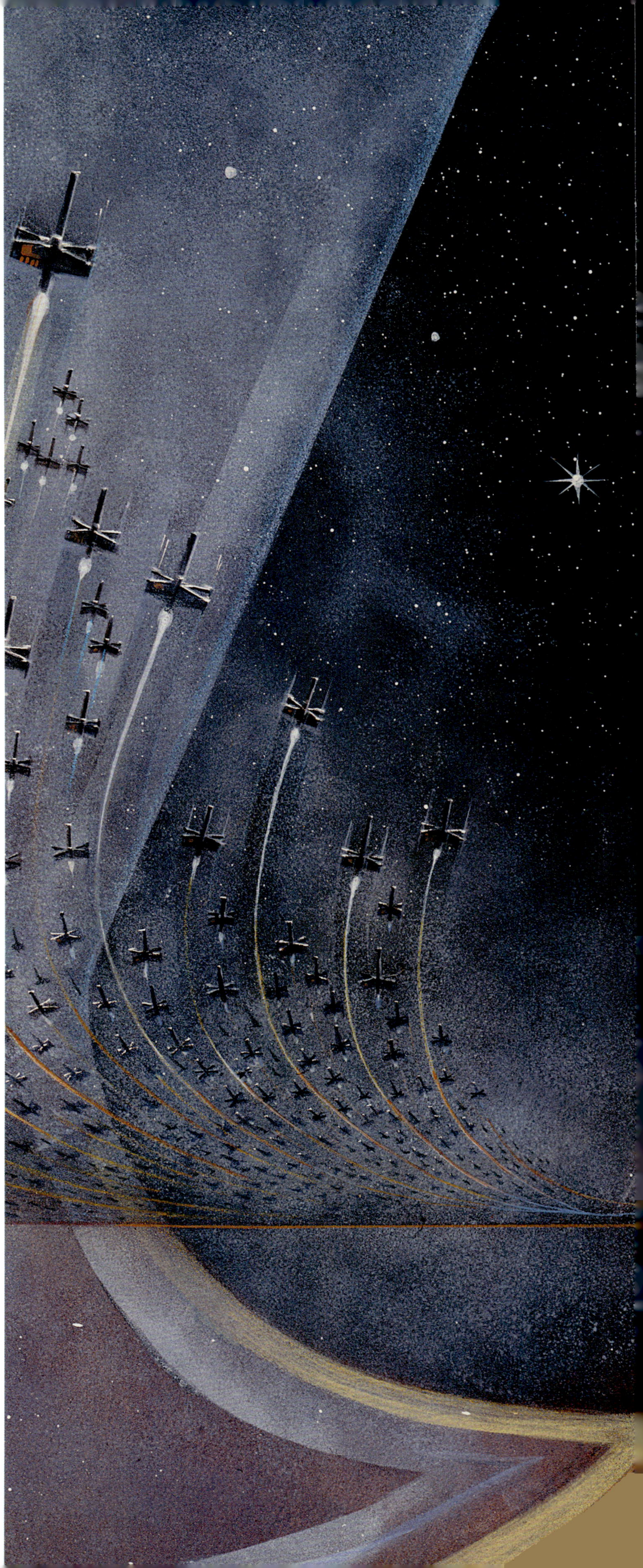

PREVIOUS SPREAD, LEFT

Tom Jung

Black-and-white concept treatment for *Star Wars* style "A" theatrical one-sheet, 1977

RIGHT (DETAIL)

Tom Jung

Final painted artwork for *Star Wars* style "A" theatrical one-sheet, 1977

PAGE SIX

Drew Struzan

Black-and-white concept treatment for *Revenge of the Jedi* theatrical advance one-sheet, 1982

PAGE NINE

Roger Kastel

Black-and-white concept treatment for *The Empire Strikes Back* style "A" ("*Gone with the Wind*") theatrical one-sheet, c. 1979

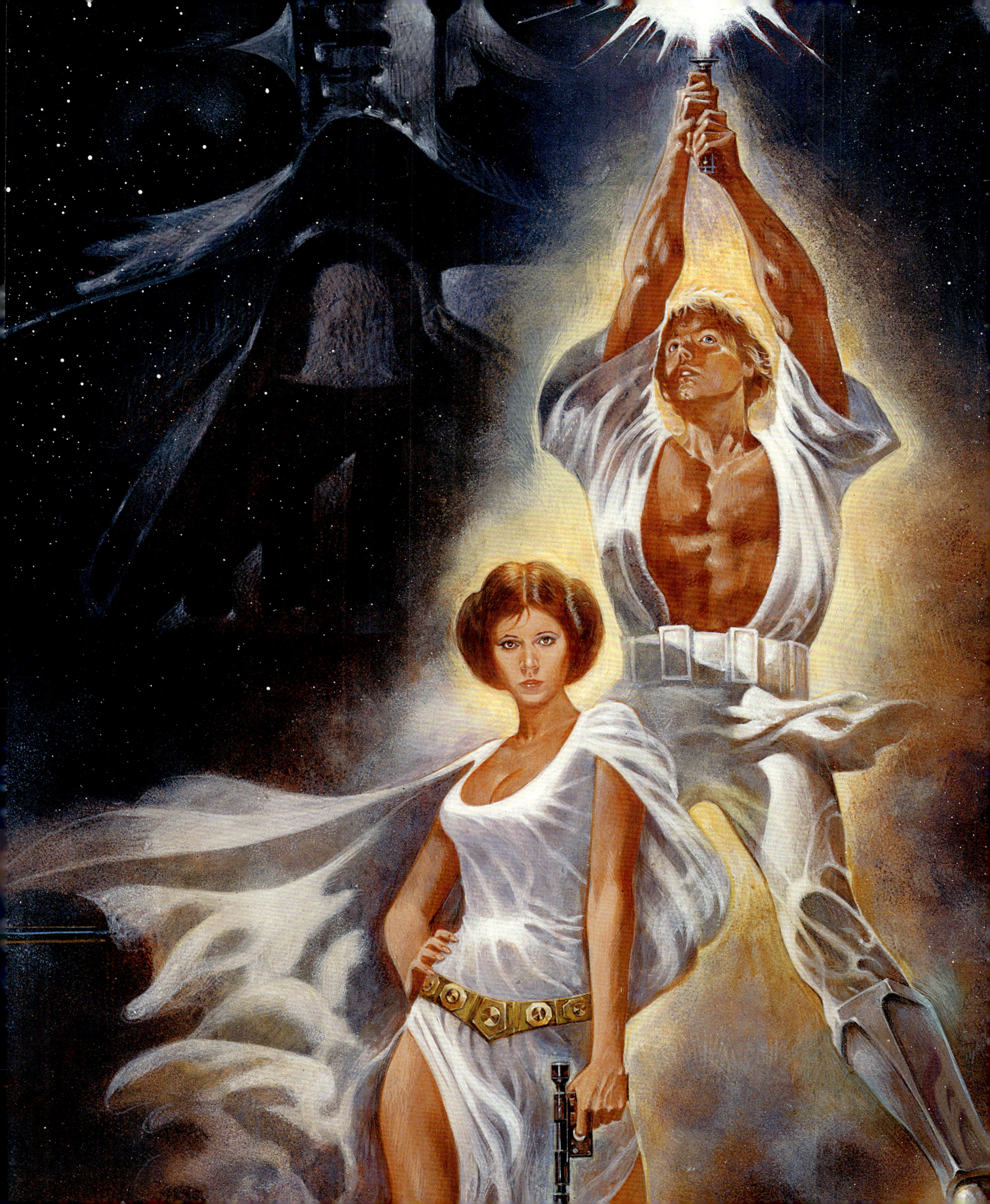

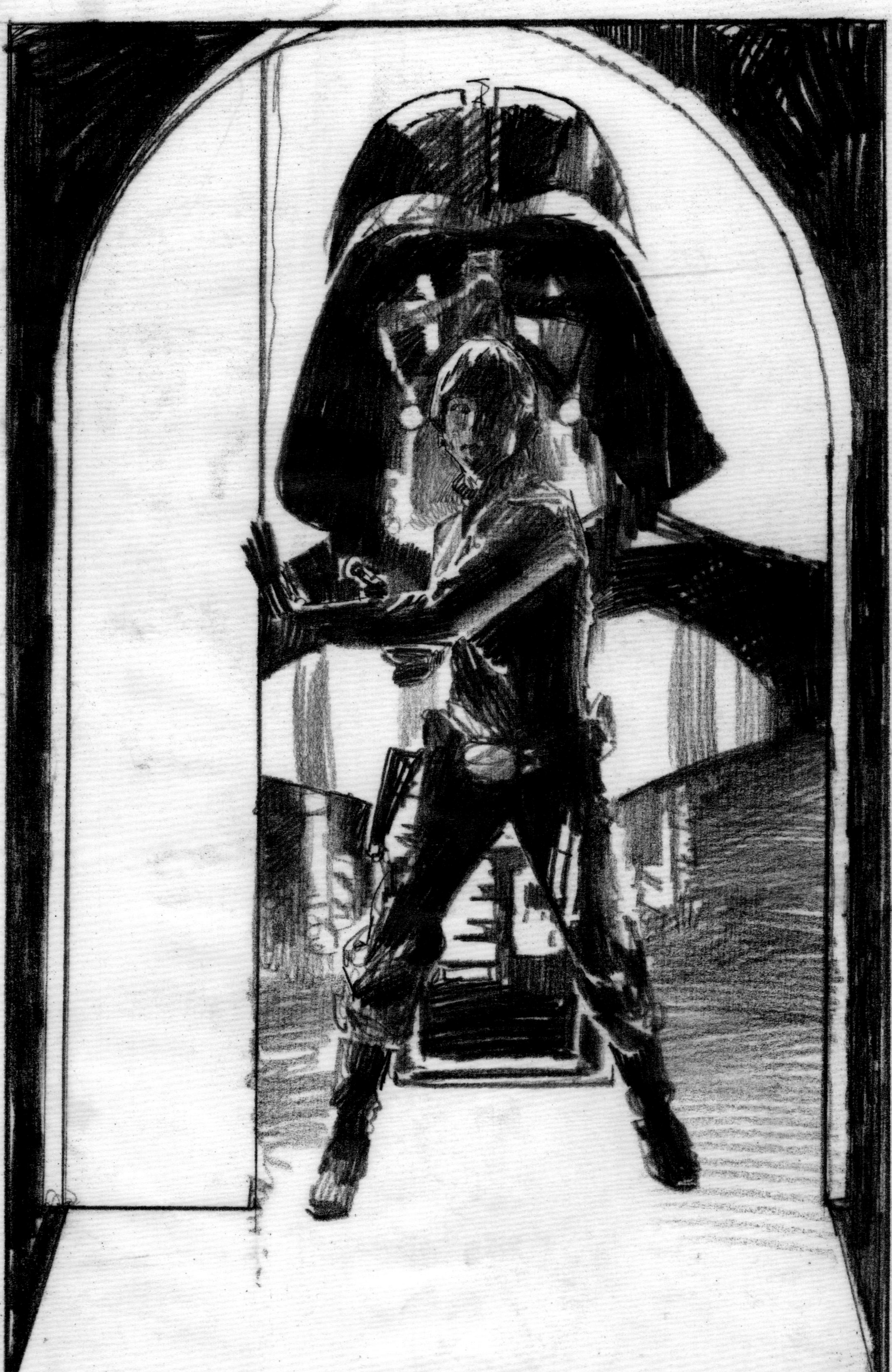

FOREWORD

Something new and exciting entered our world with the release of *Star Wars* in 1977. *Star Wars* moved the world. It changed not only movies, but also how we view ourselves, our world, our future, our language, our fantasies, our dreams, and, yes, our art. It gave us catchphrases, such as "May the Force be with you," "Let the Wookiee win," "These aren't the droids you're looking for," and (the ultimate) "Use the Force, Luke."

For me, *Star Wars* was not only a grand subject to paint; it also brought me into association with George Lucas. It was the turning point in my career. I went from relative obscurity to being a real part of a phenomenon. At the time, films generally enjoyed an opening-weekend release, saw a short run of a week or so, and were gone. But *Star Wars* kept drawing crowds. The interest did not wane for months. As a result, Lucasfilm decided to refresh the look of its marketing with a new poster.

Here's where I came in—well, not exactly.

Charles White III was commissioned to create this new poster. He was not, however, a portrait artist. Charlie had seen my work and decided to call me in as a collaborator. I painted the portraits, while he painted the hardware. Lucasfilm liked the artwork, but there was not enough space left open for the "billing block" (credits). Necessity being the mother of invention, we decided to enlarge the dimensions of the art to increase the open space and give the work an early-twentieth-century, wild-posted circus-style look. Charlie made the edges of the painting appear torn and aged. I painted a portrait of Obi-Wan that was layered "under" the edge. So it came about that it took the two of us to paint what would come to be known as the "Circus" poster for its throwback style. The poster also became the favorite of the Master, George Lucas, whom I still had not met.

It was not until 1991 that I finally encountered the *Star Wars* originator. At the time, I was working on the cover of his filmography *The Creative Impulse*. I had just finished the poster for Steven Spielberg's movie *Hook*, which had recently wrapped, and the production department was throwing a huge party. The entire parking lot of Sony Pictures was covered with three giant tents and was loaded with bands, restaurants, arcade games, cookie carts, and all manner of distractions. It seemed as if everyone who was anyone in Hollywood had been invited.

My wife and I, being pretty much out of our element, stood far to the back, watching the parade of stars pass by. Standing on the opposite side of the parade was another lone figure taking in the hoopla. My wife, Dylan, thought she recognized him from the portrait I was painting and urged me to go introduce myself. Reluctantly, I waded toward him through the crowd. "Hi, I'm Drew," I said at the top of my lungs. "Hi, I'm George," he replied at full volume, barely audible. That was all we could hear through the din. Smiling, I fought my way back to my wife. "Yup, it is George," I said. My excitement was palpable.

Later we ran into some friends who screamed, "You'll never guess who was just here, excited that he had finally met Drew Struzan." So there you have it. We had met at last, and from that day forward we have spoken and collaborated on numerous occasions. Two quiet guys. Pleased to know and be known by each other.

How can I think about or recall *Star Wars* without thinking of George? *Star Wars* is George. His mind, imagination, drive, creativity, heart, and soul are best understood by knowing his work. He is a good man, always loyal and supportive. My grand blessing in life has been the opportunity to be a part of the *Star Wars* "family" and to have been known by this good fellow, George Lucas.

Skip to December 1997.

It is the holiday season. The phone rings. George is on the line. He says something to the effect that he is releasing Special Editions of the three *Star Wars* movies. He asks me to create one work of art for the poster. Am I astonished? Uh, well, yes. "I'd be honored," I say. Well, maybe I didn't say it just that way, but that's what I felt—and then I stuck my presumptuous foot in my mouth: "Hold on . . . You have a grand opportunity here to do a triptych, three posters that will work together as one." He says, "Good idea. How do you see it?"

I began to talk off the top of my head, describing what I imagined. As I recall, six designers from Lucasfilm were listening in on the conversation. They began sketching as I was explaining. Then they sent a fax that asked, "Something like these?" Yes. Good. OK. And from there, "it" began.

Good design is simple and to the point, not rendered or flourished. The movie renders the idea. My job is to summarize and simplify a film's essence. I was given one week each to design, draw, and paint these three posters for three different films. Normally, this process takes at least a month per poster and involves comprehensive drawings that are subject to criticism, changes, and approvals even before the work goes to finish. Then the labor of love—brush to canvas. This was different.

The first piece had to be done by Christmas. The second piece was completed by New Year's. The third piece, a week into the New Year. No holidays. No weekends. Little rest for a month. Add to that the fact that I was not able to paint the images side-by-side to match and balance them. As I finished one painting, it was delivered immediately to Lucasfilm. I had to work from memory to complete the next in the series. This is the life of an illustrator. Everything is always a big rush. Everything is always a deadline. The posters all hit their openings on schedule.

Voilà! And then there were three. I could finally rest. And then, a few years later, there were six. And all along the way, dozens of book covers, postage stamps, and special projects—thirty-five years' worth of association with *Star Wars*.

When you look at my *Star Wars* works, you see my take on George's creation. When I begin a project, I look for the thing that drove the creator to make his sacrifice. People spend years of their time and power trying to bring these worlds to fruition. For my part, I think hard on their expression. I feel my way through their heart and soul and try to capture that in a single image.

One thing I've learned recently is that we think we are beings of reason and that reason is our power, but we have to admit the heart is stronger than the mind. Our hearts are at the center of our power. We can be more than what we are if we just let the Force flow within us so that we are present in every waking hour. All you have to do is choose.

George's vision has lasted nearly forty years. *Star Wars* is preparing to go for another round, offering a new generation of artists an opportunity to express their creative insight. I count it as an honor to have been granted the autonomy to circulate in the *Star Wars* orbit by its creator, to bring my talents to bear on this grand vision. I am not alone. This book is a testimony to the adage that the whole becomes greater than the sum of its parts.

Though I write of my experiences in the *Star Wars* universe, I know that all the artists represented in this volume are stars in the fantastic universe of George Lucas. I believe their experiences are all much the same as mine. Enjoy their art, their hearts, and their dreams, and get carried away with me in their wonder and visions.

God bless you my friend, George Lucas. Thirty-seven years a blessing and counting.

"May the Force be with you."

Drew Struzan

INTRODUCTION

Where to begin? I feel like a *Star Wars* interloper. . . . My connection to *The Empire Strikes Back* probably began in 1975, when I did the paperback book cover for Peter Benchley's *Jaws.* This image was also used for the movie poster, and, after *Jaws* became such a success, I started getting calls to do other movie posters, such as *The Great Train Robbery* and *Doc Savage: The Man of Bronze.*

When *Star Wars* debuted, it was a sensation. The movie posters for that first *Star Wars* film were wonderful, perfect images, and, of course, they made you want to go see the movie. For my part, as a busy illustrator, I was concentrating on my own work. Despite the attention I received from *Jaws,* doing movie posters wasn't anything I was angling for. I was mostly working on illustrations for paperbacks, as well as some for mainstream magazines, such as *Good Housekeeping* and *Argosy.* I thoroughly enjoyed illustrating paperback covers, since the subject matter was greatly varied and my use of different techniques evolved while working on them. They ranged from classics and romances to mysteries and thrillers, but none of them were space fantasy, so *The Empire Strikes Back* would turn out to be unique to me in that regard.

One Sunday, out of the blue, I received a call from someone at Lucasfilm, asking if I wanted to be involved in creating the poster for the new *Star Wars* movie. They did not have to ask me twice. I believe that they mentioned my *Jaws* poster during our conversation, and also a recent paperback cover I had illustrated for Pocket Books, *Tenants of the Earth,* a period piece about a wealthy family during the railroad era.

I wasn't the only artist that Lucasfilm called to take a crack at the poster. In all, including myself, six artists were recruited to submit designs for a poster. A week later, I was asked to go to Manhattan for a meeting, to learn about the movie and receive movie stills to work from. All the illustrators were given the same instructions, and from these we each had to come up with our own concept, or layout, for the poster.

At the time, Lucasfilm had space in a brownstone building on the East Side of Manhattan, specially set up for *The Empire Strikes Back.* After the contracts had been explained and signed, I had time to look over the movie stills—and the one that impressed me the most was of Luke Skywalker riding a tauntaun in the snow. I thought about the image and how wonderful it would be to paint. So I worked up a rough layout to show the art director, whom I had yet to meet.

When we finally did have our first meeting with him, he explained what the poster was to be about: Everything would be built around a romantic image of Princess Leia and Han Solo. It was mentioned that the *Gone with the Wind* poster, the one with Rhett Butler embracing Scarlett O'Hara, was one of George Lucas's favorite movie posters. Of course this meant that Luke on the tauntaun in the white snow, and Darth Vader, representing the dark universe endangering them, would have to shift from the central focus of my early roughs to smaller, supporting details. Even so, I liked my original layout so much that in 2008 I painted a second version for myself using that concept—it appears on page 174 of this book.

At the next meeting with the art director, we showed him pencil roughs that were then sent to Northern California for approval. Pencil roughs are usually unfinished drawings that are sketched enough to show how you want to lay out the poster, book cover, etc. For *The Empire Strikes Back,* I did a number of pencil sketches with different ideas. From my rough sketches, one was accepted, and then it was time to start painting the poster. I was excited and really looked forward to doing it.

Of course, Han Solo and Princess Leia's embrace was the main focus of the painting and became known as the *"Gone with the Wind"* poster. During the time that I worked on the poster, many adjustments were made, such as wardrobe changes, the moving of rudiments in the background, and the adding and deleting of images. Luke and the tauntaun were made larger, and feet were also added to the tauntaun. (It was a total surprise to me that the tauntaun actually had feet. In all the original movie stills I'd seen, its feet were completely covered with snow.)

While working on the poster, there was a lot of starting and stopping, as the painting was sent back and forth to California and other places for approval. This was difficult, since every change meant that I had to paint out what was already painted in and then paint a new scene over what had been there before. Amidst all the back and forth, I was also doing work for other clients, and yet somehow everything seemed to work out. In all, from that first phone call through all the revisions, starts, and stops, it took four or five months to complete the illustration for the movie poster.

Later, I had a call from Lucasfilm, asking me to come to New York City again. There was to be some additional work on the painting. It was a warm day, and I decided to go into the city dressed the way I was—for studio work—in jeans and a casual shirt. Wrong decision. I arrived at the space for what appeared to be a cocktail party in progress, with elegantly dressed people enjoying hors d'oeuvres and wine on the terrace while looking at all the *Empire* poster paintings leaning against the wall.

I met with the Lucasfilm representative. He told me that they liked what I had done and just needed me to make one more change to my painting, which he explained before handing me new stills to work from. I retrieved my painting and headed back to my studio to do the additional work and finish the poster.

The last time I saw that original was when I did the final changes and handed it back. In all the years since, I have always been impressed by the legions of fans. They are very knowledgeable about *The Empire Strikes Back* movie and my poster. When I do conventions, the fans are fun to meet and have taught me a lot about the individual characters. They ask a lot of questions about the painting of the poster, and some of them have told me that they came to the convention specifically to meet me and to have their posters signed! I am always amazed at how loyal and friendly they are. All in all, *The Empire Strikes Back* has been an exciting space trip for me.

Roger Kastel

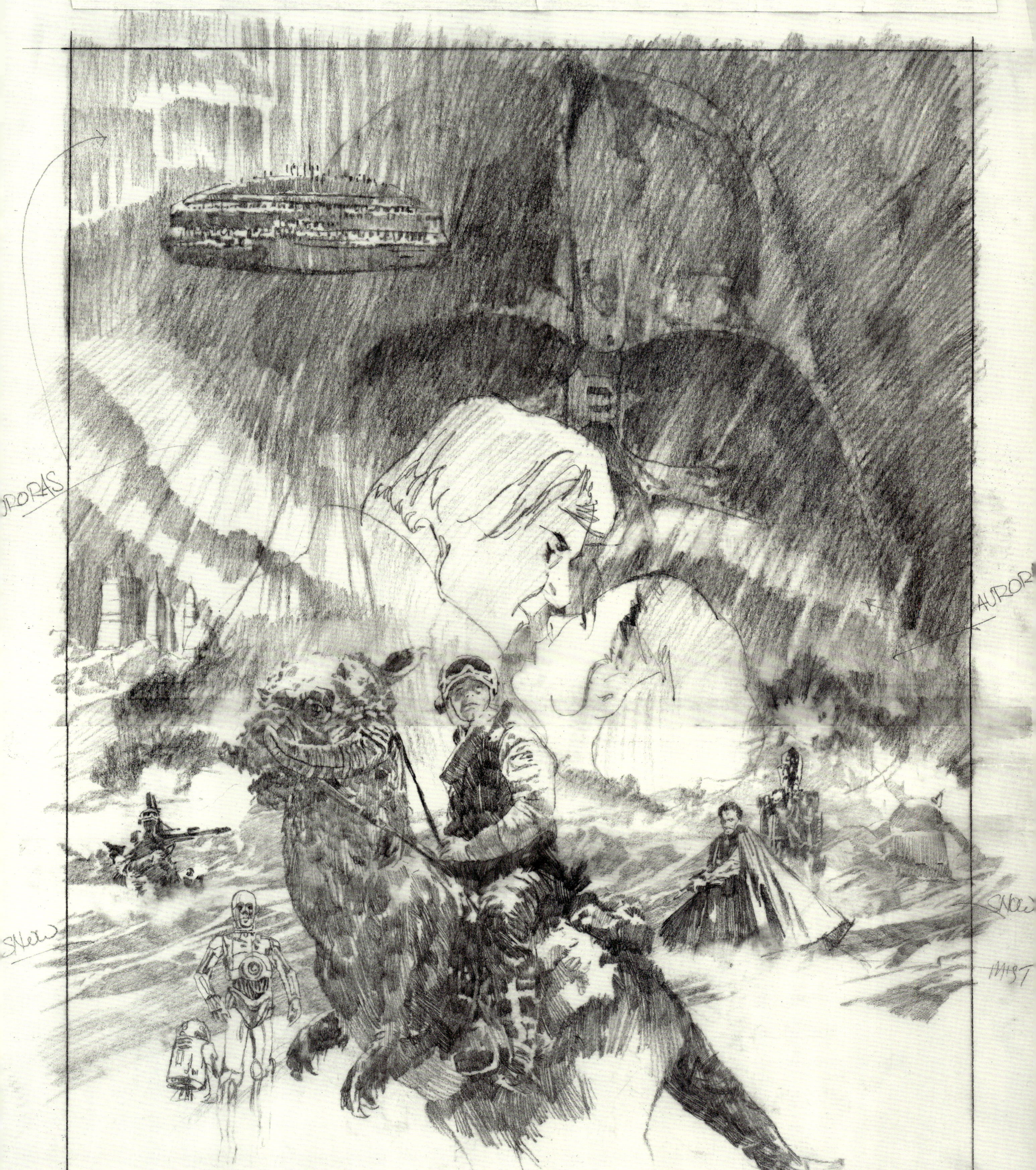

URORAS
AUROR
SNOW
SNOW
MIST

STAR WARS ART™

POSTERS

THE PLATES

RIGHT

Ralph McQuarrie

Full-color painted concept treatment for early *Star Wars* poster, 1975

Based on McQuarrie's preproduction conceptual art

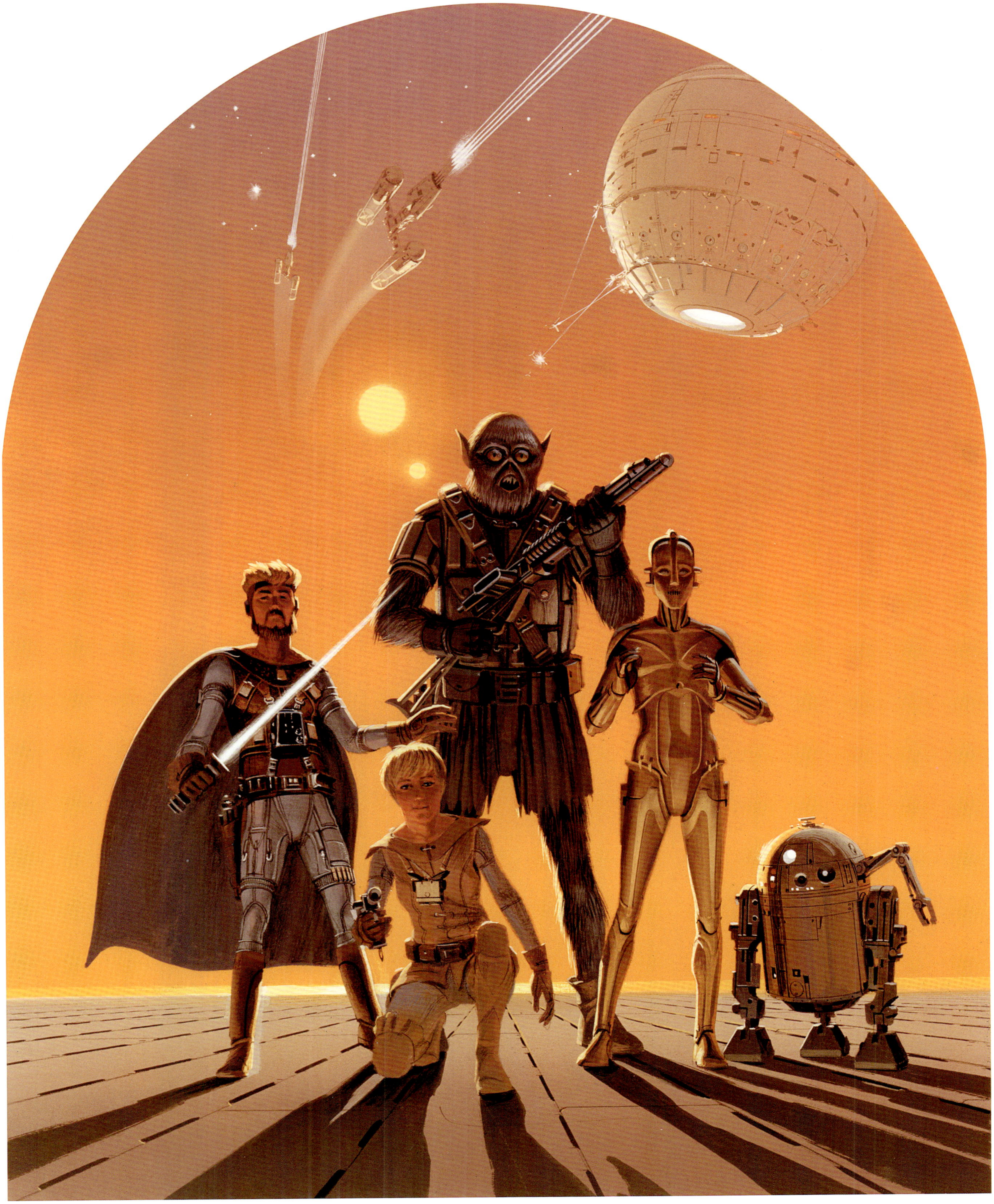

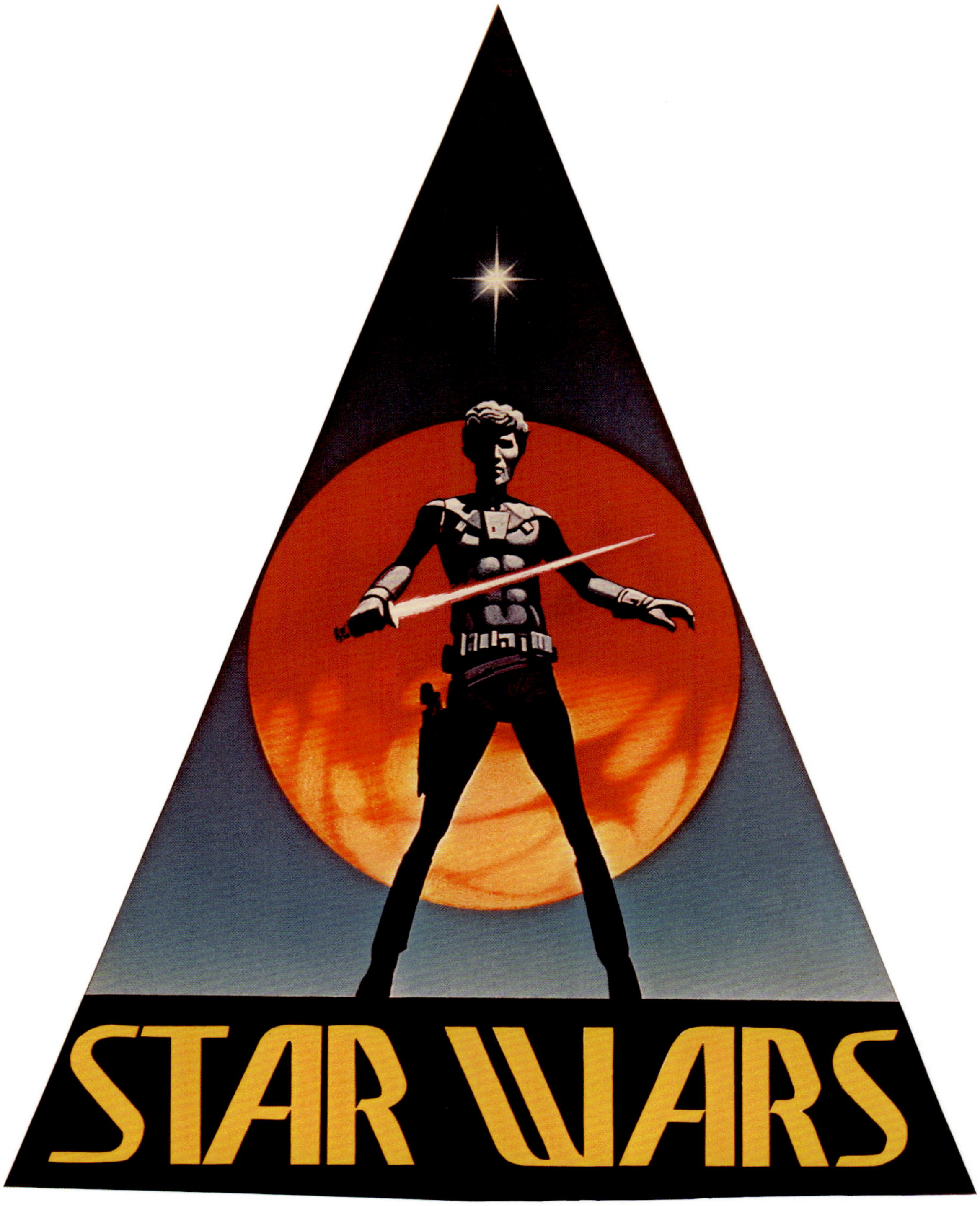

ABOVE

Ralph McQuarrie

Full-color painted concept treatment for early *Star Wars* logo, 1975

Based on McQuarrie's conceptual art; logo first produced as sticker during film production

RIGHT AND FOLLOWING SPREAD (DETAIL)

Howard Chaykin

Final painted artwork for *Star Wars* "Poster 1," 1976

First promotional *Star Wars* poster

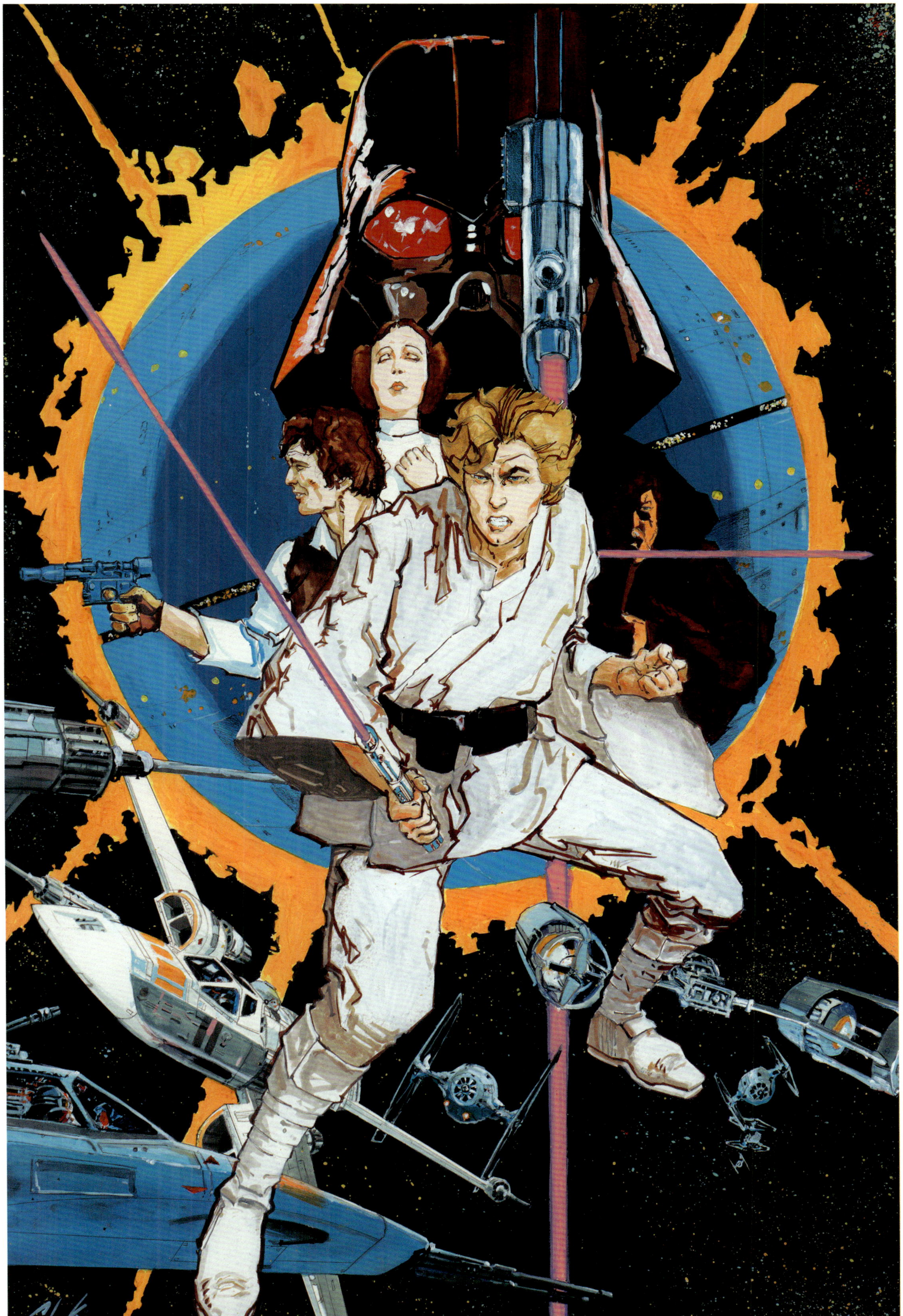

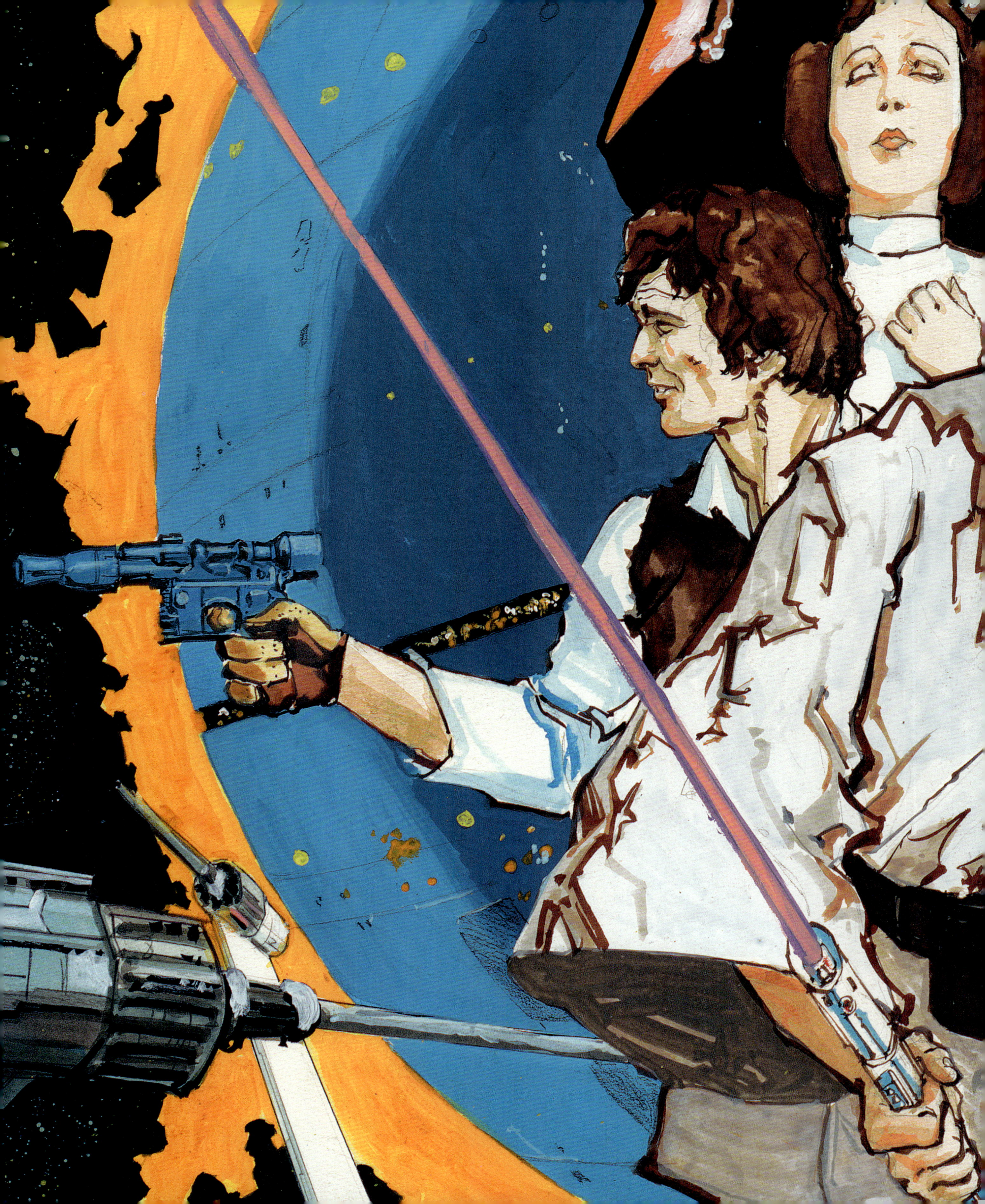

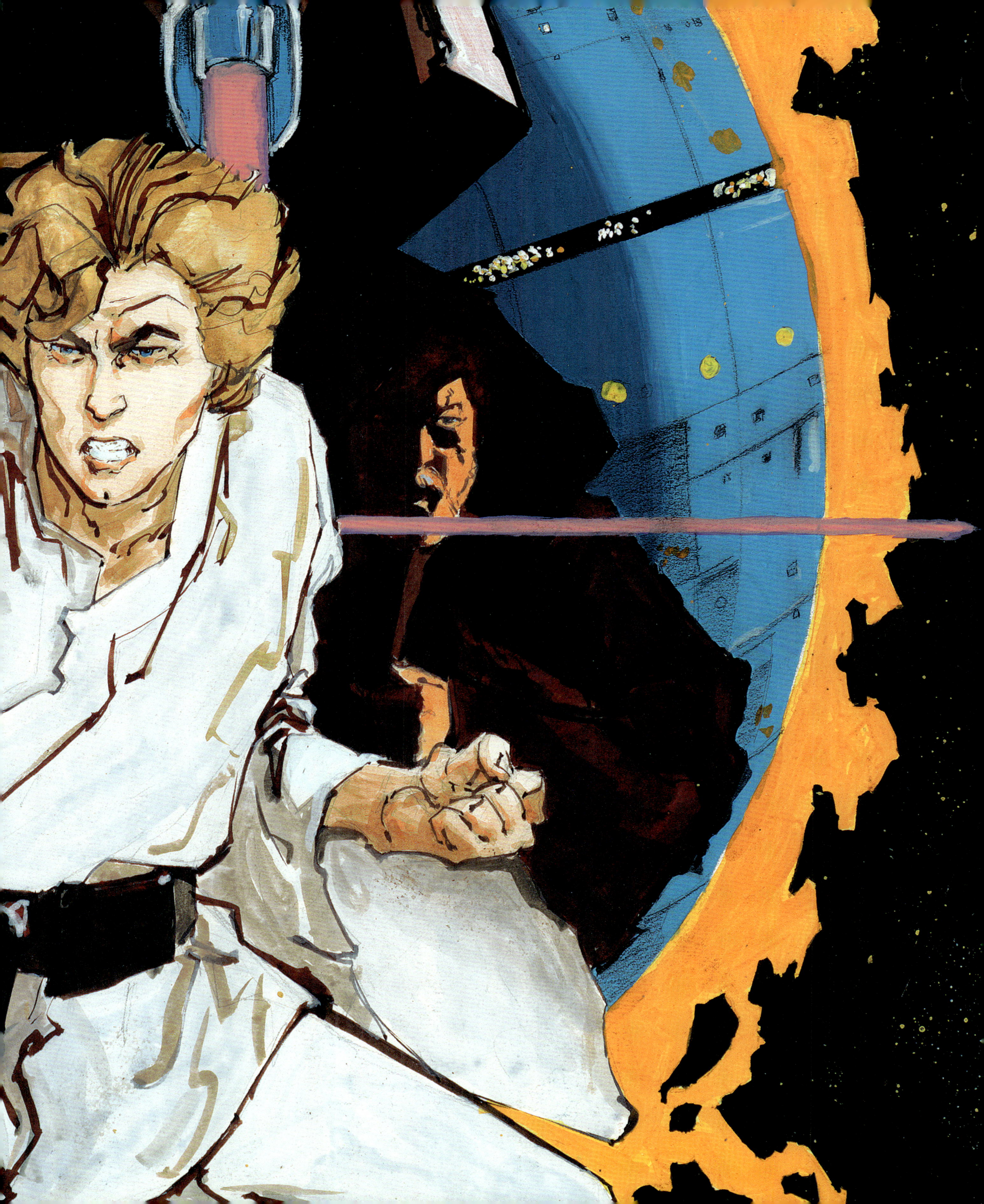

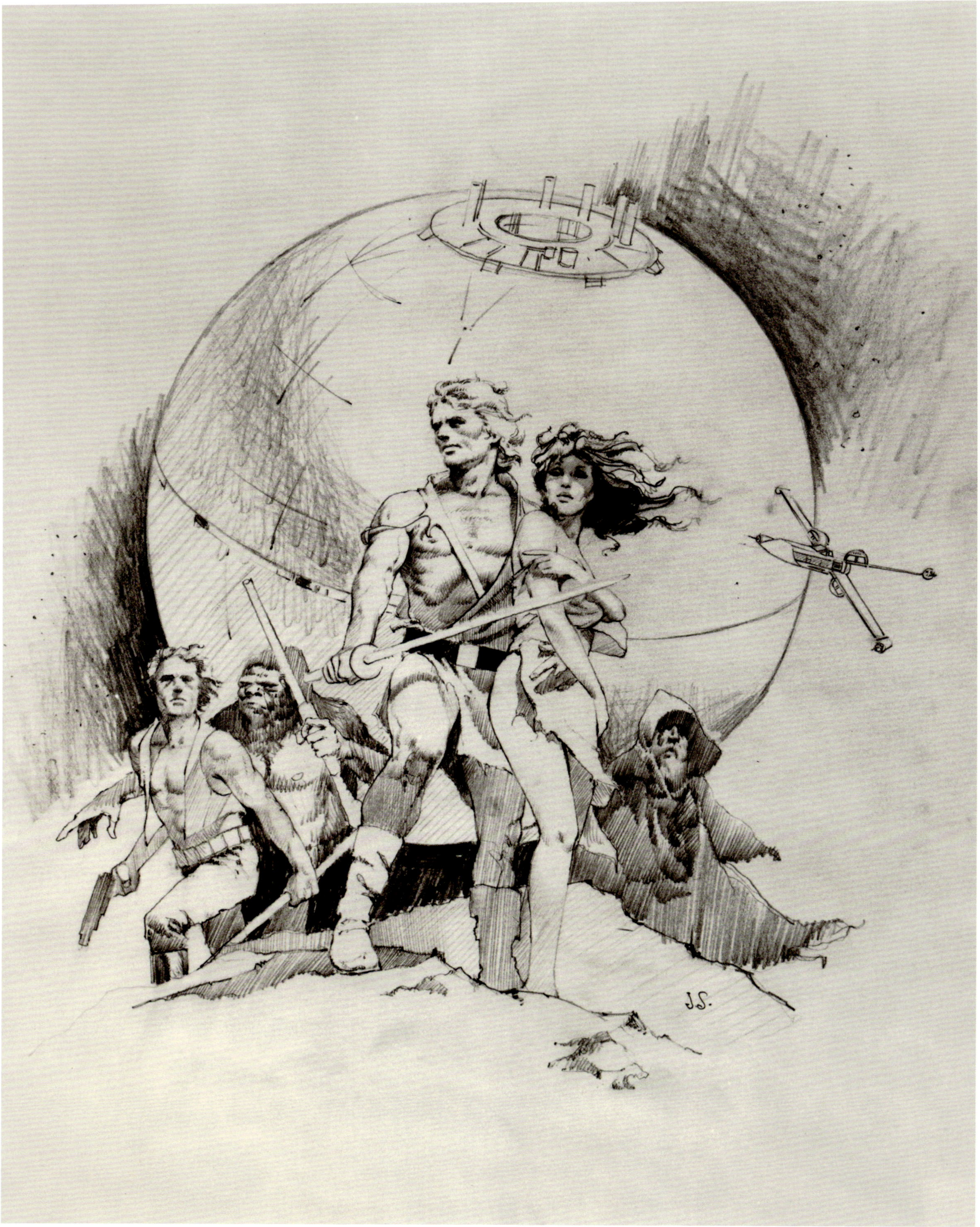

ABOVE AND FOLLOWING SPREAD (DETAIL)

John Solie

Black-and-white concept treatment for *Star Wars* poster, c. 1976

RIGHT

Tom Jung

Final painted artwork for *Star Wars* style "A" theatrical one-sheet, 1977

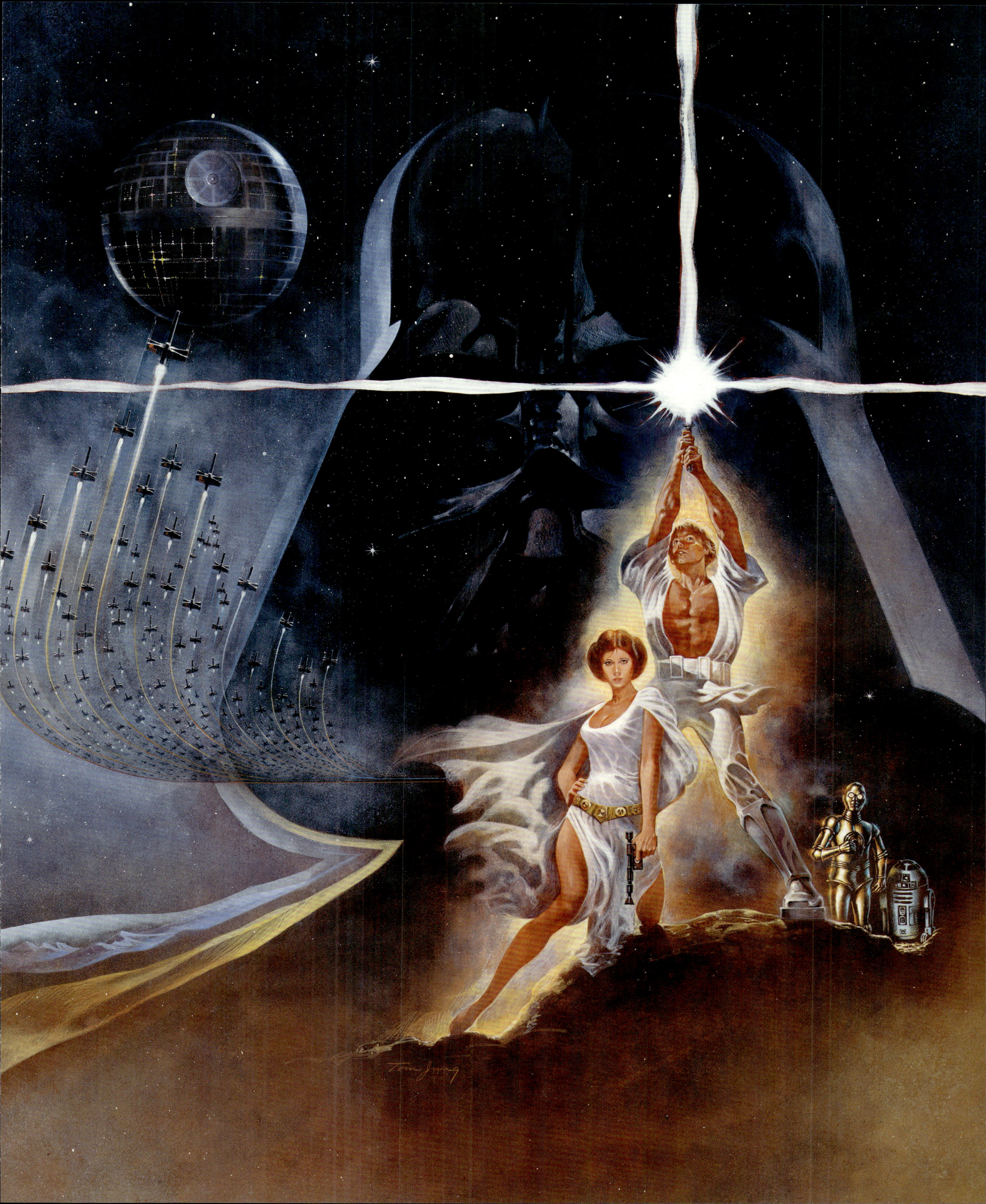

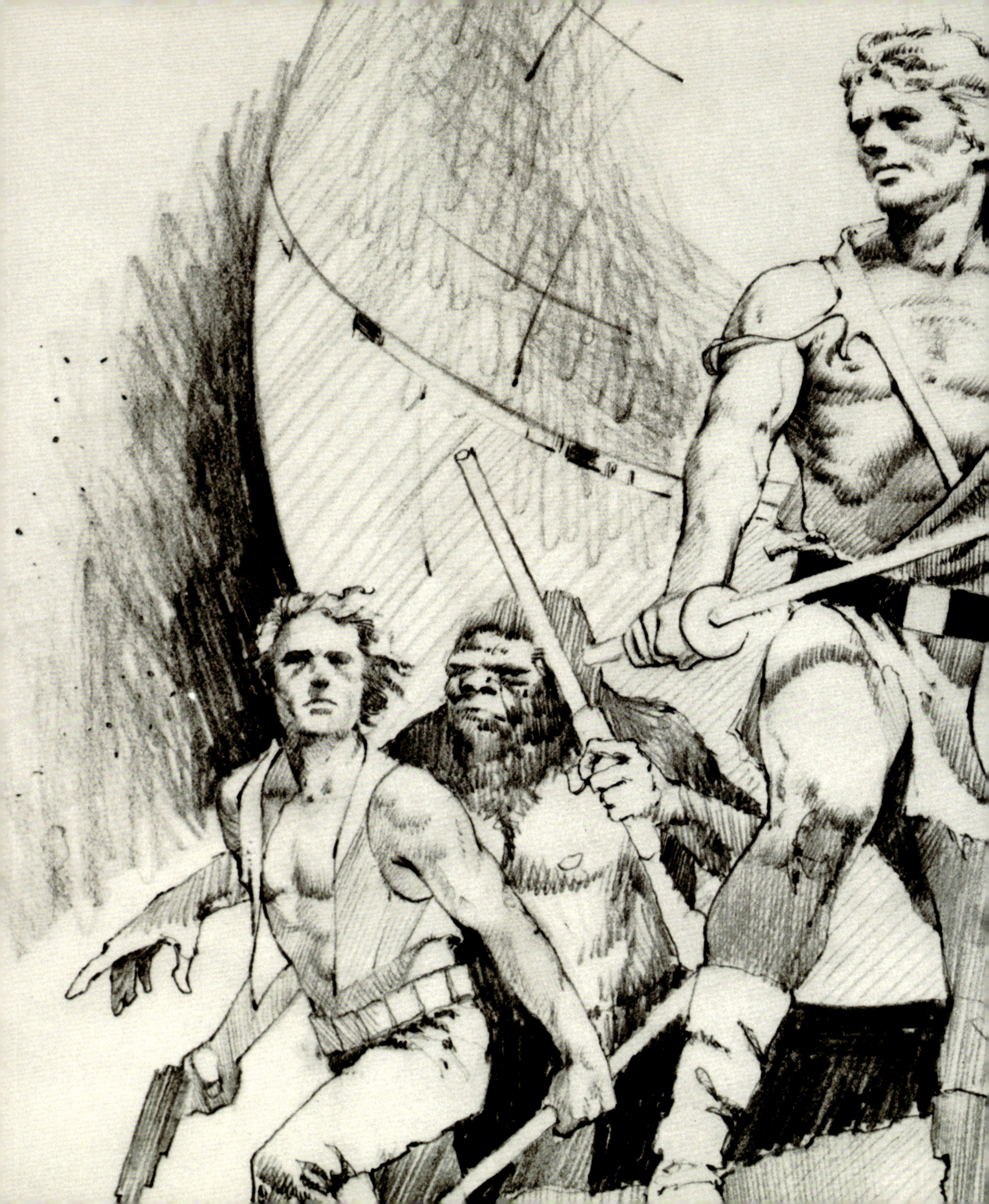

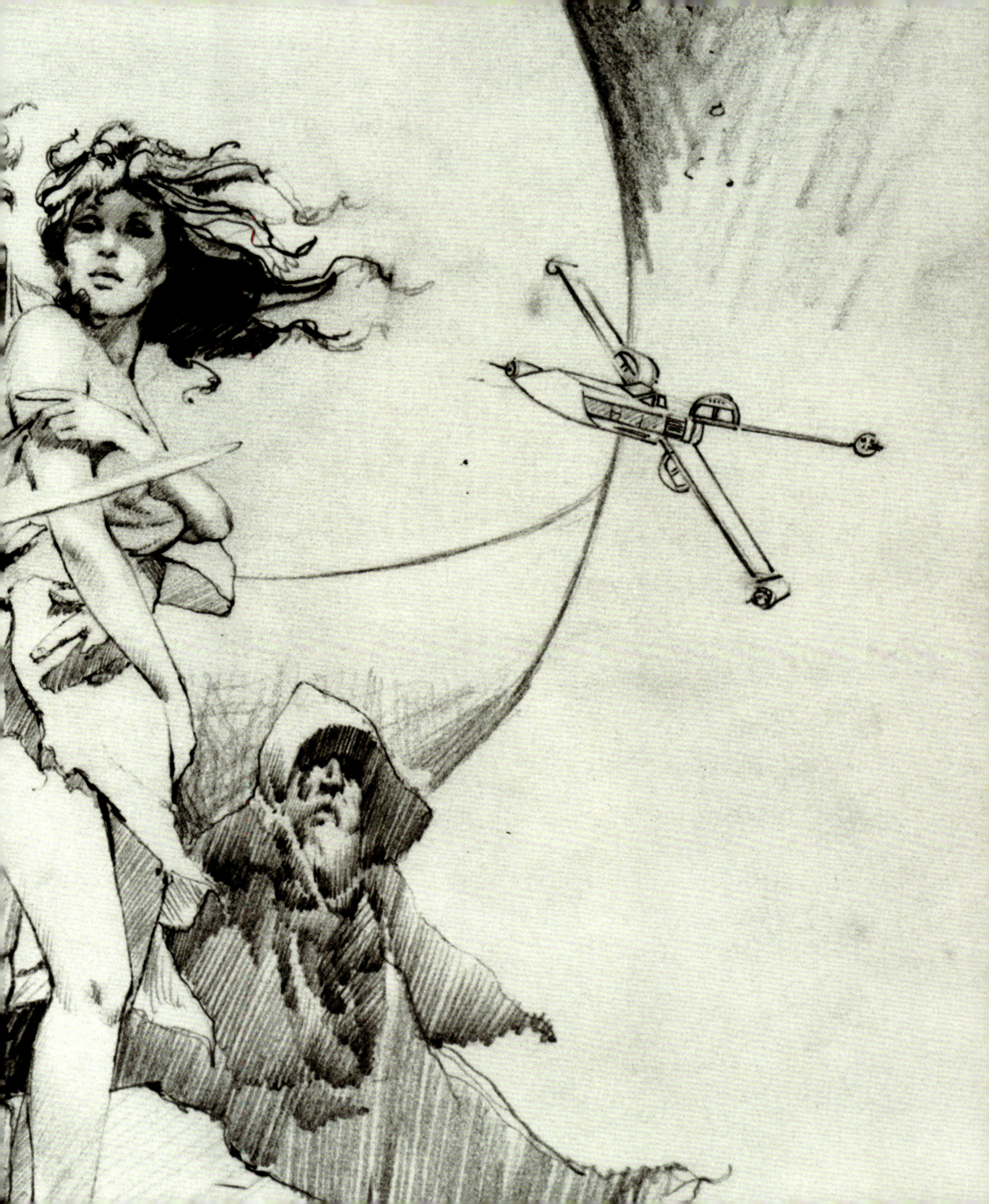

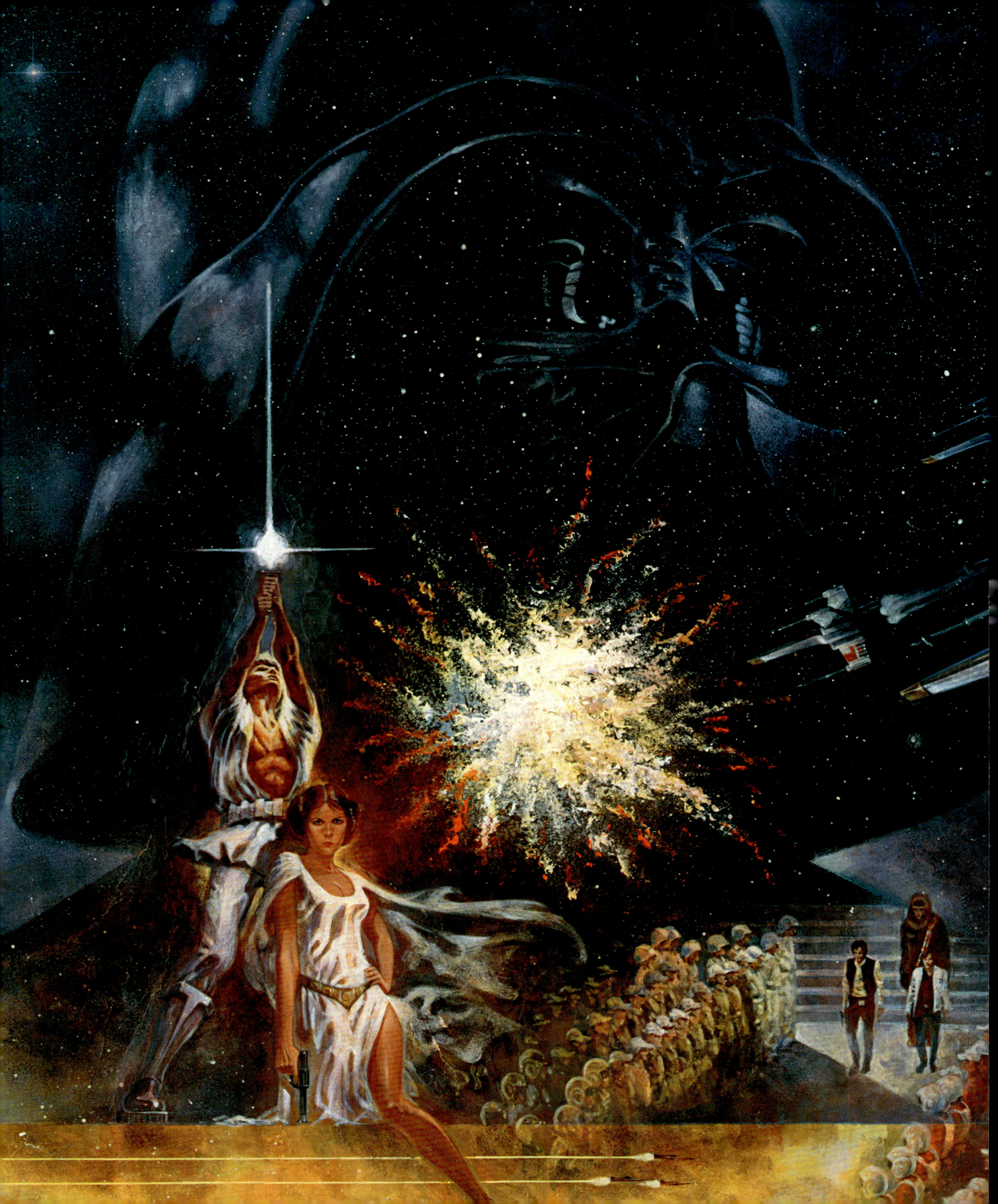

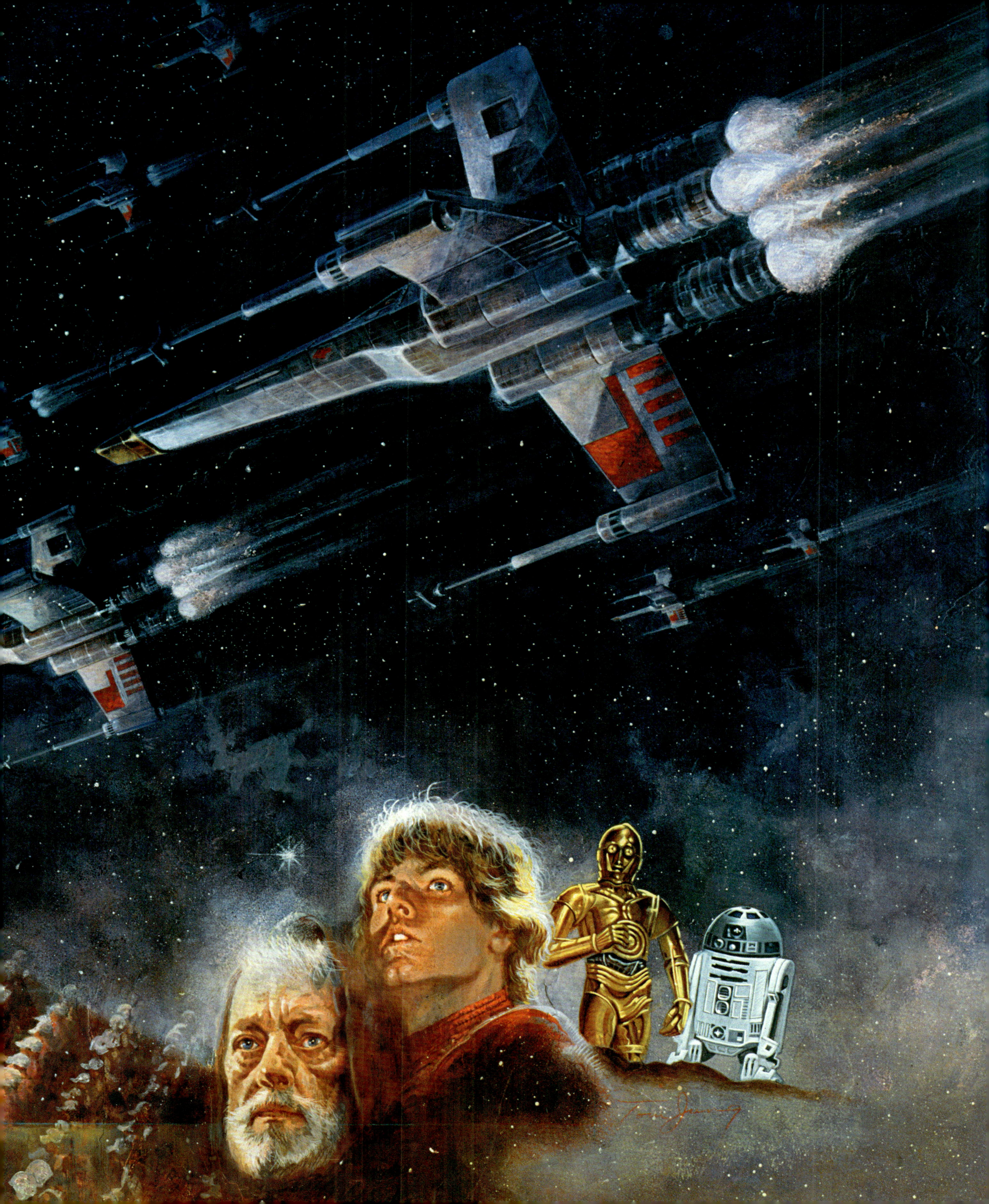

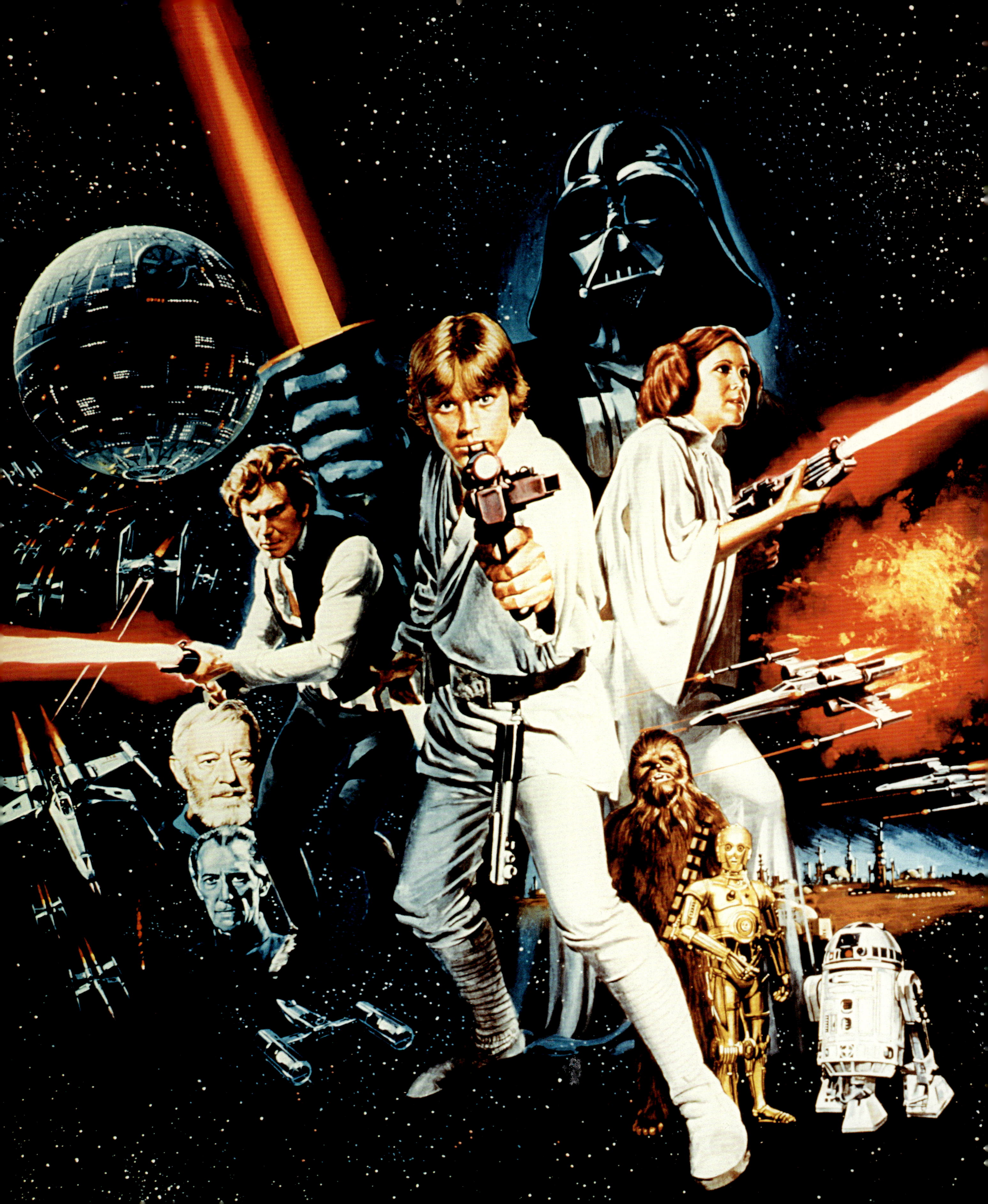

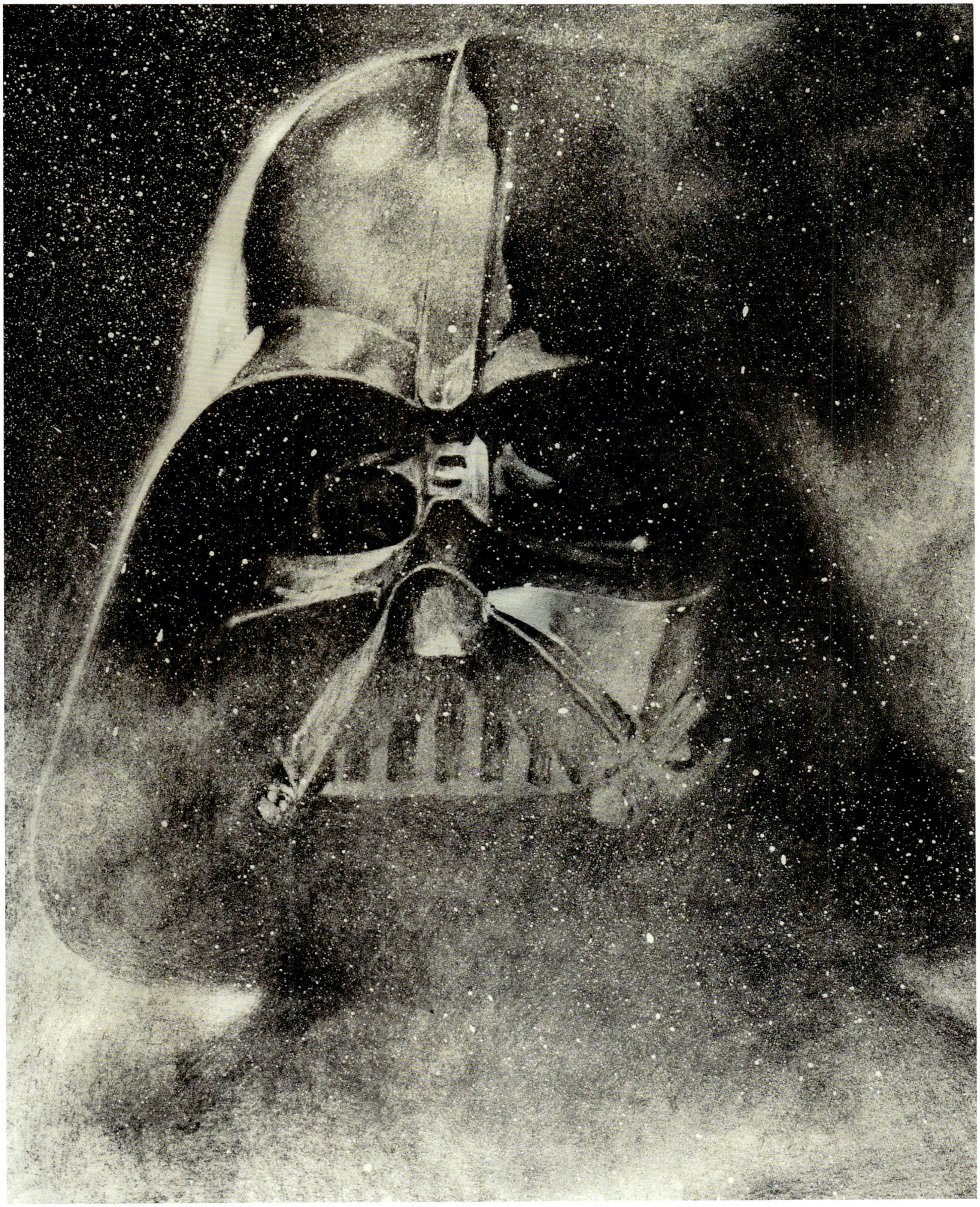

PREVIOUS SPREAD

Tom Jung

Final painted artwork for *Star Wars* style "A" theatrical half-sheet, 1977

LEFT

Tom Chantrell

Final painted artwork for *Star Wars* style "C" theatrical one-sheet, 1977

Produced for international distribution

ABOVE

Tom Jung

Final black-and-white artwork for *Star Wars* poster, 1977

Foil poster released to promote *Star Wars* soundtrack album

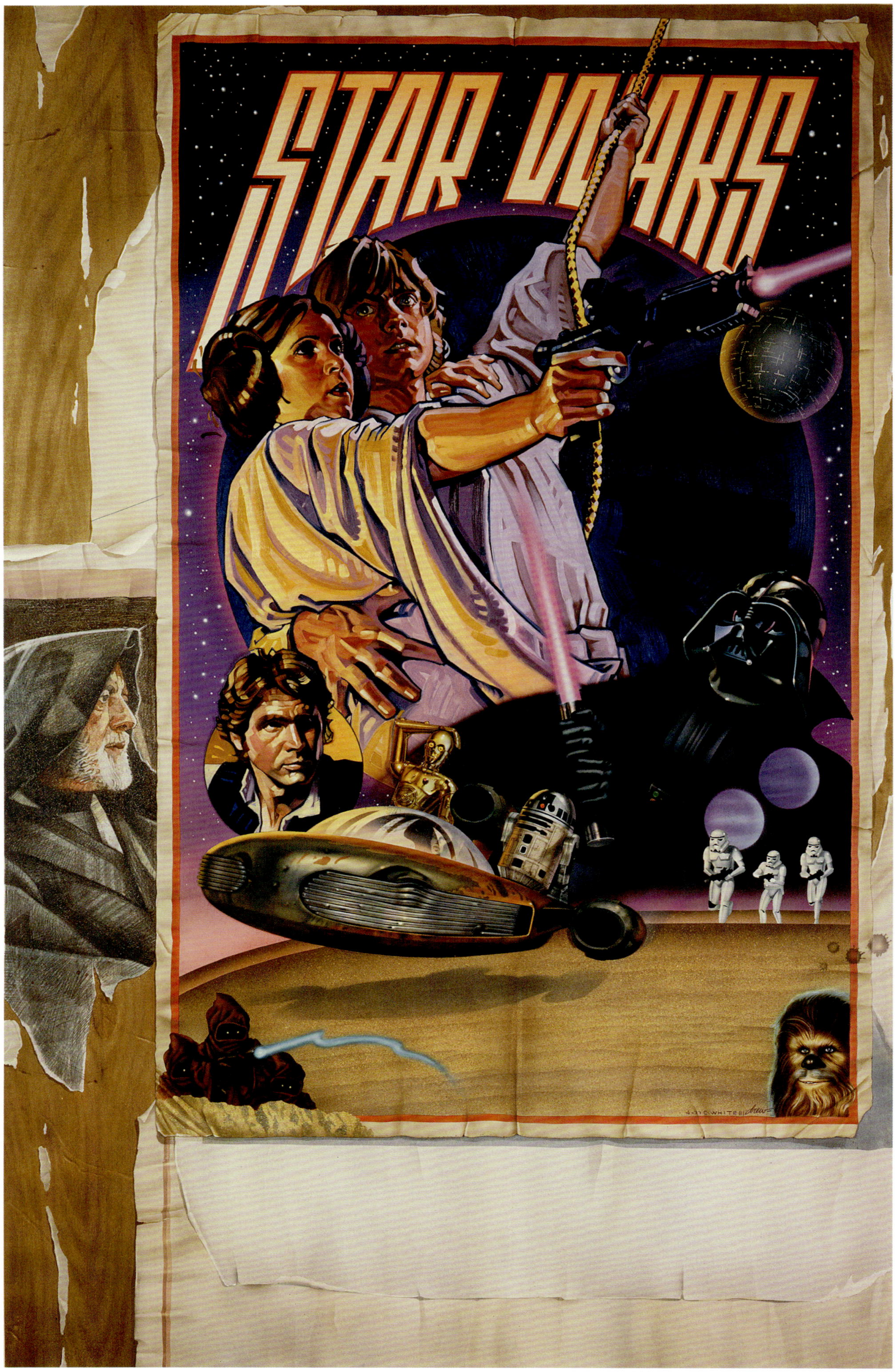

LEFT

Charles White III/Drew Struzan

Final painted artwork for *Star Wars* style "D" ("Circus") theatrical one-sheet, 1978

RIGHT

John Berkey

Final painted artwork for *Star Wars* poster, 1977

Insert premium for *Star Wars* soundtrack album

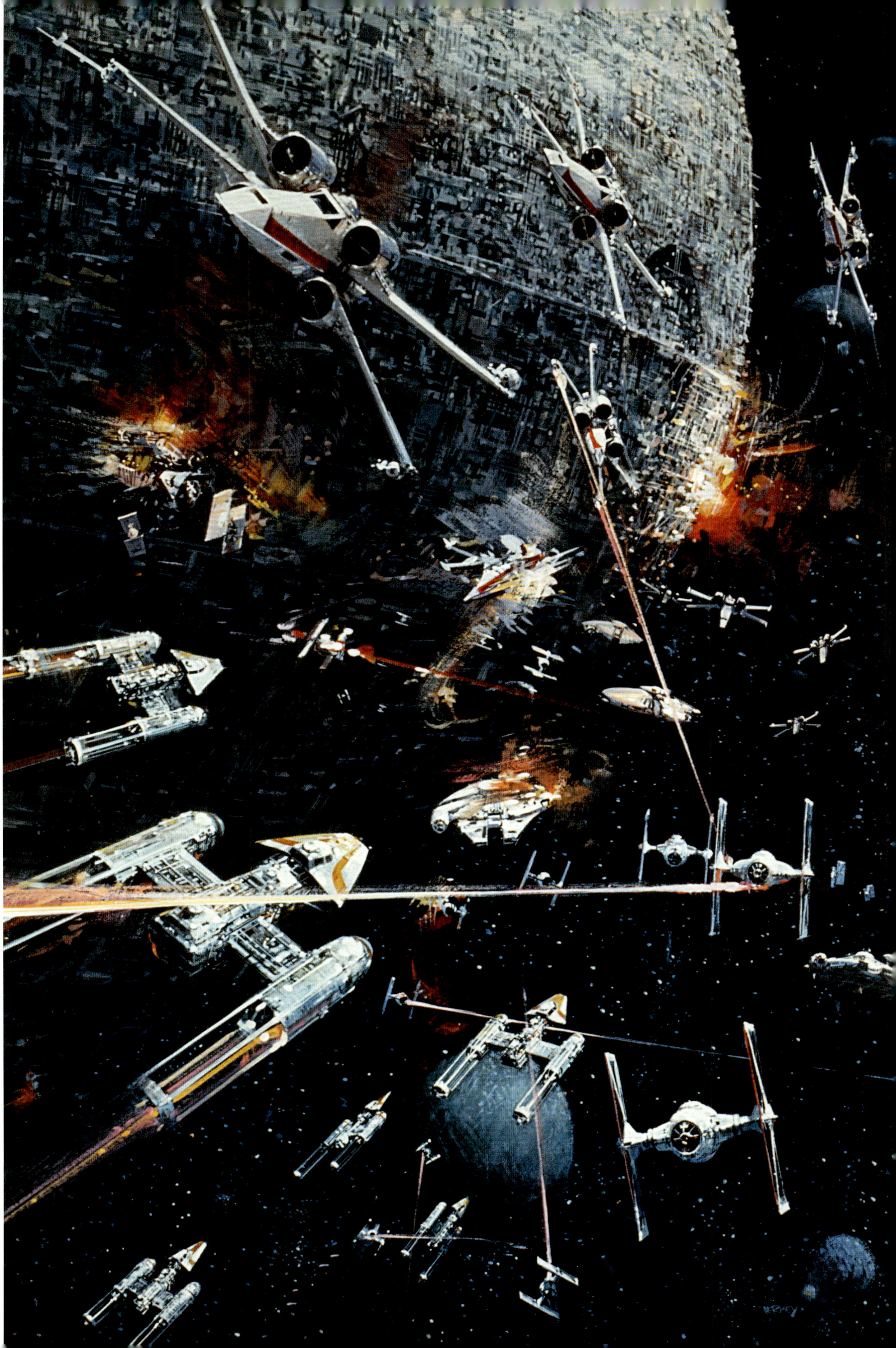

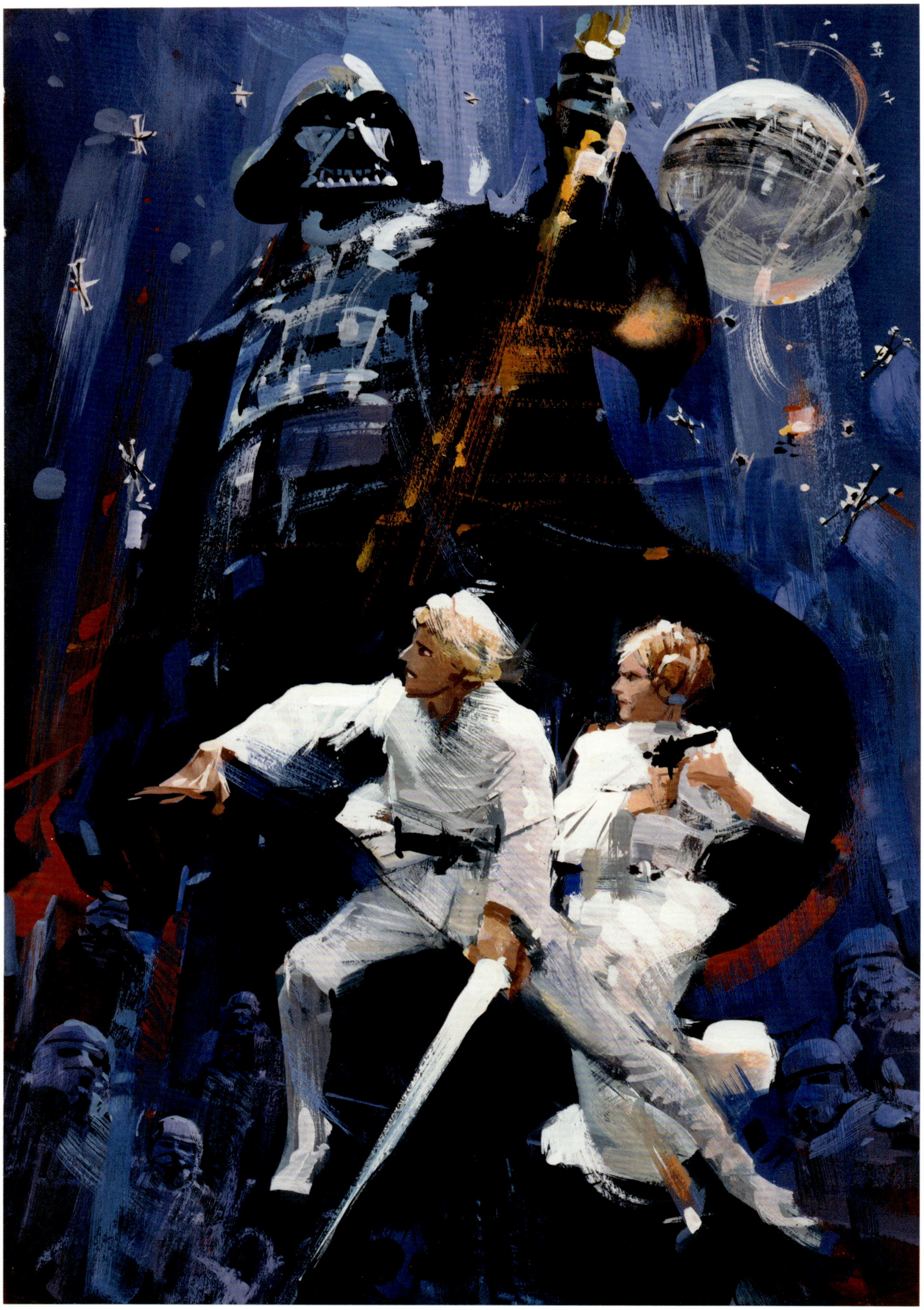

ABOVE

John Berkey

Full-color painted concept treatment for *Star Wars* novelization rerelease cover, c. 1977

RIGHT

John Berkey

Full-color painted concept treatment for *Star Wars* novelization rerelease cover, c. 1977

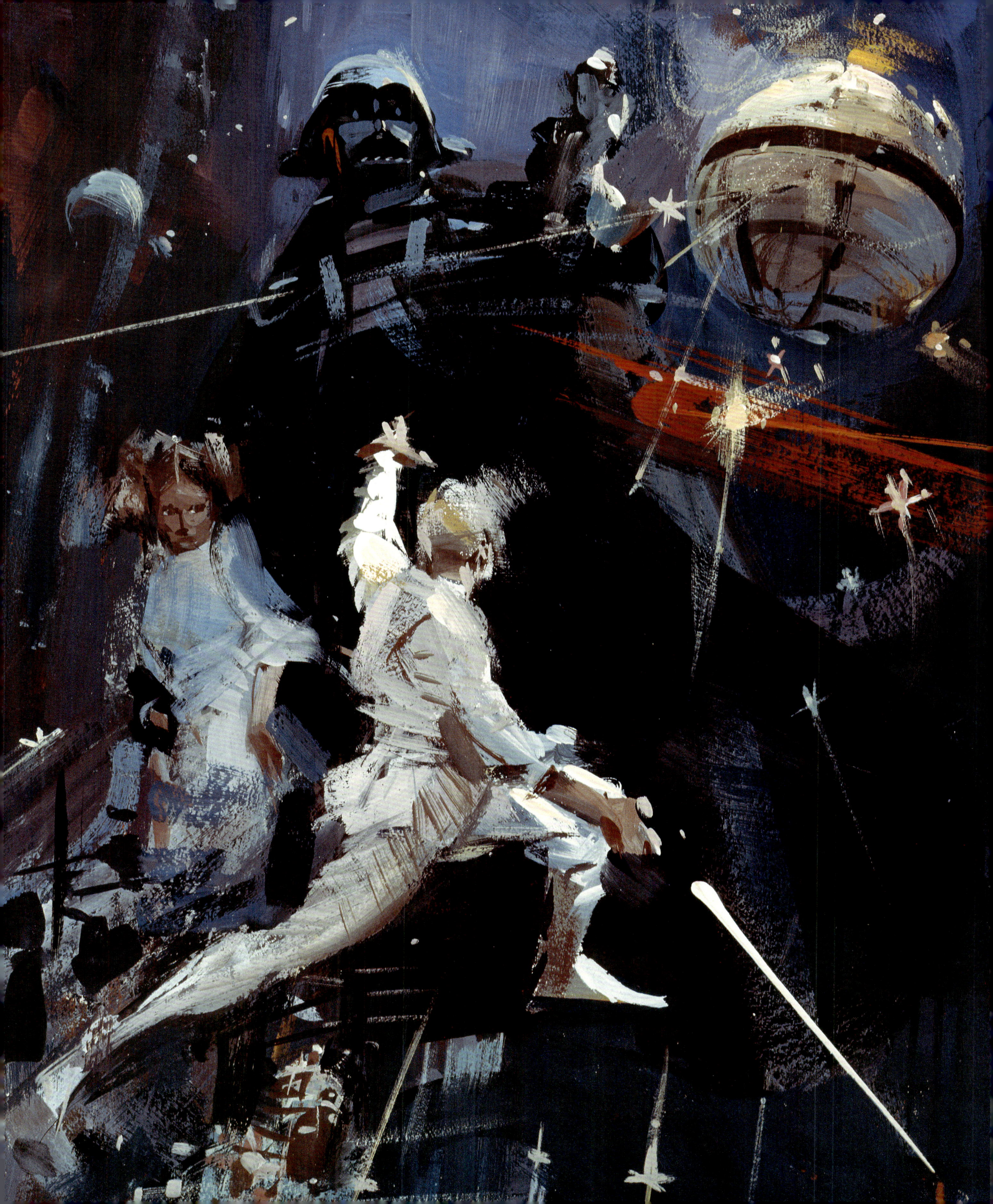

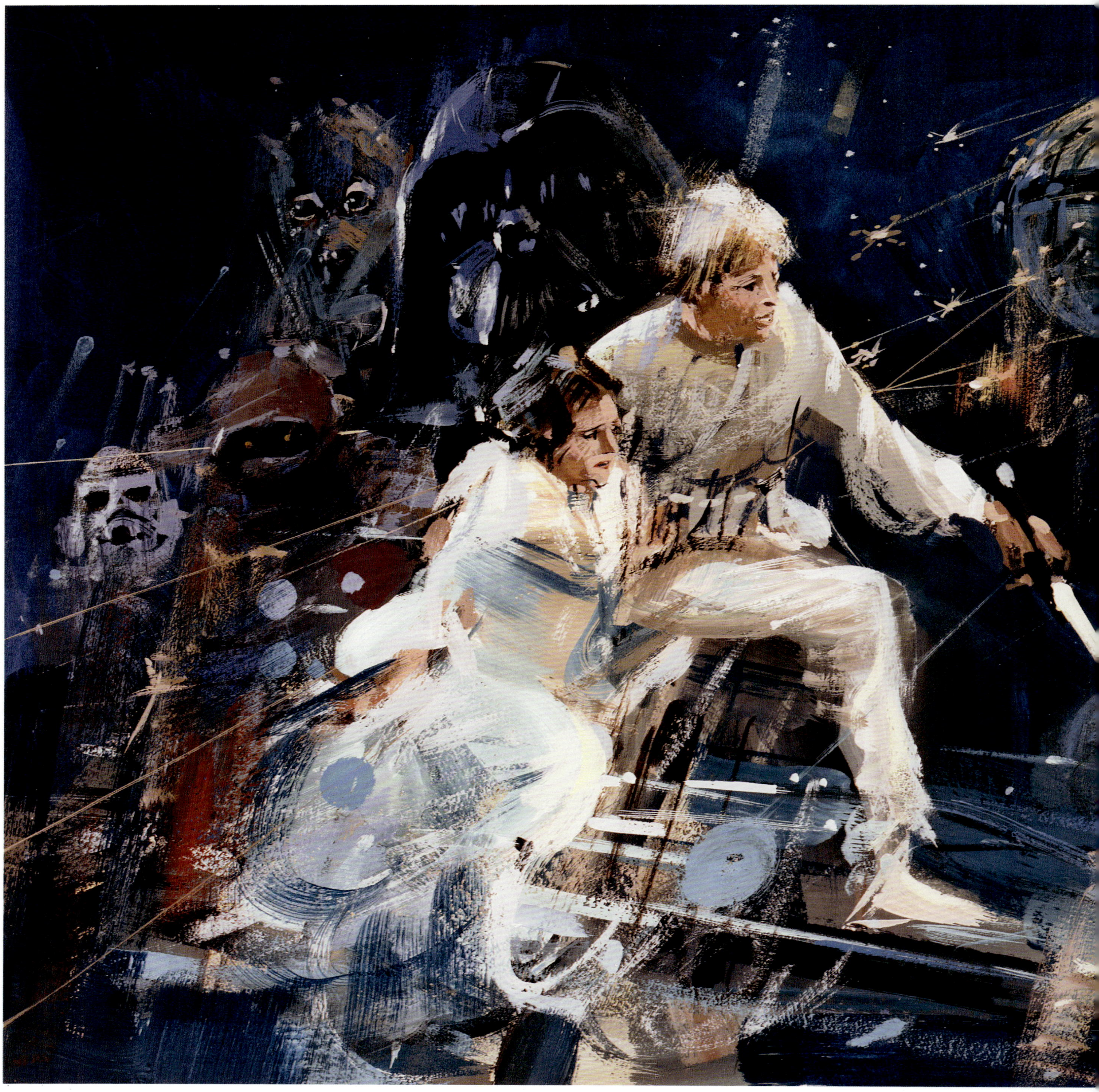

ABOVE

John Berkey

Full-color painted concept treatment for *Star Wars* novelization rerelease cover, c. 1977

RIGHT AND FOLLOWING SPREAD (DETAIL)

John Berkey

Final painted artwork for *Star Wars* novelization rerelease cover, c. 1977

This image was "flopped" horizontally for the printed cover, so that lightsabers would be shown in the characters' right hands; repurposed as shown here on a poster for Trends International in 1996

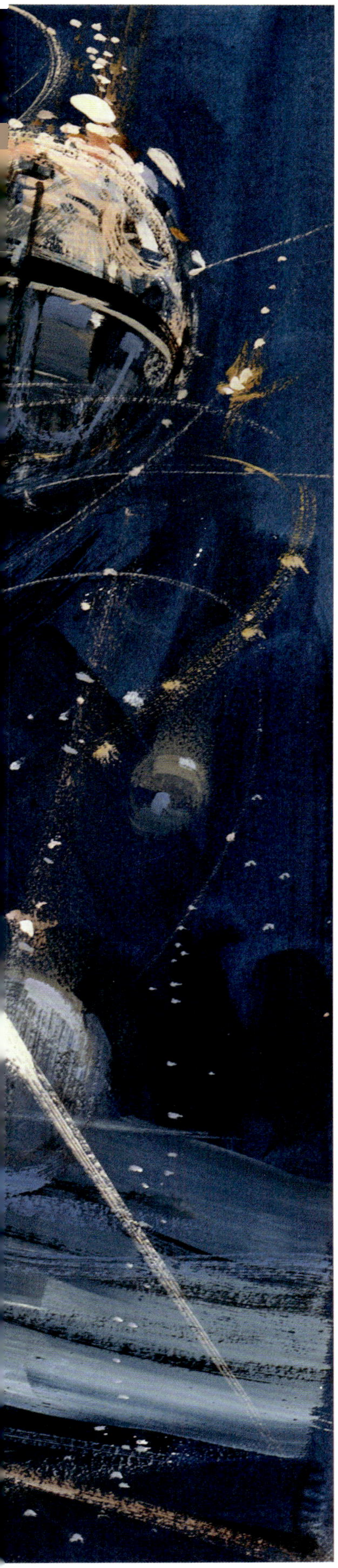

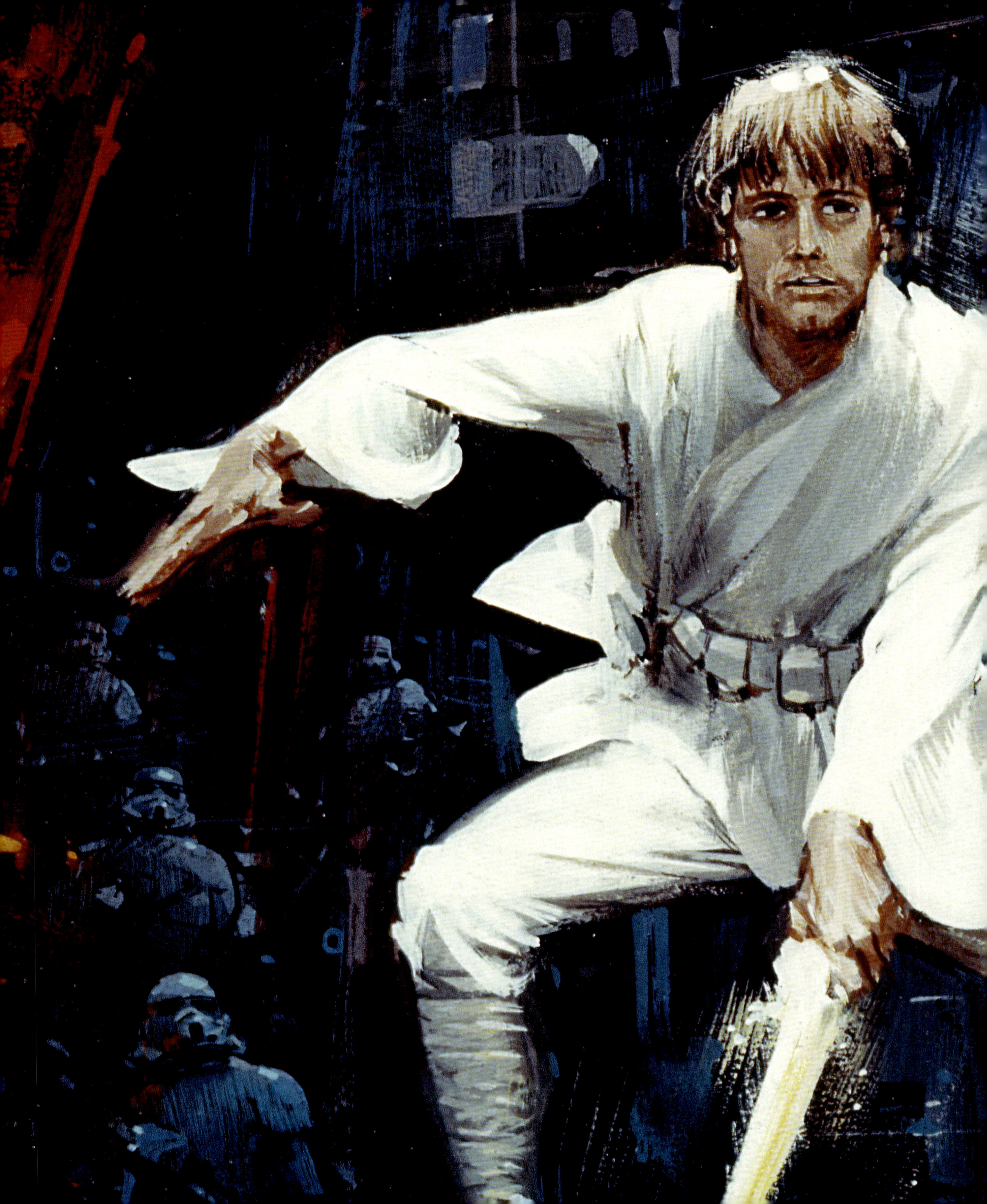

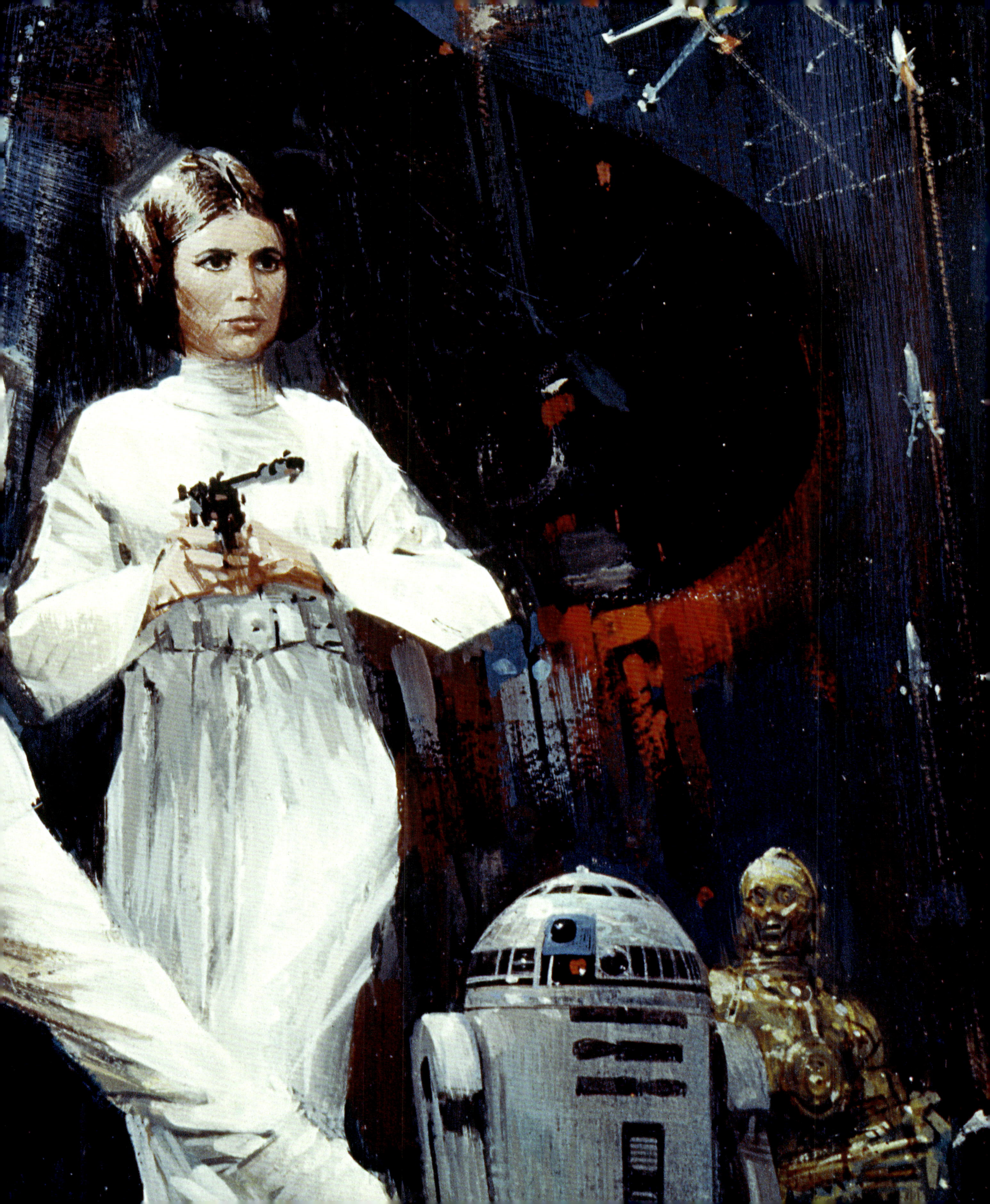

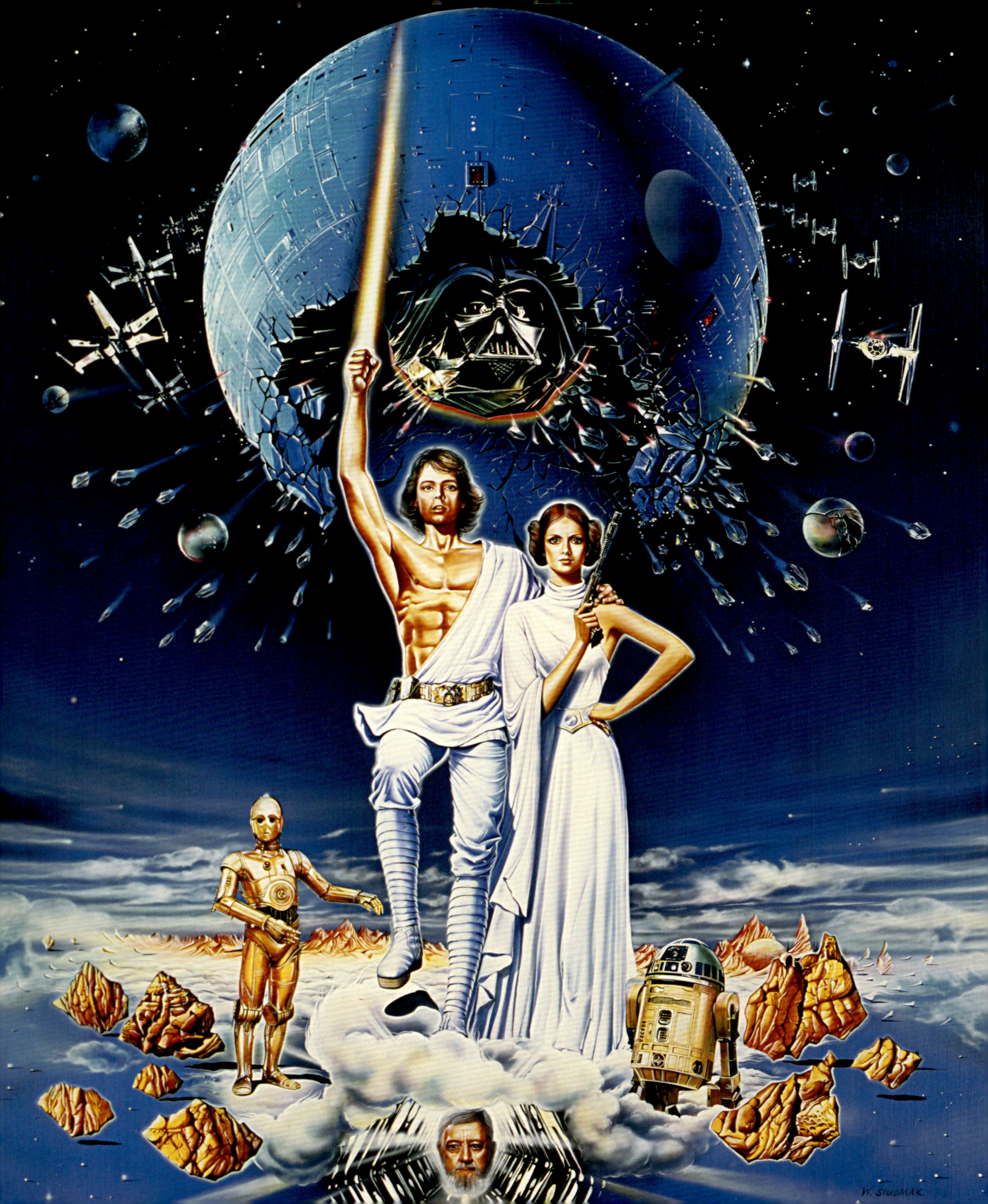
W. SIUDMAK

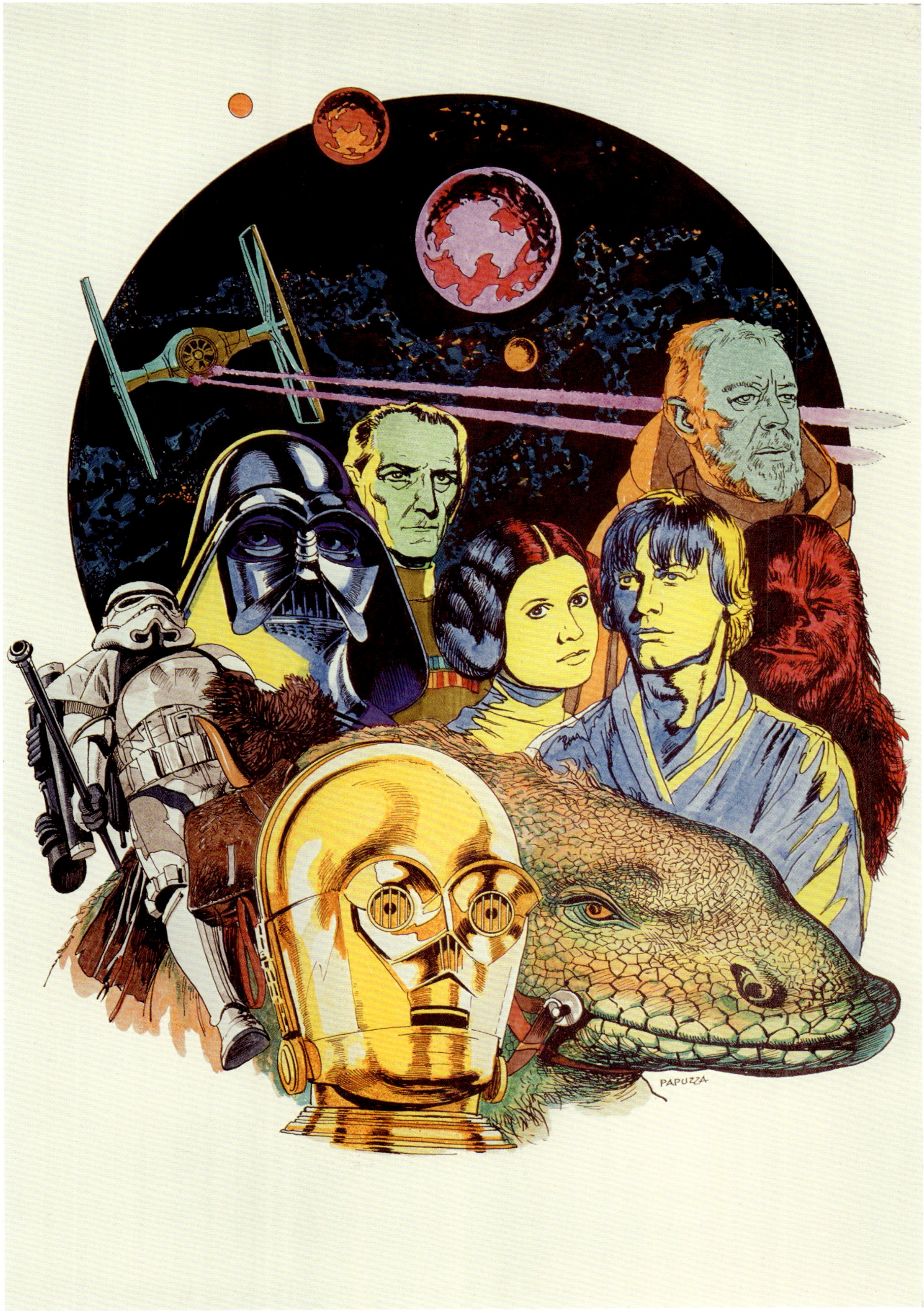

LEFT

Wojtek Siudmak

Full-color painted concept treatment for *Star Wars* poster, Poland, c. 1977

RIGHT

Michelangelo Papuzza

Full-color painted concept treatment for *Star Wars* poster, Italy, c. 1977

FOLLOWING SPREAD

Noriyoshi Ohrai

Full-color painted concept treatment for *Star Wars* "Vehicles" poster, 1978

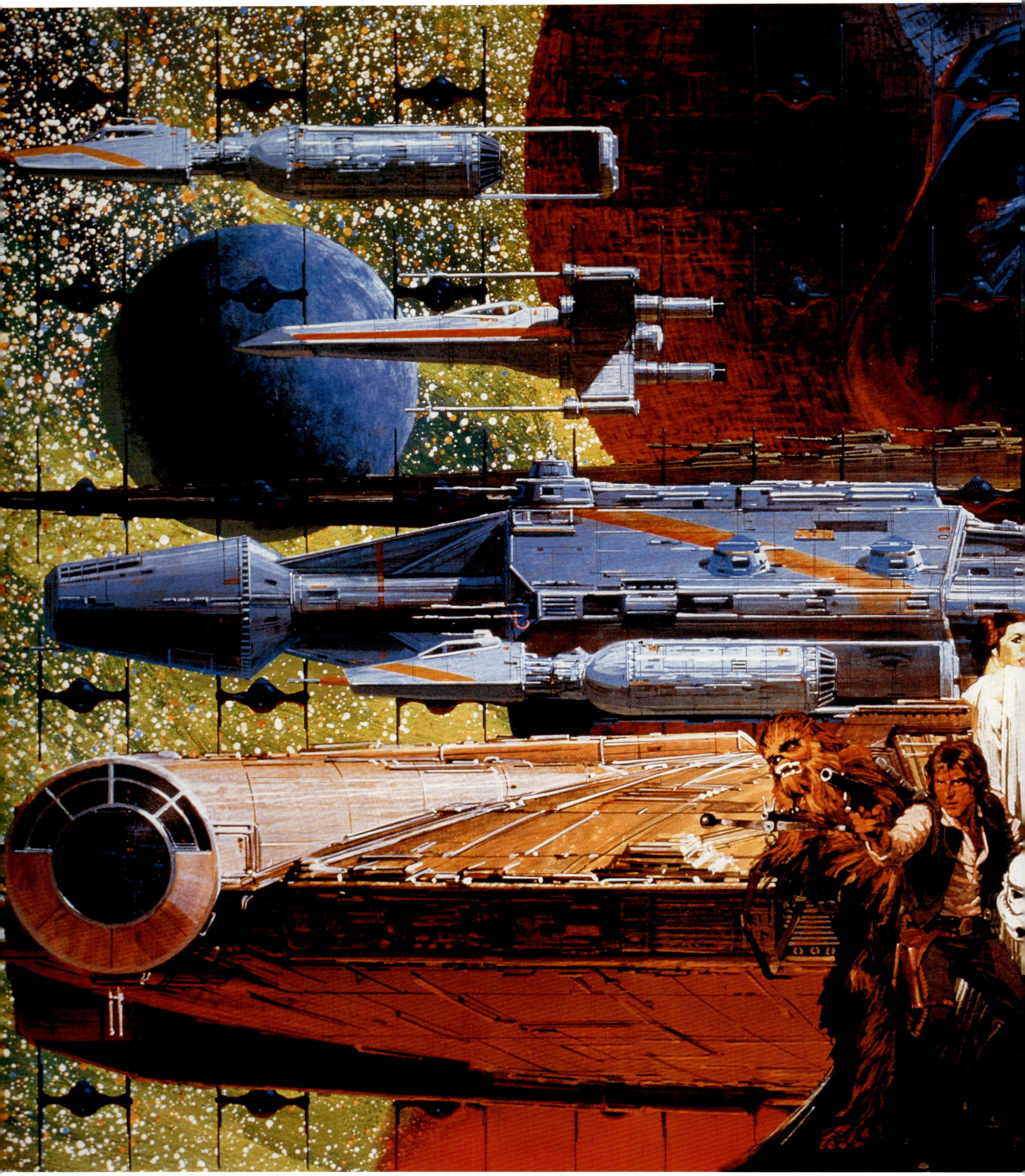

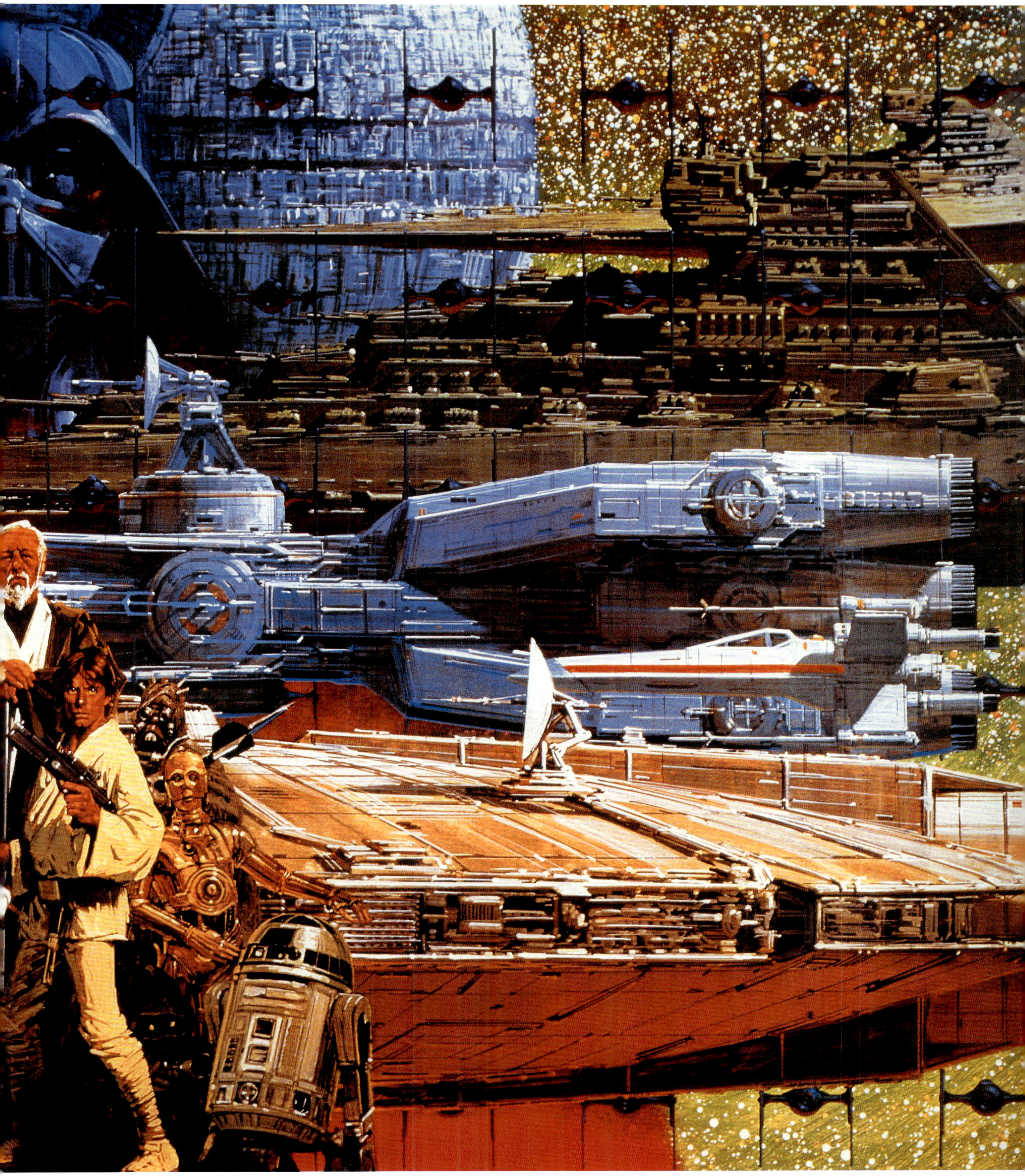

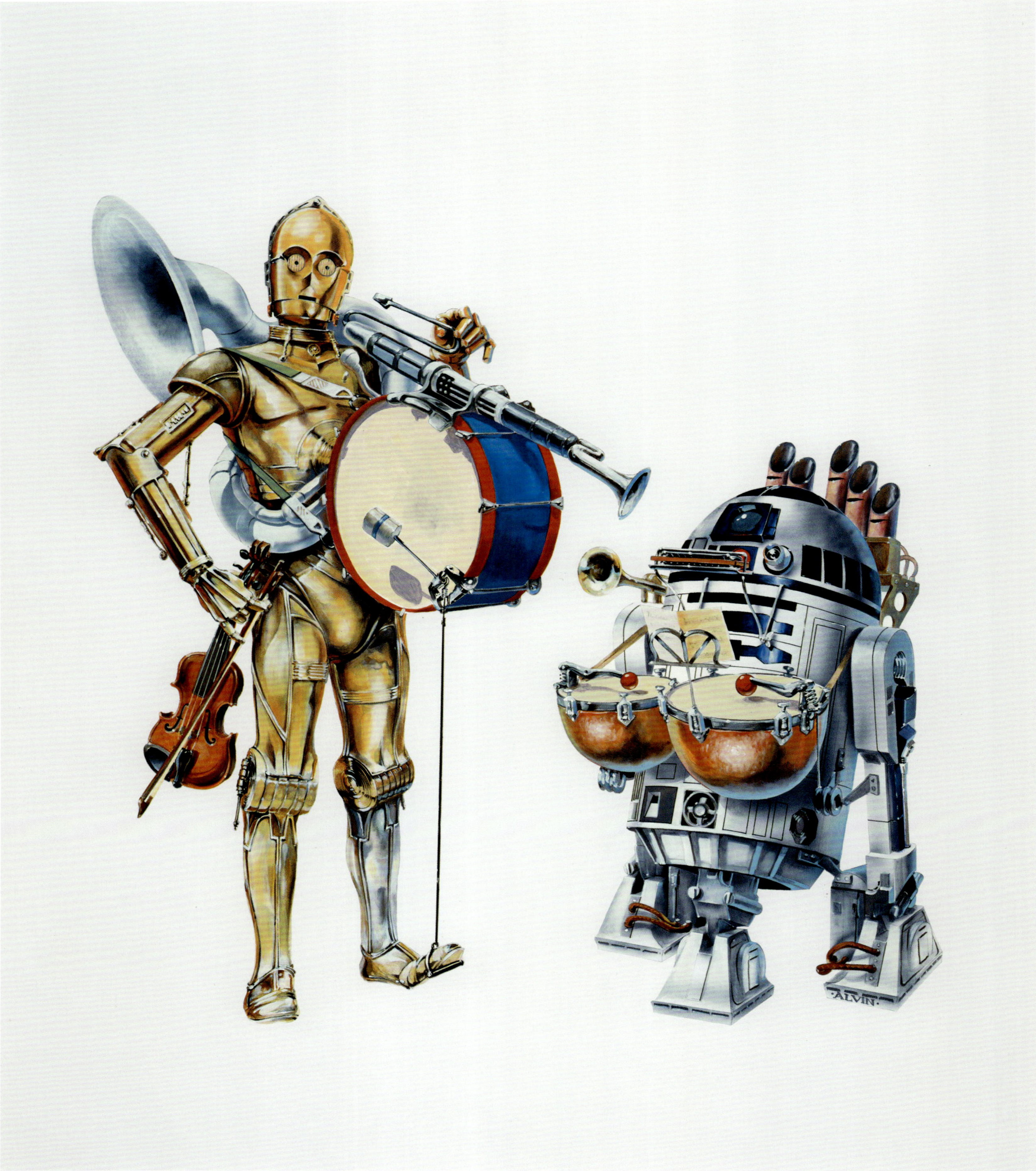

ABOVE

John Alvin

Final painted artwork for *Star Wars in Concert* promotional poster, 1978

Proposed symphonic concert series poster

RIGHT

Noriyoshi Ohrai

Final painted artwork for *Star Wars* poster, Japan, 1982

Localized dubbed theatrical rerelease

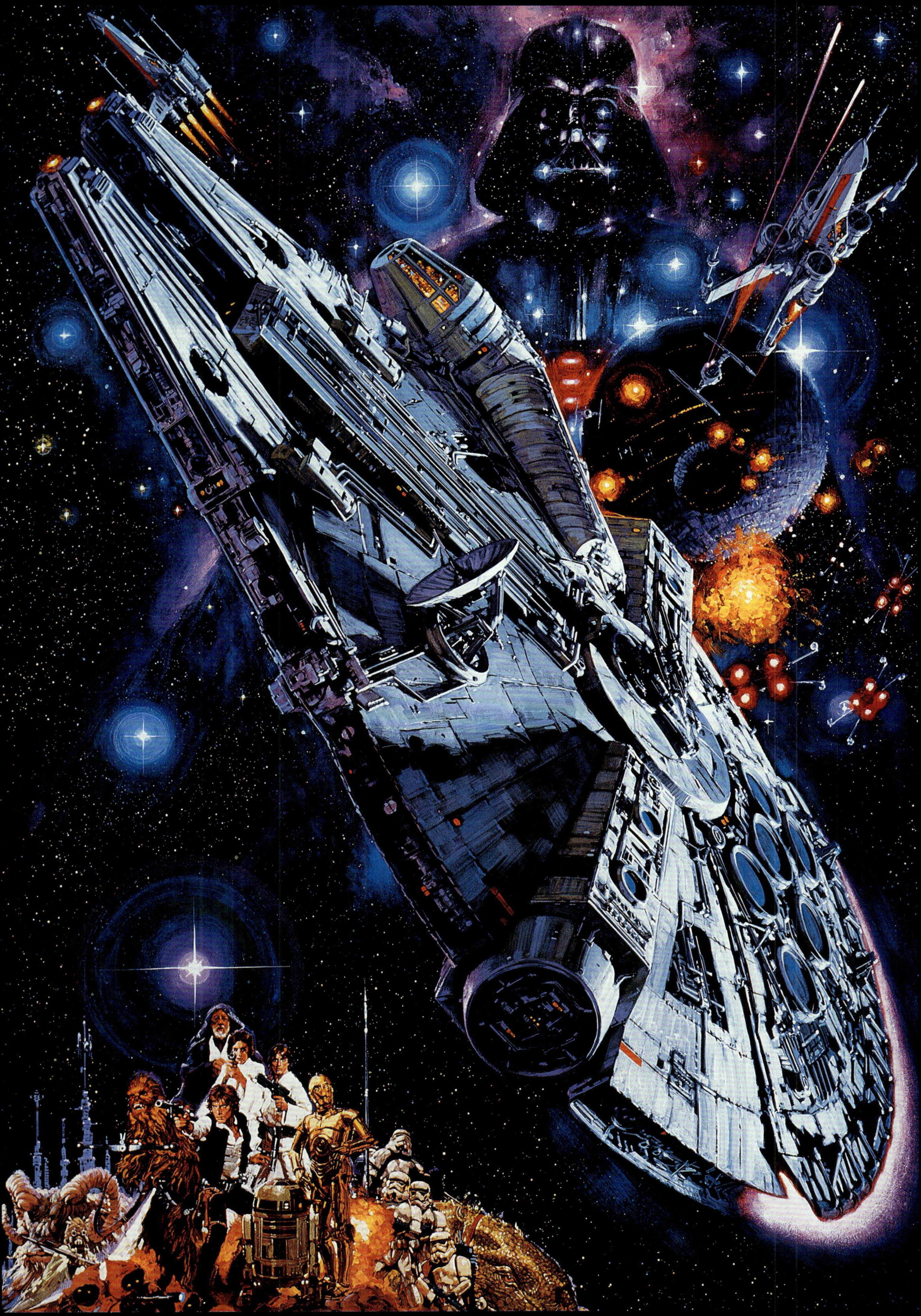

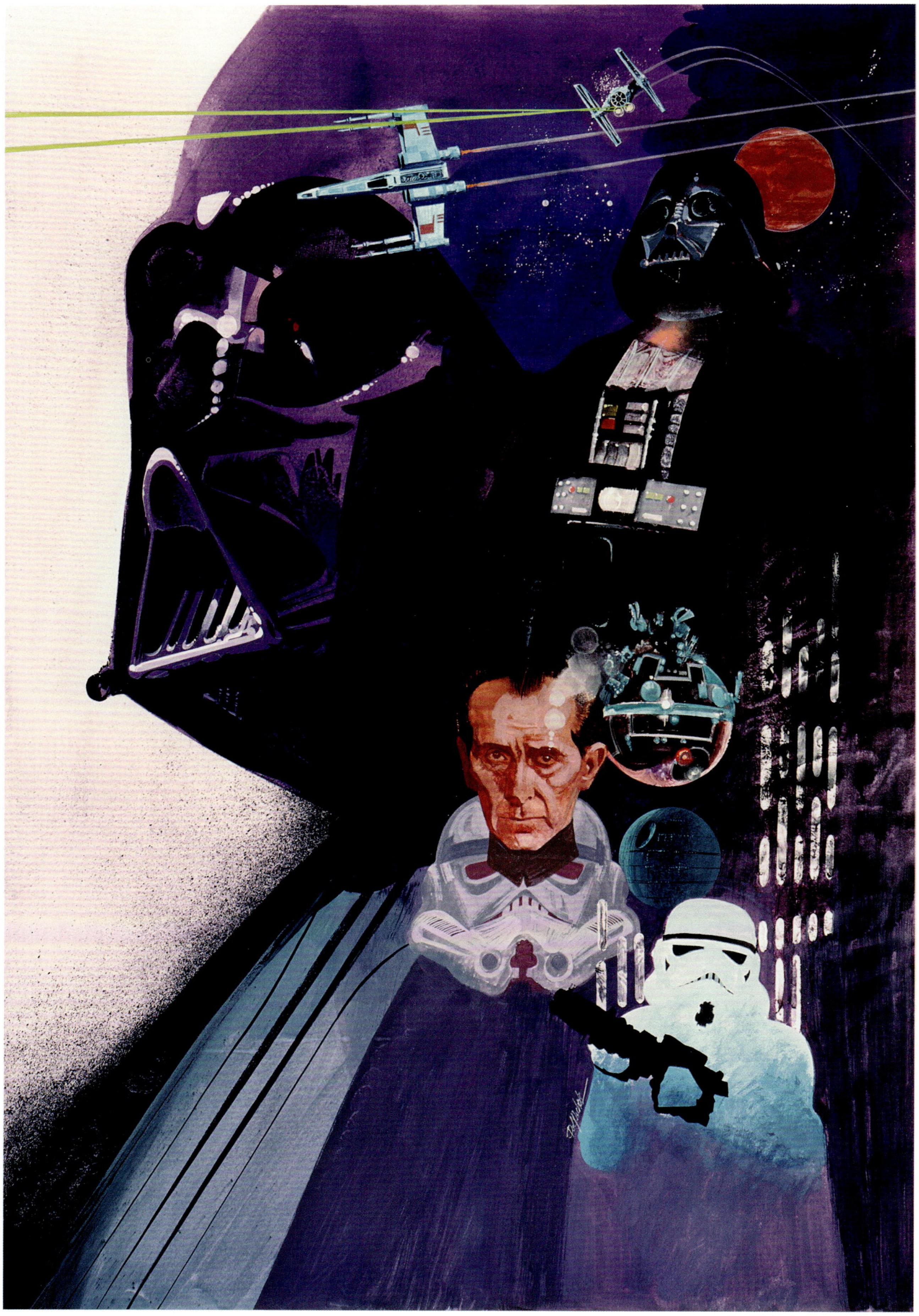

LEFT

Del Nichols

Final painted artwork for *Star Wars* Coca-Cola poster, 1977

Poster used as a premium in Coca-Cola/Burger King/ Burger Chef promotion

RIGHT

Del Nichols

Final painted artwork for *Star Wars* Coca-Cola poster, 1977

Poster used as a premium in Coca-Cola/Burger King/ Burger Chef promotion

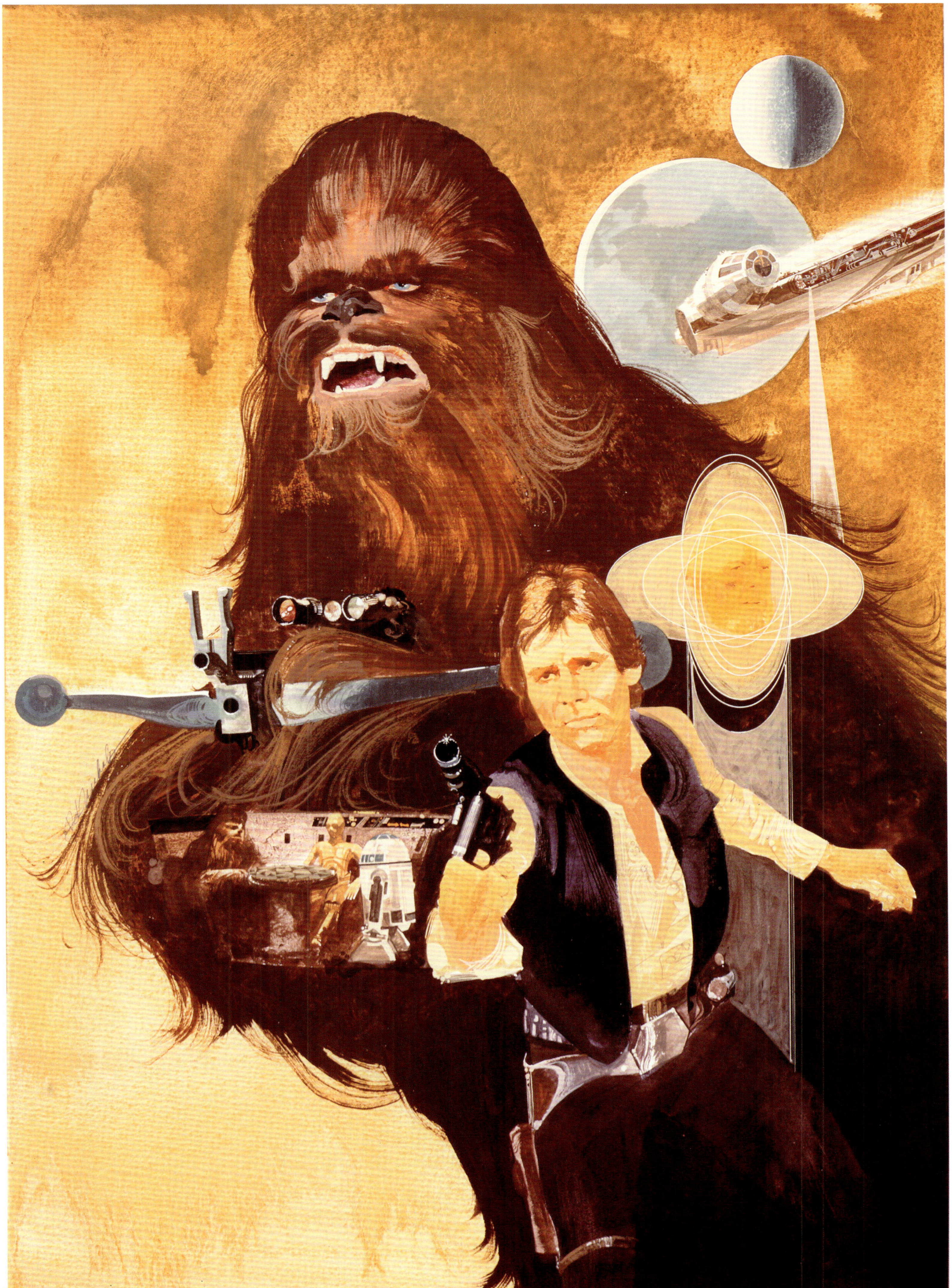

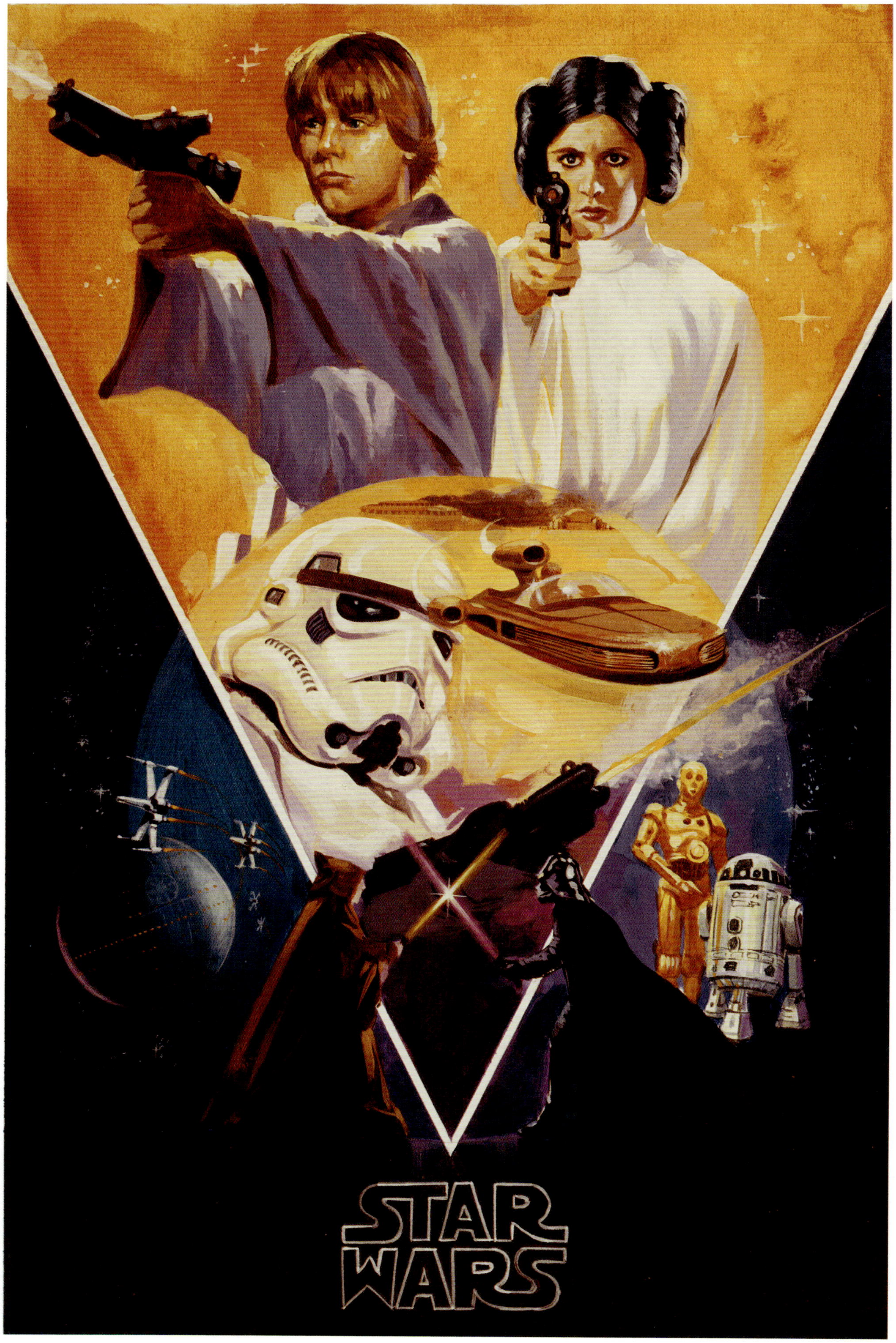

LEFT

Unknown

Full-color painted concept treatment for *Star Wars* poster, c. 1977

RIGHT

Del Nichols

Final painted artwork for *Star Wars* Coca-Cola poster, 1977

Poster used as a premium in Coca-Cola/Burger King/ Burger Chef promotion

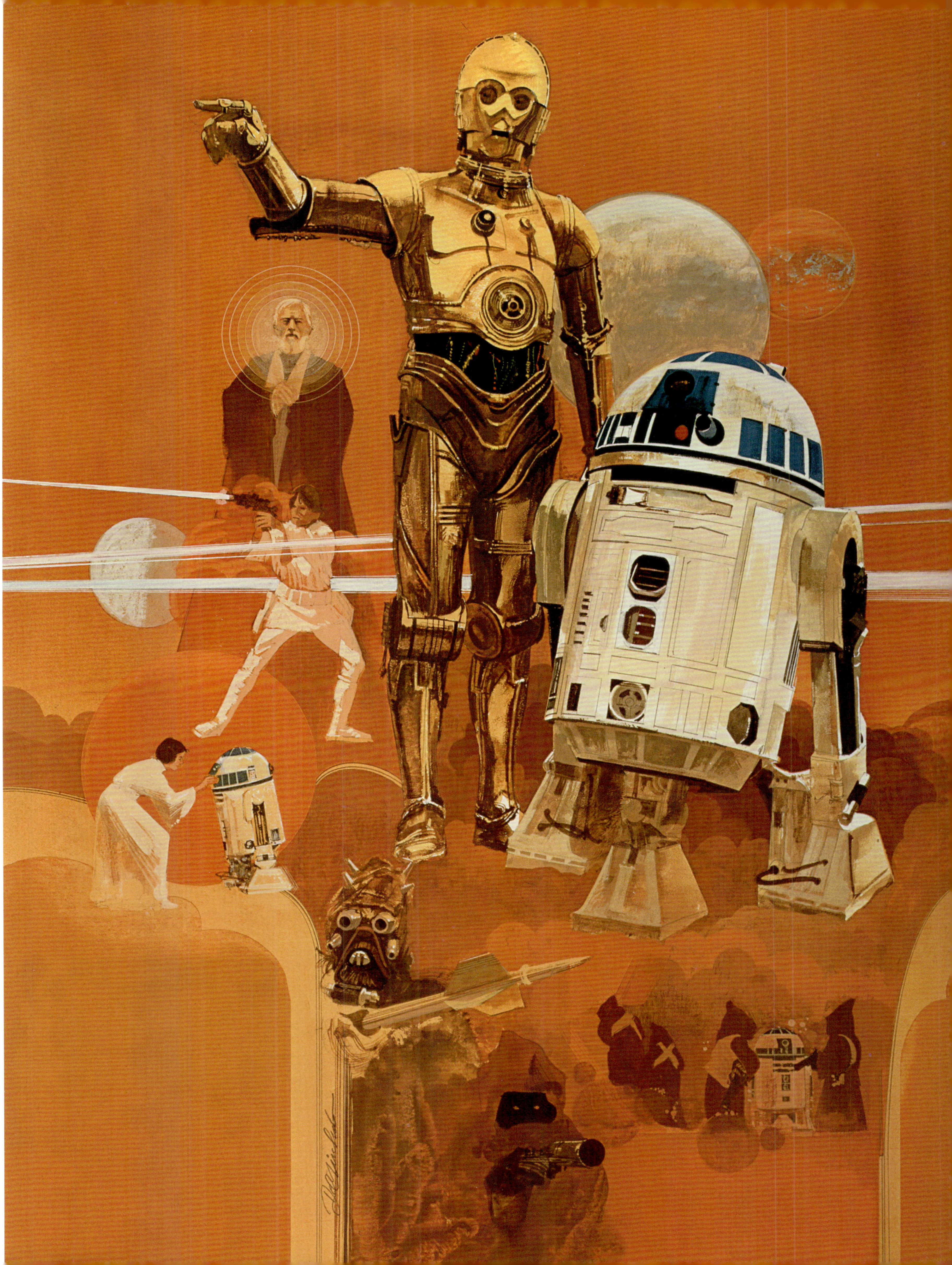

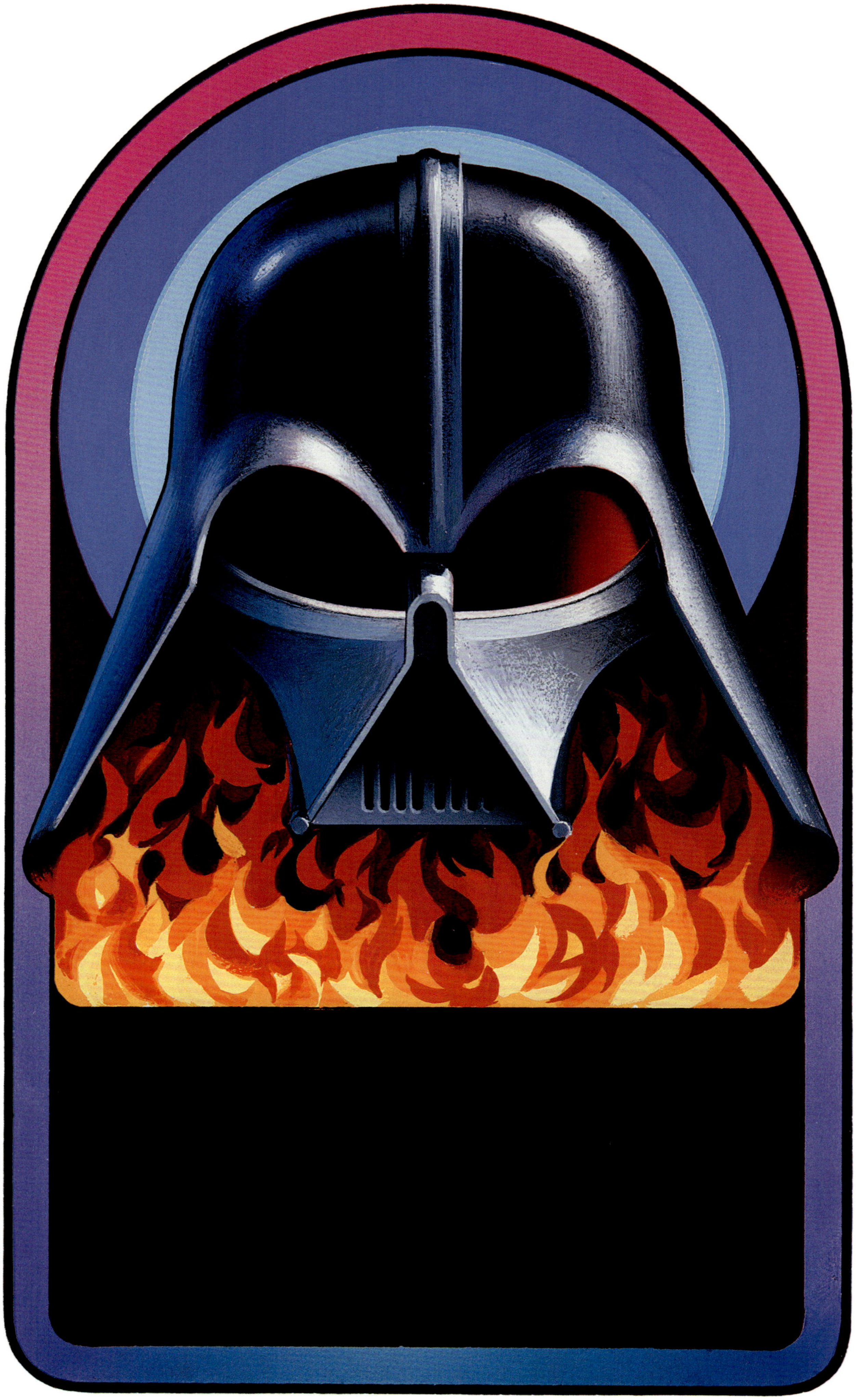

LEFT

Ralph McQuarrie

Final painted artwork for *The Empire Strikes Back* logo, 1979

Logo first produced as sticker during film production

RIGHT

Ralph McQuarrie

Full-color painted concept treatment for *The Empire Strikes Back* logo, 1979

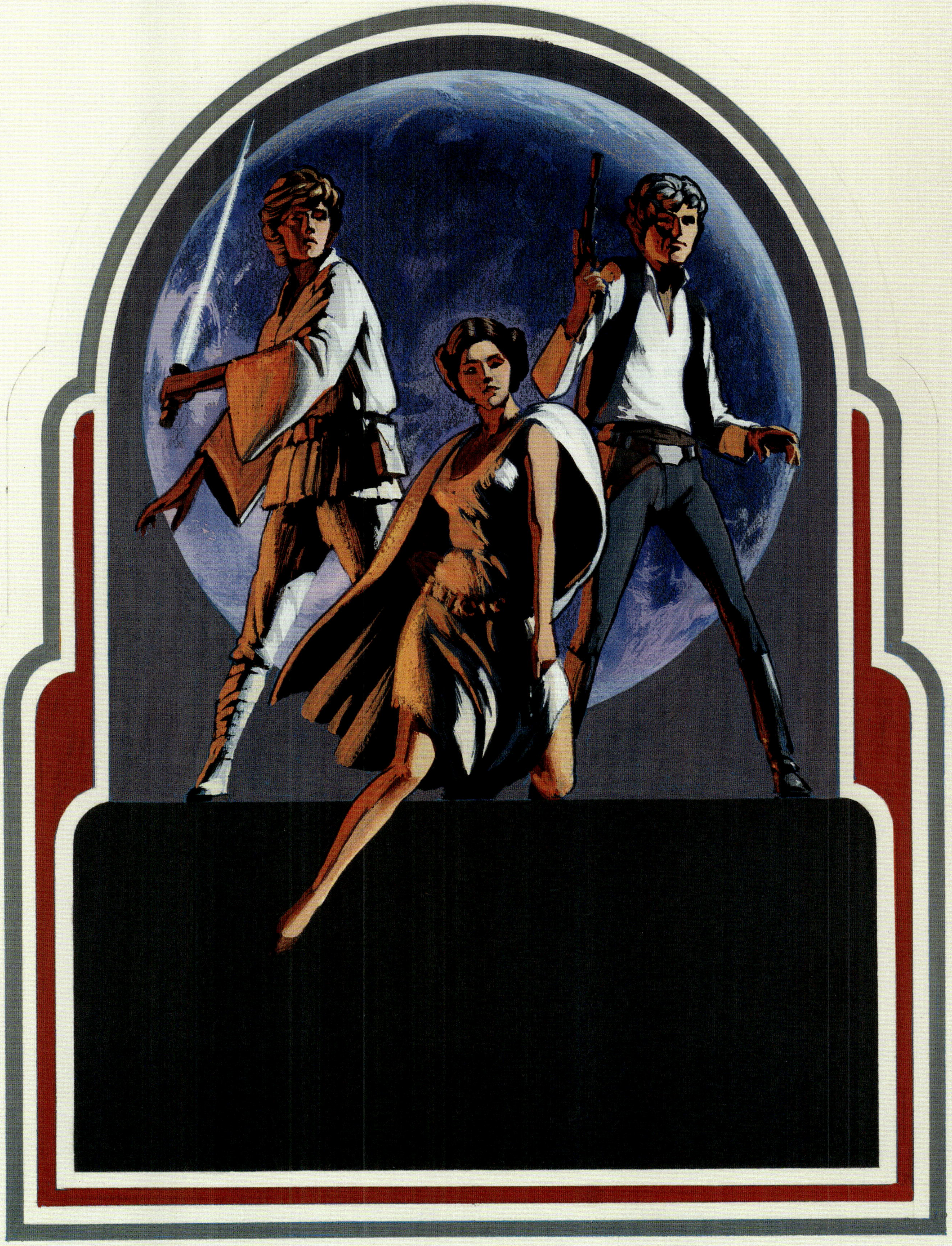

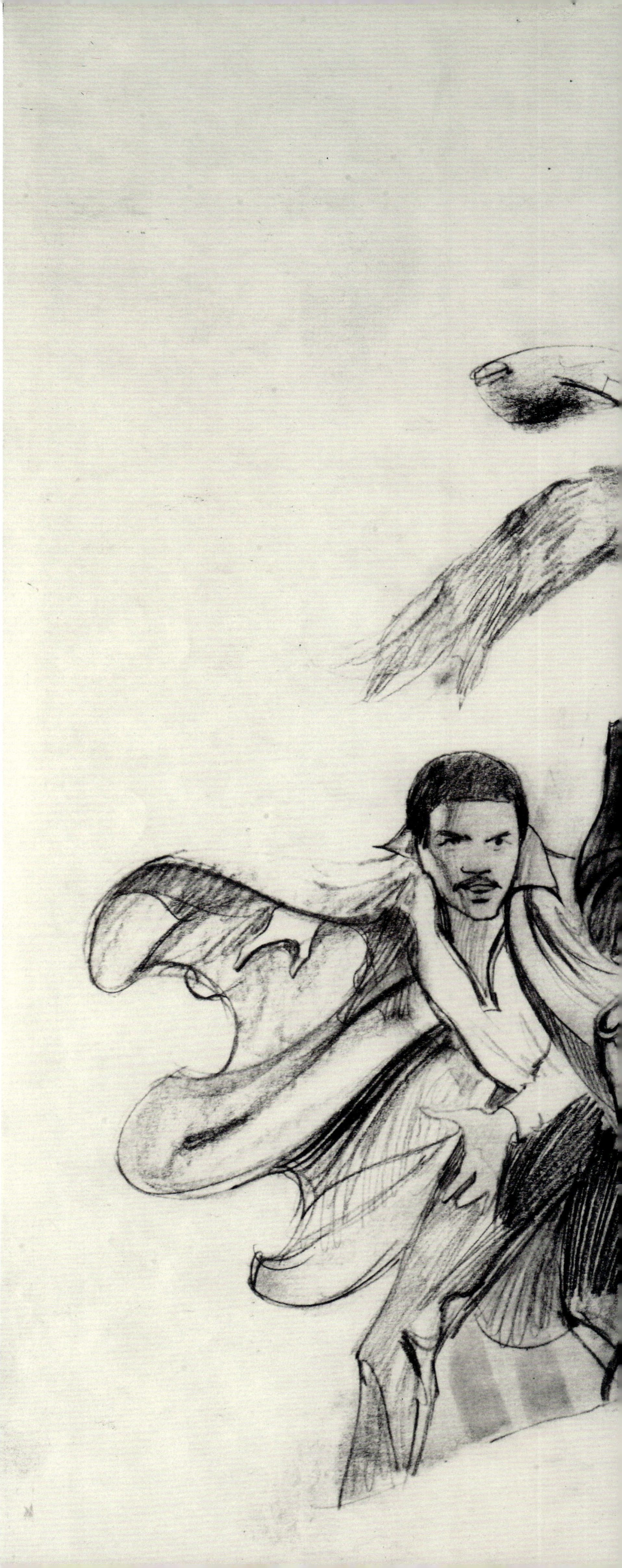

RIGHT

Tom Jung

Black-and-white concept treatment for *The Empire Strikes Back* poster, 1979

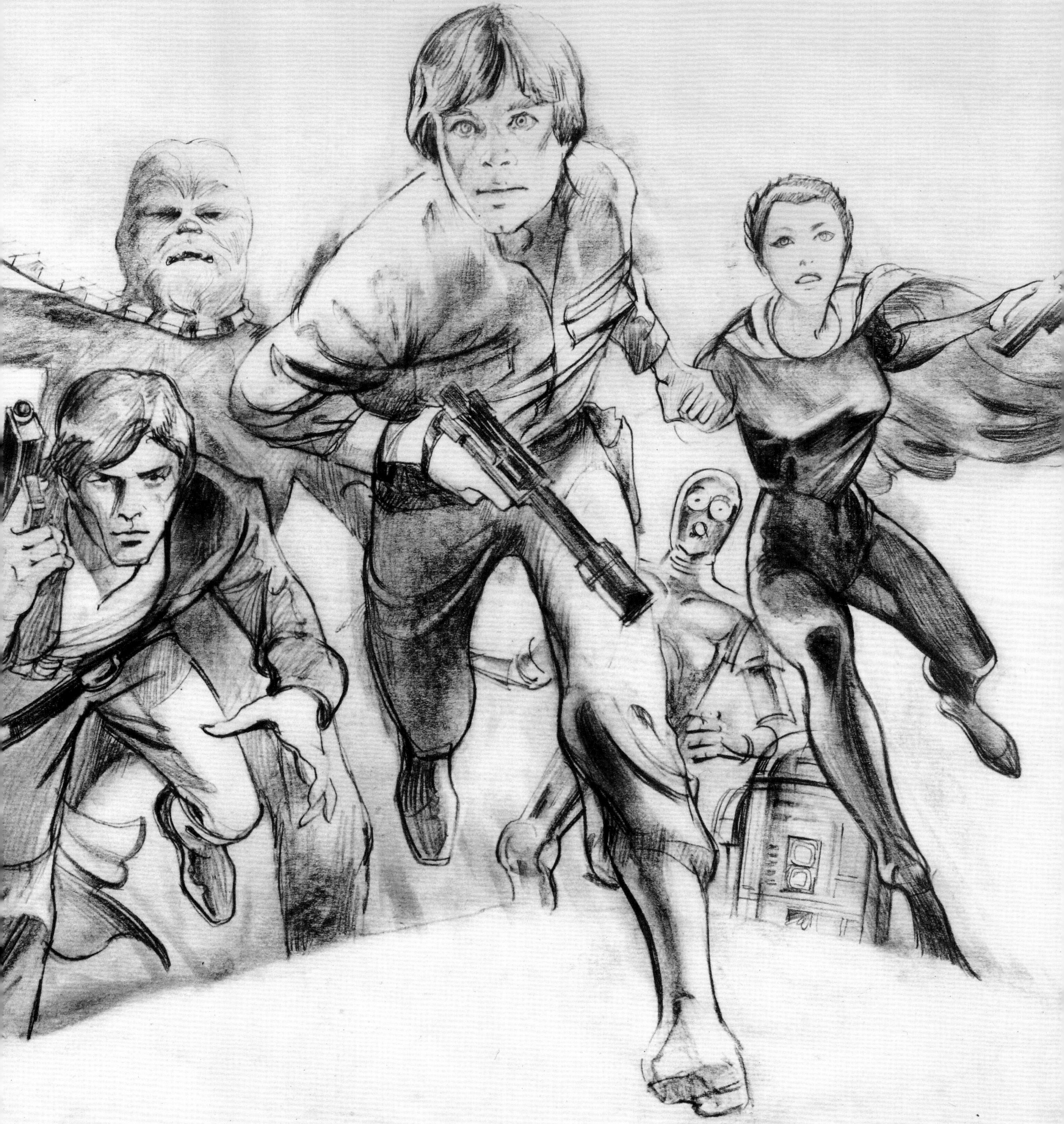

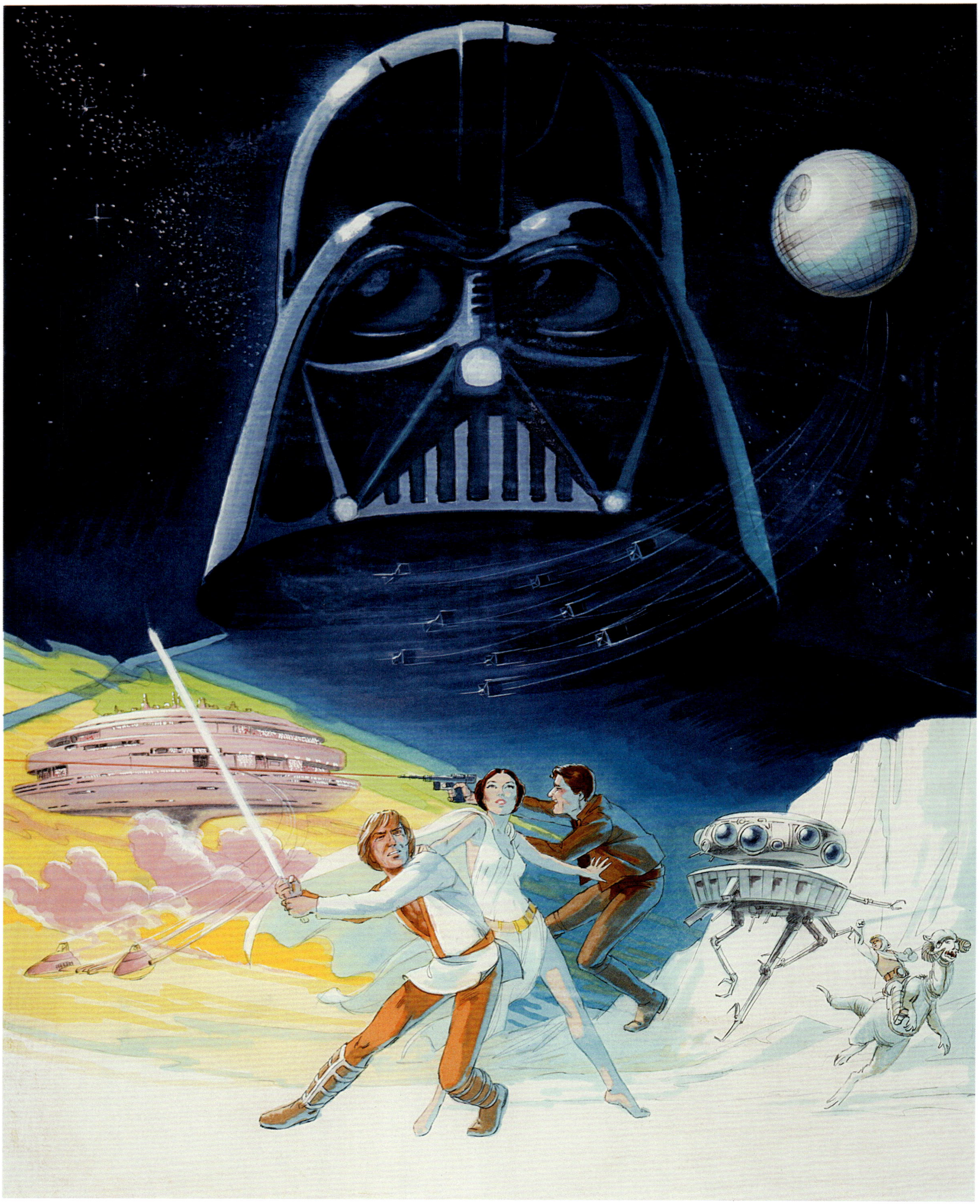

ABOVE

Unknown

Full-color painted concept treatment for *The Empire Strikes Back* poster, 1979

RIGHT

Noriyoshi Ohrai

Full-color painted concept treatment for *The Empire Strikes Back* poster, 1979

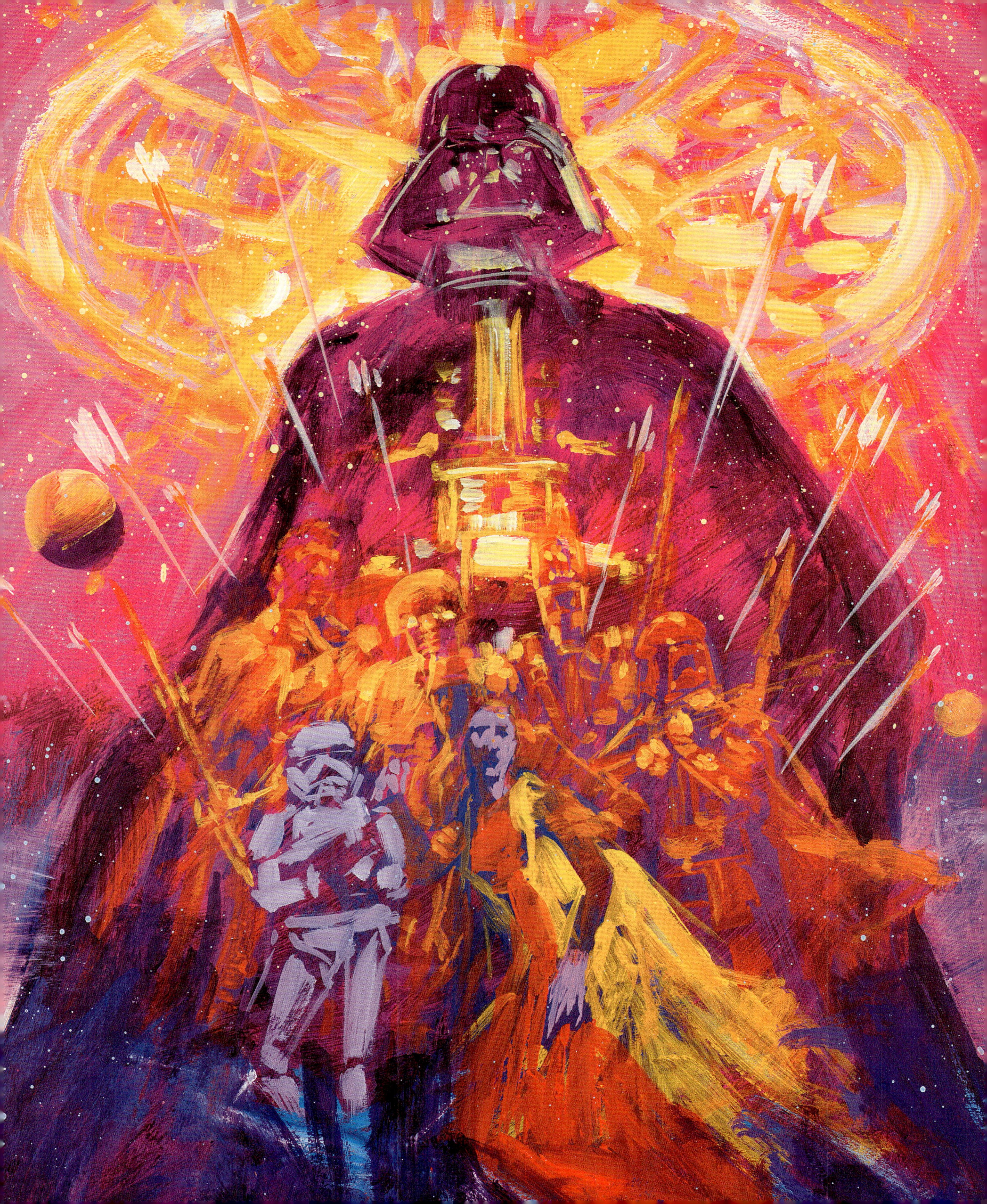

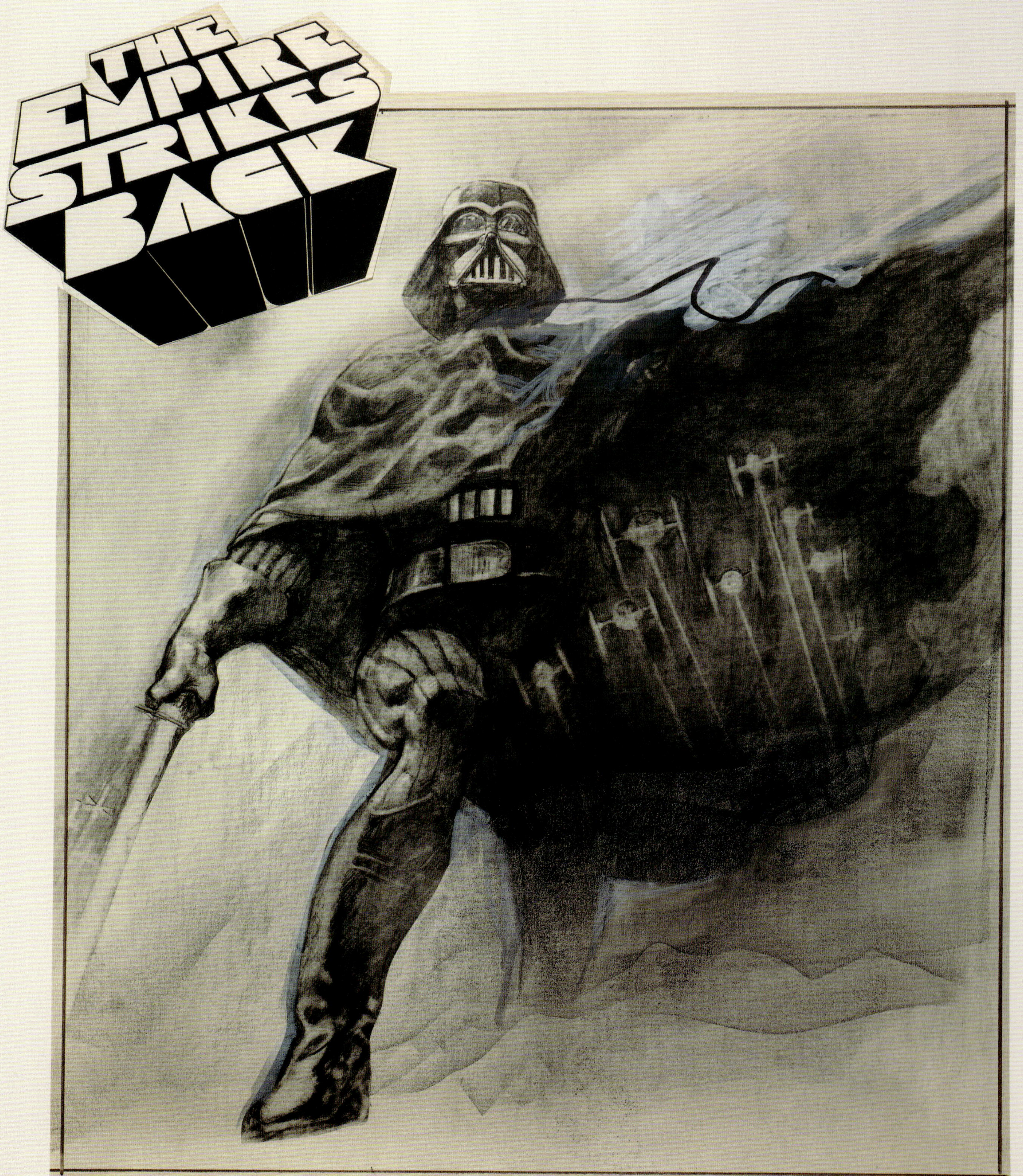
THE
EMPIRE
STRIKES
BACK

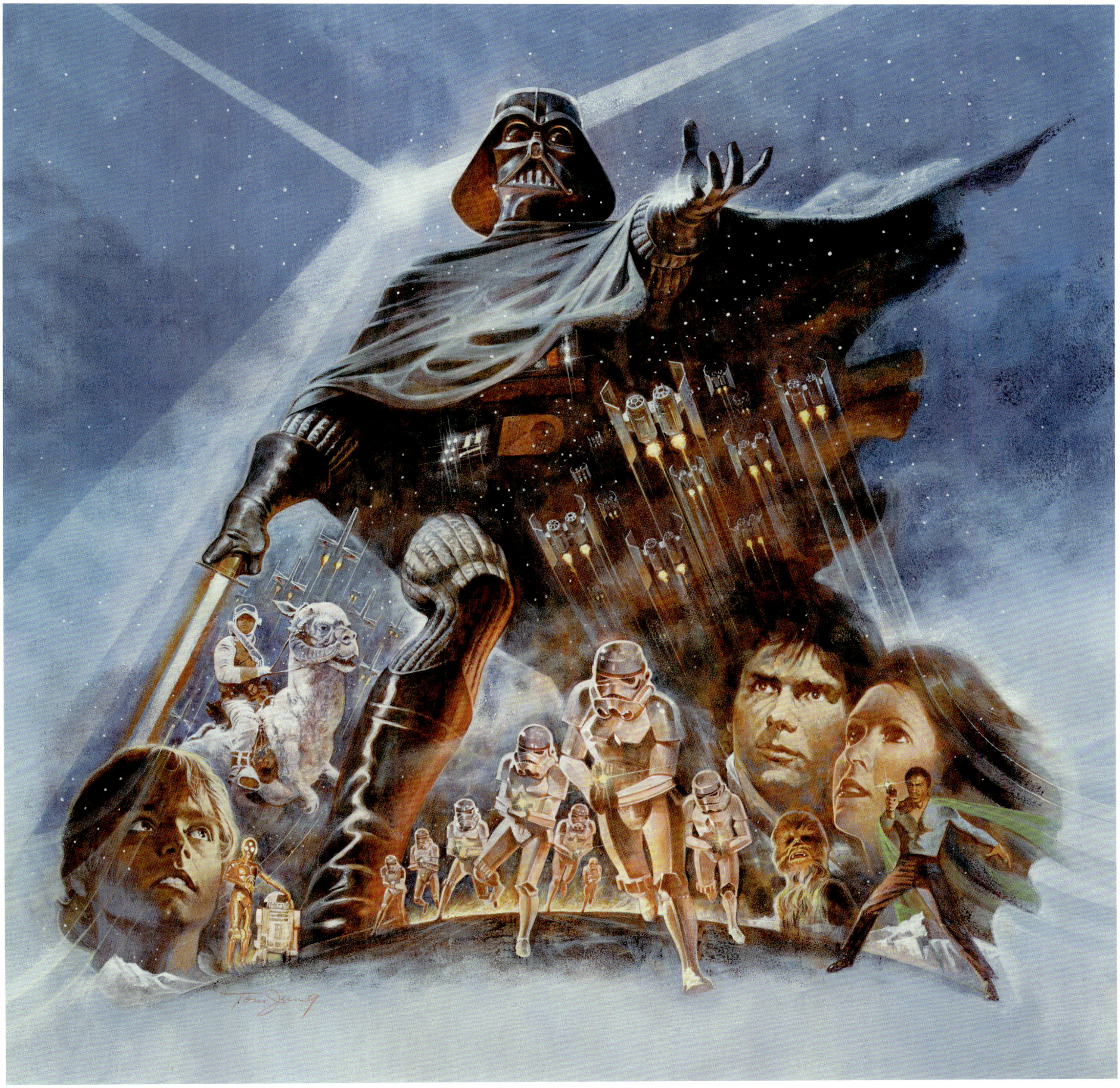

LEFT

Tom Jung

Black-and-white concept treatment for *The Empire Strikes Back* poster, c. 1979

ABOVE AND FOLLOWING SPREAD (DETAIL)

Tom Jung

Final painted artwork for *The Empire Strikes Back* style "B" theatrical one-sheet, 1980

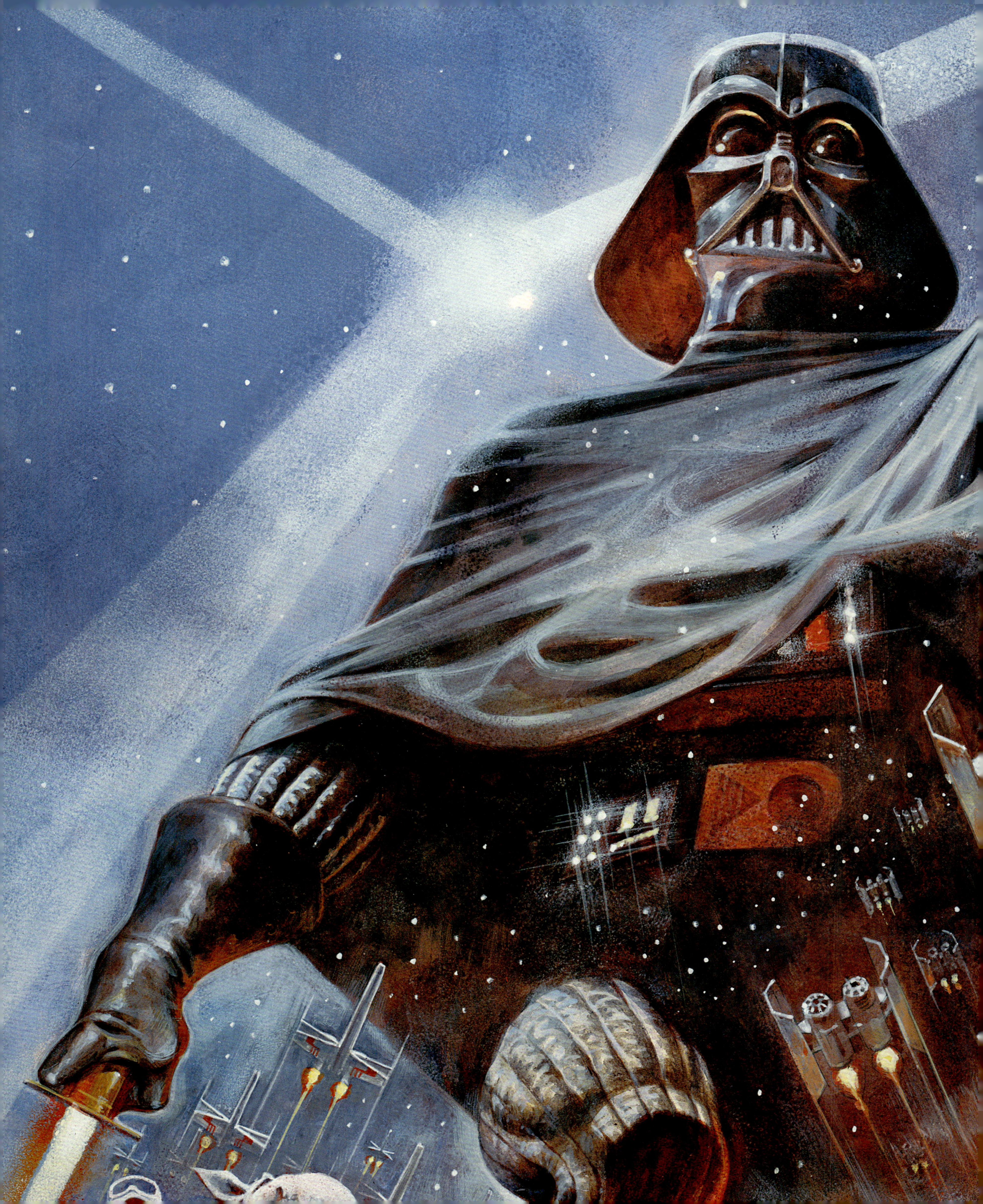

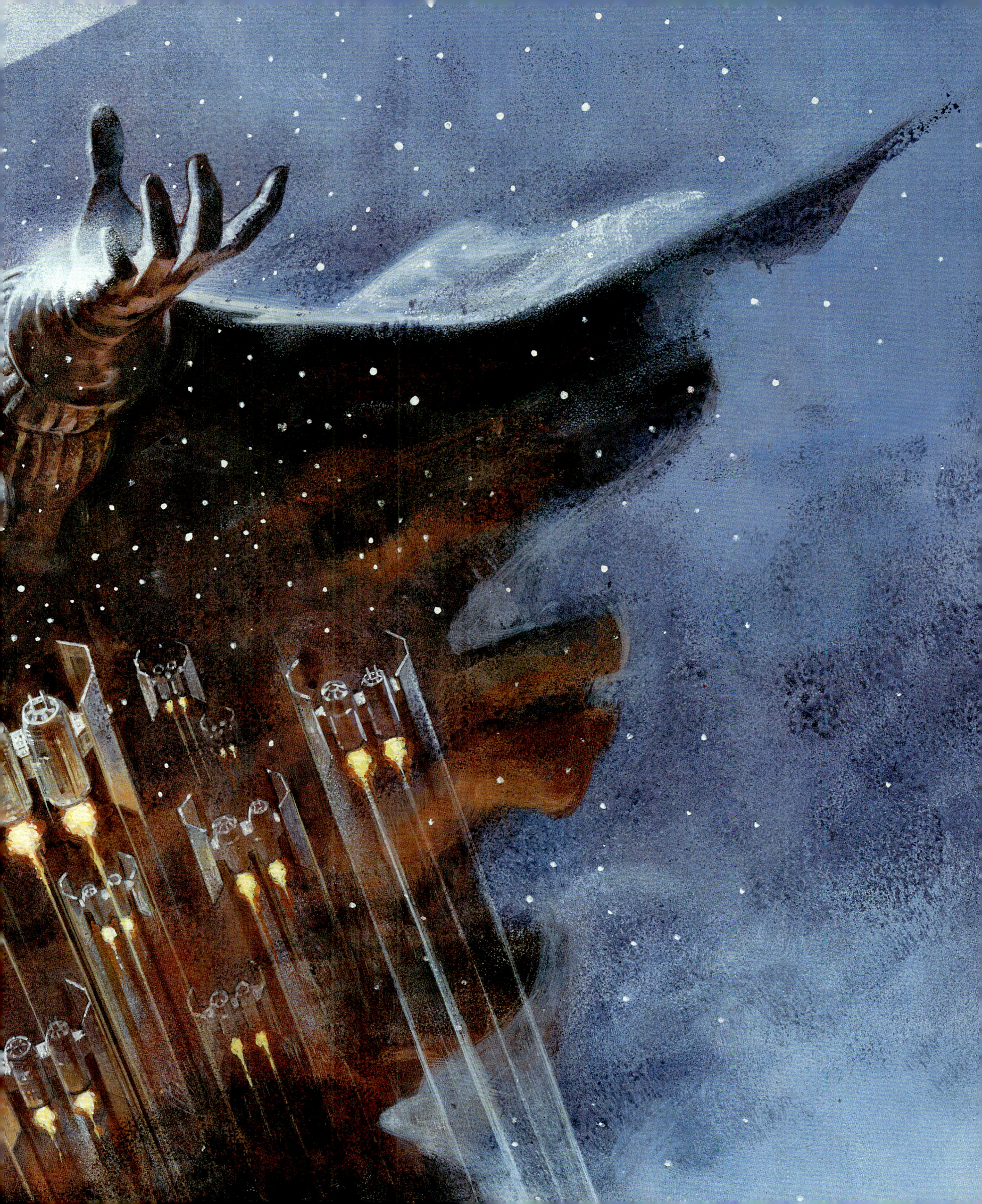

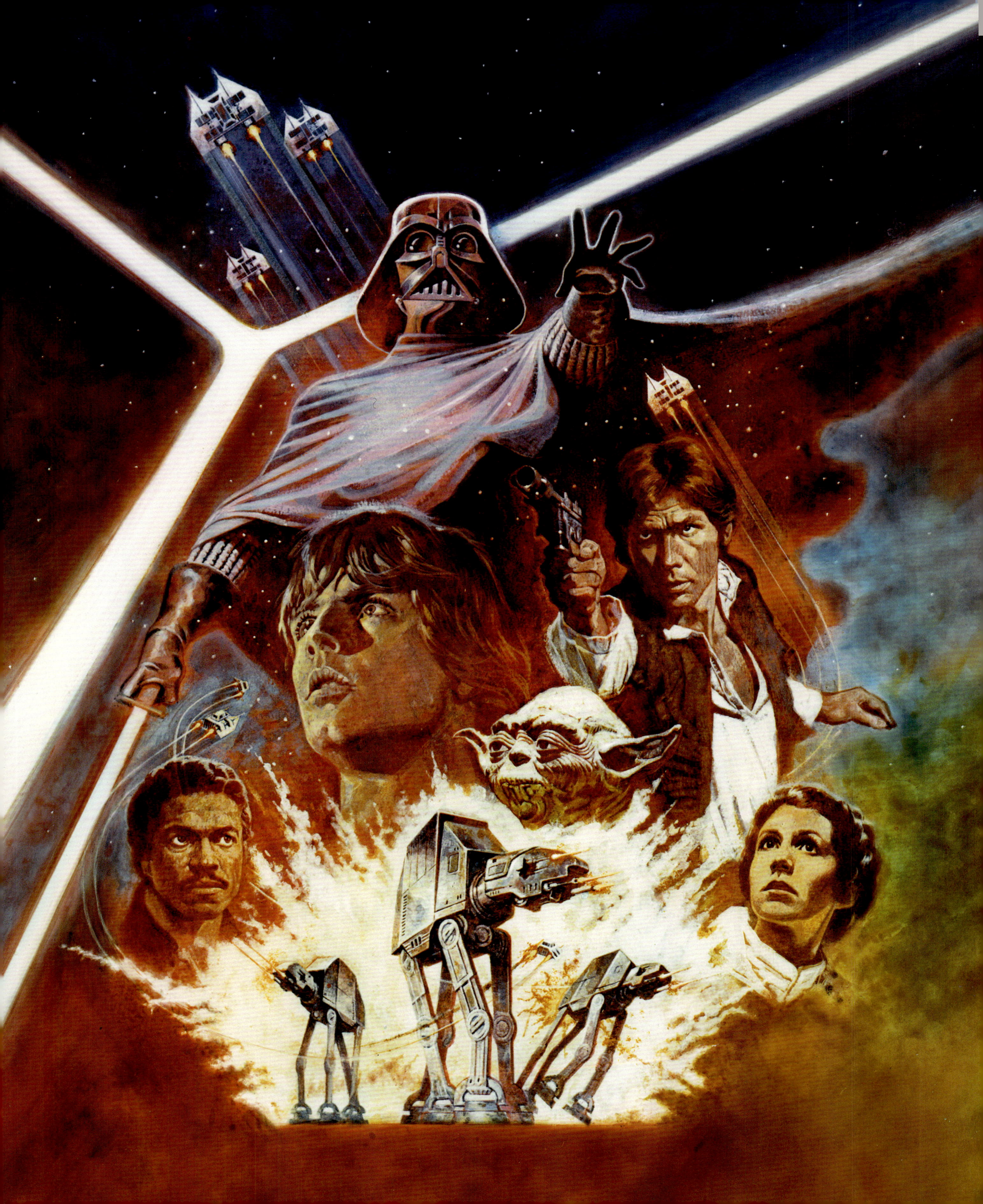

LEFT

Tom Jung

Final painted artwork for *The Empire Strikes Back* theatrical rerelease one-sheet, 1981

RIGHT

Manuel Sanjulián

Black-and-white concept treatment for *The Empire Strikes Back* poster, c. 1979

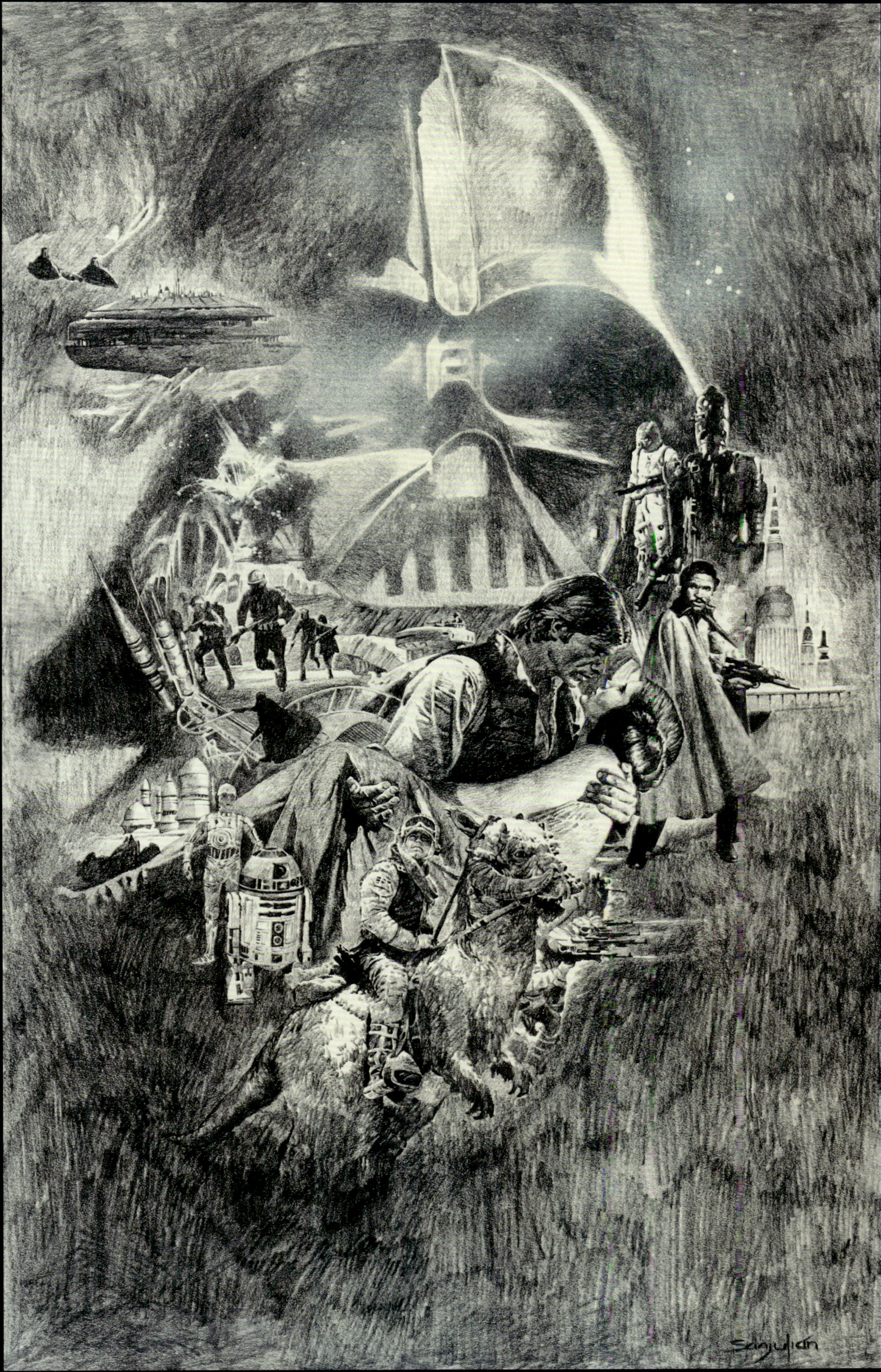

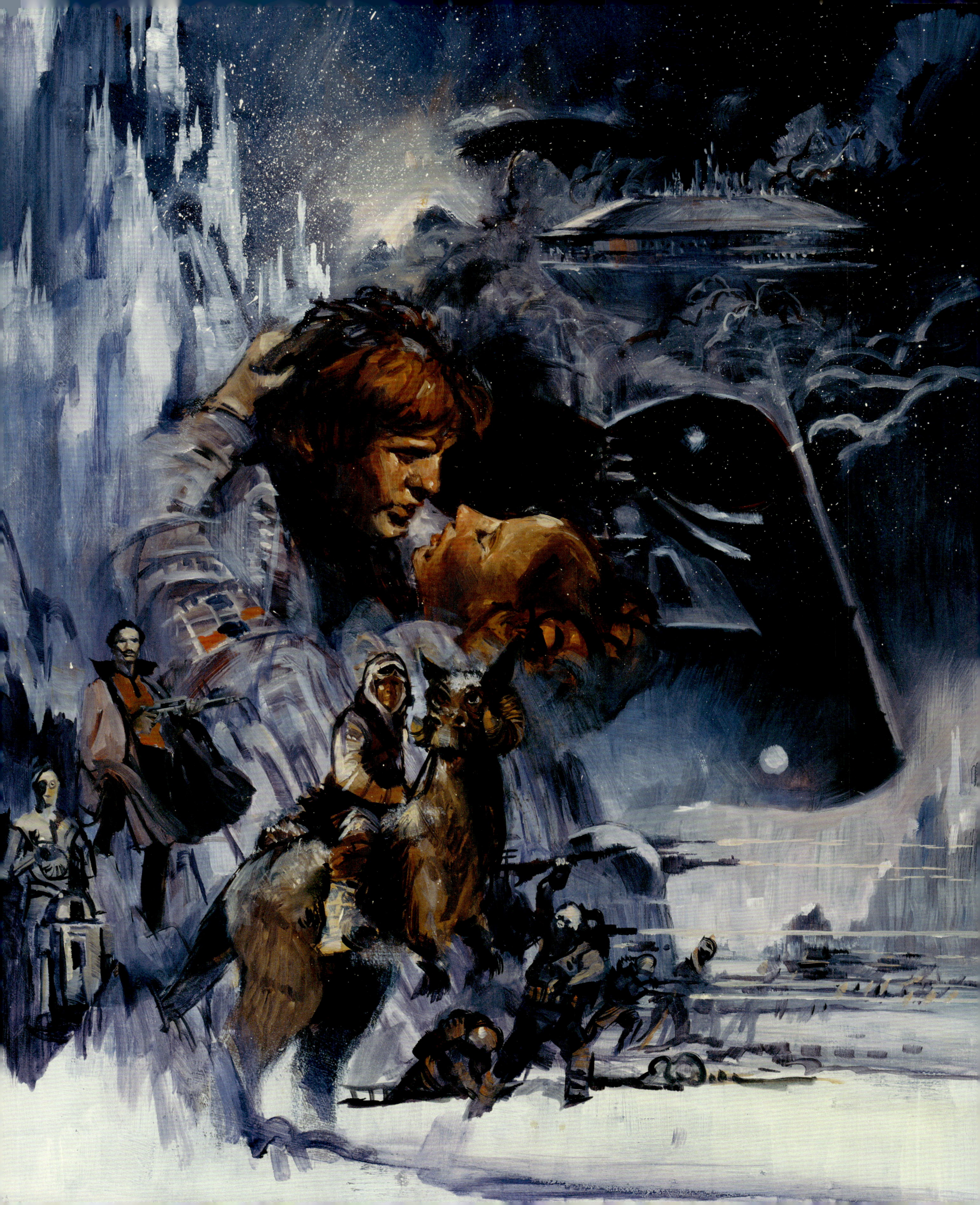

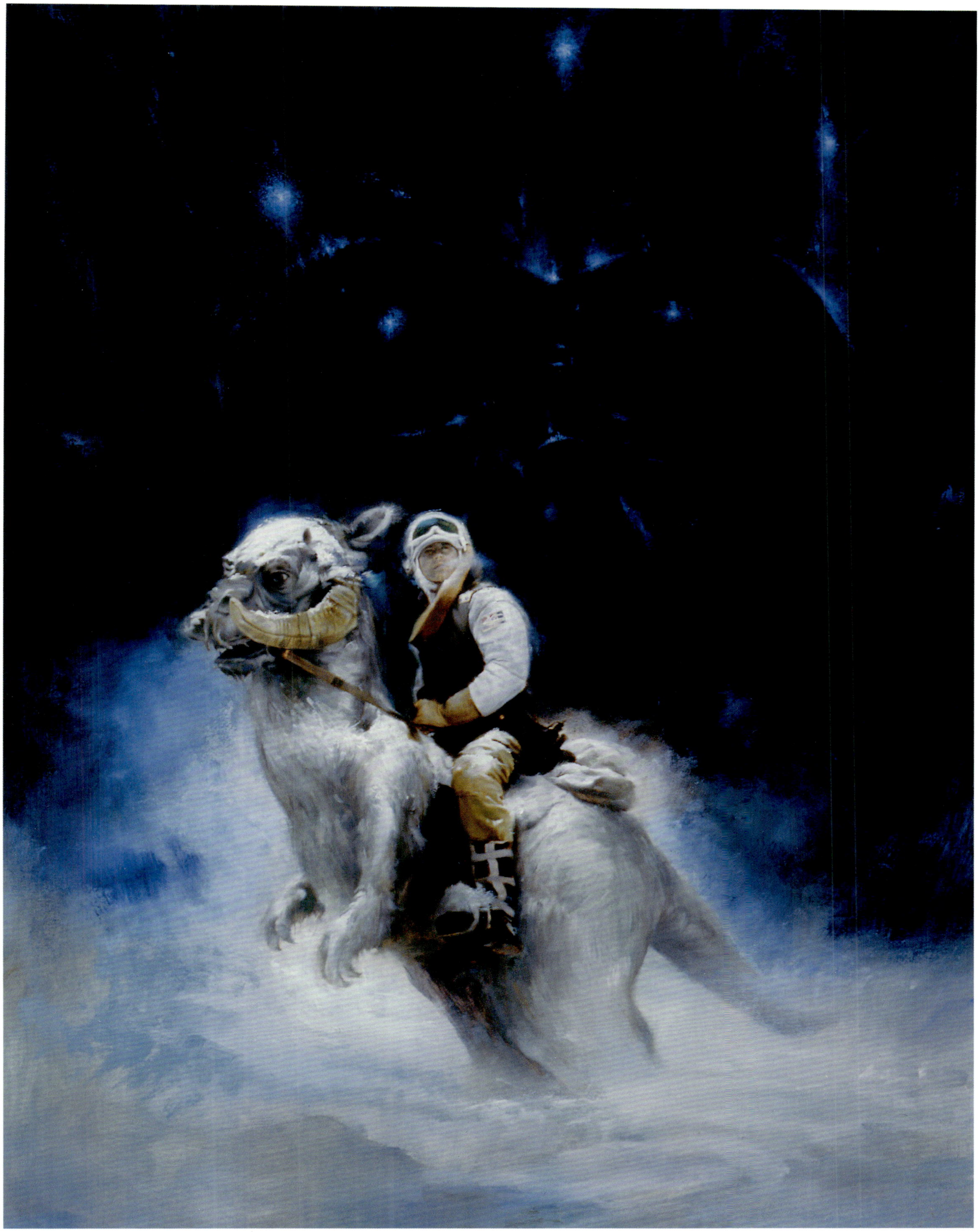

LEFT

Unknown

Full-color painted concept treatment for *The Empire Strikes Back* poster, c. 1979

ABOVE

Roger Kastel

Full-color painted concept treatment for *The Empire Strikes Back* style "A" theatrical one-sheet, c. 1979

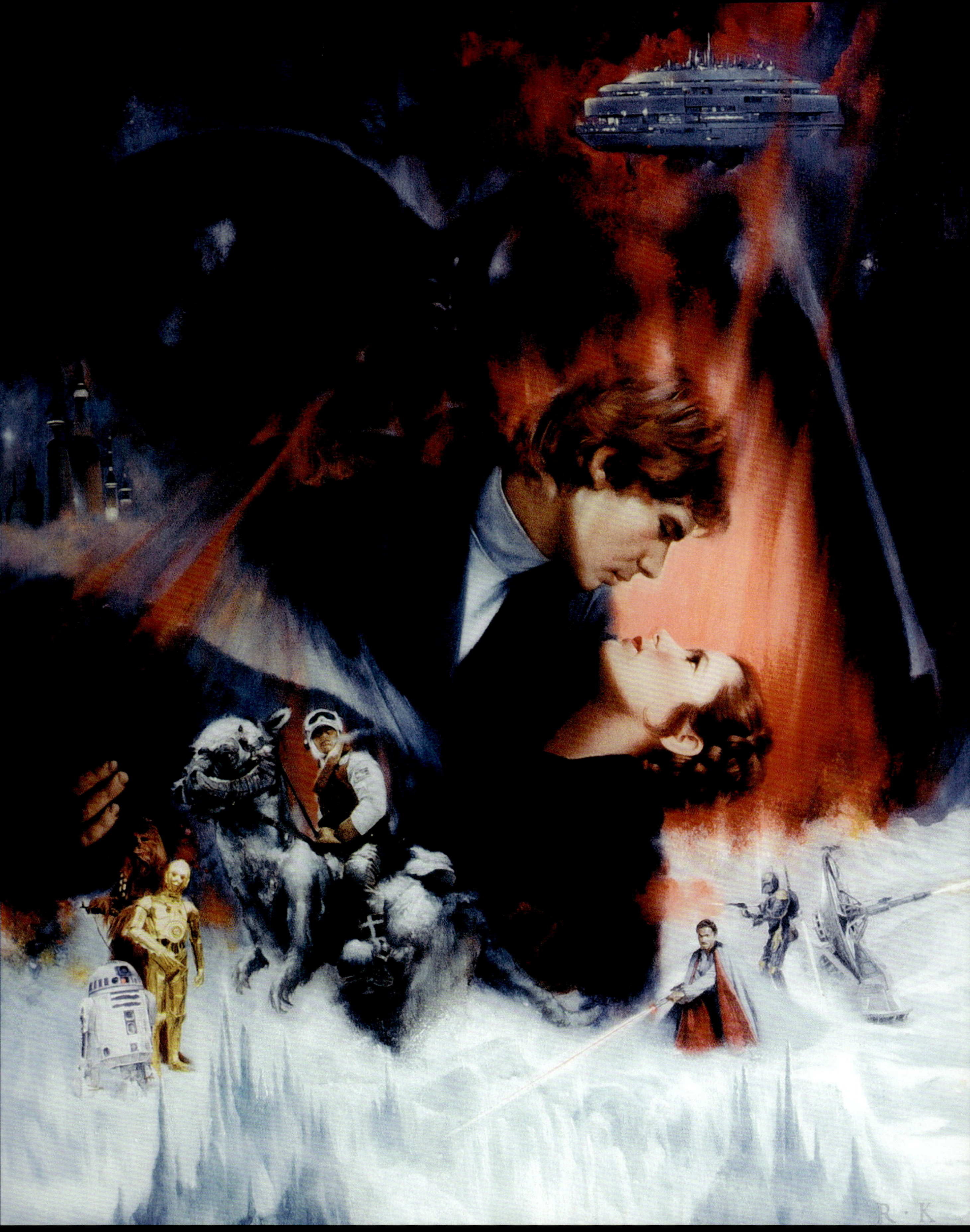

ABOVE

Roger Kastel

Full-color painted concept treatment for *The Empire Strikes Back* style "A" ("*Gone with the Wind*") theatrical one-sheet, c. 1979

RIGHT AND FOLLOWING SPREAD (DETAIL)

Roger Kastel

Final painted artwork for *The Empire Strikes Back* style "A" ("*Gone with the Wind*") theatrical one-sheet and novelization cover, 1980

For the U.S. one-sheet, the elements of Cloud City on the left, and Lando Calrissian, Boba Fett, and the Hoth cannon on the right, were painted out. They remained in many international-release posters.

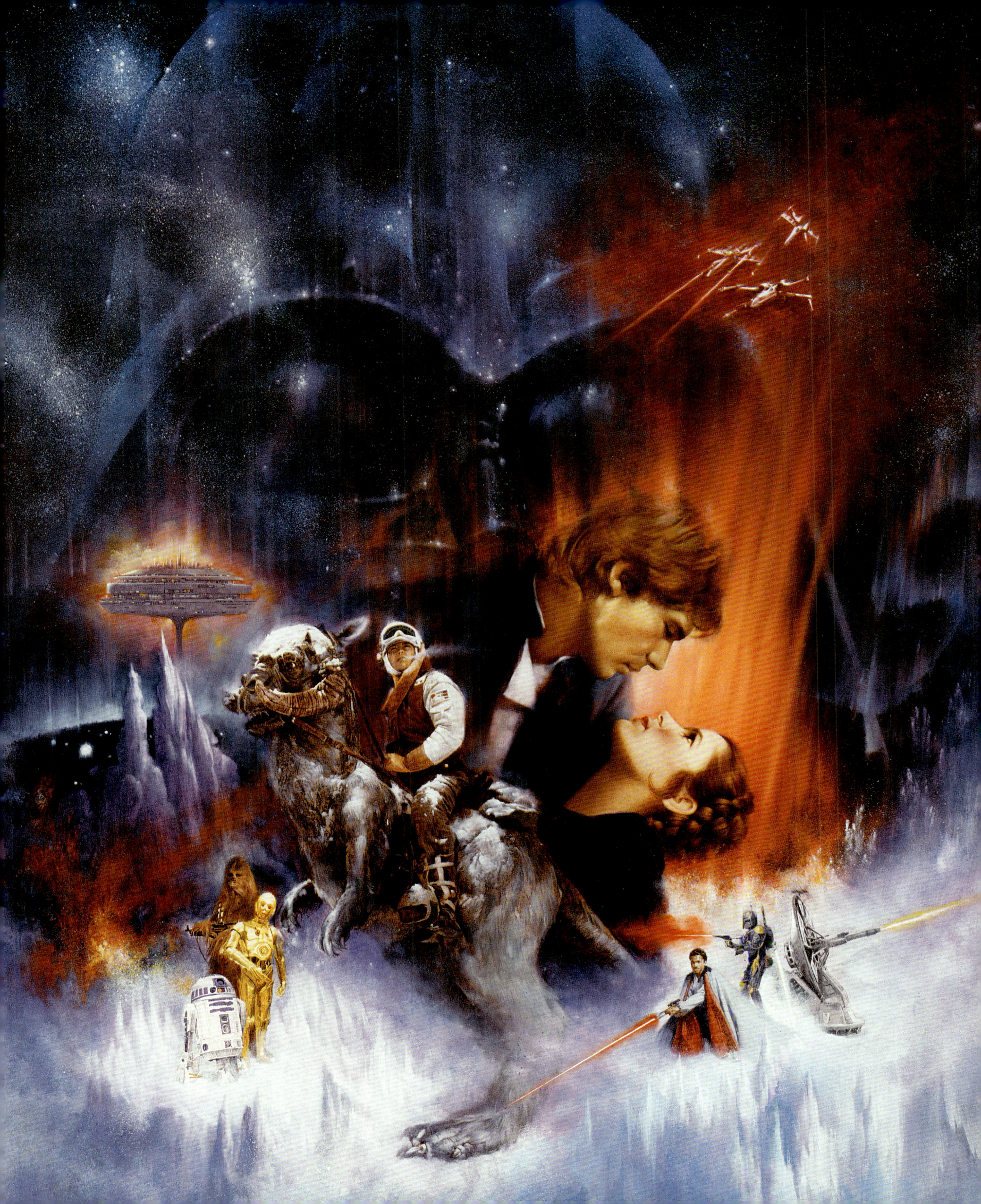

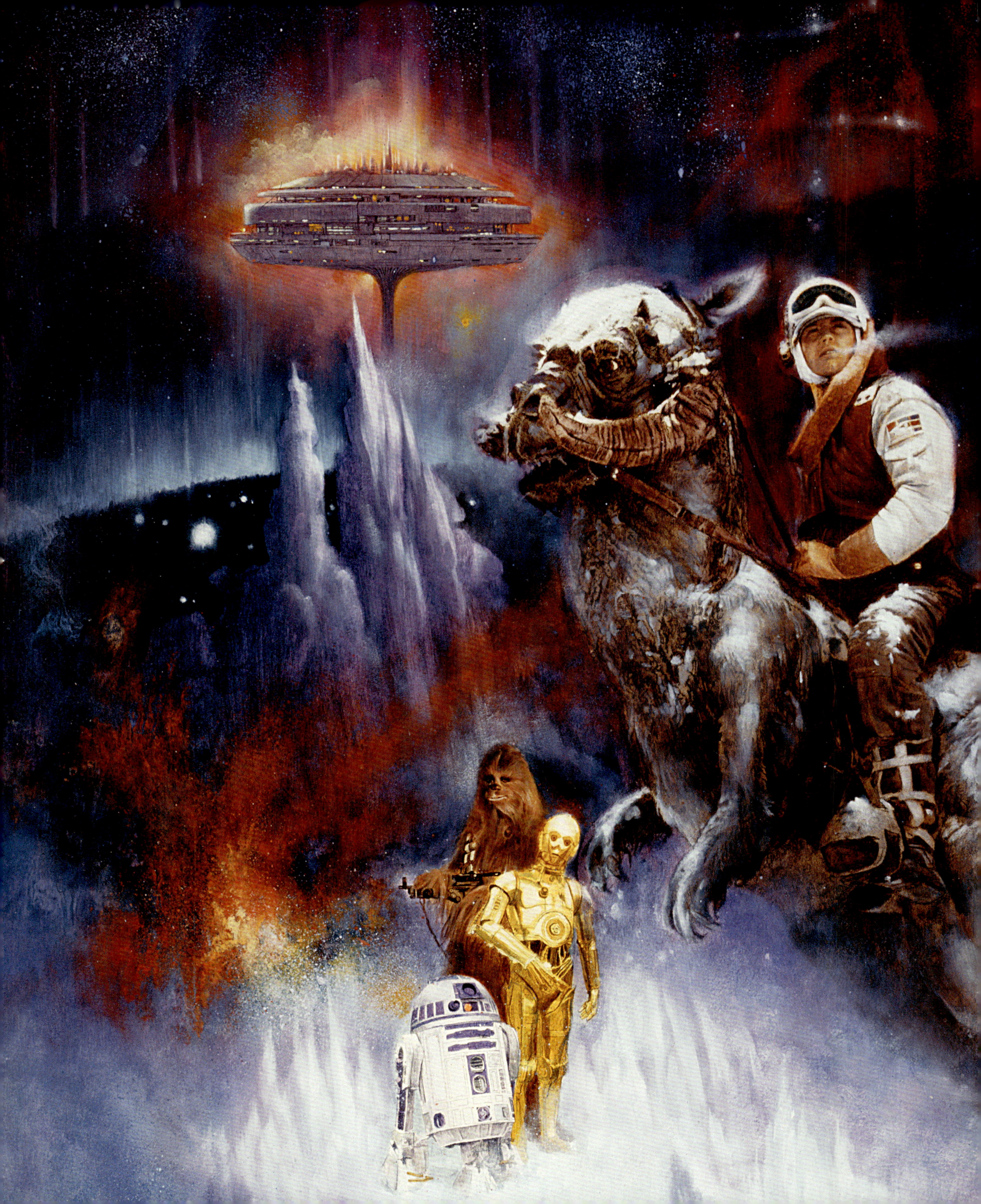

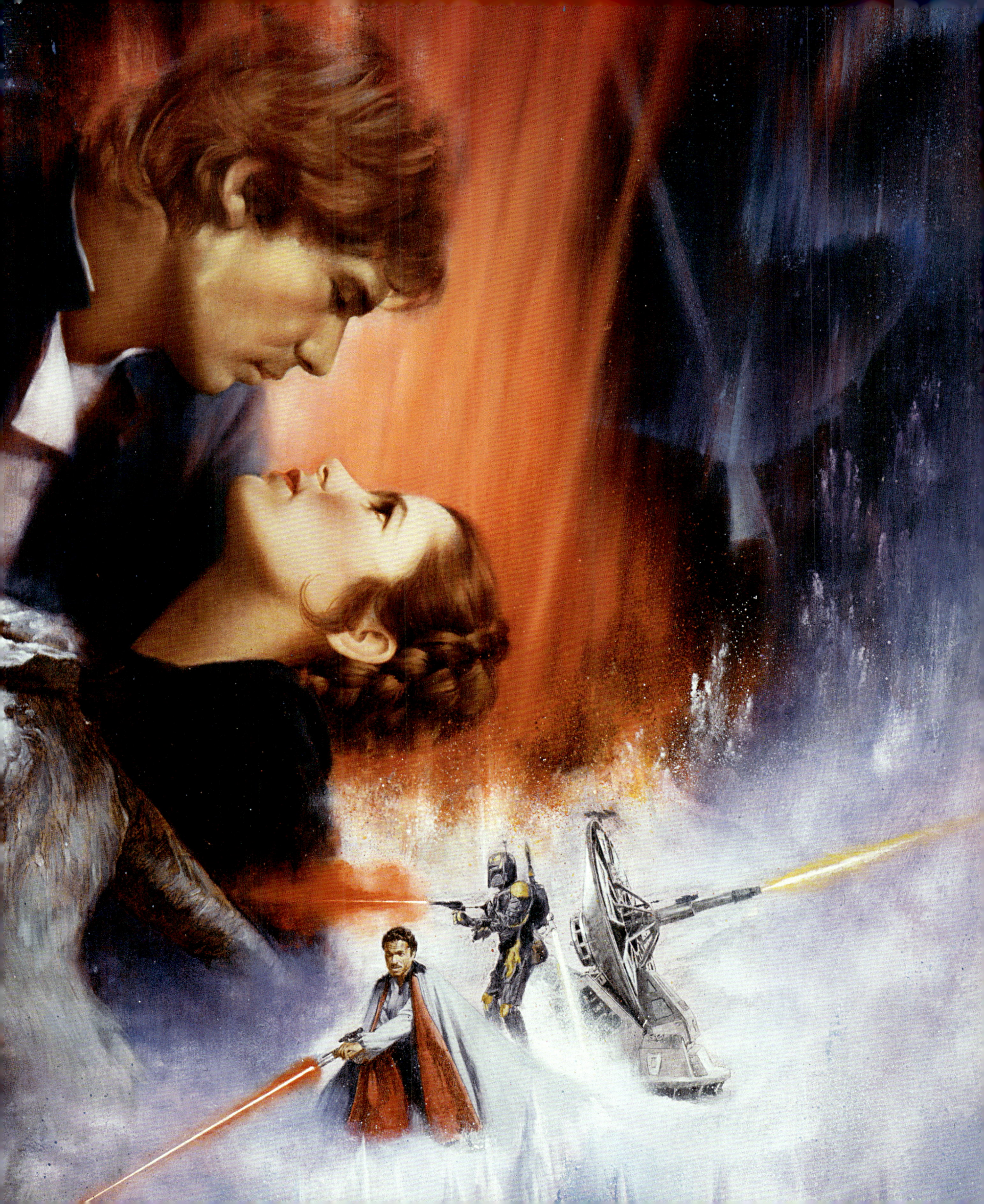

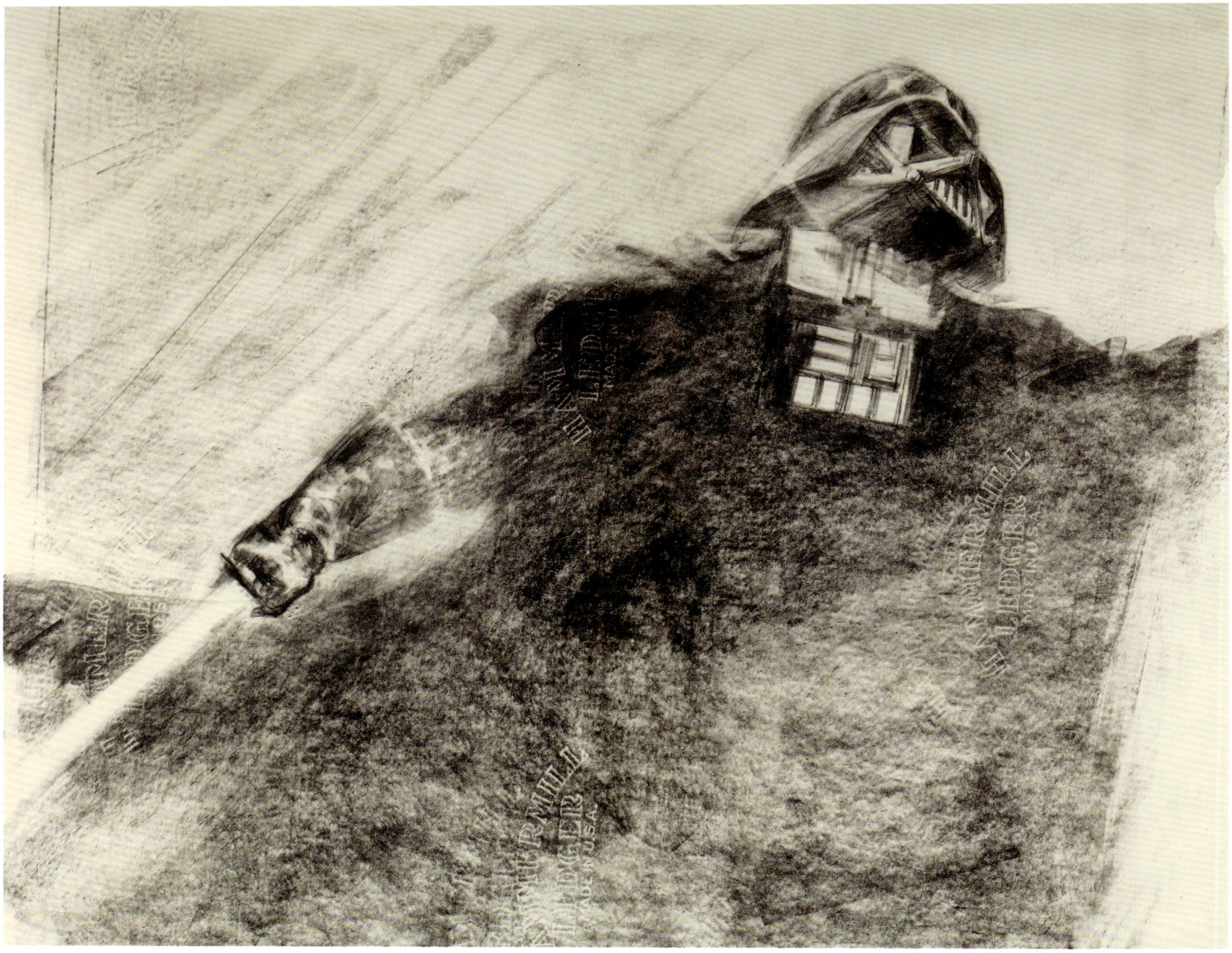

ABOVE

Tom Jung

Black-and-white concept treatment for *The Empire Strikes Back* poster, c. 1979

RIGHT

Tom Jung

Black-and-white concept treatment for *The Empire Strikes Back* poster, c. 1979

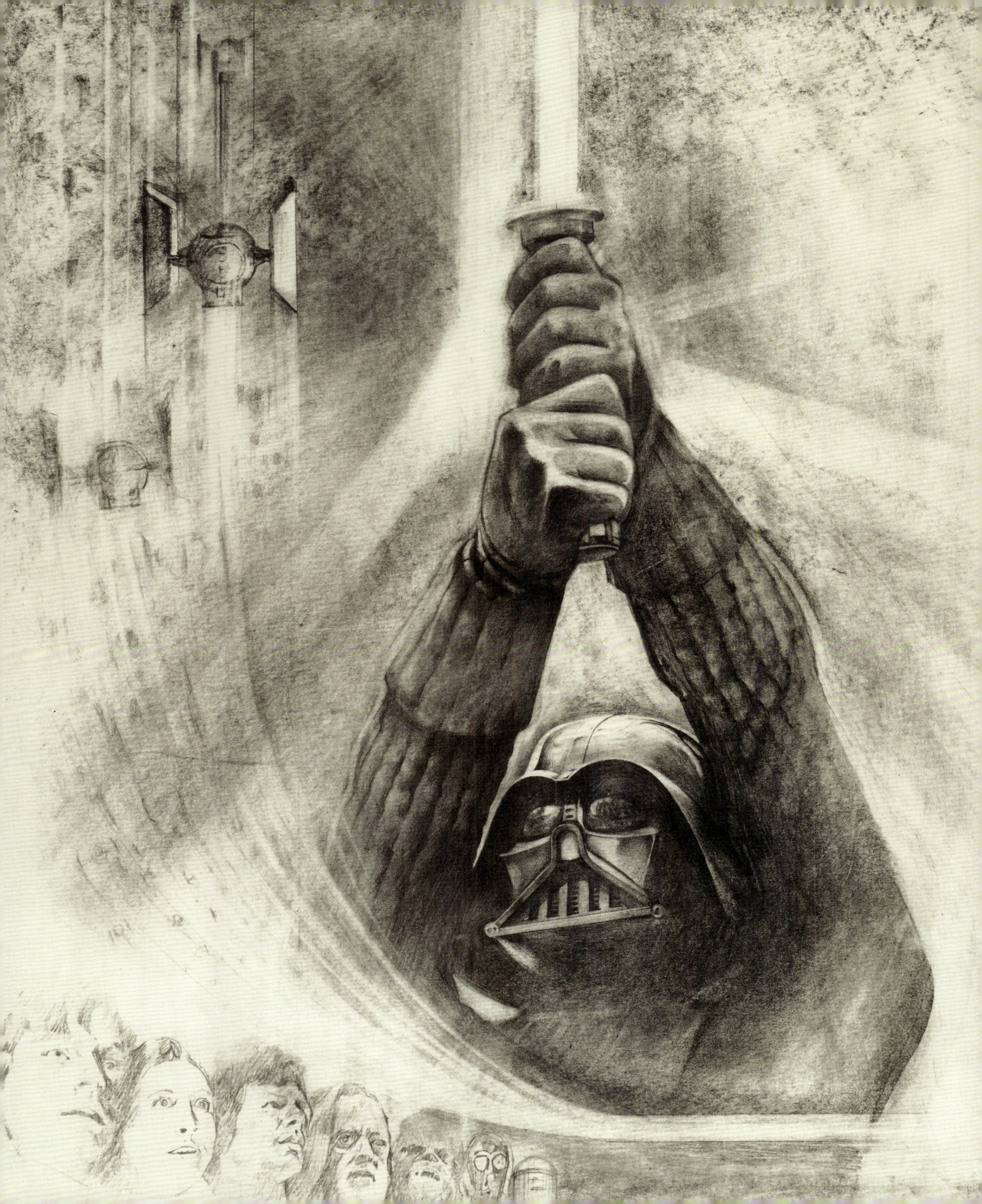

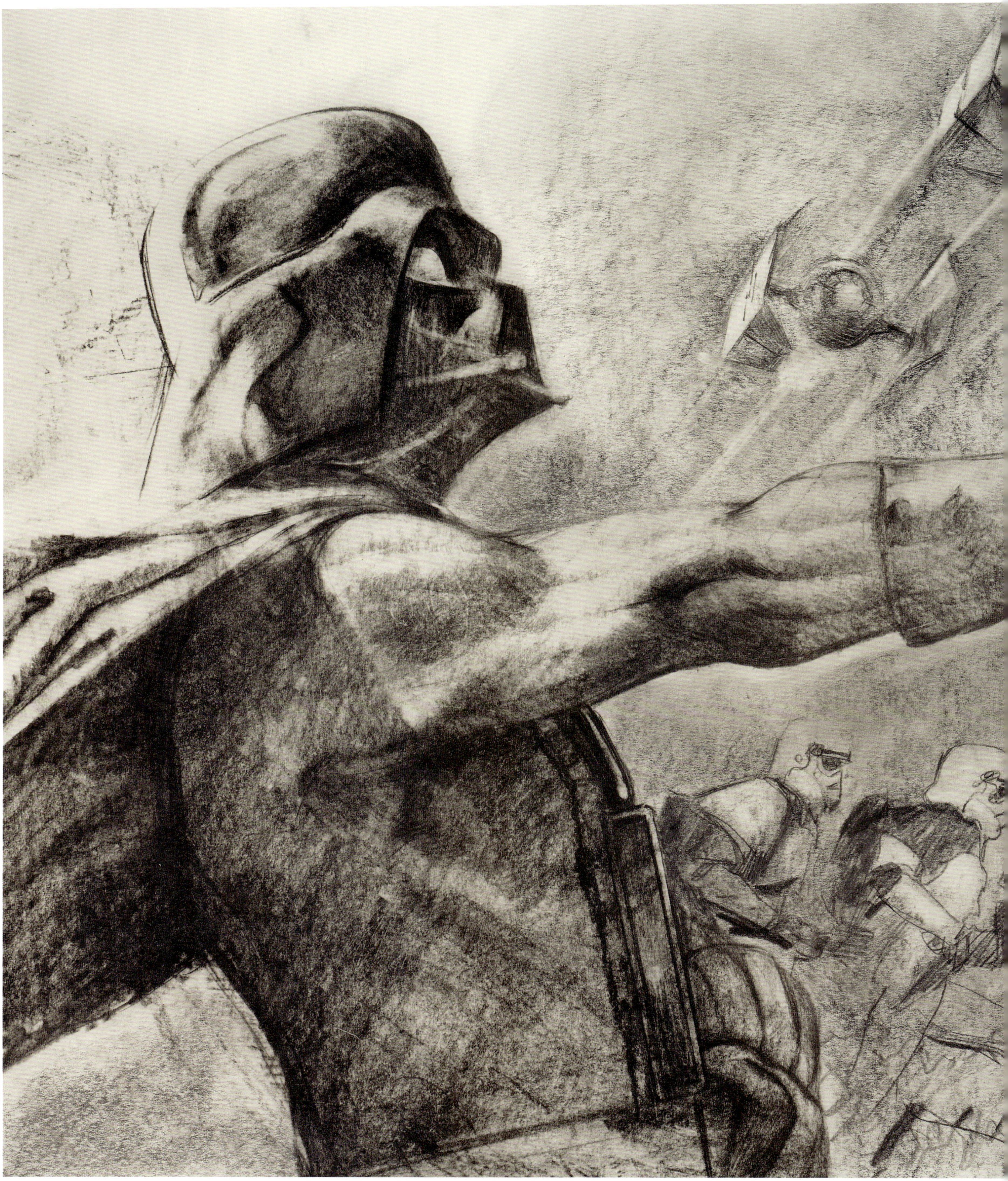

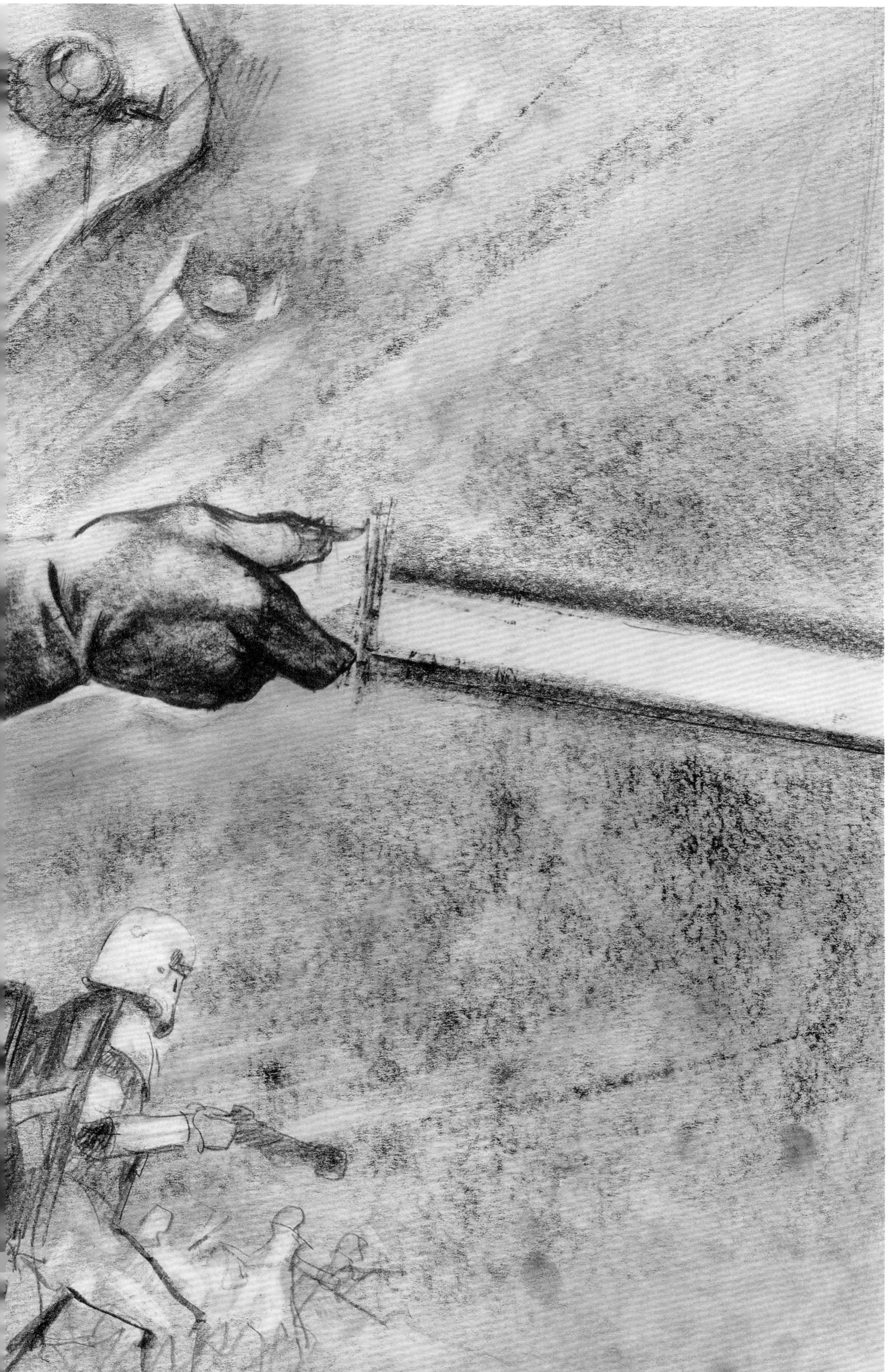

LEFT

Tom Jung

Black-and-white concept treatment for *The Empire Strikes Back* poster, c. 1979

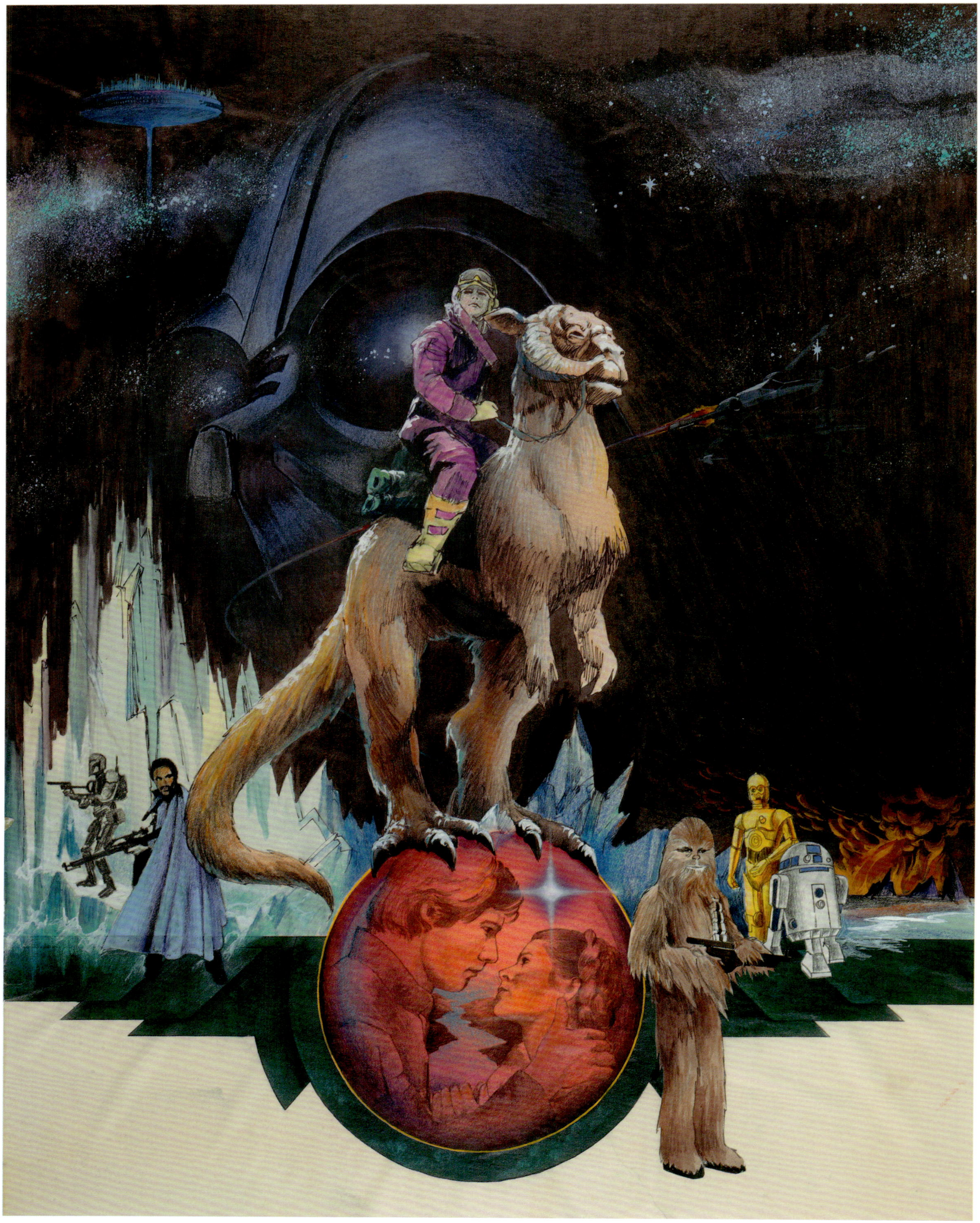

ABOVE

Unknown

Full-color painted concept treatment for *The Empire Strikes Back* poster, c. 1979

RIGHT AND FOLLOWING SPREAD (DETAIL)

Noriyoshi Ohrai

Pre-final painted artwork for *The Empire Strikes Back* theatrical one-sheet, Japan, 1980

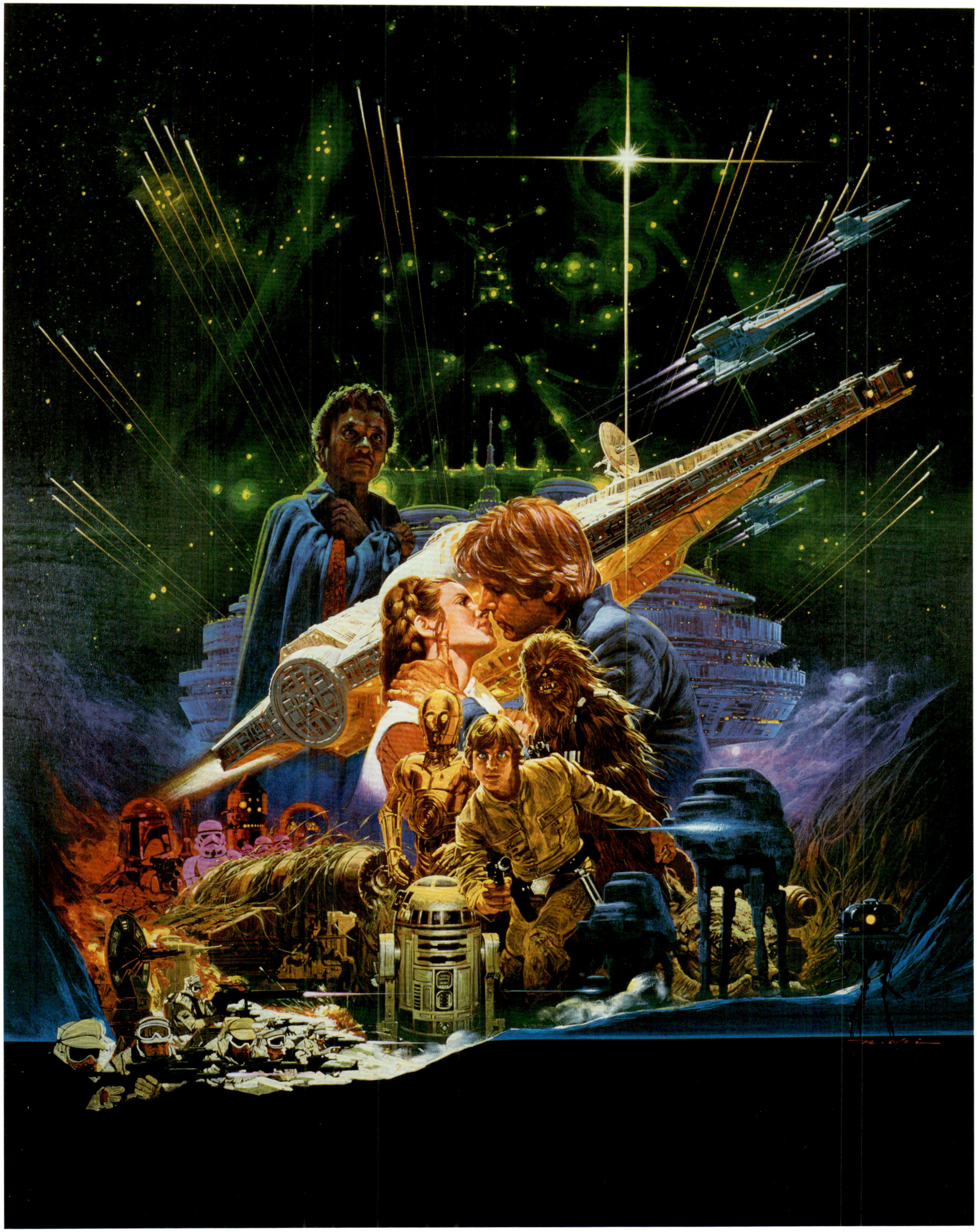

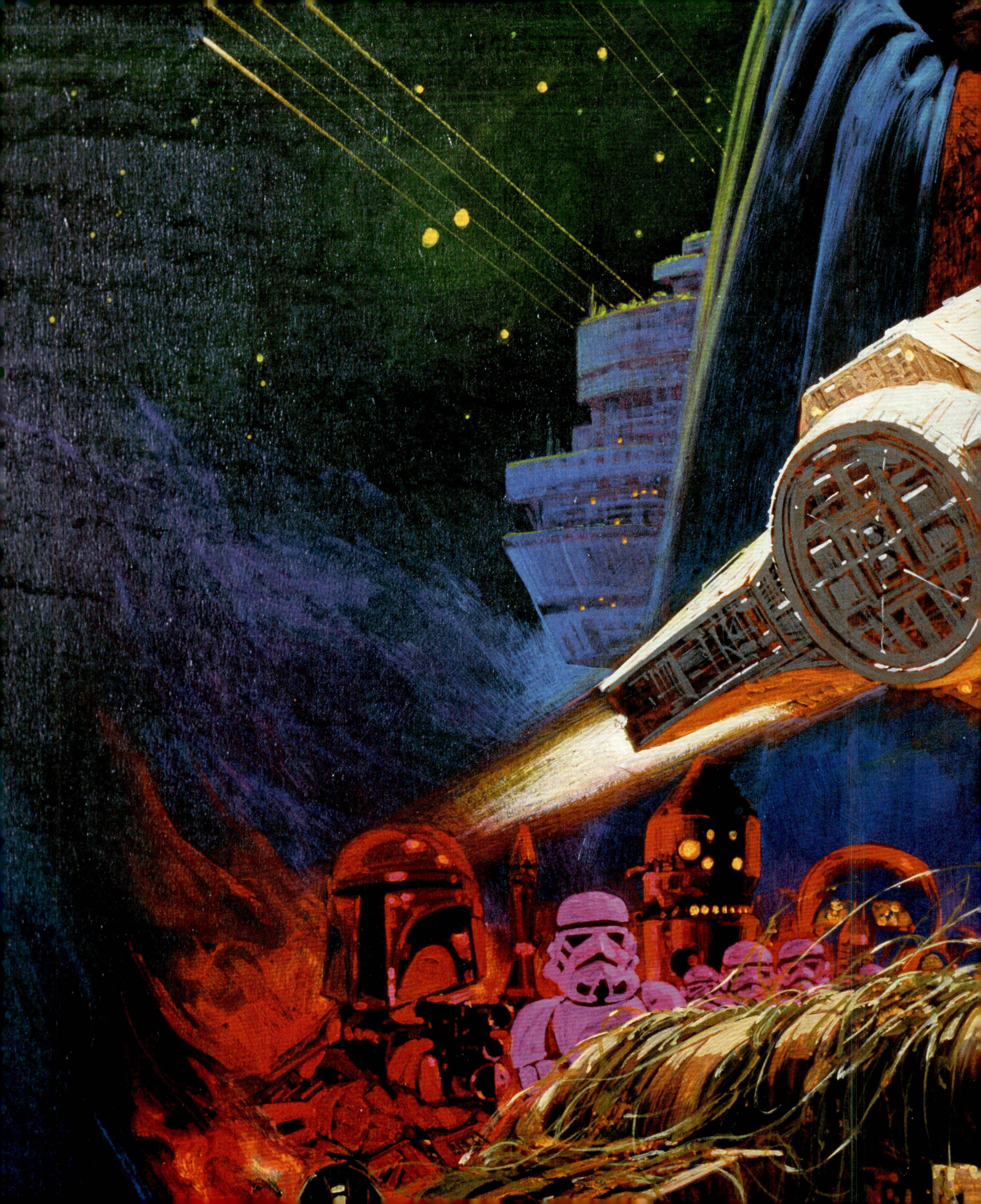

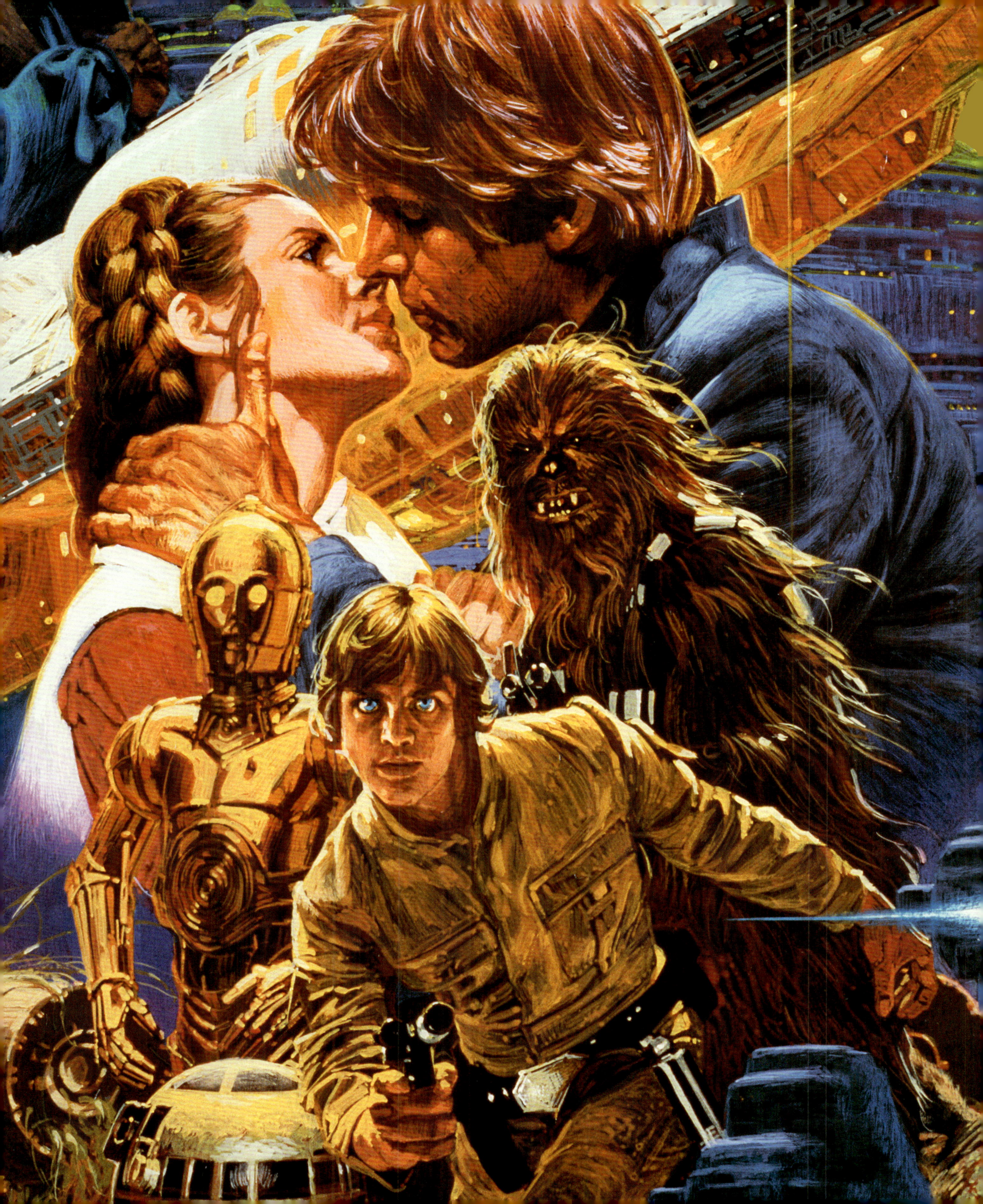

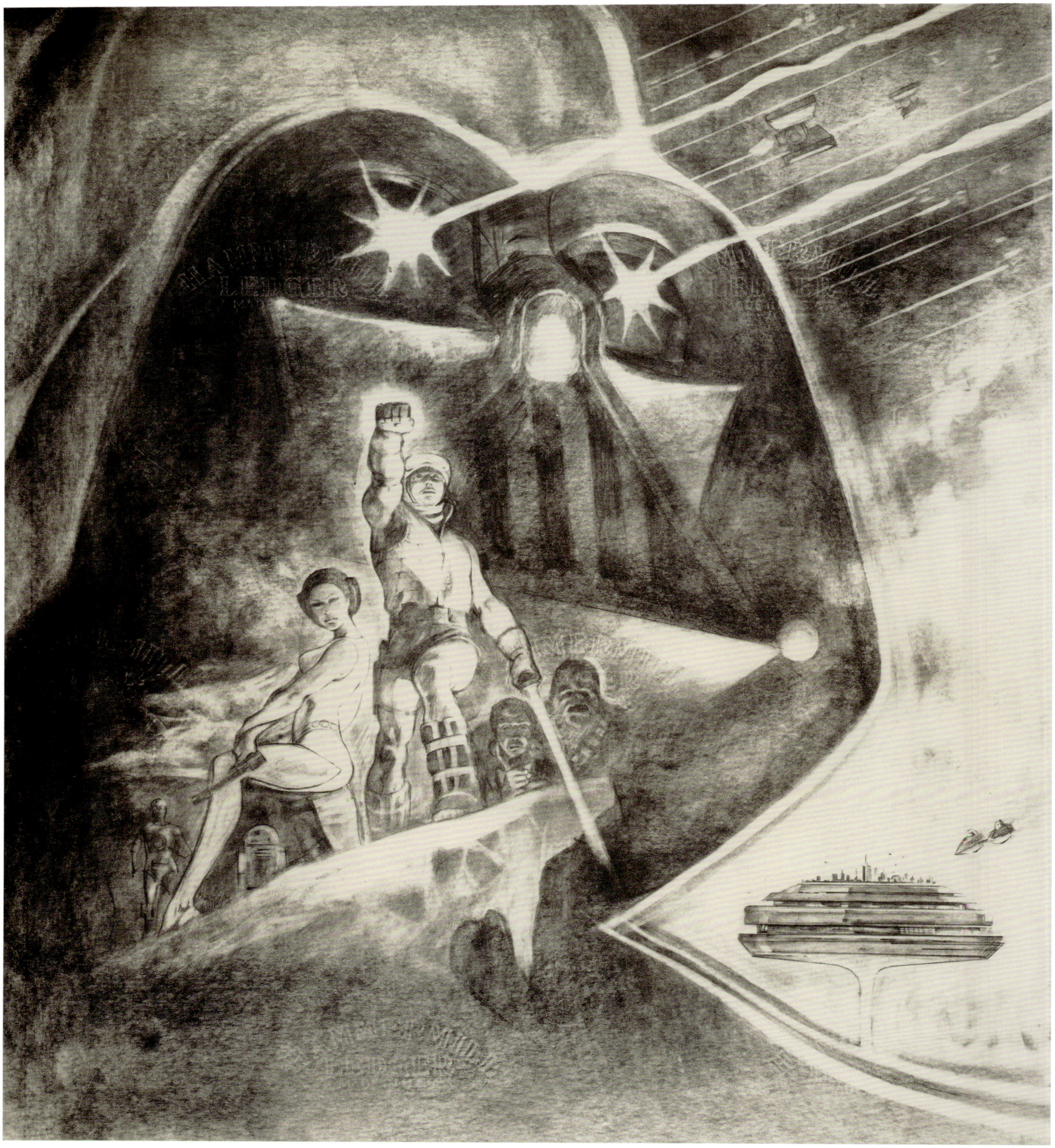

ABOVE

Tom Jung

Black-and-white concept treatment for *The Empire Strikes Back* poster, c. 1979

RIGHT

Noriyoshi Ohrai

Full-color painted concept treatment for *The Empire Strikes Back* poster, c. 1979

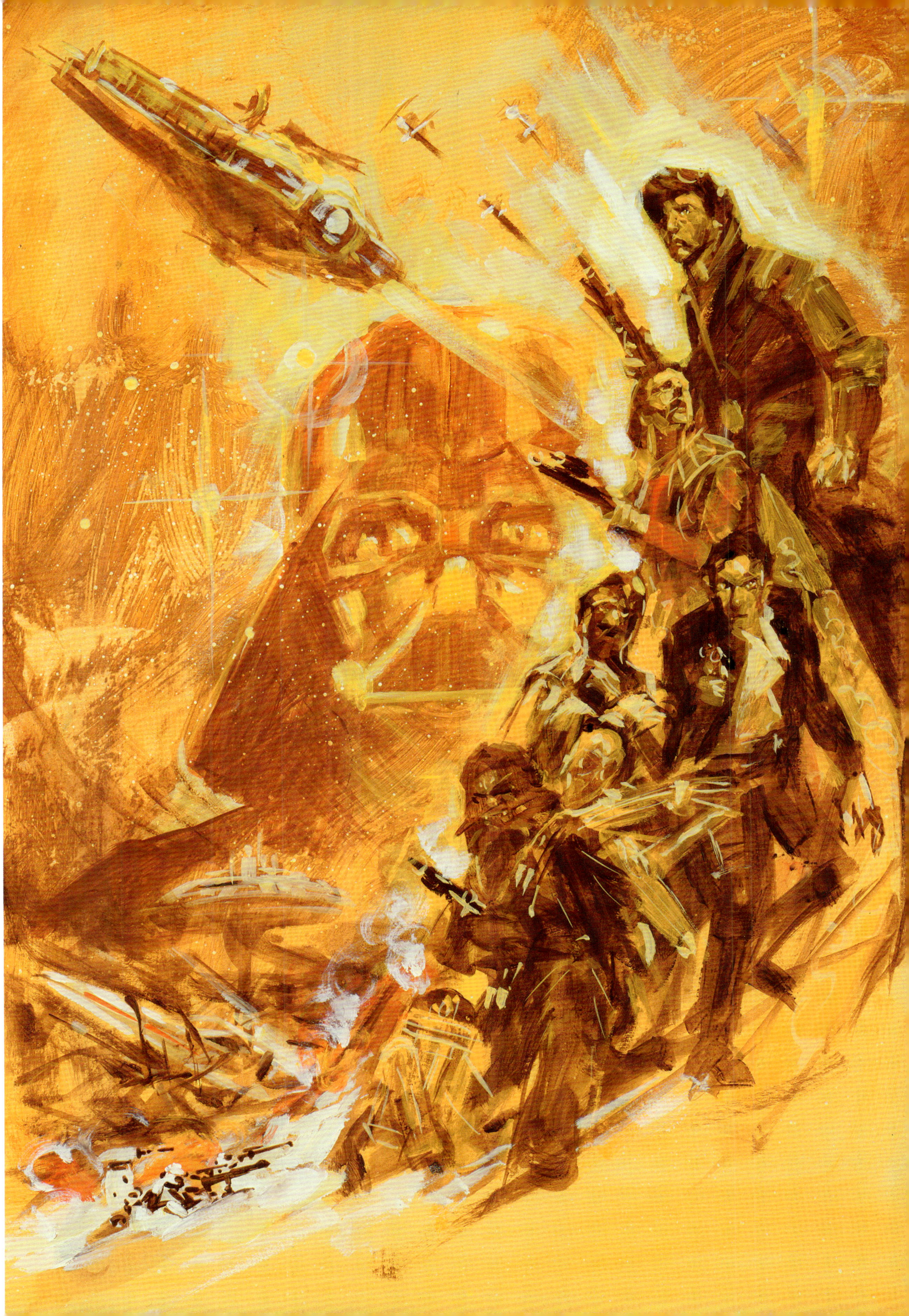

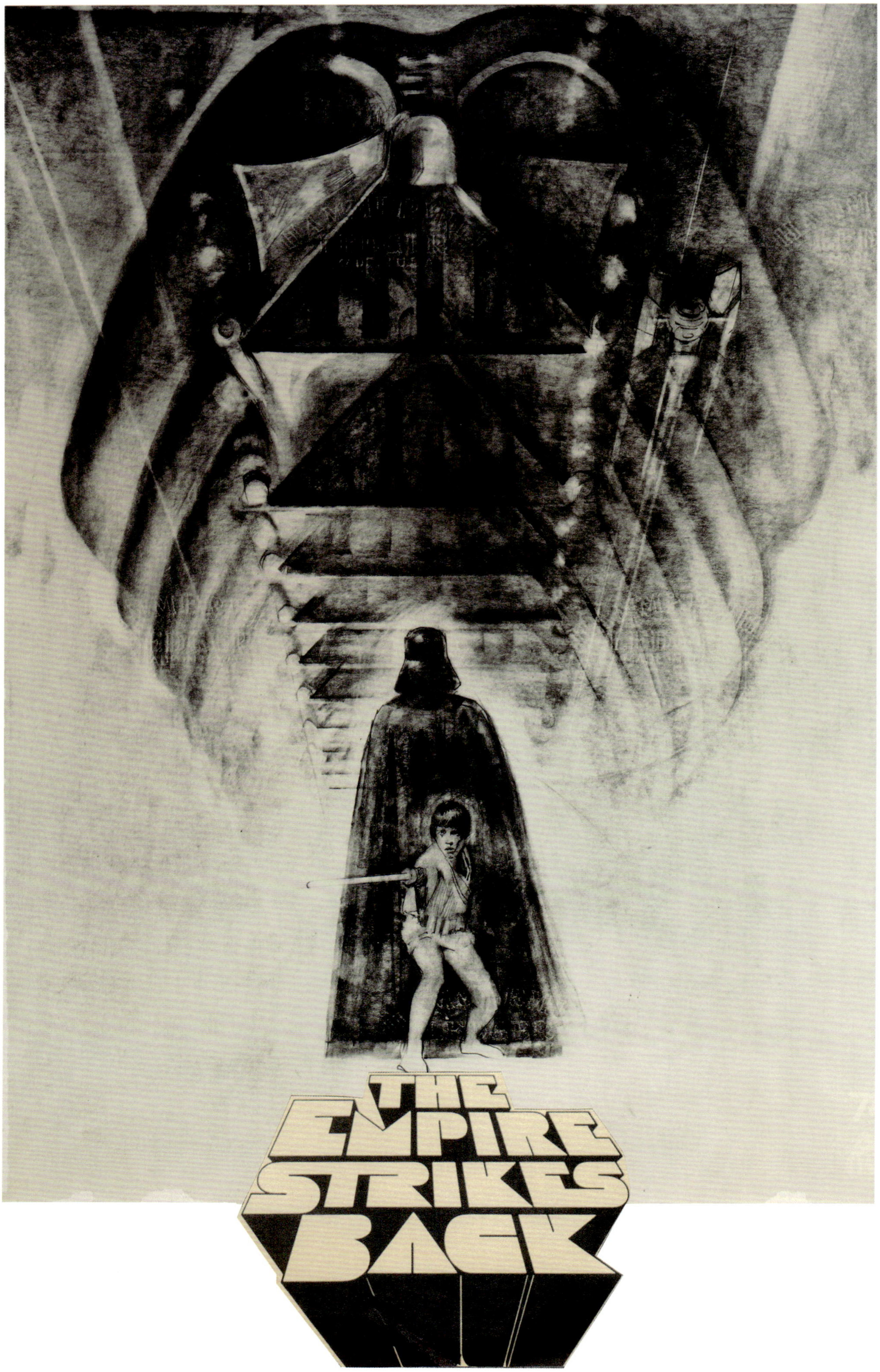

LEFT

Tom Jung

Black-and-white concept treatment for *The Empire Strikes Back* poster, c. 1979

RIGHT

Tom Jung

Black-and-white concept treatment for *The Empire Strikes Back* poster, c. 1979

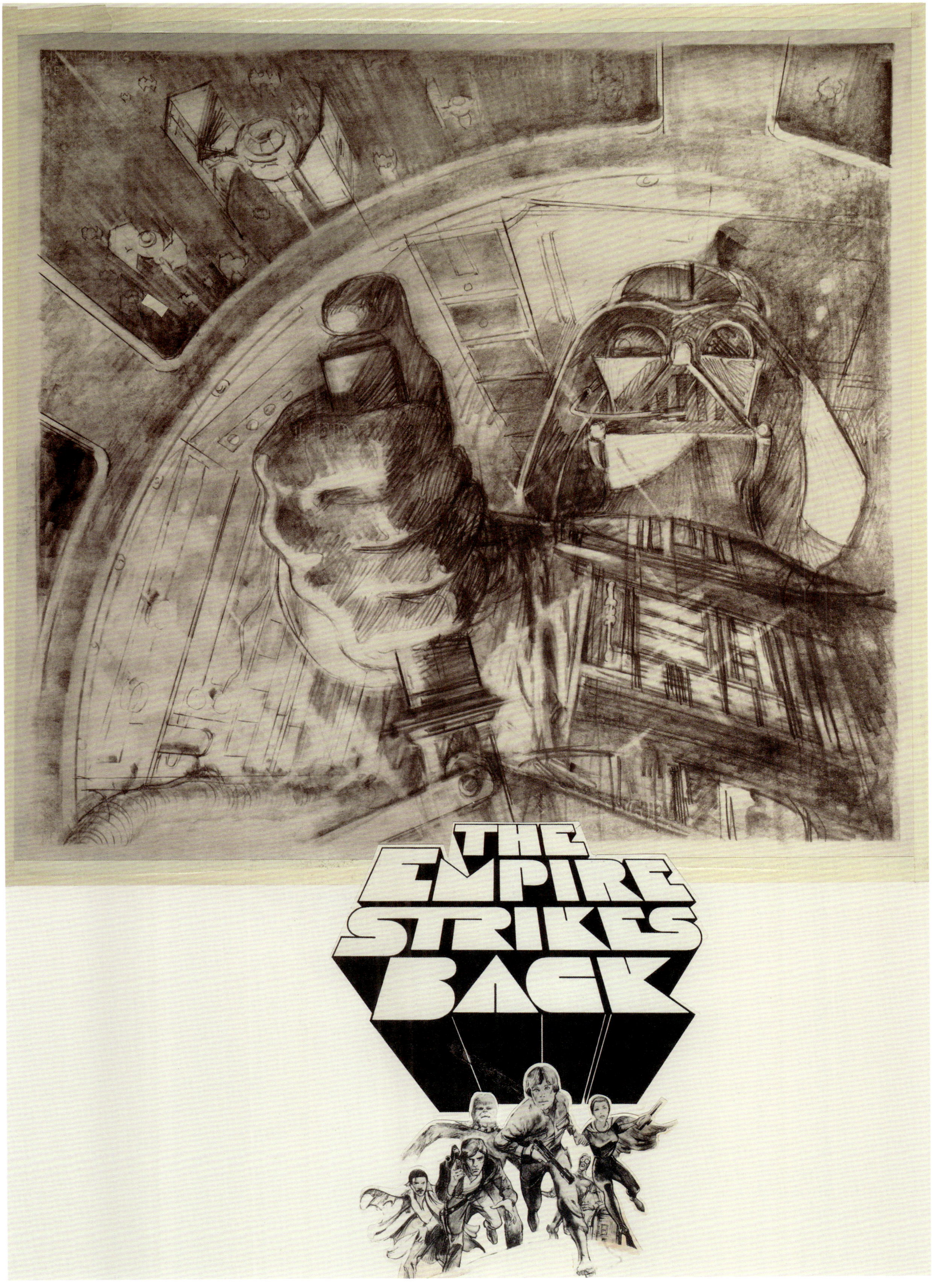
THE EMPIRE STRIKES BACK

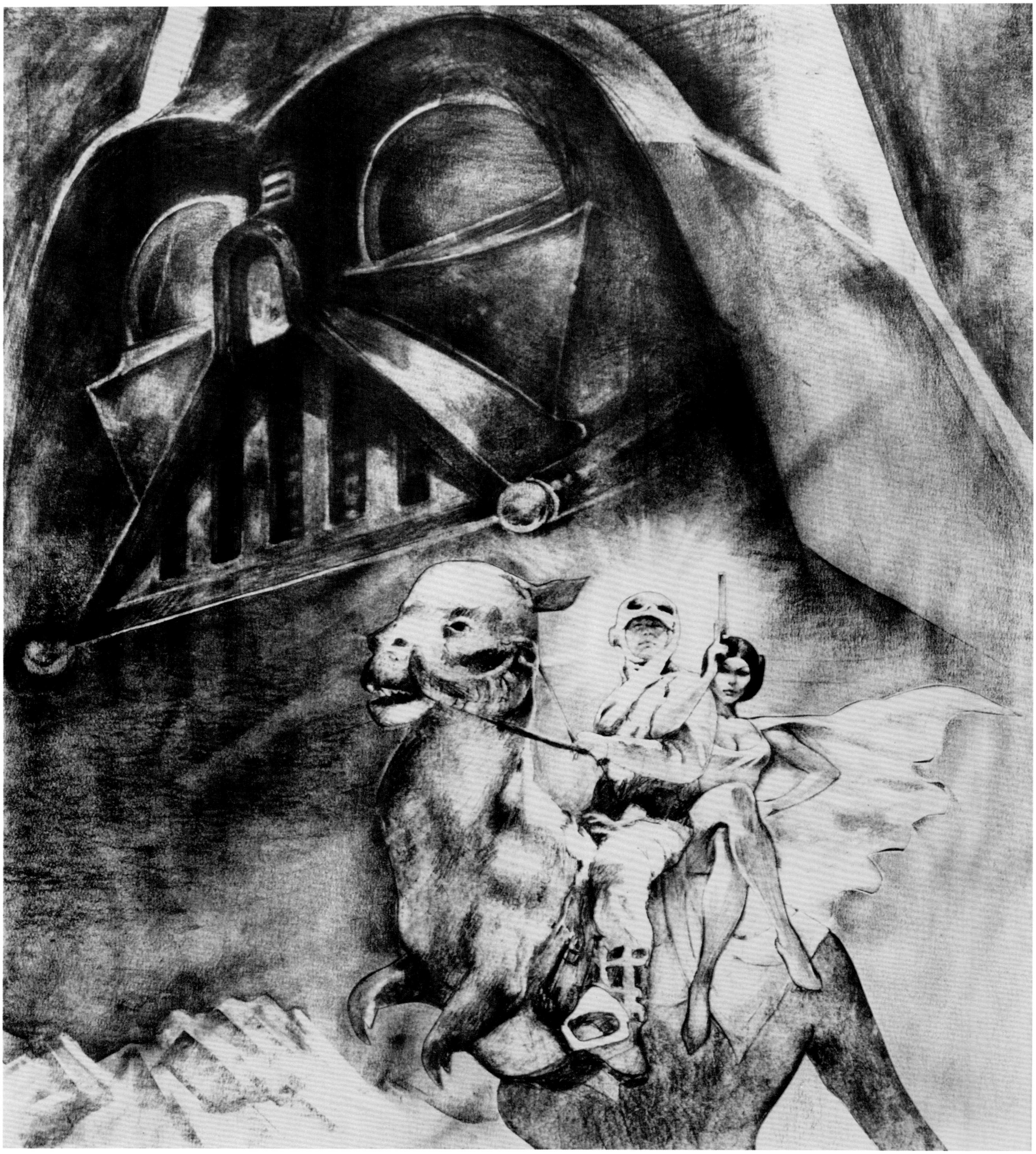

ABOVE

Tom Jung

Black-and-white concept treatment for *The Empire Strikes Back* poster, c. 1979

RIGHT AND FOLLOWING SPREAD (DETAIL)

Boris Vallejo

Final painted artwork for *The Empire Strikes Back* Coca-Cola poster, 1980

Poster used as a premium Coca-Cola/Burger Chef promotion

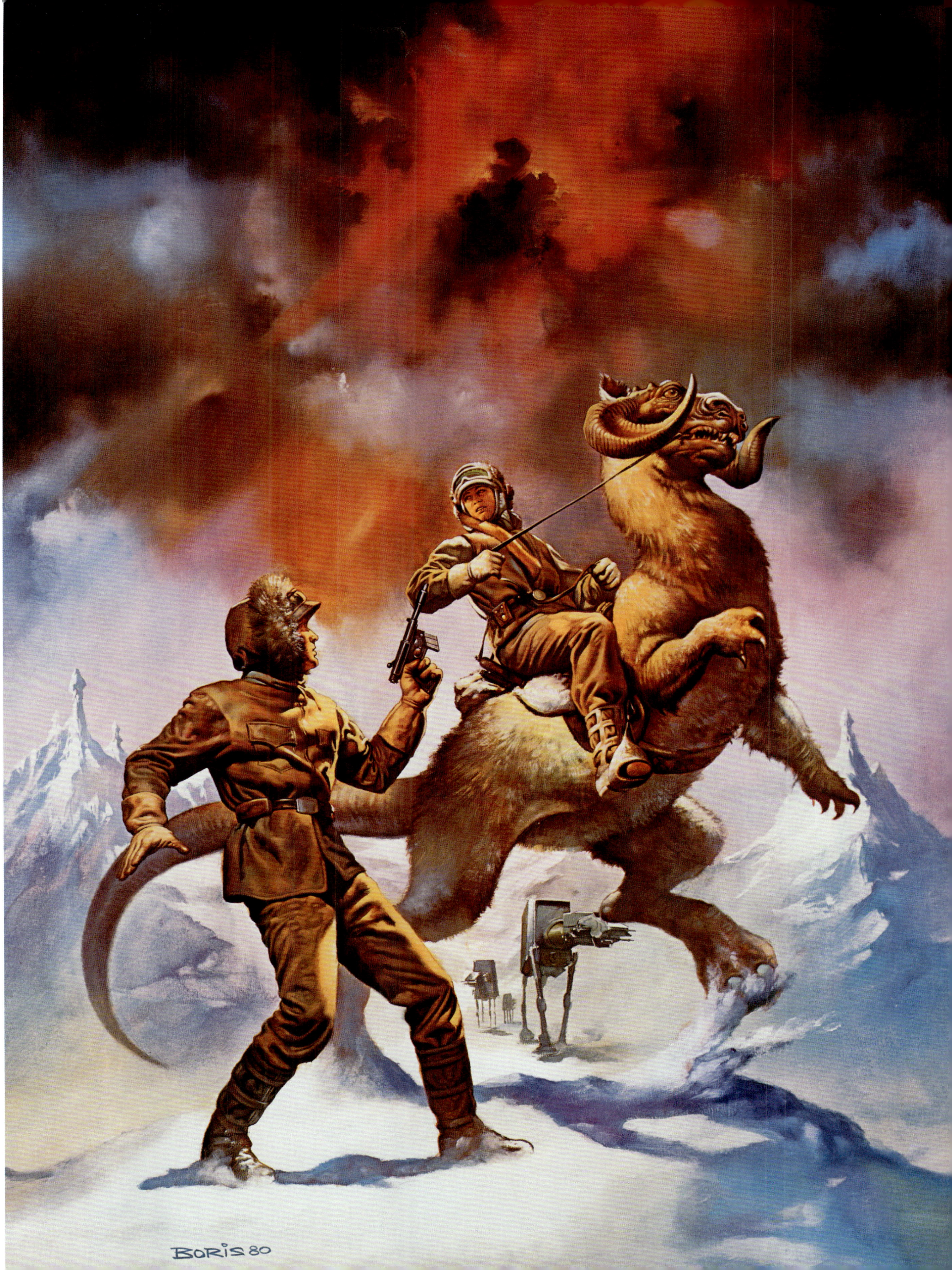
BORIS 80

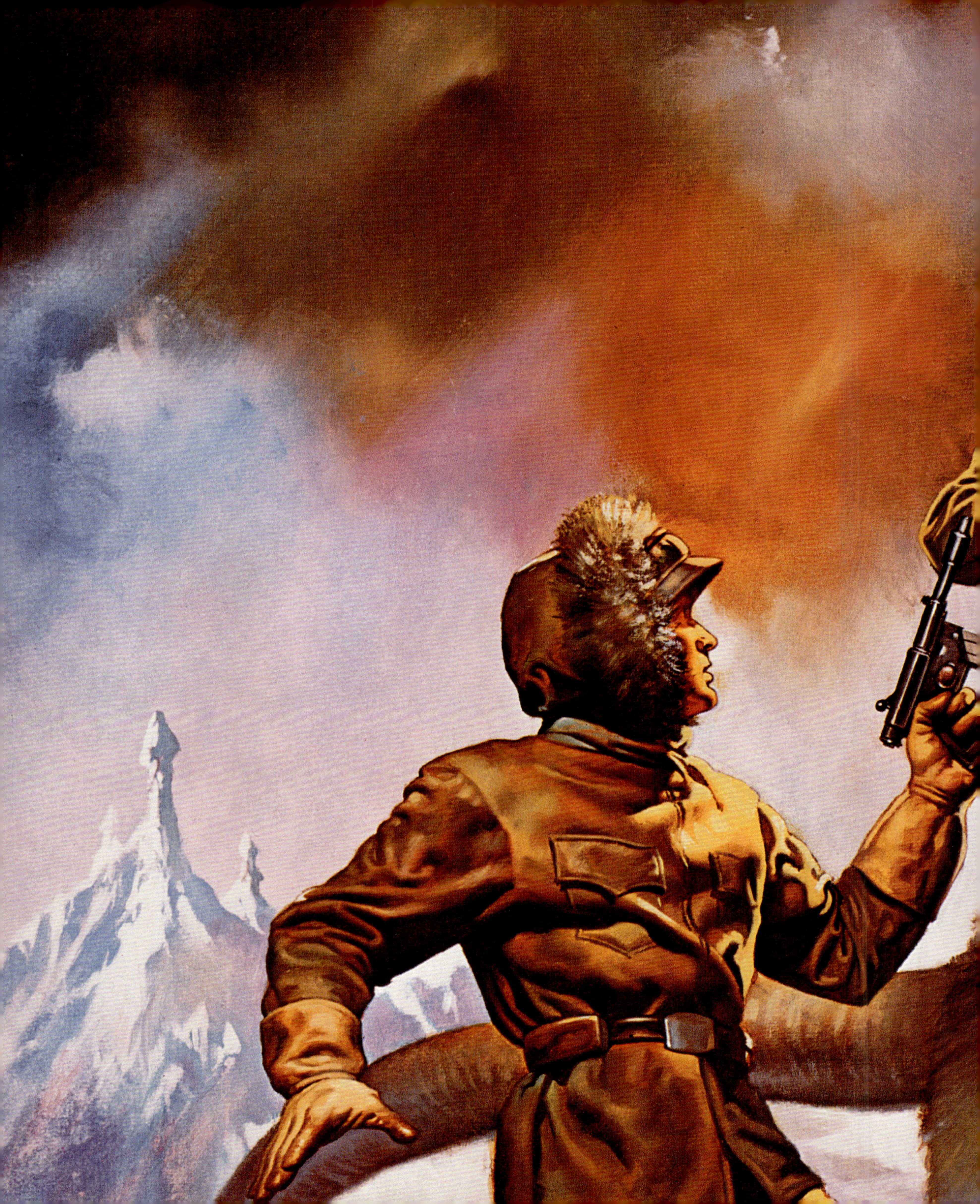

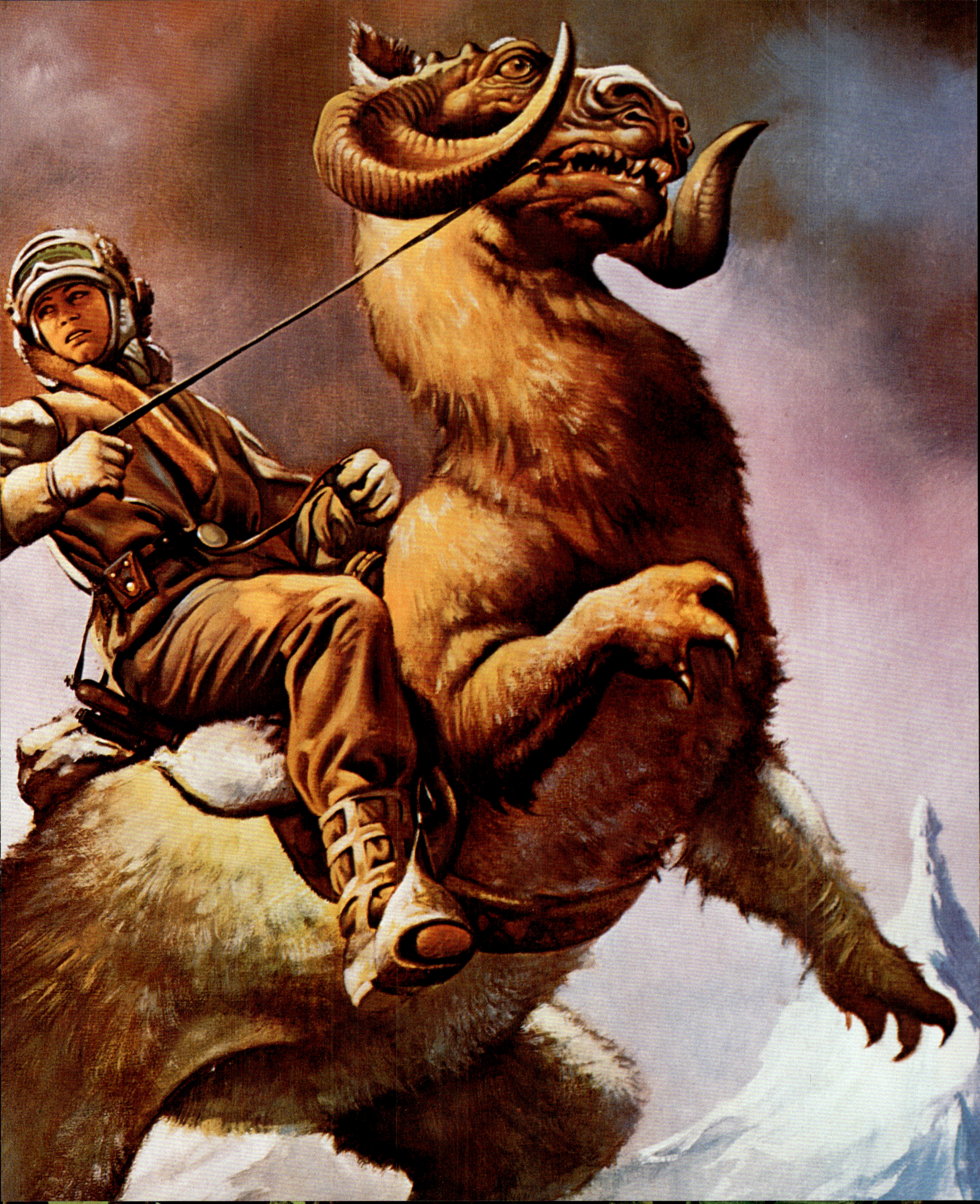

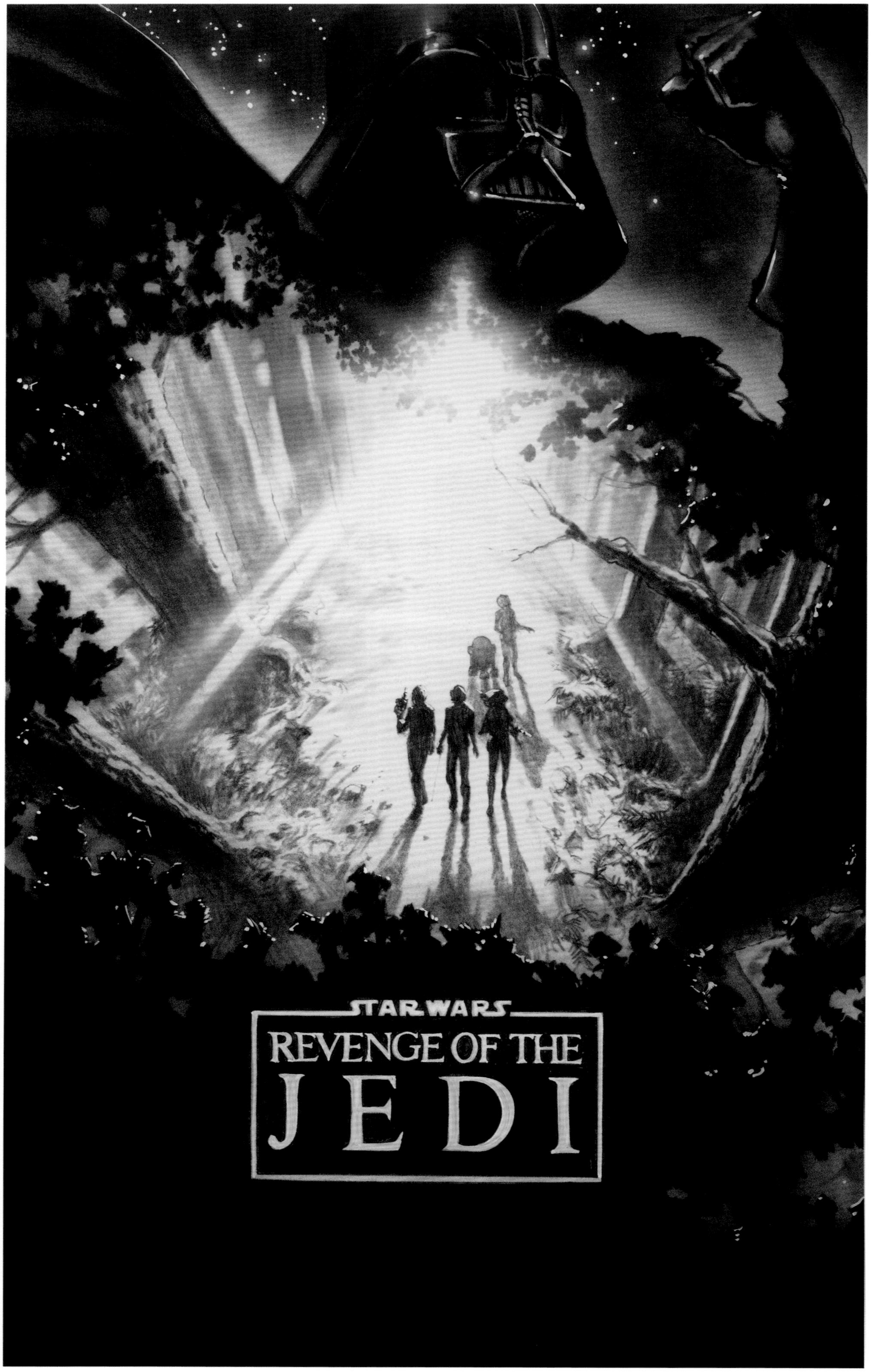

LEFT

John Alvin

Black-and-white concept treatment for *Revenge of the Jedi* poster, c. 1982

RIGHT

John Alvin

Black-and-white concept treatment for *Revenge of the Jedi* poster, c. 1982

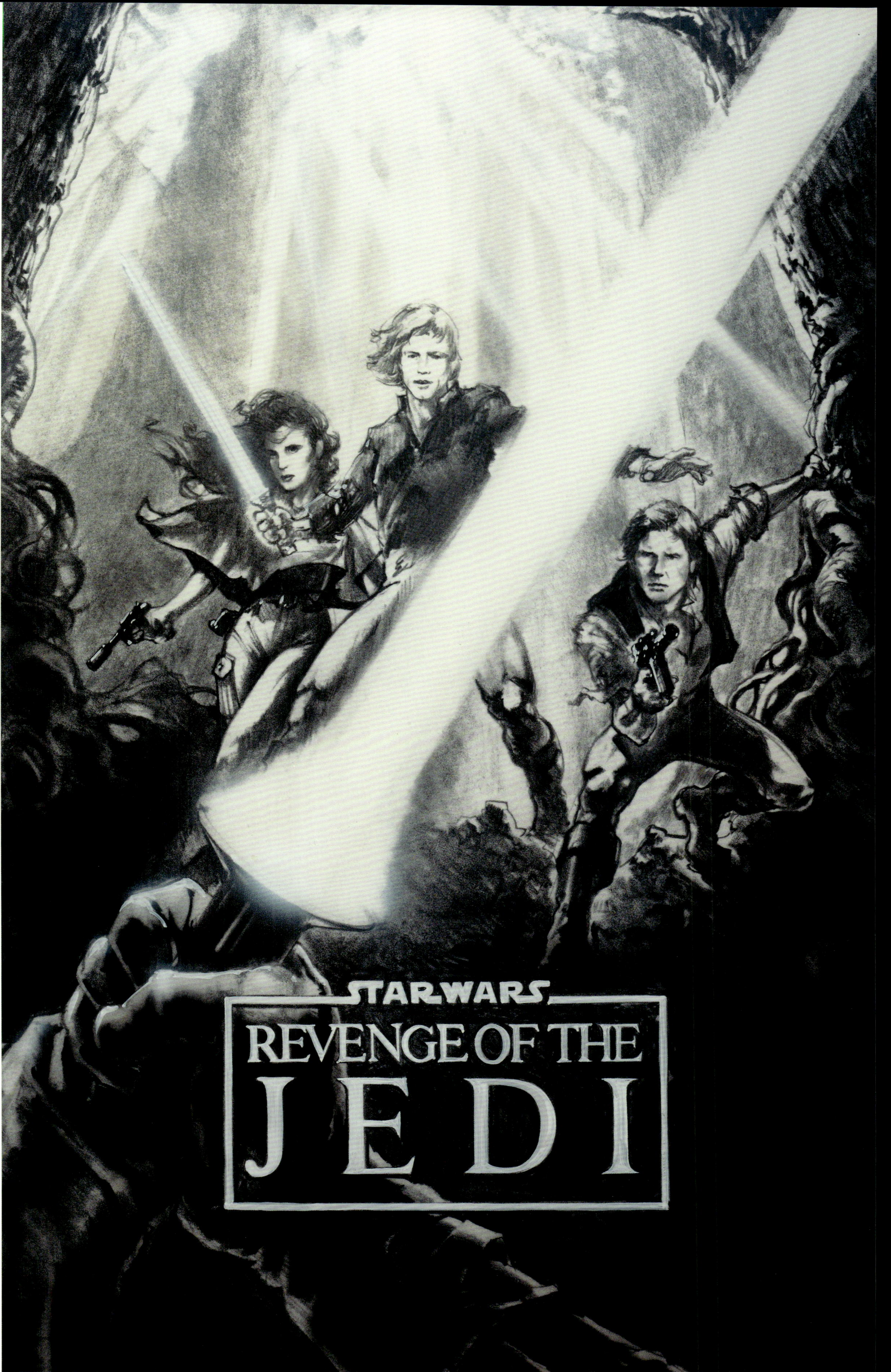
STAR WARS
REVENGE OF THE
JEDI

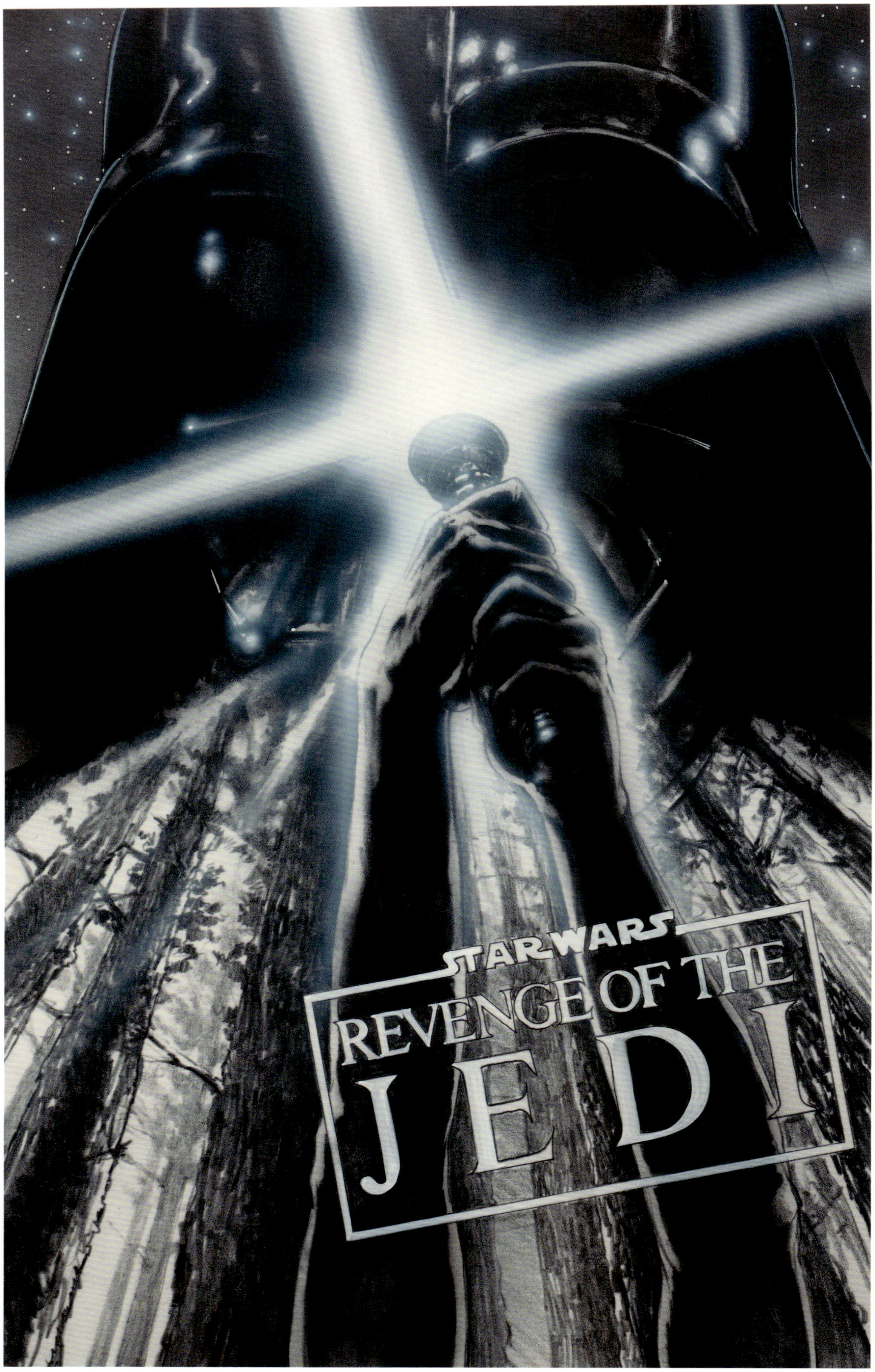

LEFT

John Alvin

Black-and-white concept treatment for *Revenge of the Jedi* poster, c. 1982

RIGHT

Tim Reamer

Final painted artwork for *Return of the Jedi* style "A" theatrical one-sheet, 1983

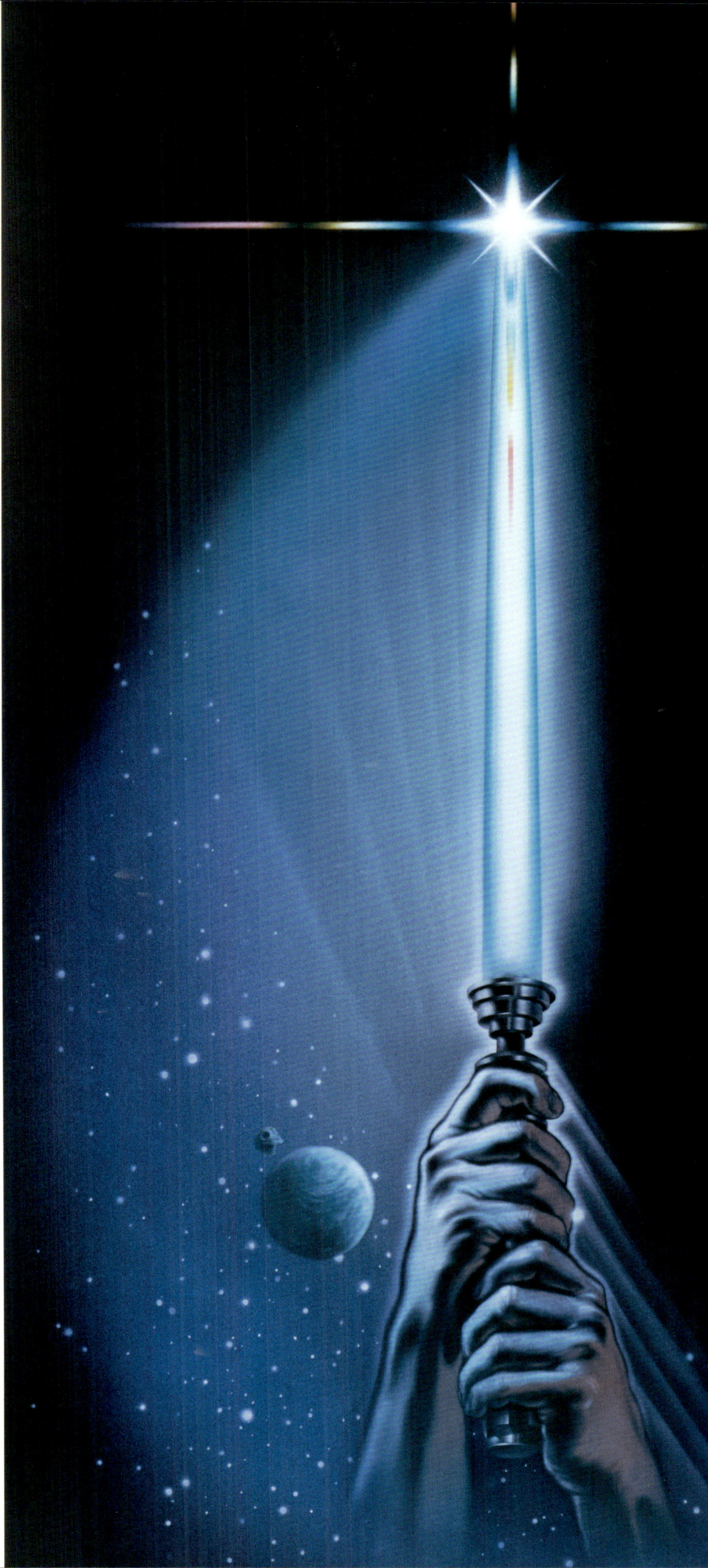

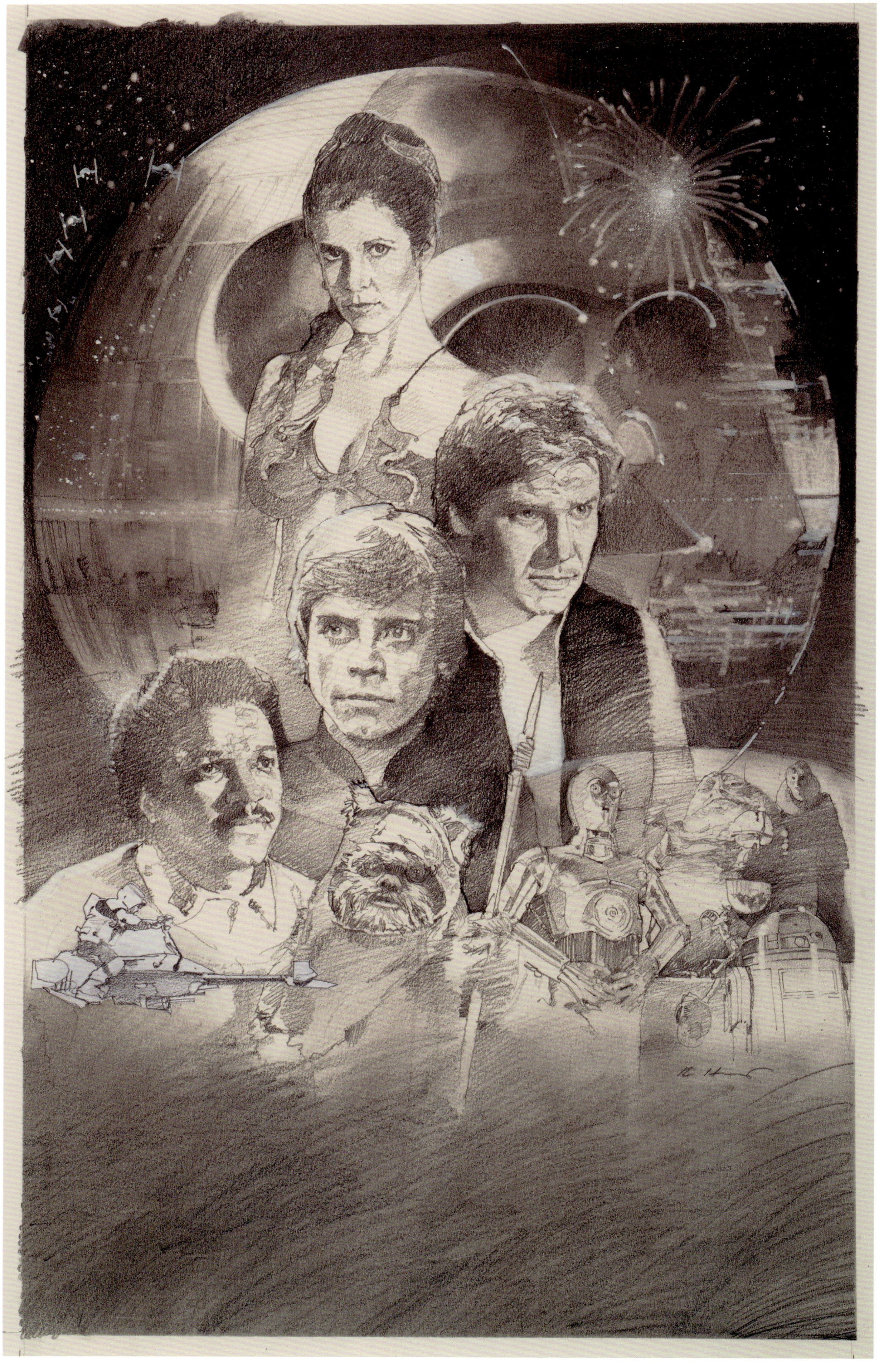

LEFT

Robert Hunt

Black-and-white concept treatment for *Return of the Jedi* style "B" theatrical one-sheet, 1982

RIGHT AND FOLLOWING SPREAD (DETAIL)

Kazuhiko Sano

Final painted artwork for *Return of the Jedi* style "B" theatrical one-sheet, 1983

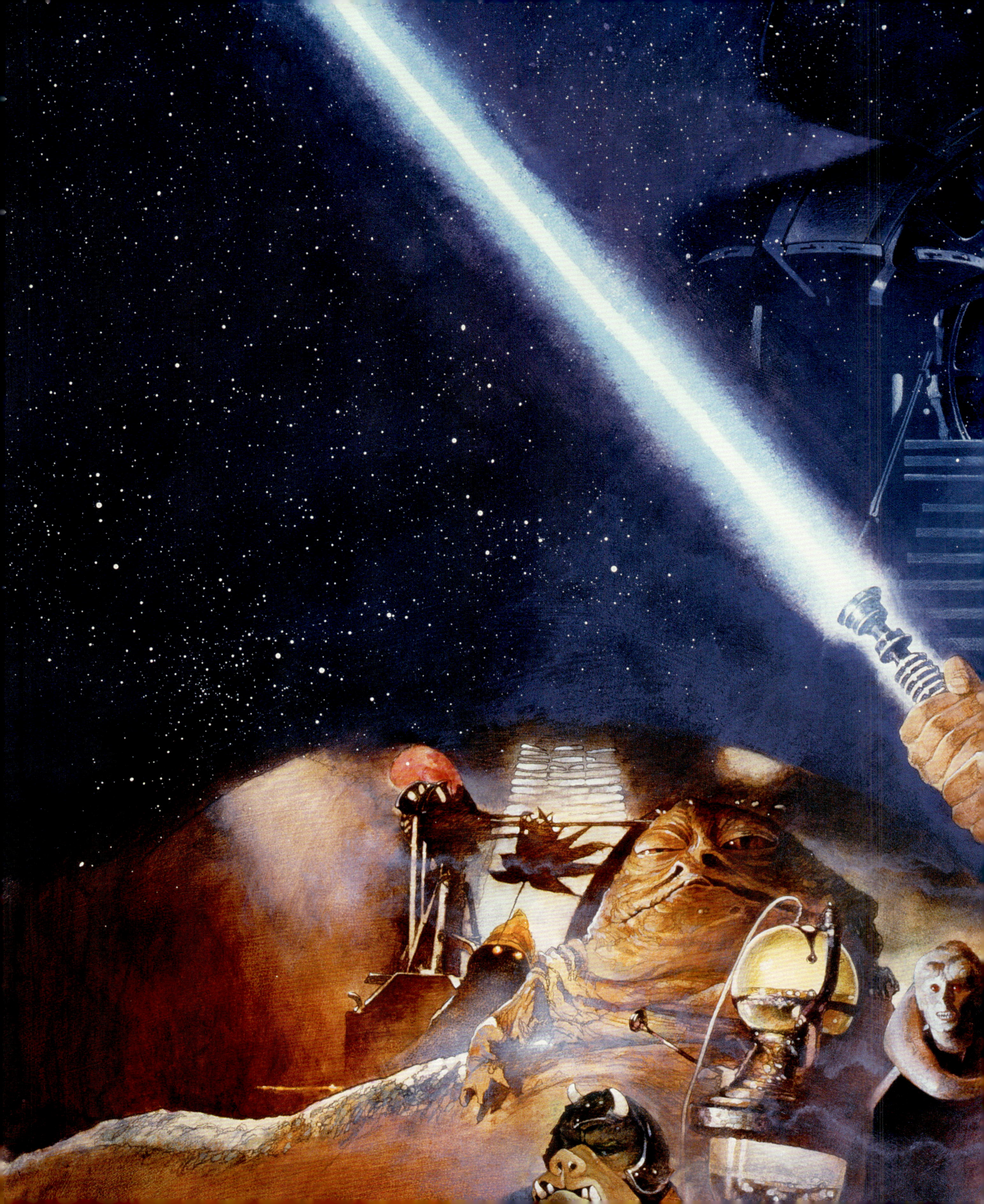

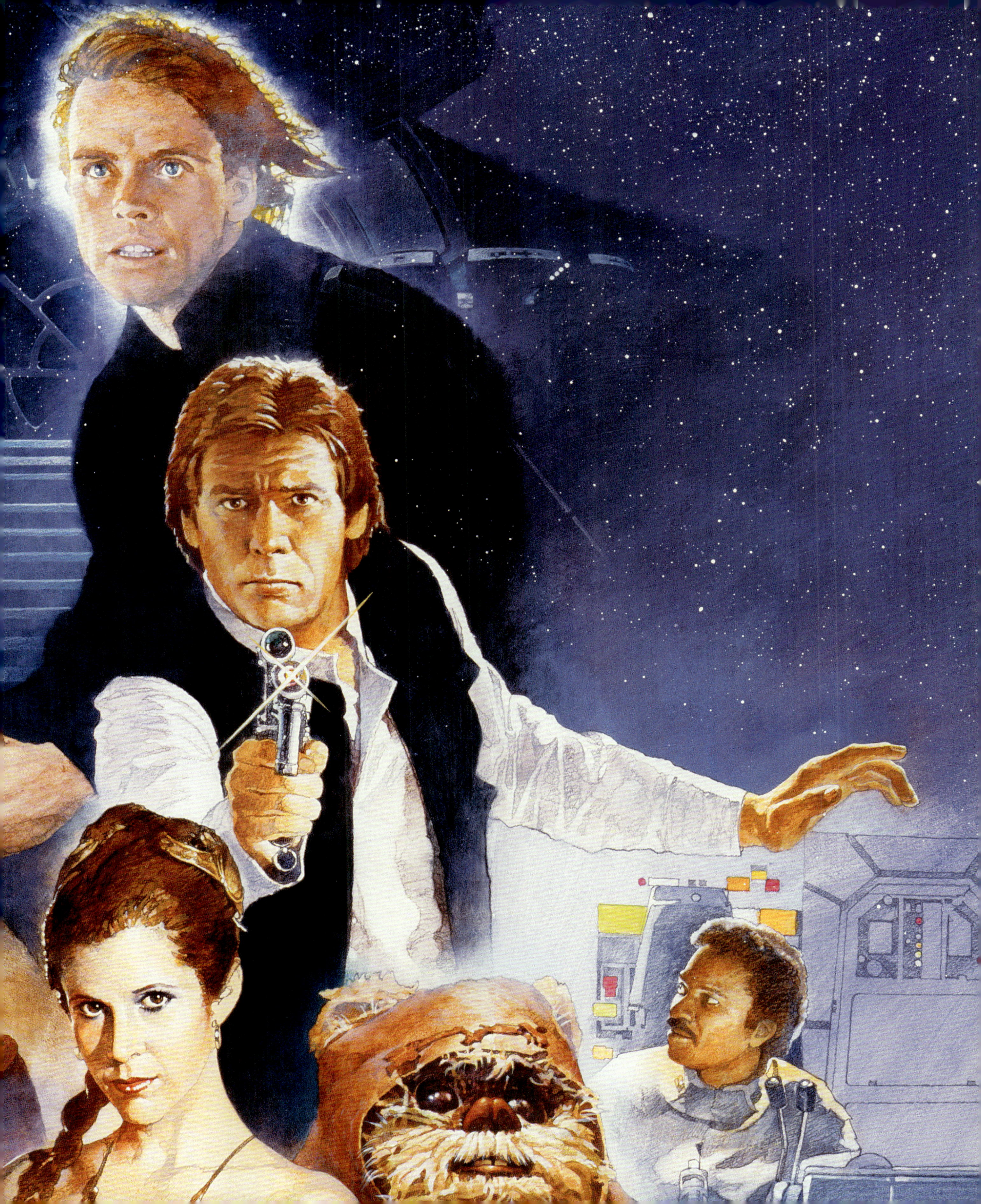

ABOVE

Drew Struzan

Final painted artwork for *Revenge of the Jedi* theatrical advance one-sheet, 1982

RIGHT

Tom Jung

Black-and-white concept treatment for *Return of the Jedi* poster, 1982

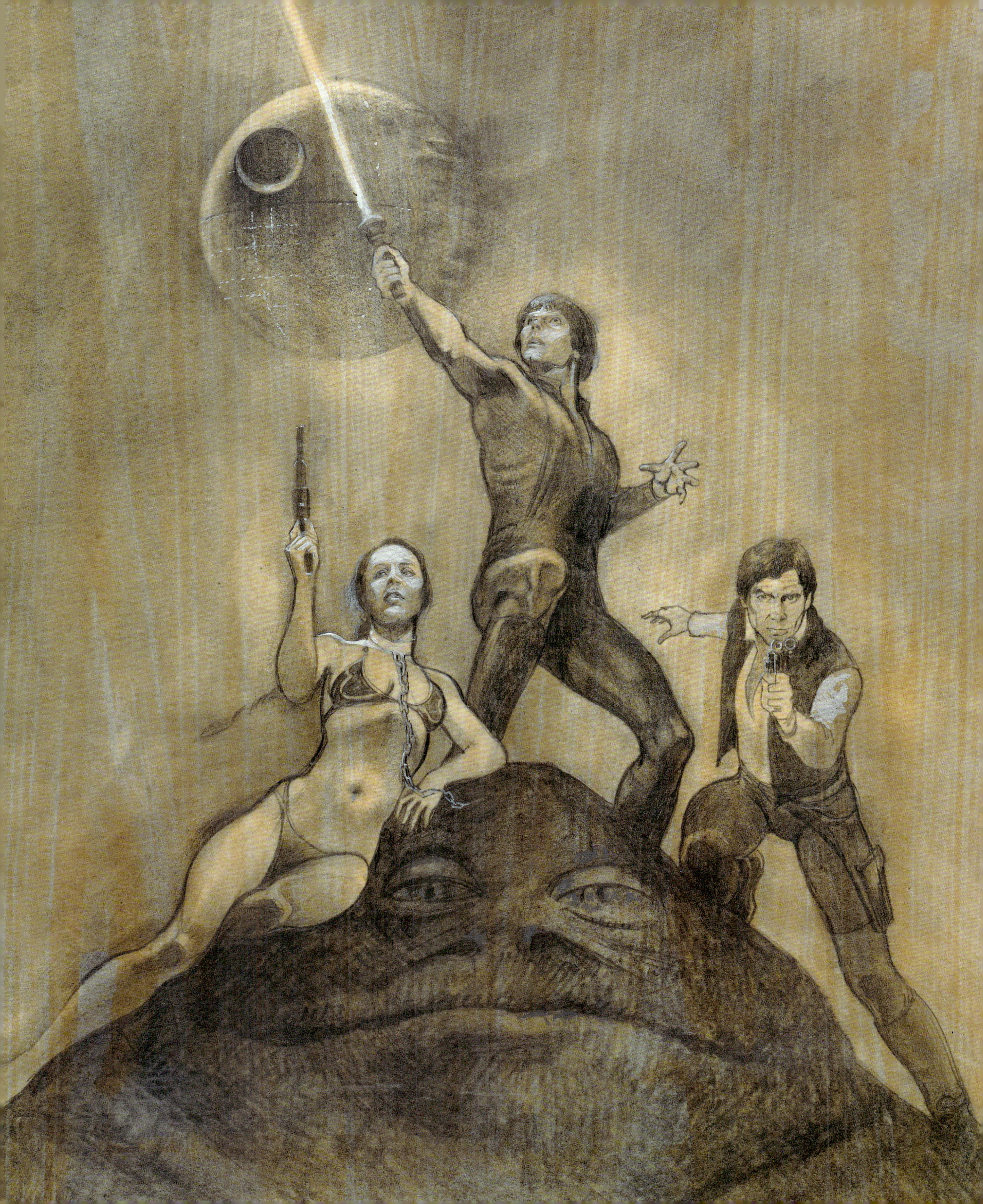

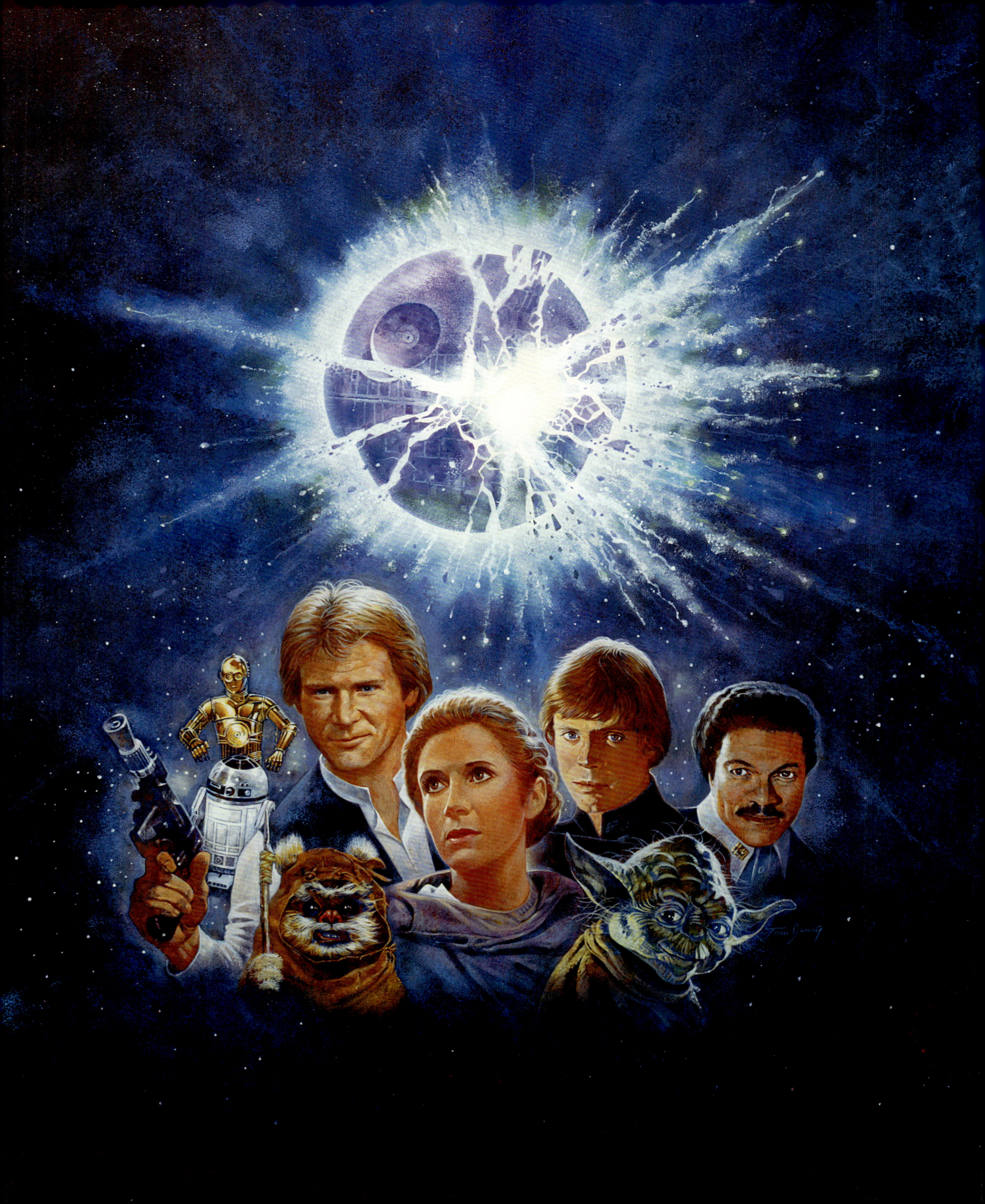

LEFT

Tom Jung

Final painted artwork for *Return of the Jedi* theatrical rerelease one-sheet, 1985

RIGHT

Noriyoshi Ohrai

Final printed artwork for *Return of the Jedi* "Starfall" poster, Japan, 1983

Localized theatrical release

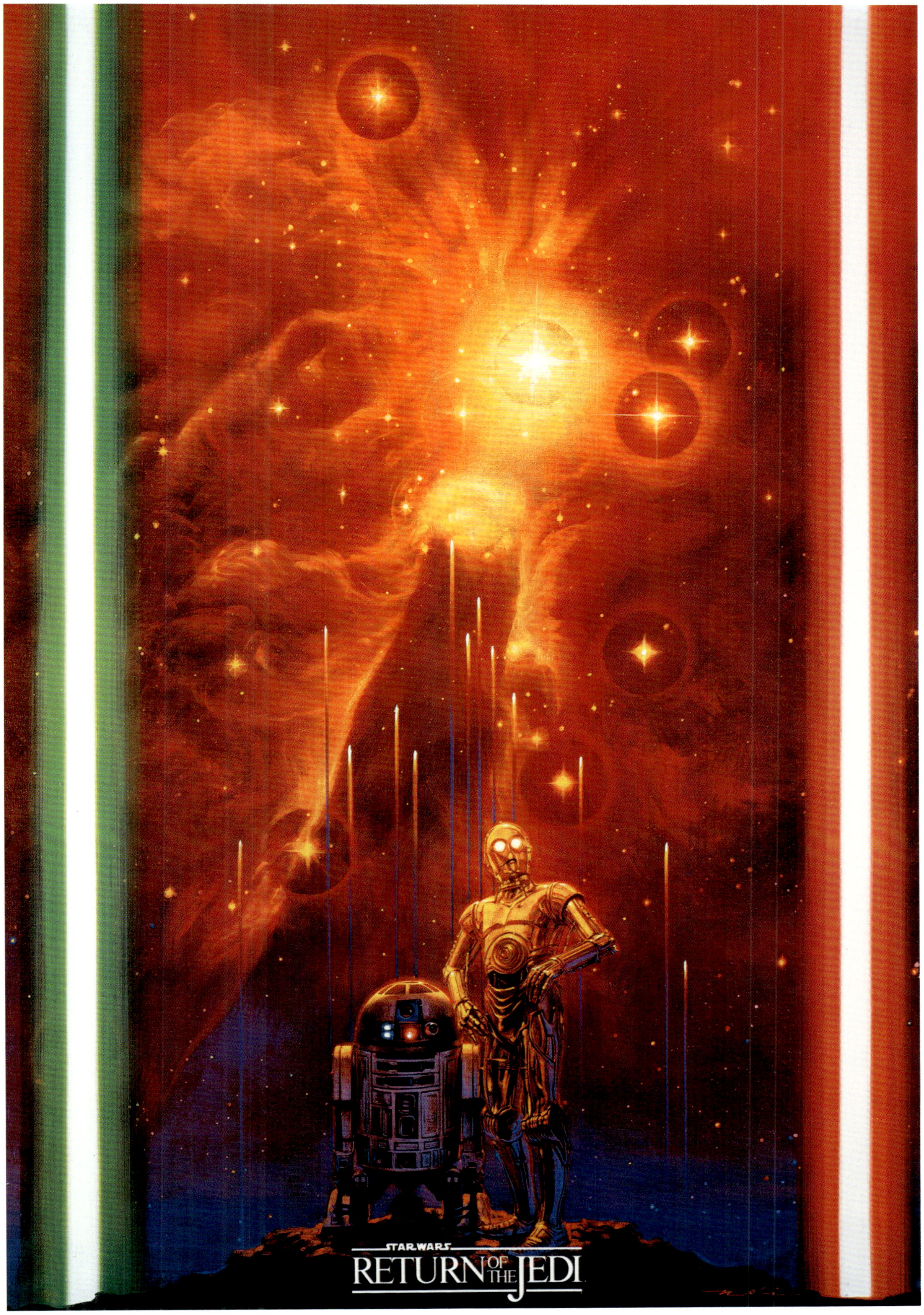

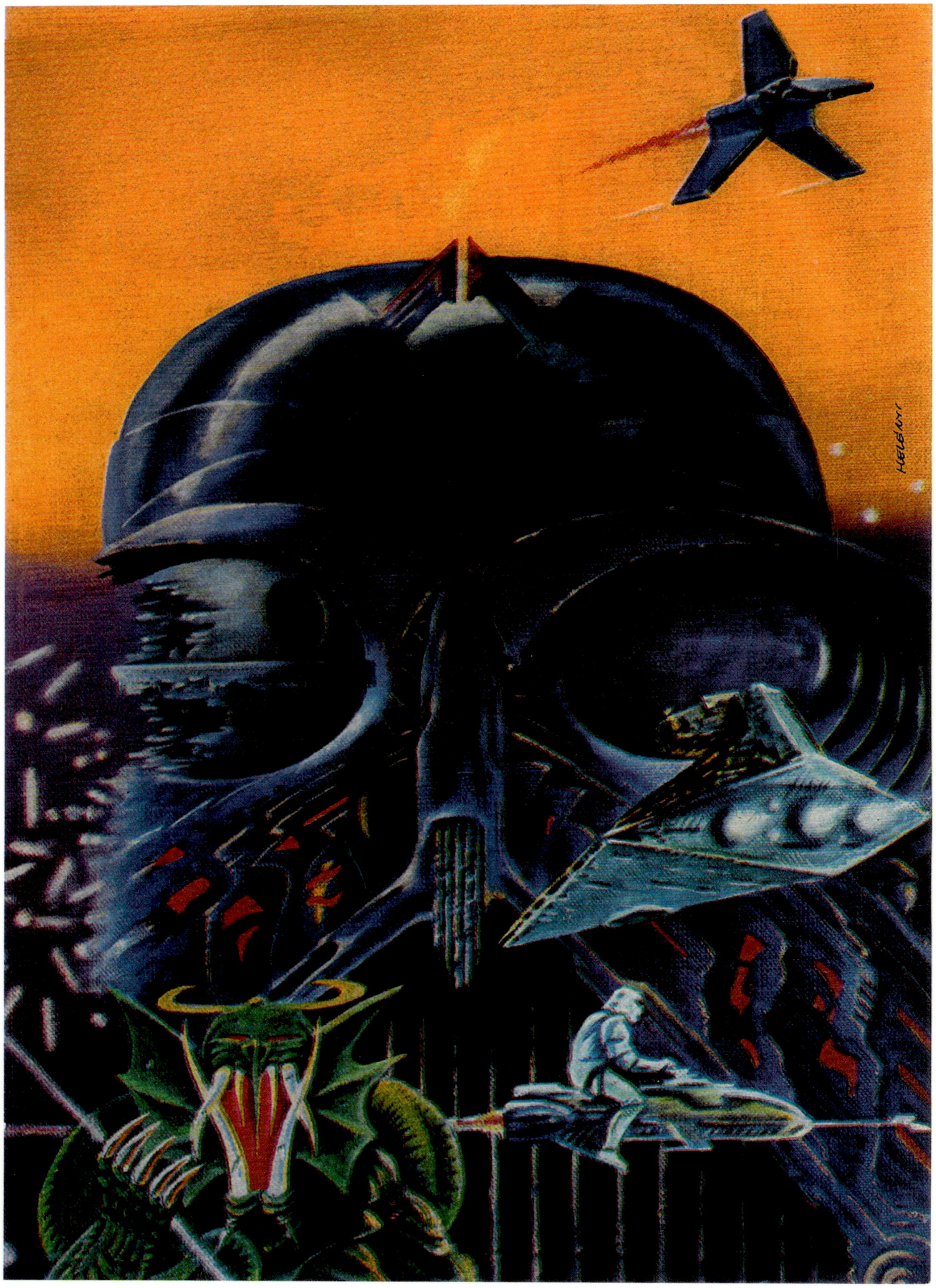

LEFT

Tibor Helényi

Final painted artwork for *Return of the Jedi* theatrical one-sheet, Hungary, 1984

Localized theatrical release

RIGHT

Witold Dybowski

Final painted artwork for *Return of the Jedi* theatrical one-sheet, Poland, 1984

Localized theatrical release

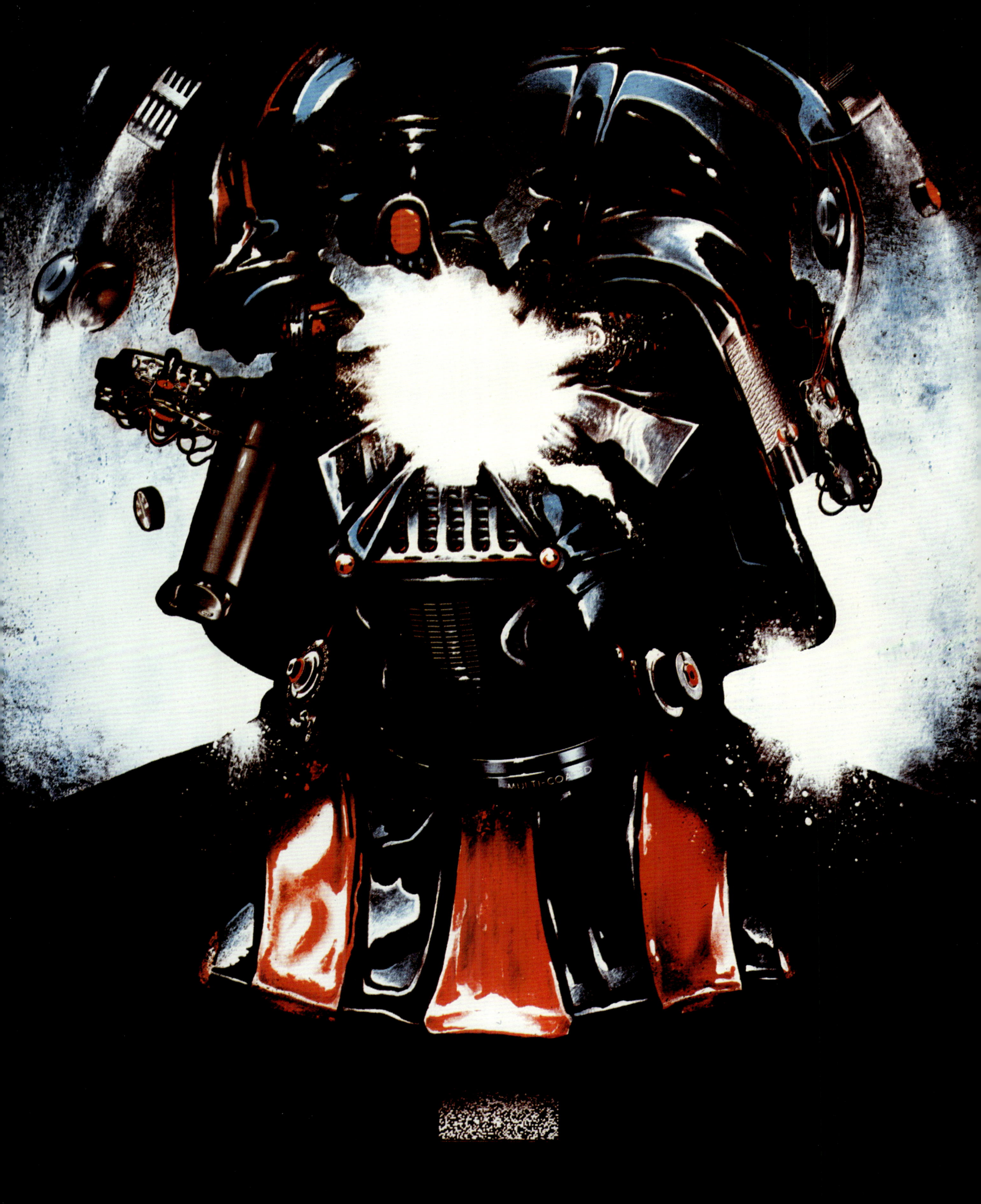

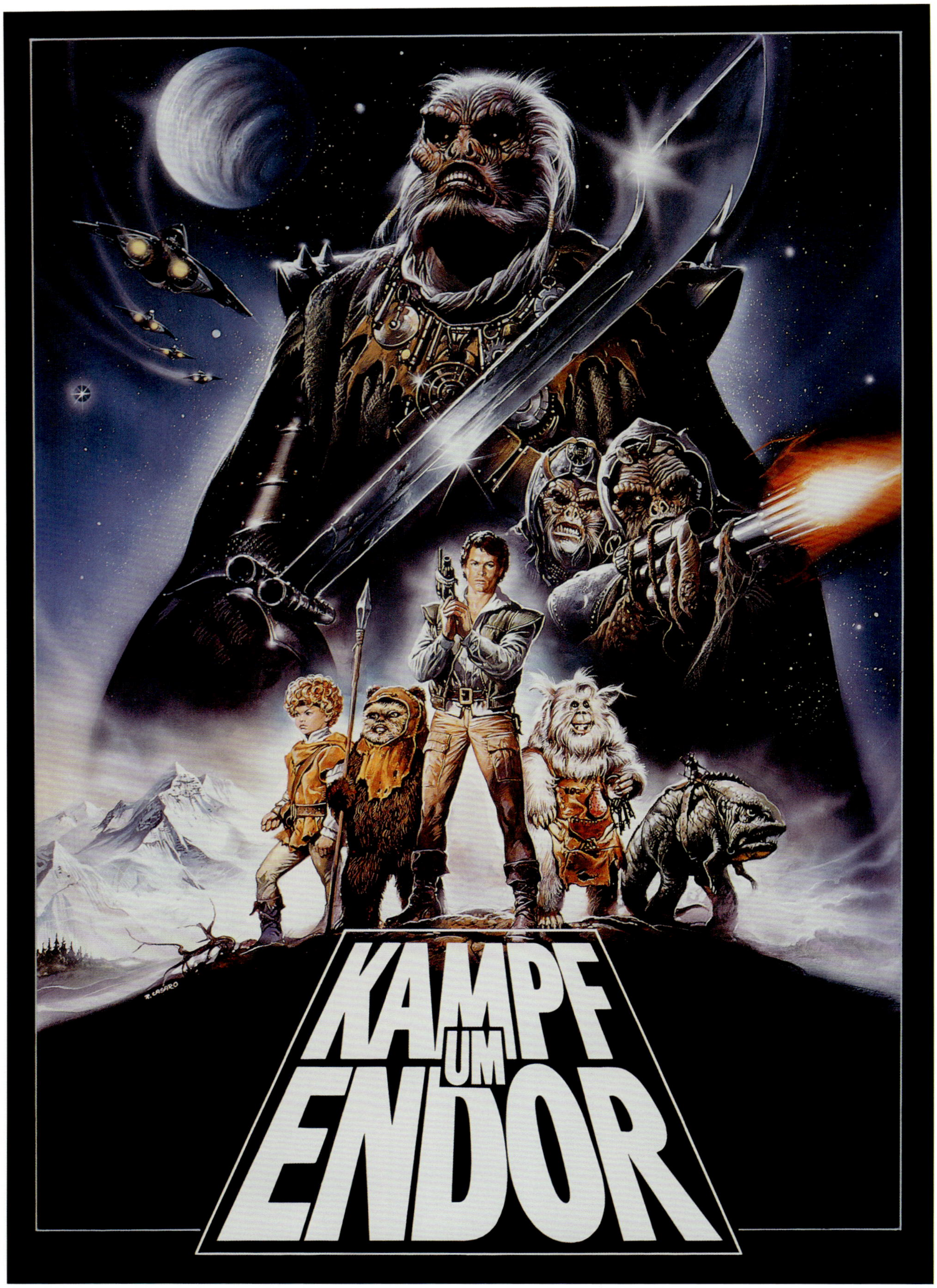

LEFT

Renato Casaro

Final printed artwork for *Ewoks: The Battle for Endor* theatrical one-sheet, Germany, 1986

Localized theatrical release of TV movie

RIGHT

Drew Struzan

Full-color painted concept treatment for *Caravan of Courage: An Ewok Adventure* style "B" poster, 1984

Localized theatrical release of TV movie

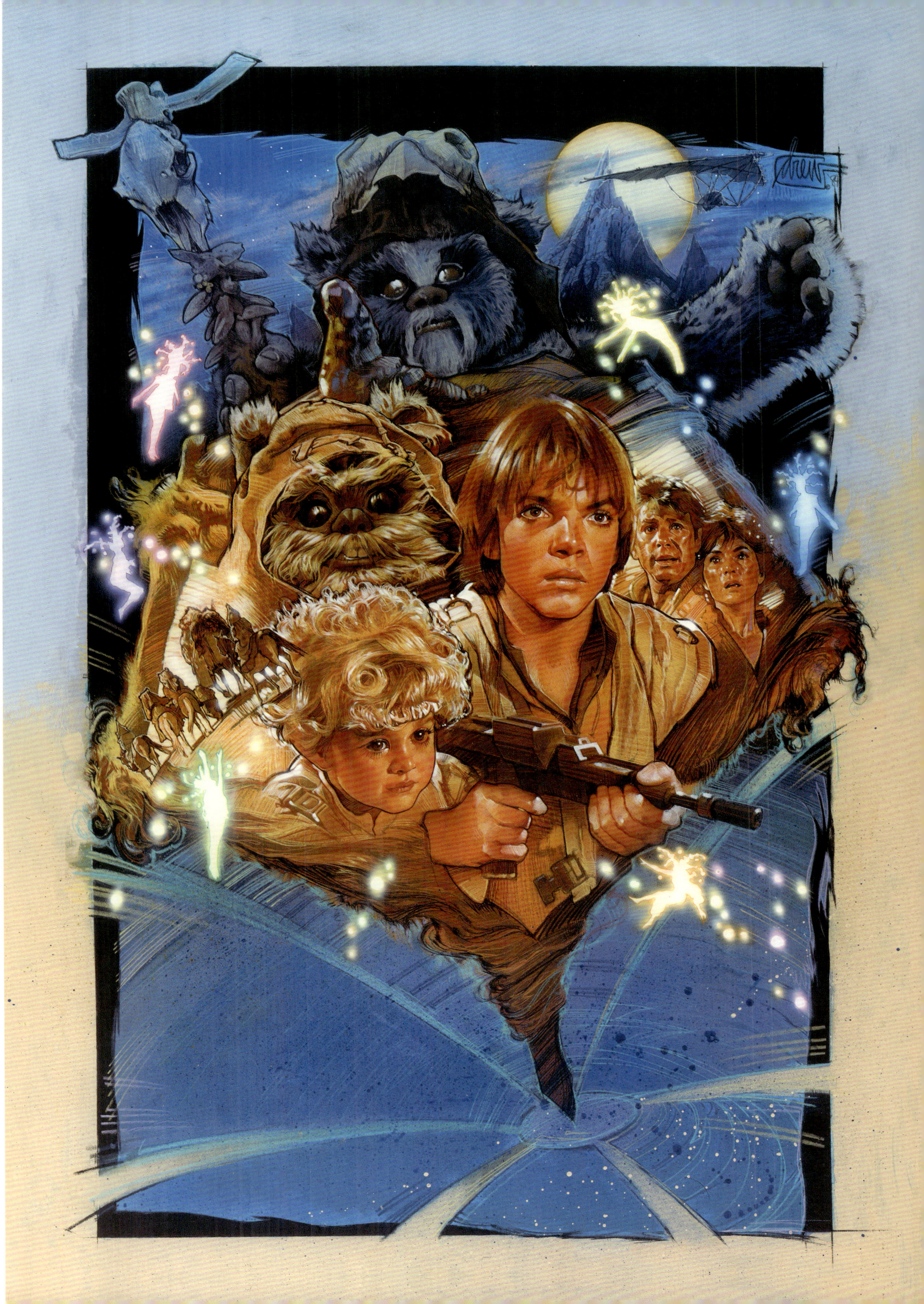

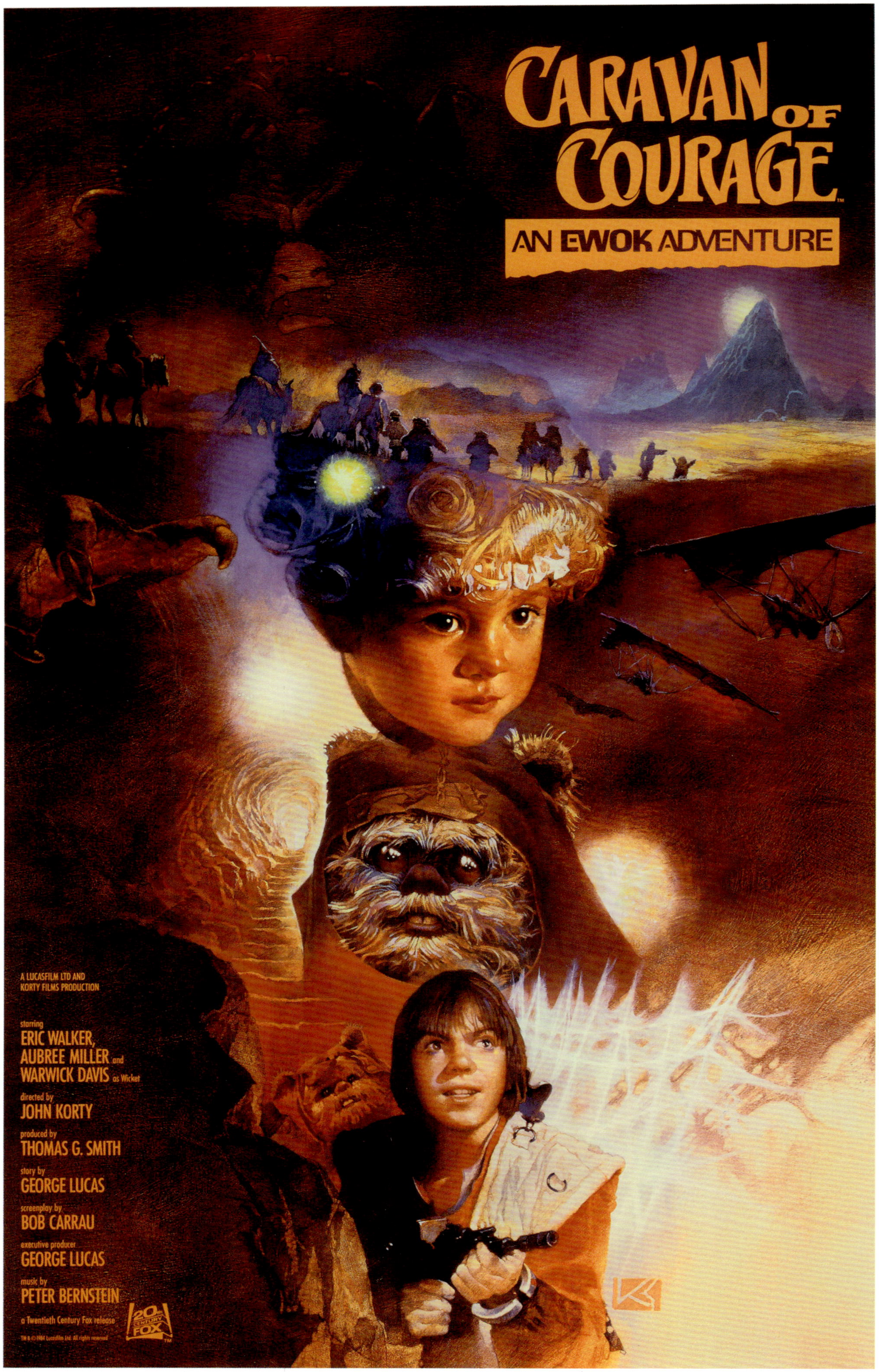

LEFT

Kazuhiko Sano

Final printed artwork for *Caravan of Courage: An Ewok Adventure* style "A" theatrical one-sheet, 1984

Localized theatrical release of TV movie

RIGHT

Randy Berrett

Final painted artwork for *Ewoks: The Battle for Endor* poster, Australia and New Zealand, 1986

Localized theatrical release of TV movie, under the title *Ewoks & the Marauders of Endor*

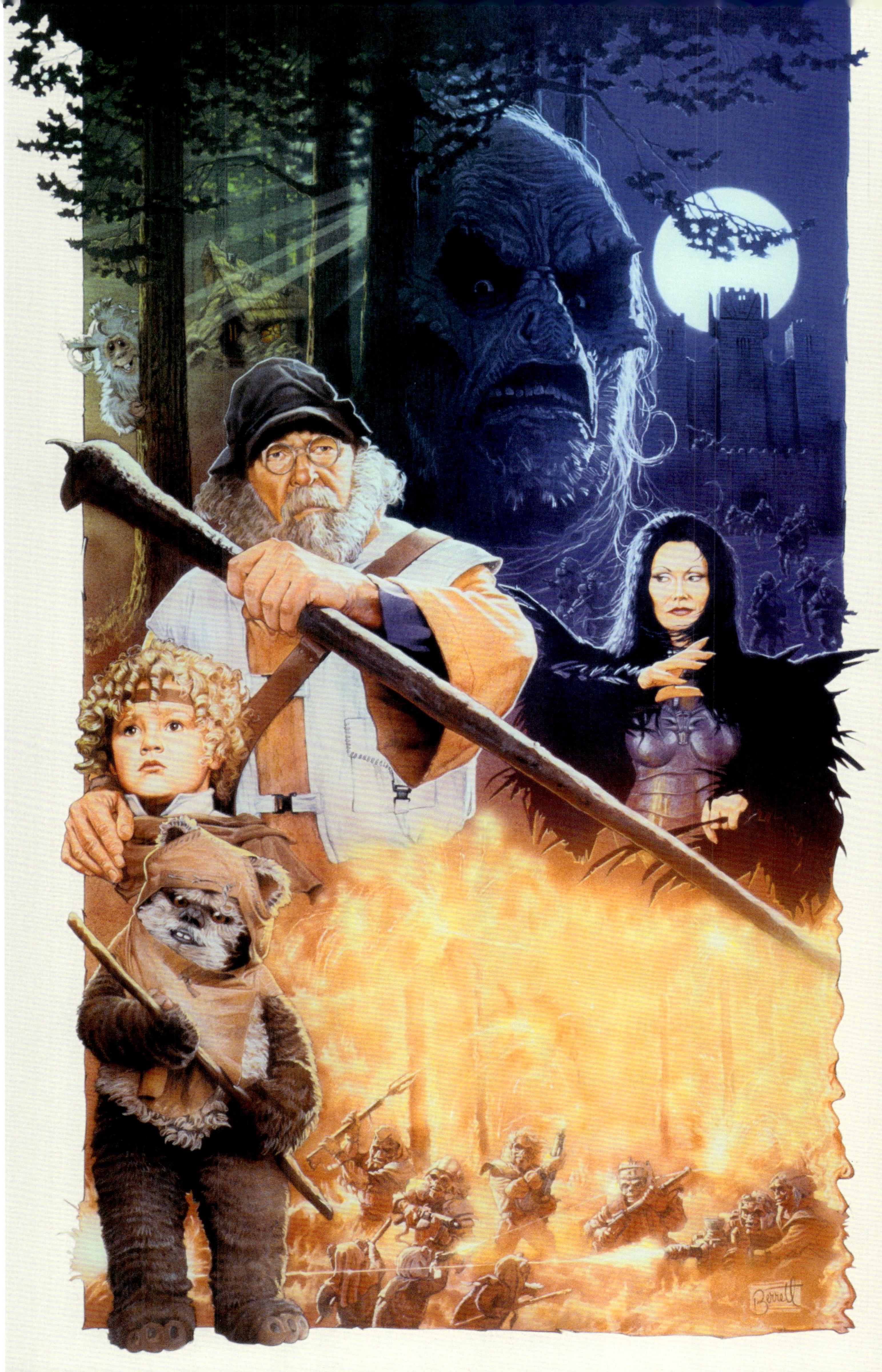
Berrett

RIGHT

Drew Struzan

Final painted artwork for *Star Wars* 10th Anniversary poster, 1987

Promotional poster for Killian Enterprises

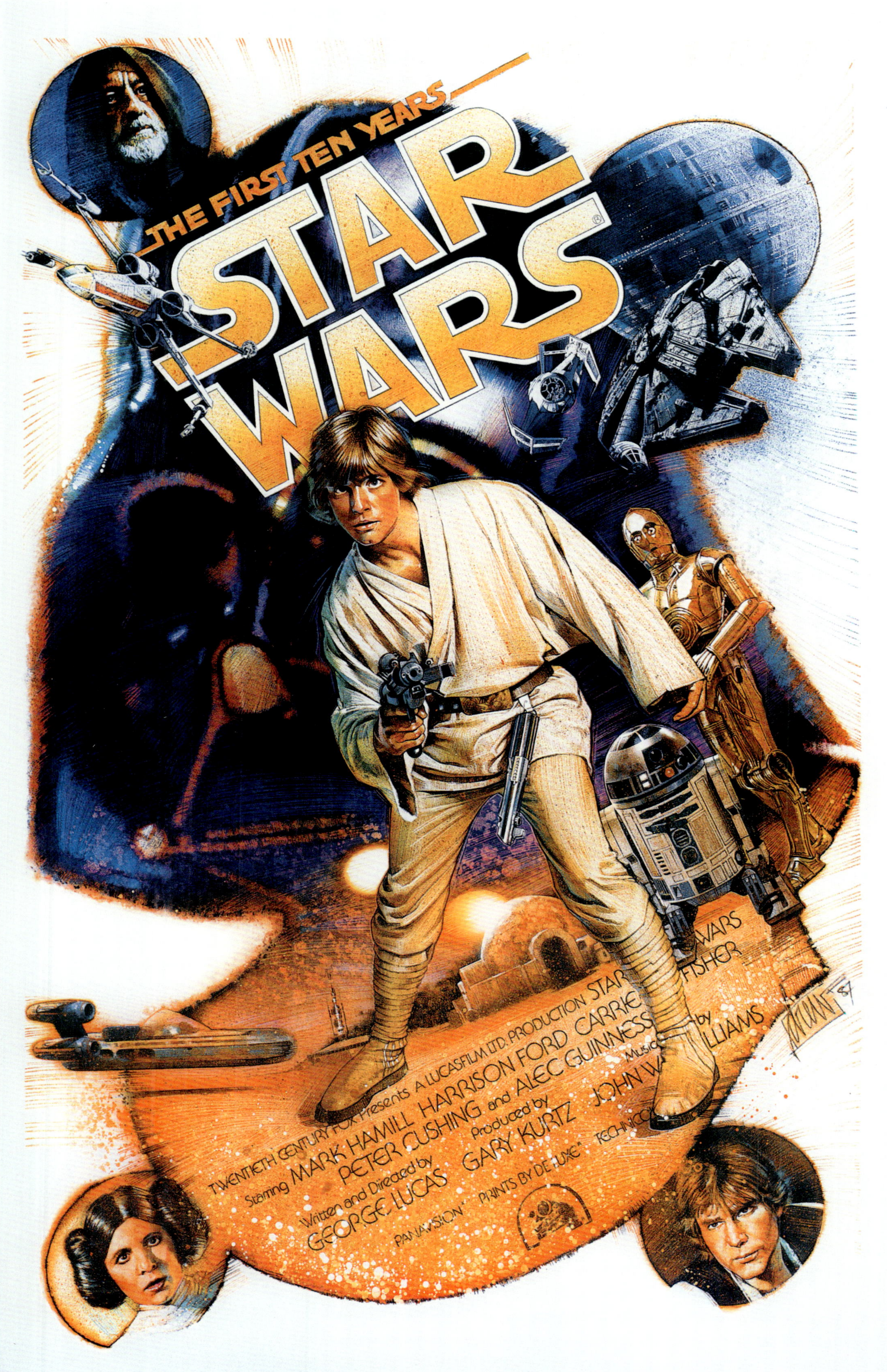
THE FIRST TEN YEARS
STAR WARS
TWENTIETH CENTURY FOX Presents A LUCASFILM LTD. PRODUCTION STAR
WARS
Starring MARK HAMILL HARRISON FORD CARRIE
FISHER
PETER CUSHING and ALEC GUINNESS
Written and Directed by GEORGE LUCAS
Produced by GARY KURTZ
Music
by
JOHN W
LLIAMS
PANAVISION
PRINTS BY DE LUXE
TECHNICO

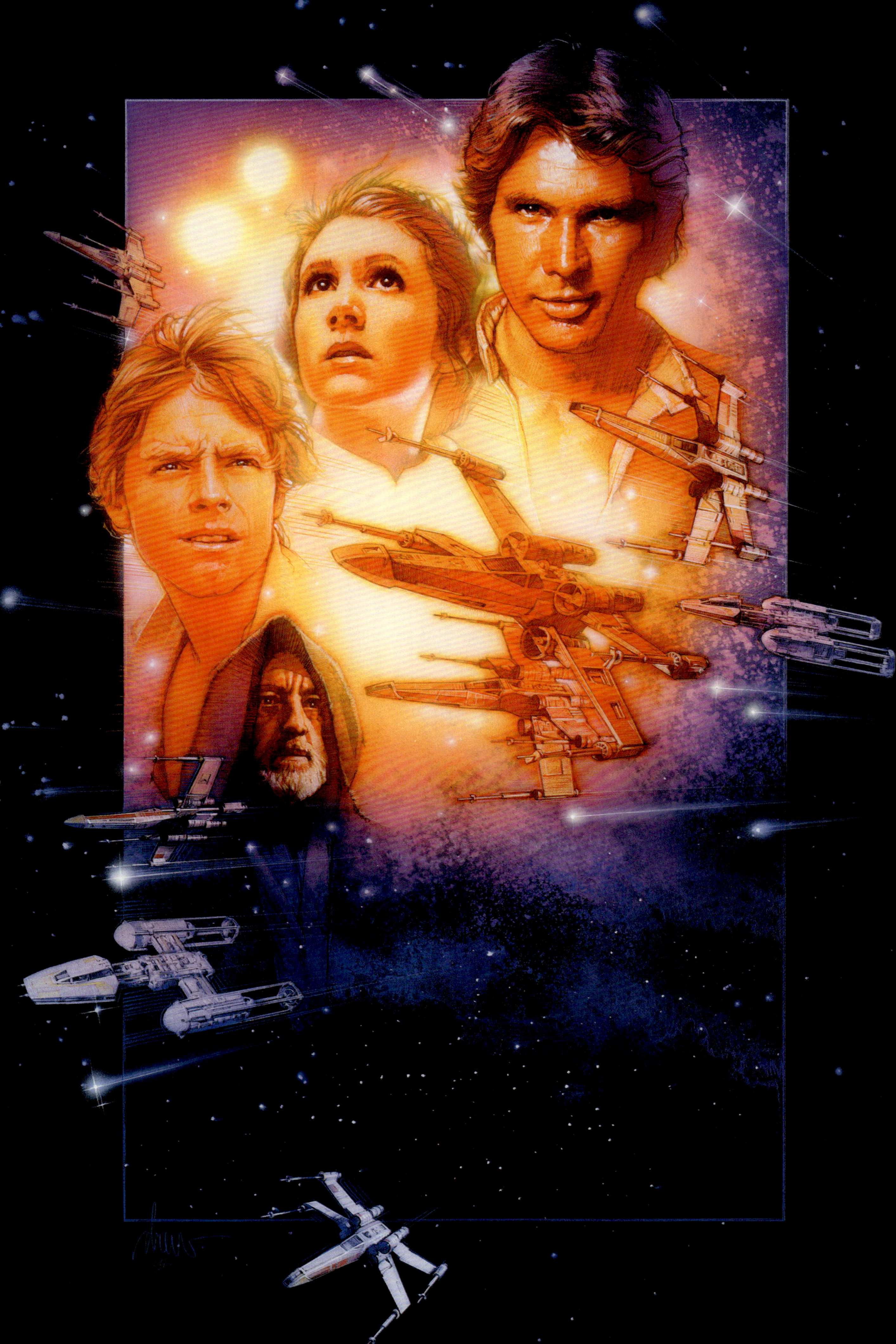

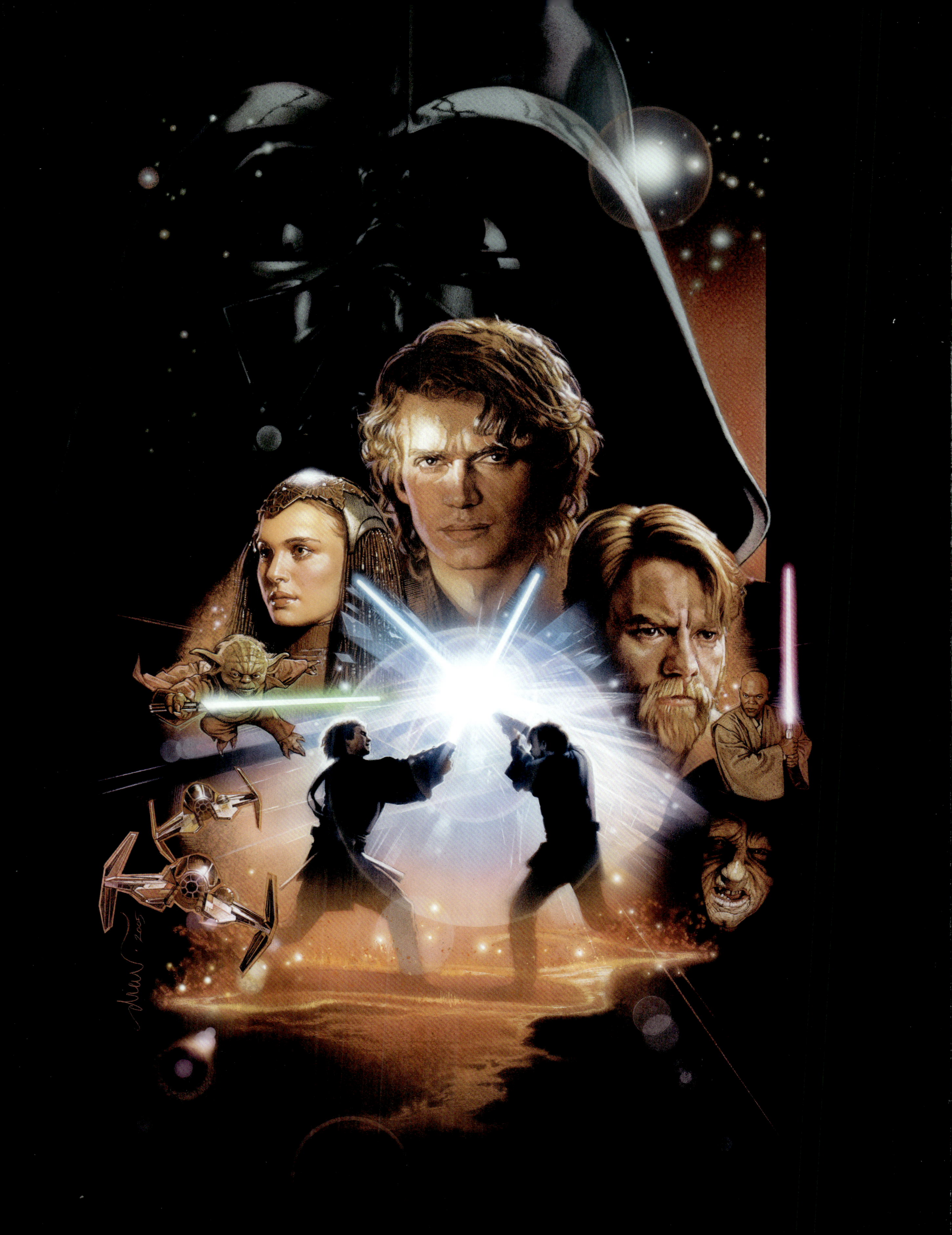

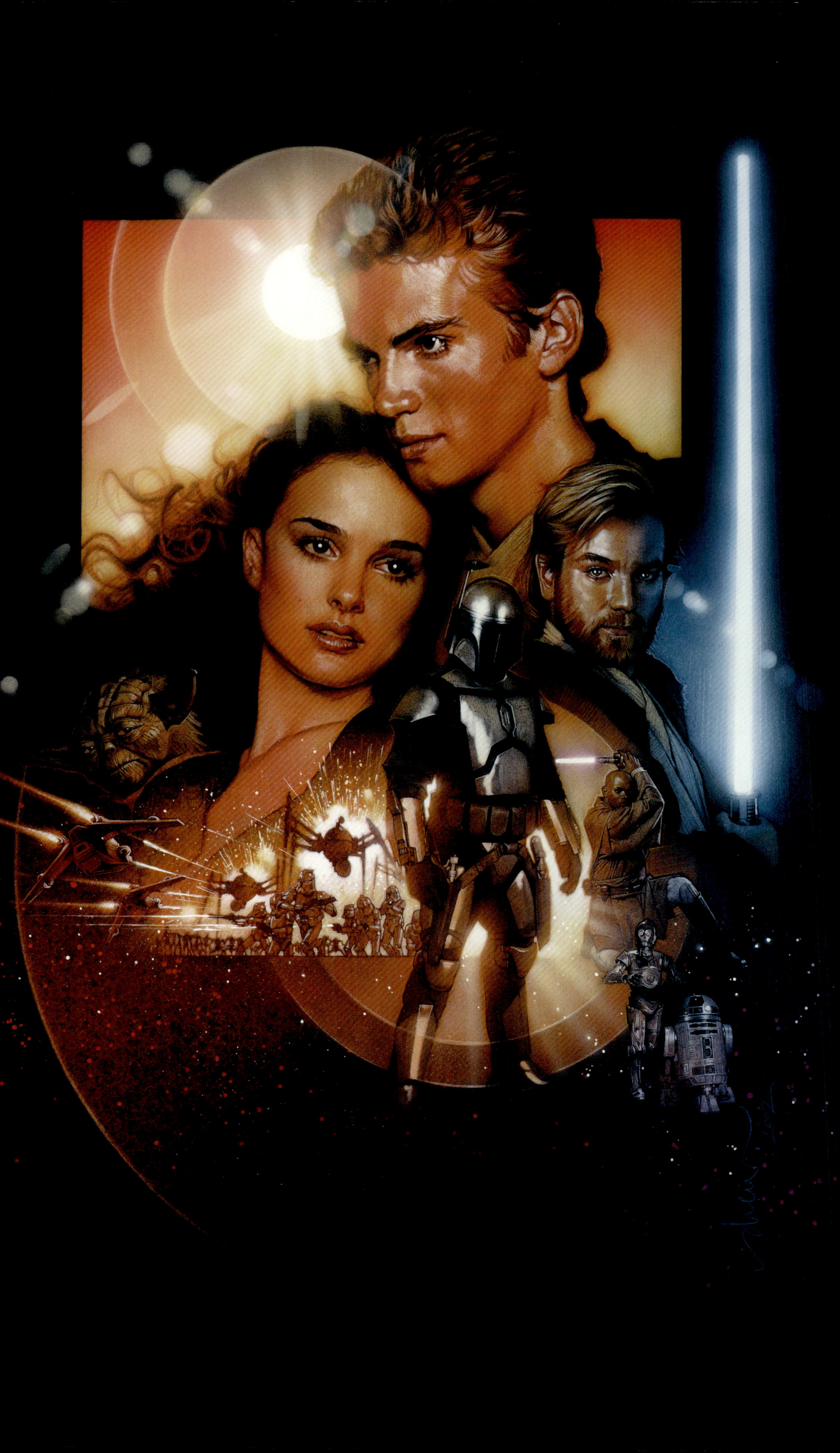

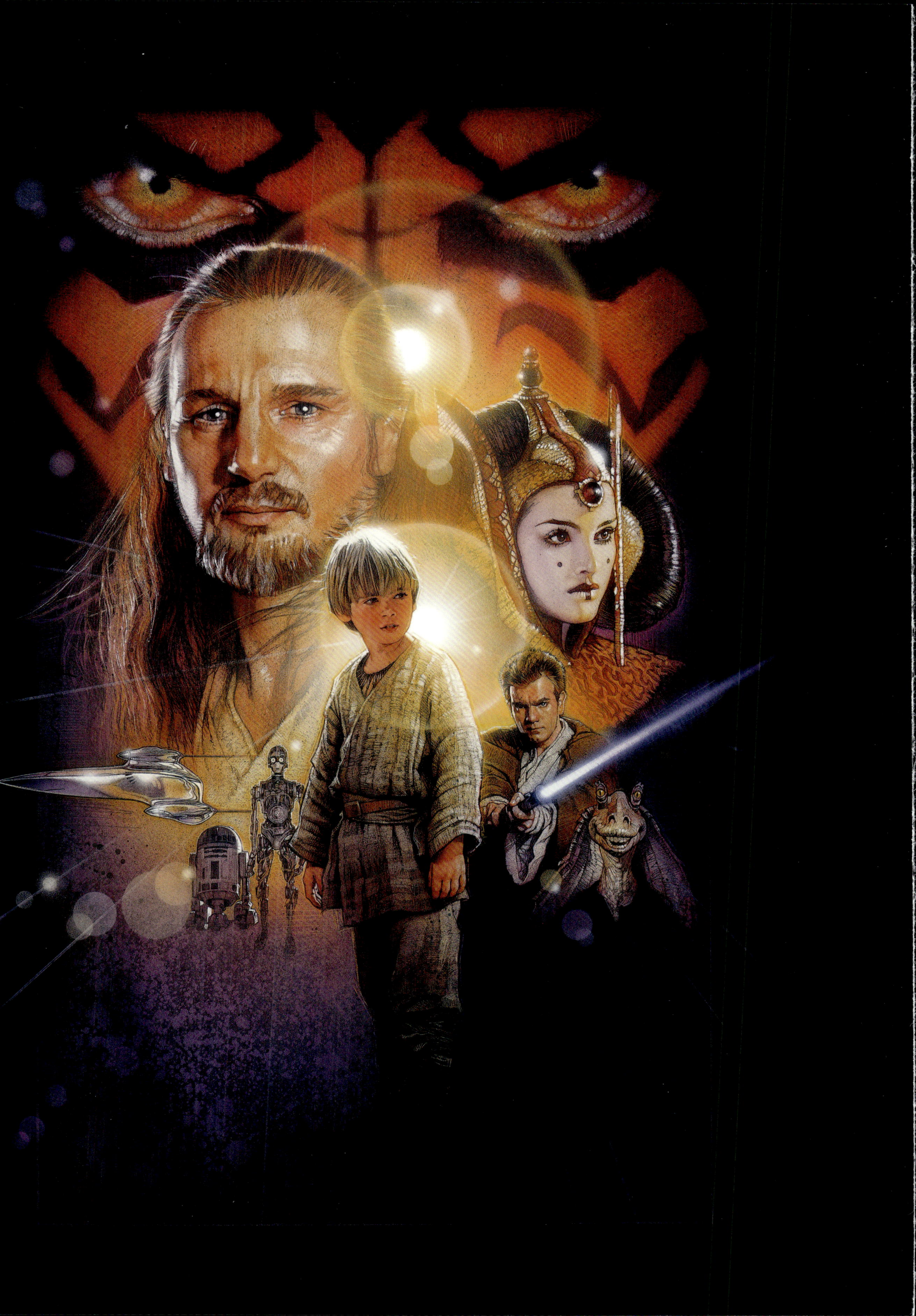

GATEFOLD PANEL ONE

Drew Struzan

Final painted artwork for *Star Wars: The Special Edition* theatrical one-sheet, 1996

GATEFOLD PANEL TWO

Drew Struzan

Final painted artwork for *The Empire Strikes Back: The Special Edition* theatrical one-sheet, 1996

GATEFOLD PANEL THREE

Drew Struzan

Final painted artwork for *Return of the Jedi: The Special Edition* theatrical one-sheet, 1996

GATEFOLD PANEL FOUR

Drew Struzan

Final painted artwork for *The Phantom Menace* theatrical one-sheet, 1999

GATEFOLD PANEL FIVE

Drew Struzan

Final painted artwork for *Attack of the Clones* theatrical one-sheet, 2002

GATEFOLD PANEL SIX

Drew Struzan

Final painted artwork for *Revenge of the Sith* theatrical one-sheet, 2005

RIGHT

Ellen Lee

Final mixed-media/digital artwork for *The Phantom Menace* theatrical advance poster, 1998

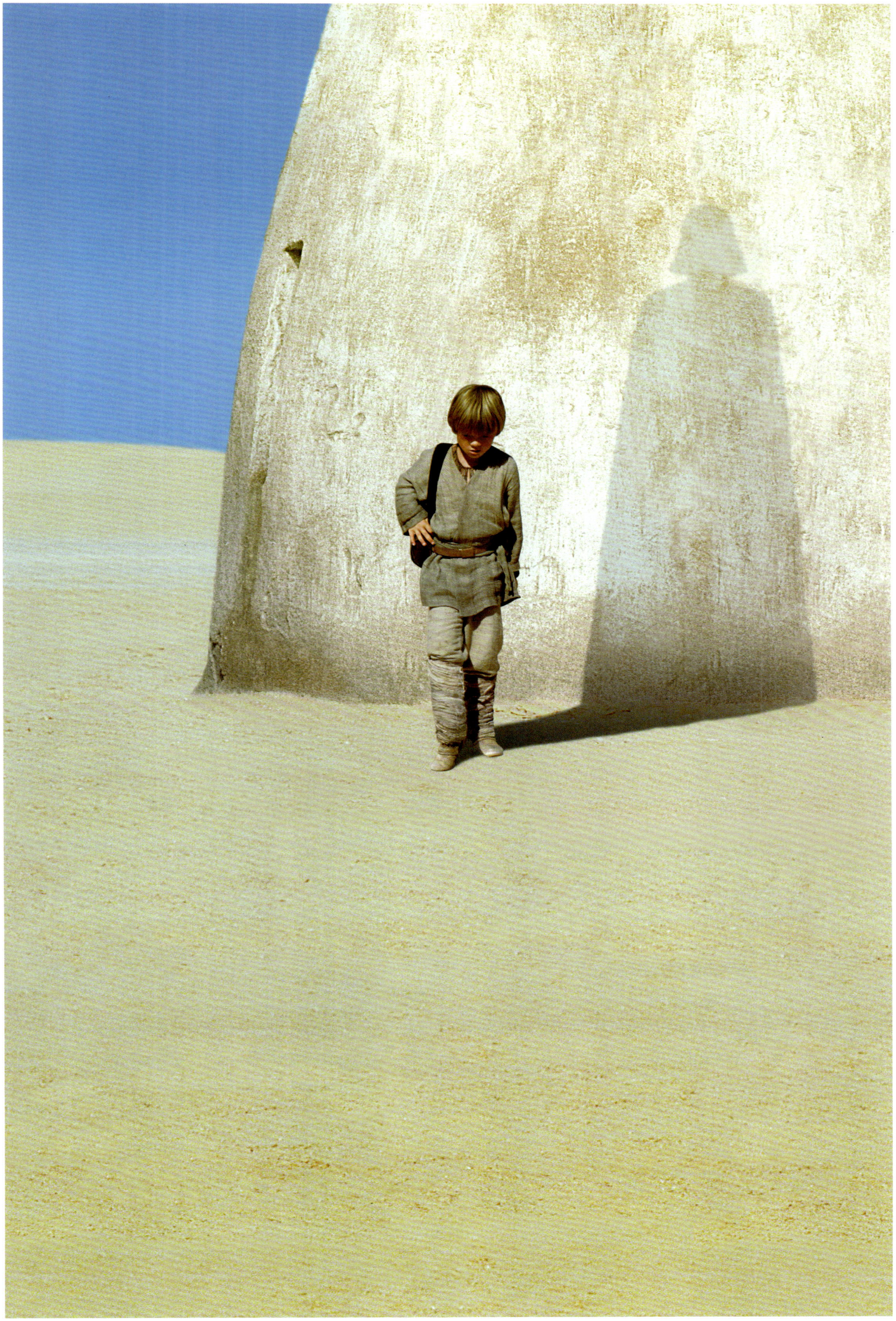

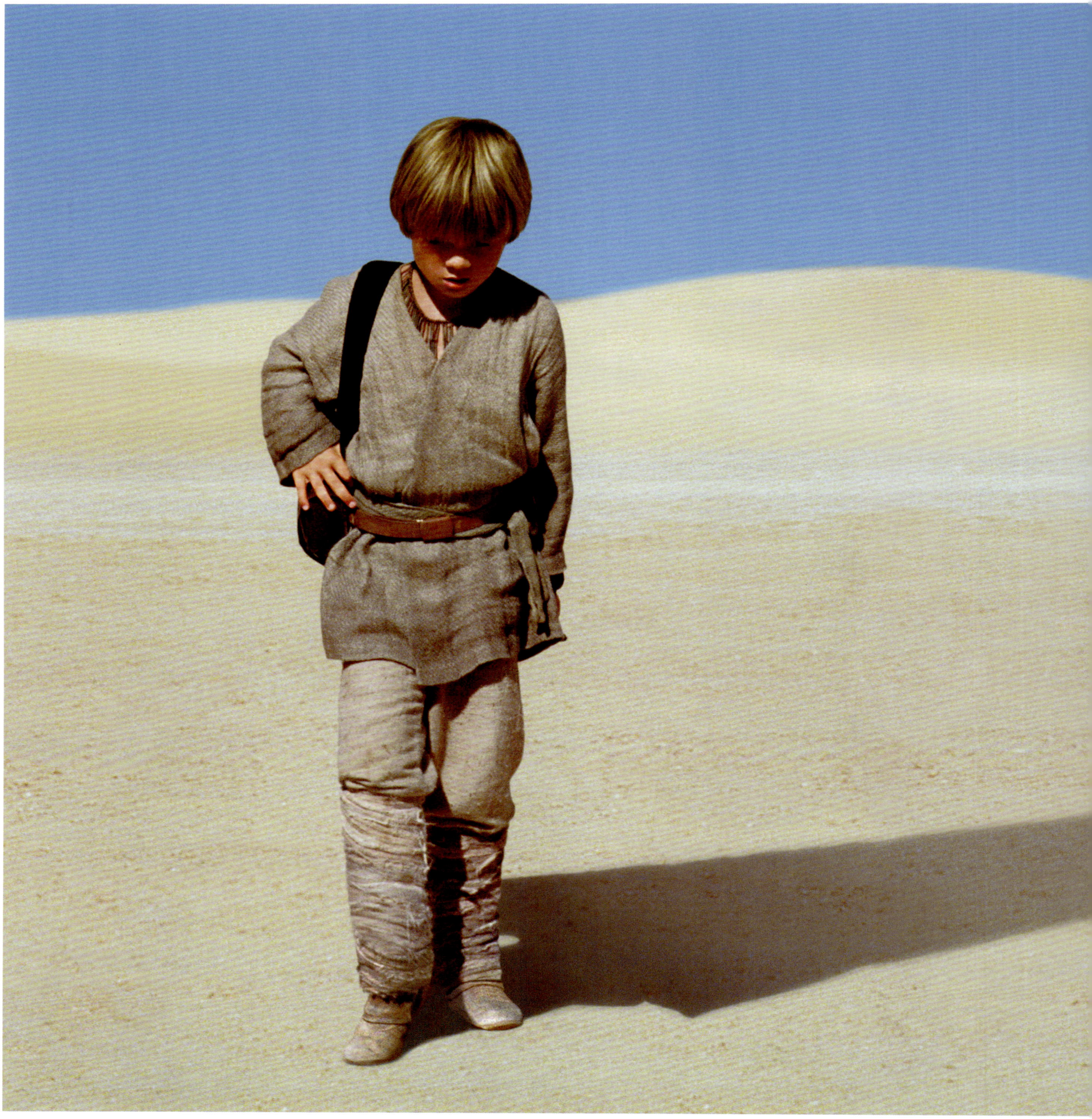

ABOVE

Ellen Lee

Final mixed-media/digital artwork for *The Phantom Menace* theatrical advance banner, 1998

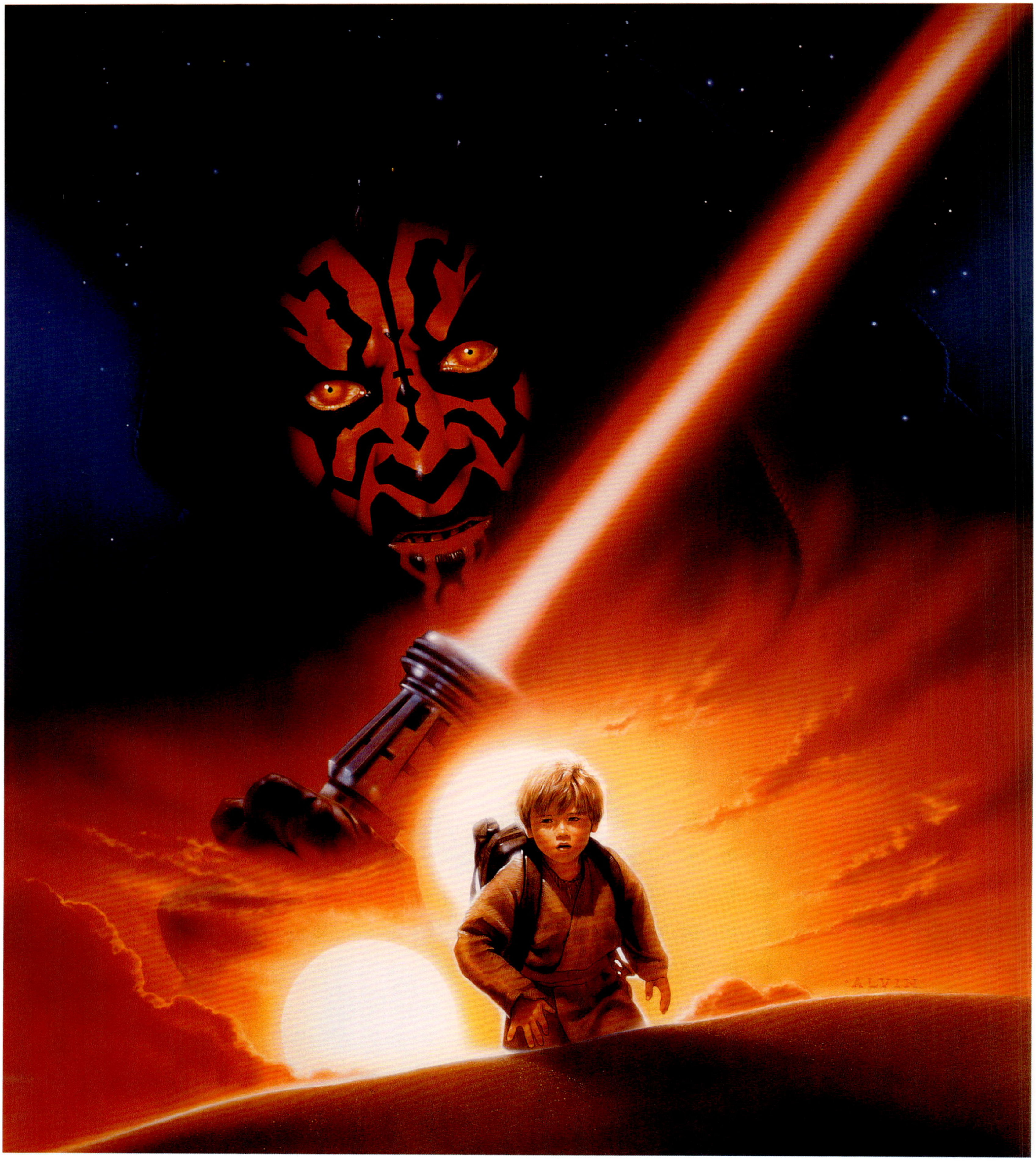

ABOVE

John Alvin

Final painted artwork for *Star Wars* Celebration I promotional poster, 1999

RIGHT AND FOLLOWING SPREAD (DETAIL)

Robert Silvers

Final photomosaic for *The Phantom Menace* poster, 1999

Produced to promote the British edition of *Star Wars Fact File*

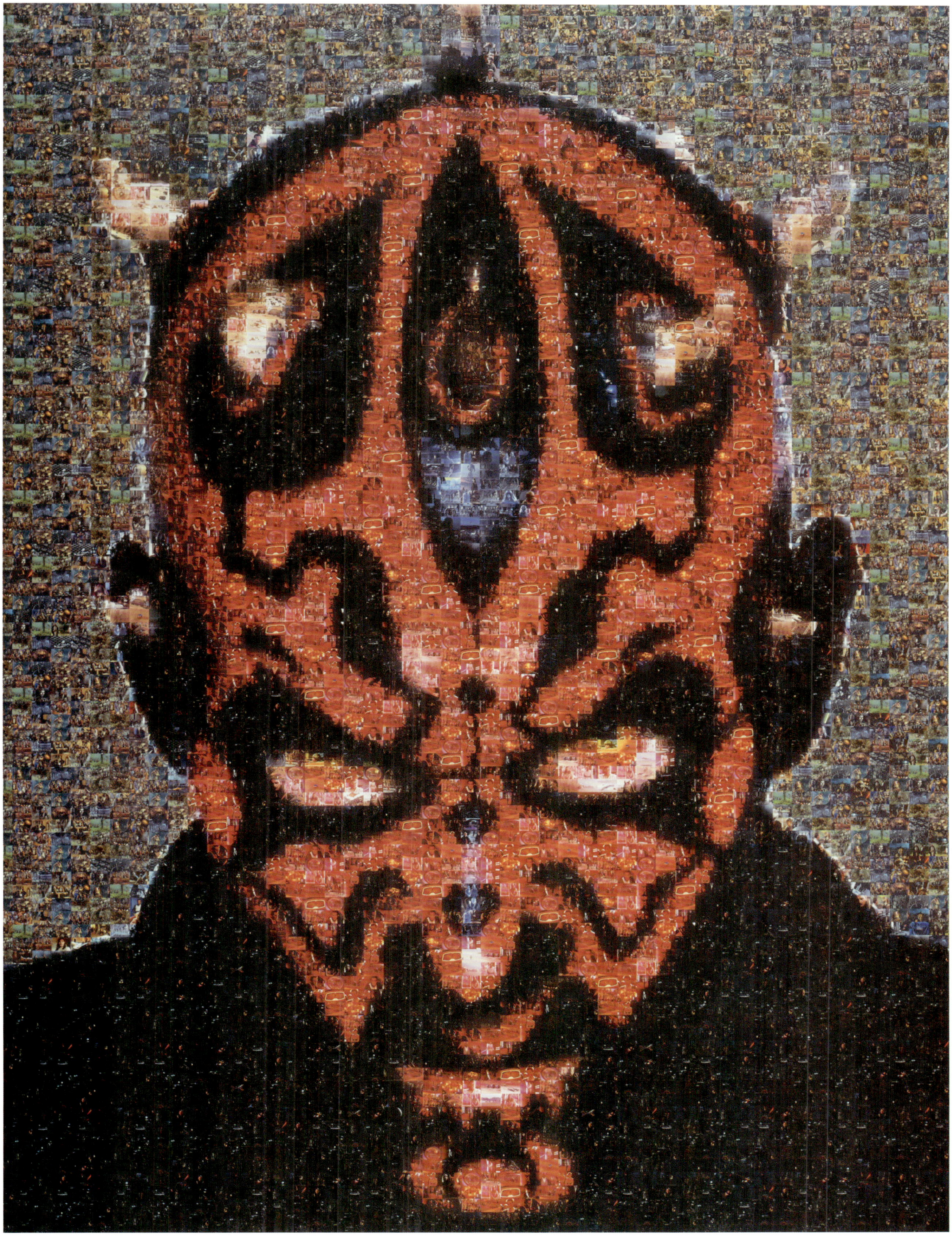

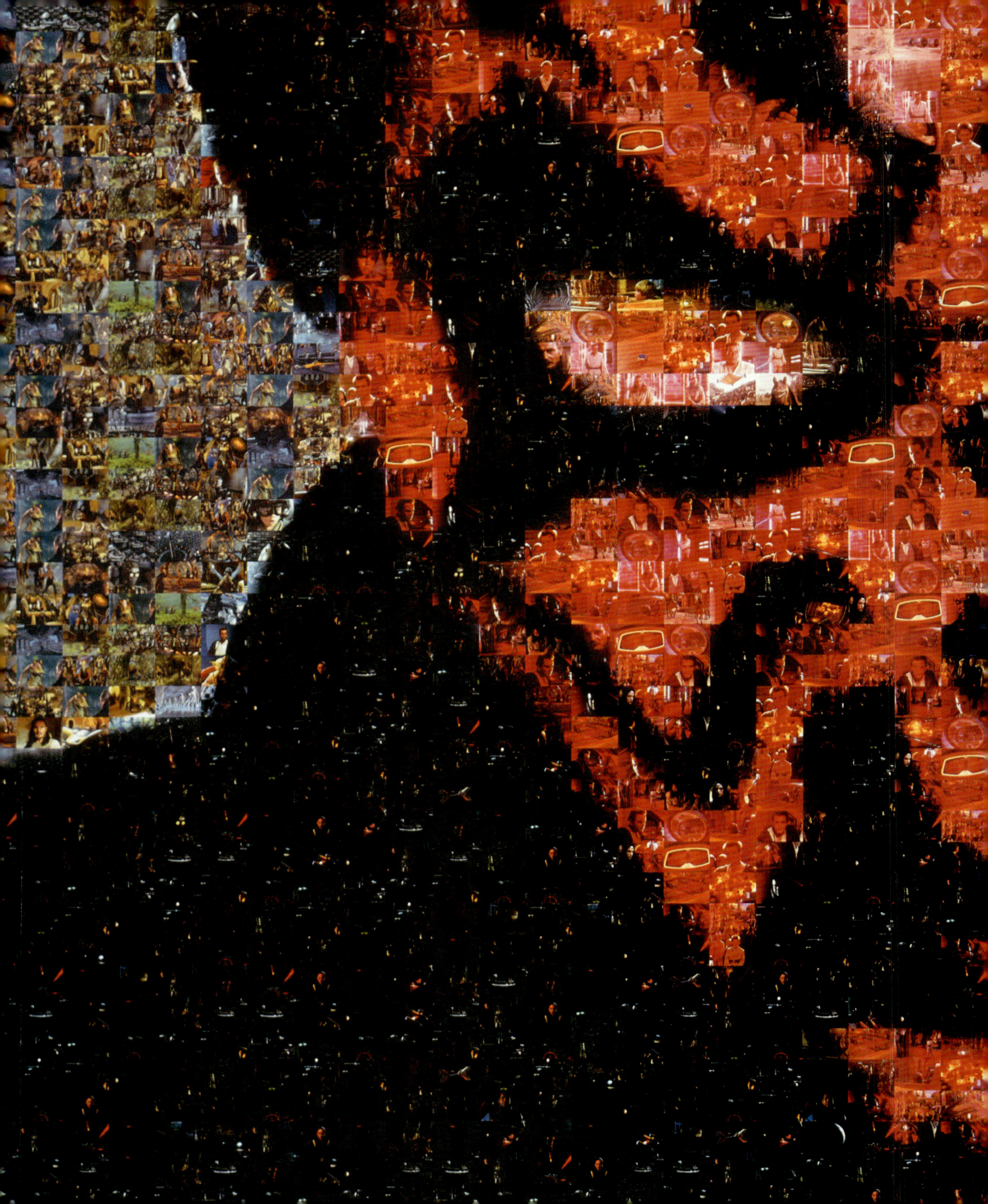

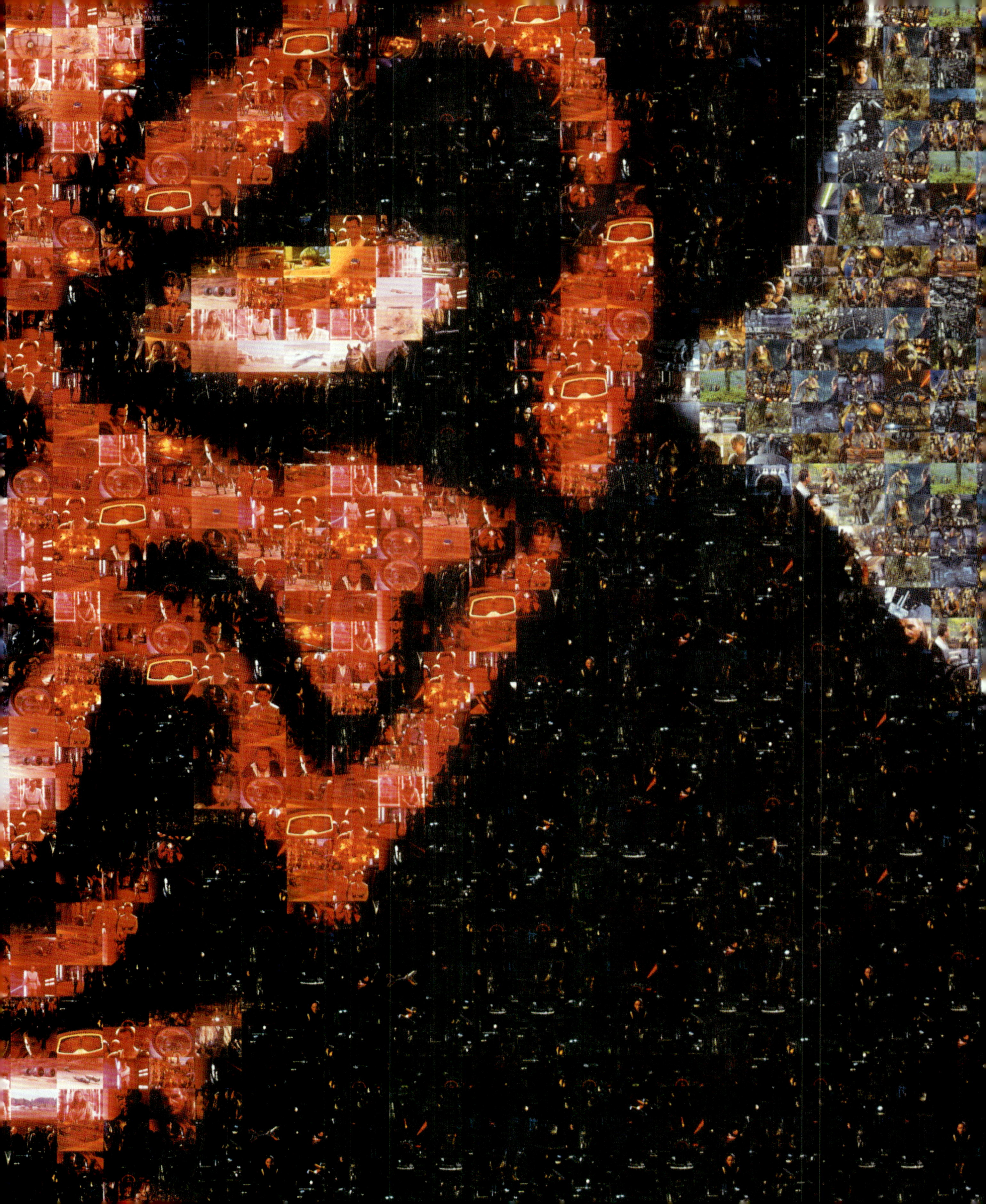

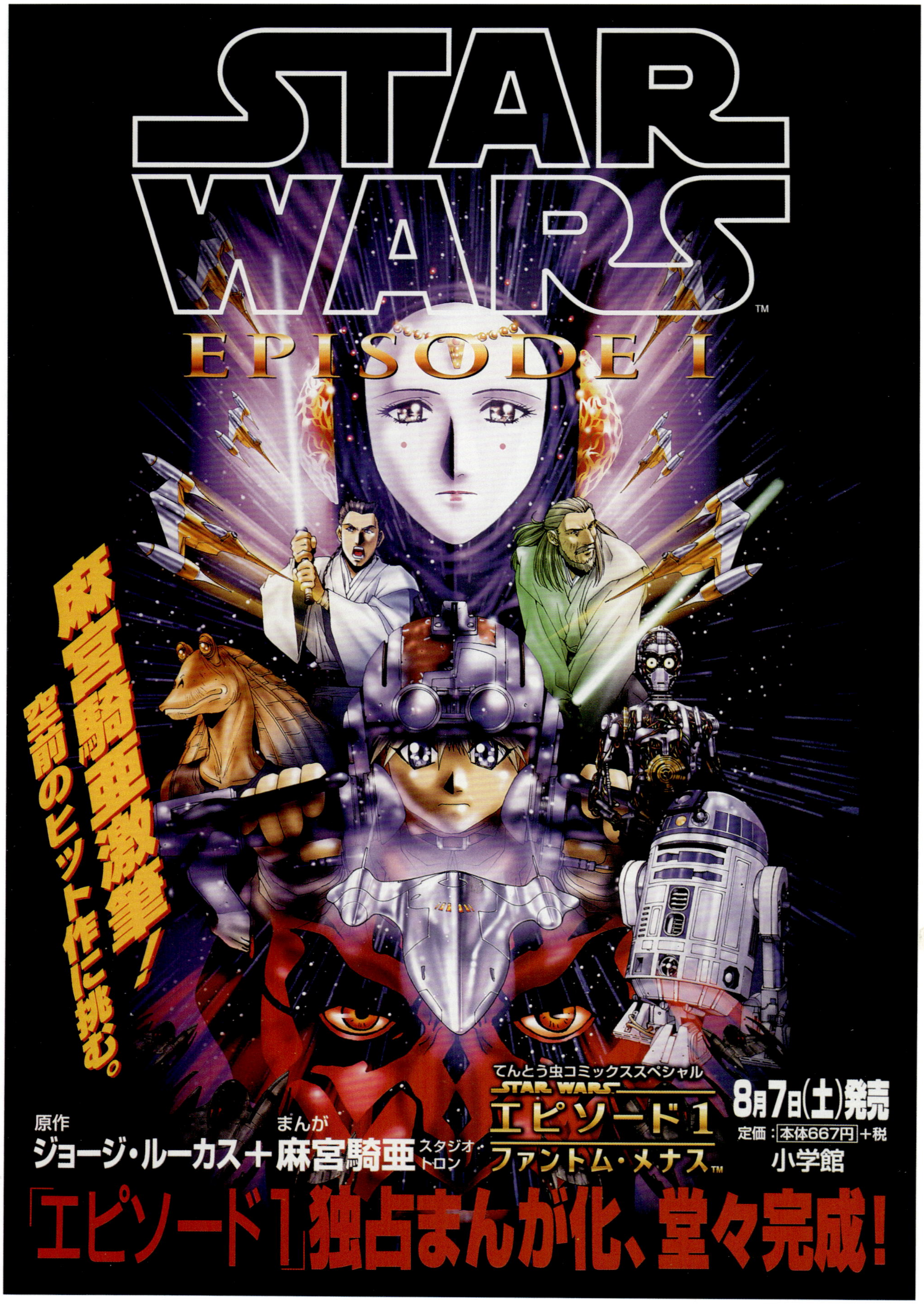

LEFT

Kia Asamiya

Final printed artwork for *The Phantom Menace* poster

Promotional reproduction of original manga art for Tentomushi Comics, 1999

RIGHT

David McMacken

Final printed artwork for *Attack of the Clones* IMAX theatrical one-sheet, 2002

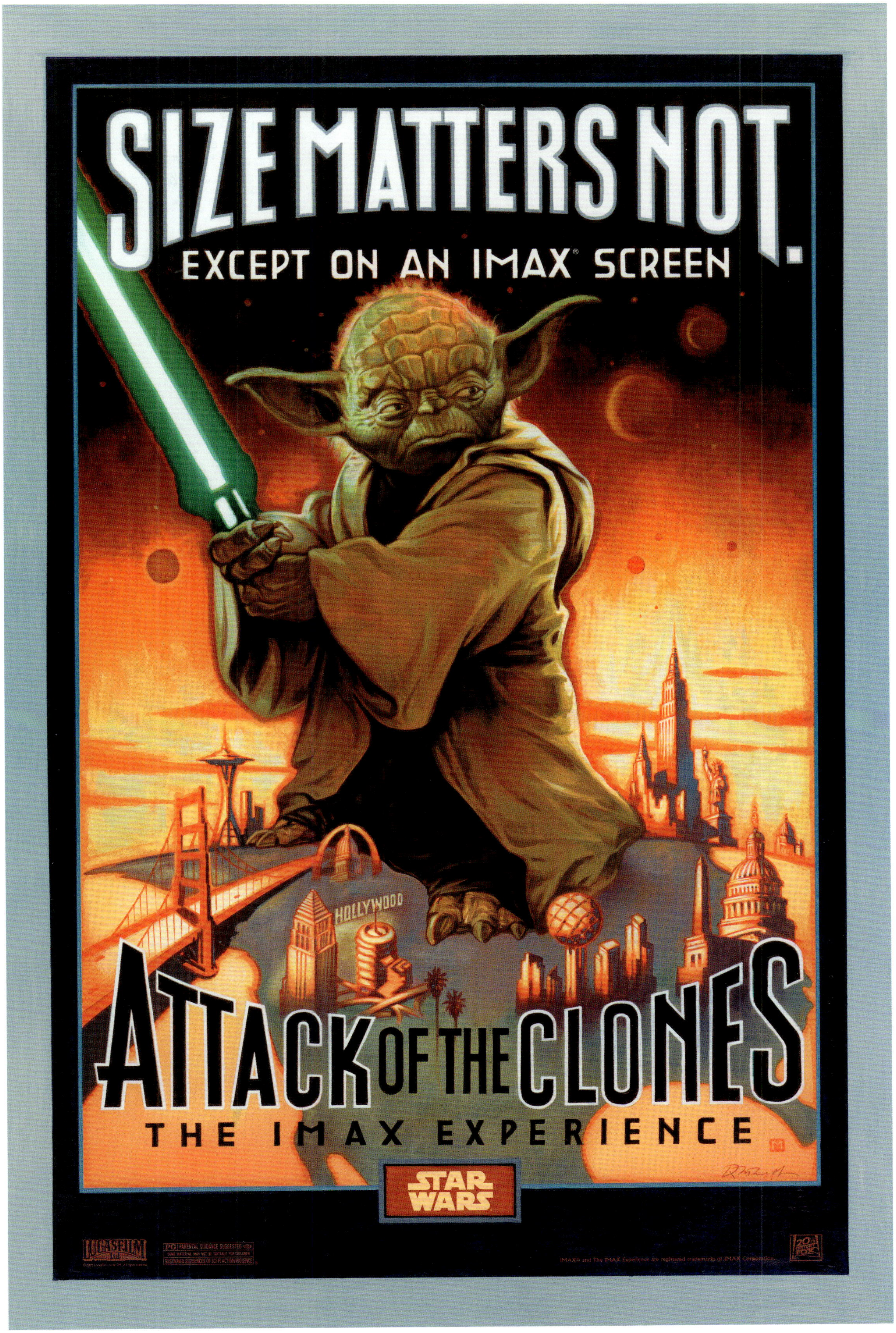

SIZE MATTERS NOT.
EXCEPT ON AN IMAX® SCREEN
HOLLYWOOD
ATTACK OF THE CLONES
THE IMAX EXPERIENCE
STAR WARS
PG PARENTAL GUIDANCE SUGGESTED
SOME MATERIAL MAY NOT BE SUITABLE FOR CHILDREN
SUSTAINED SEQUENCES OF SCI-FI ACTION/VIOLENCE
IMAX® and The IMAX Experience are registered trademarks of IMAX Corporation.

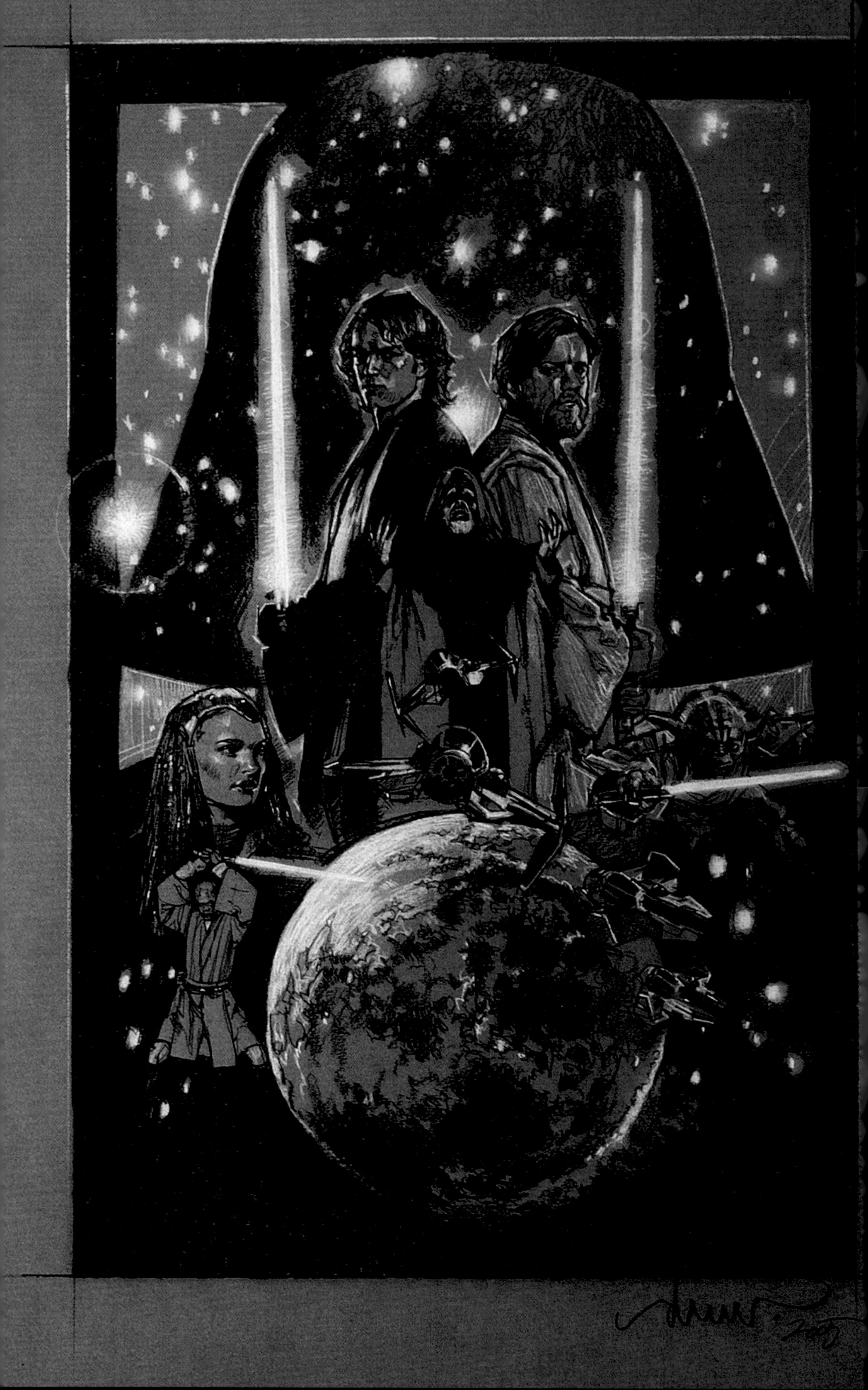

ABOVE

Drew Struzan

Black-and-white concept treatment for *Revenge of the Sith* poster, 2005

RIGHT

New Wave Entertainment

Final mixed-media/digital artwork for *Revenge of the Sith* theatrical advance one-sheet, 2004

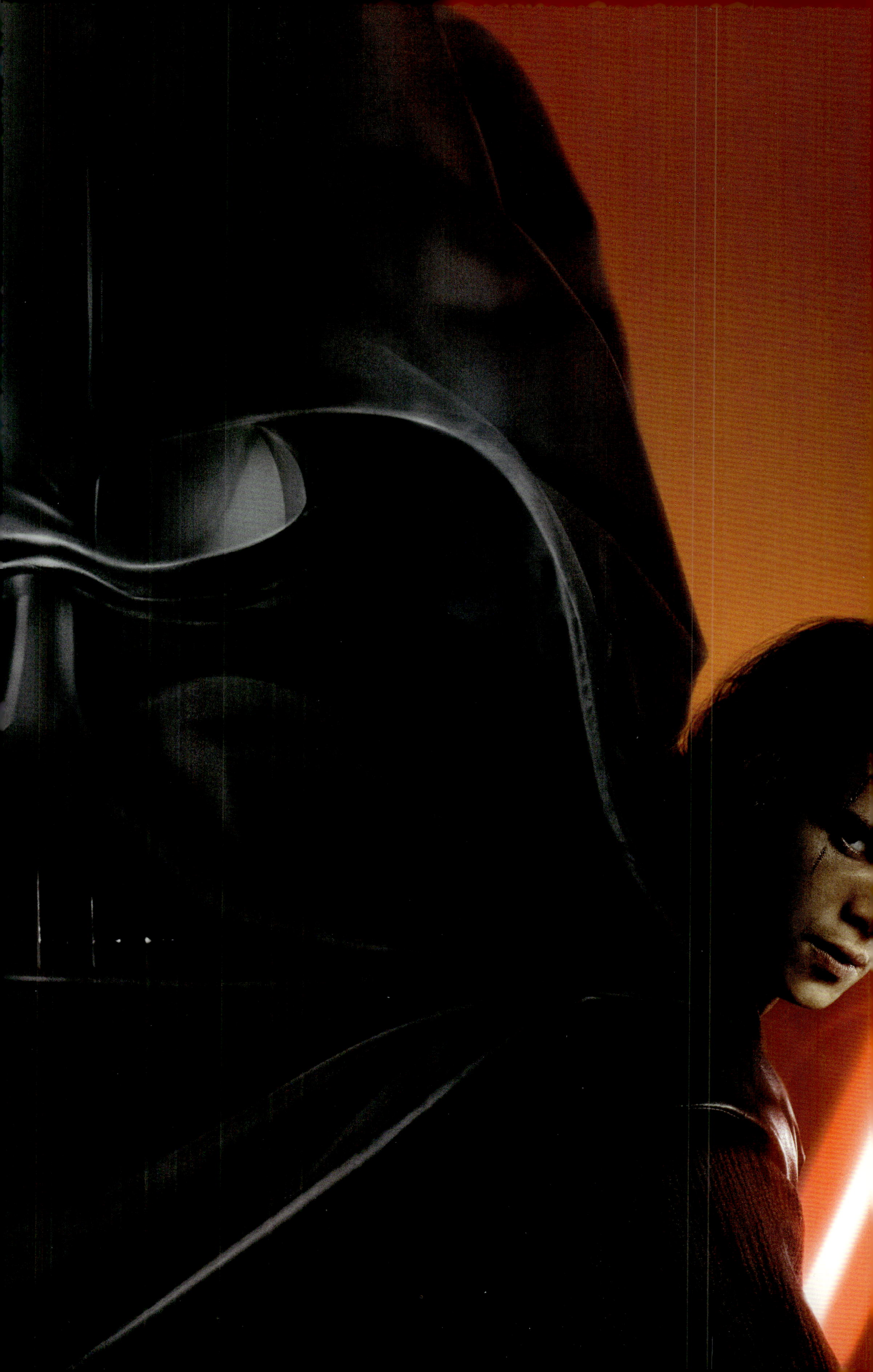

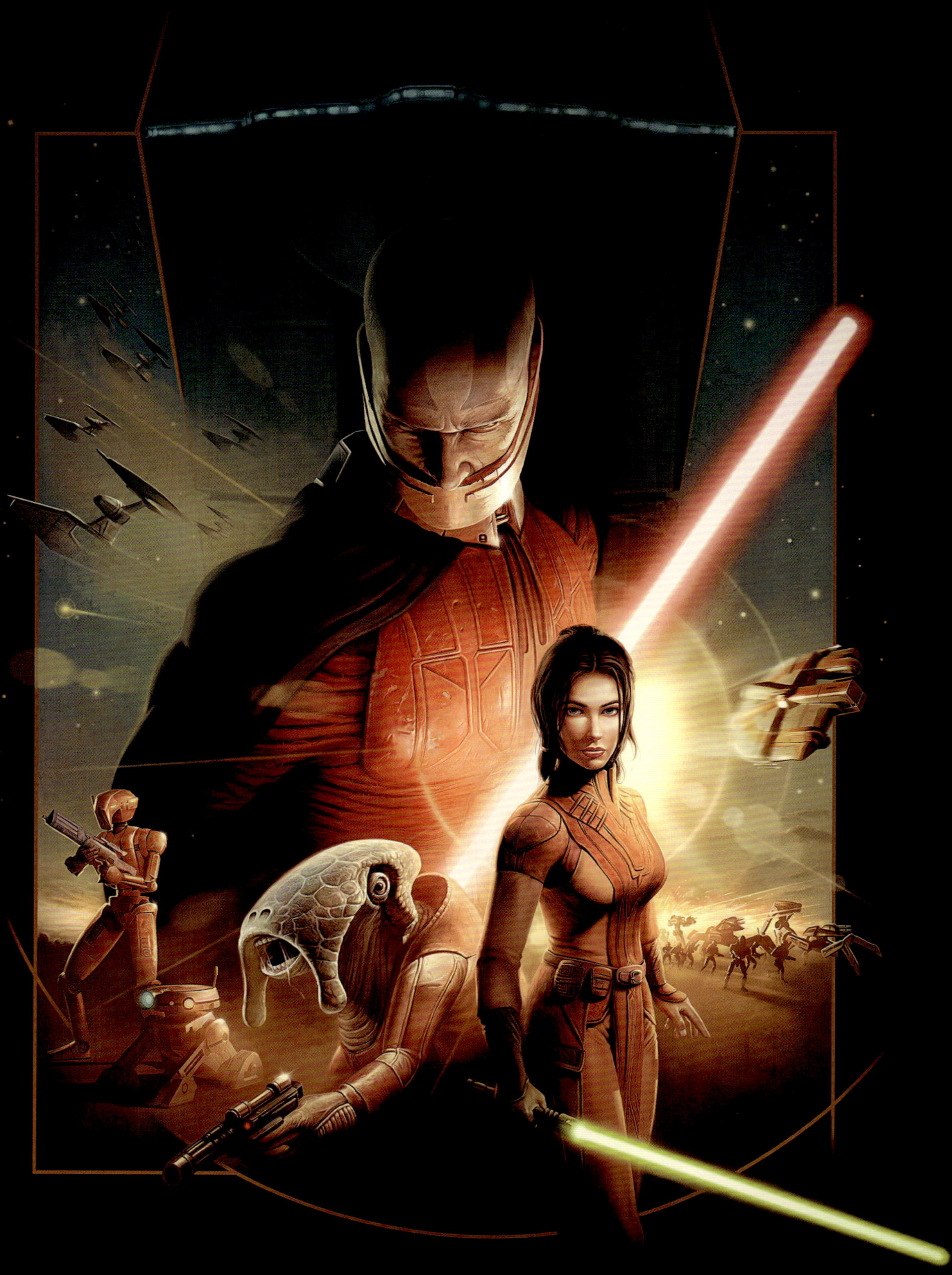

ABOVE

Mike Sadd

Final digital artwork for *Knights of the Old Republic* video game promotional poster, 2003

RIGHT

Amy Beth Christenson

Final digital artwork for *The Force Unleashed* video game promotional poster, 2008

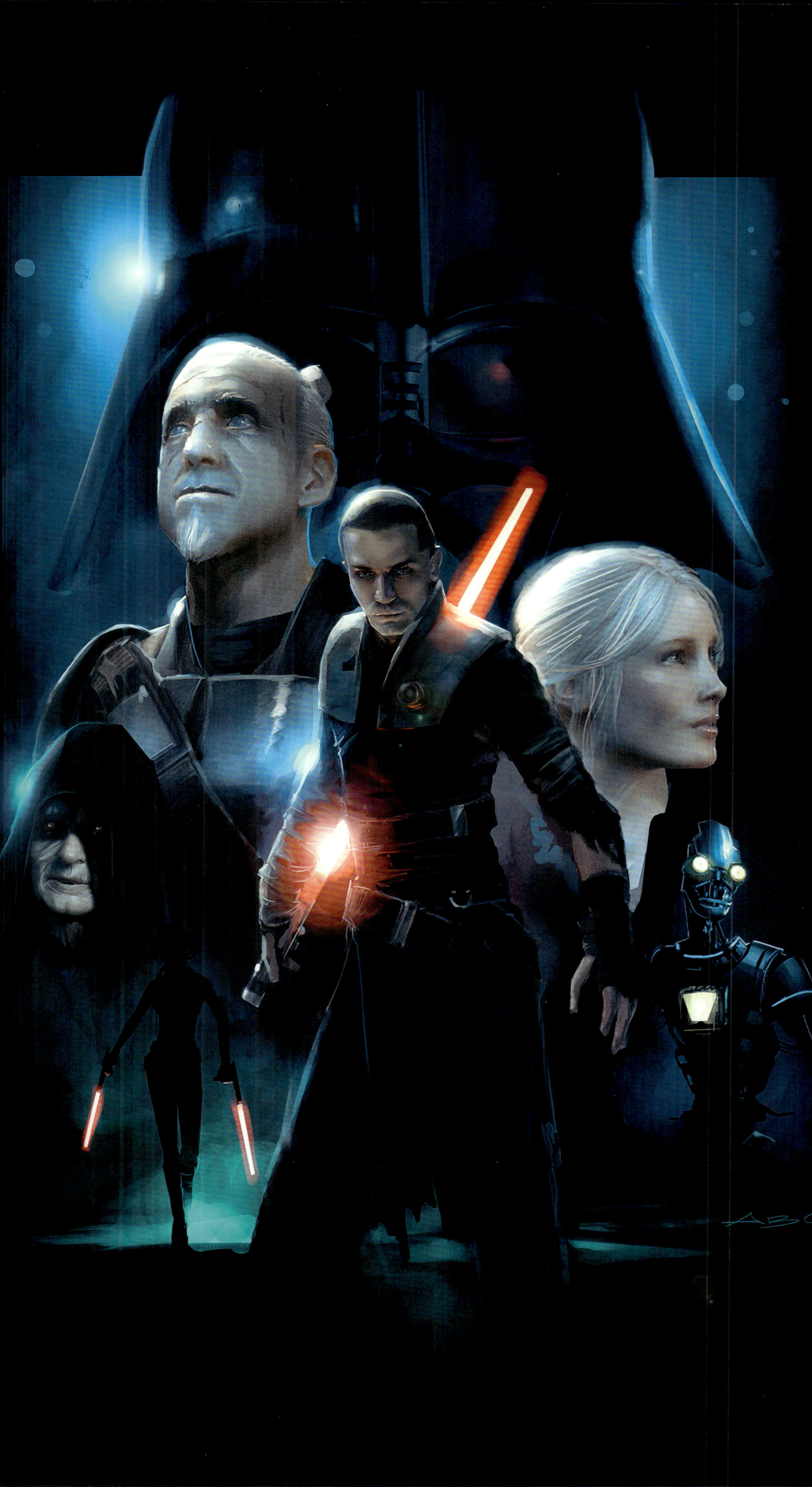

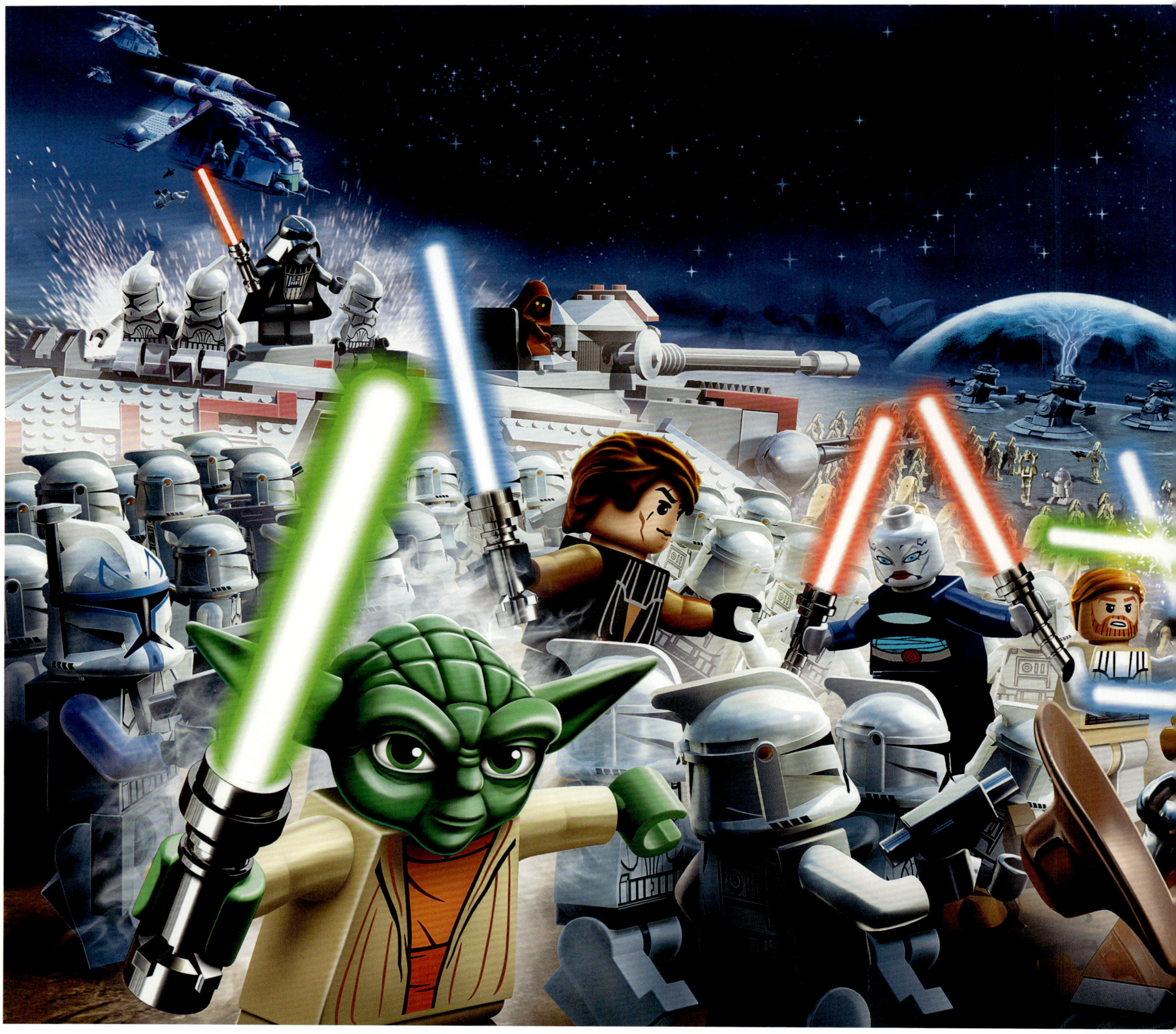

ABOVE

Hez Chorba (art direction); Hamagami/Carroll Inc. (agency)

Final digital artwork for *LEGO Star Wars III: The Clone Wars* video game key art, 2011

RIGHT

Unknown

Final digital artwork for *LEGO Star Wars II: The Original Trilogy* video game key art, 2006

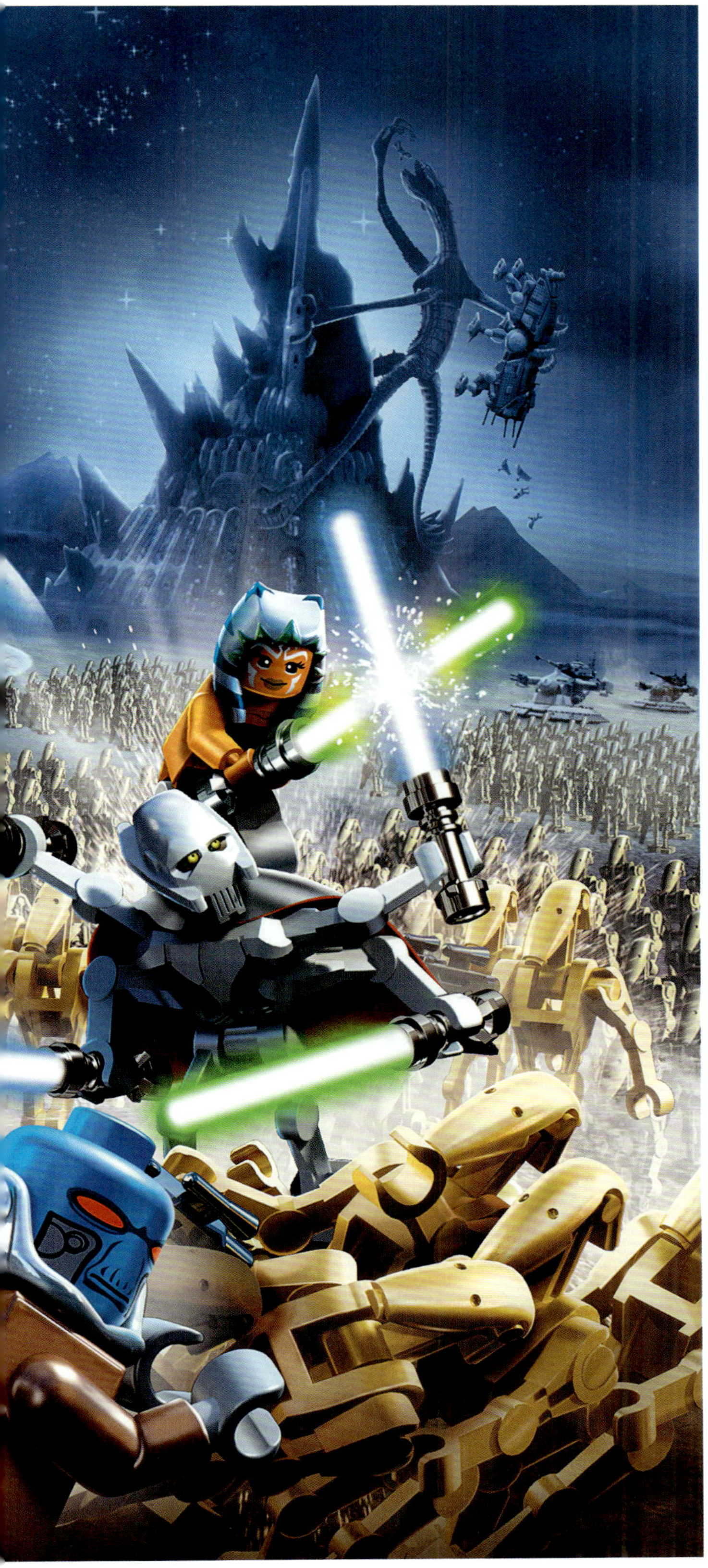

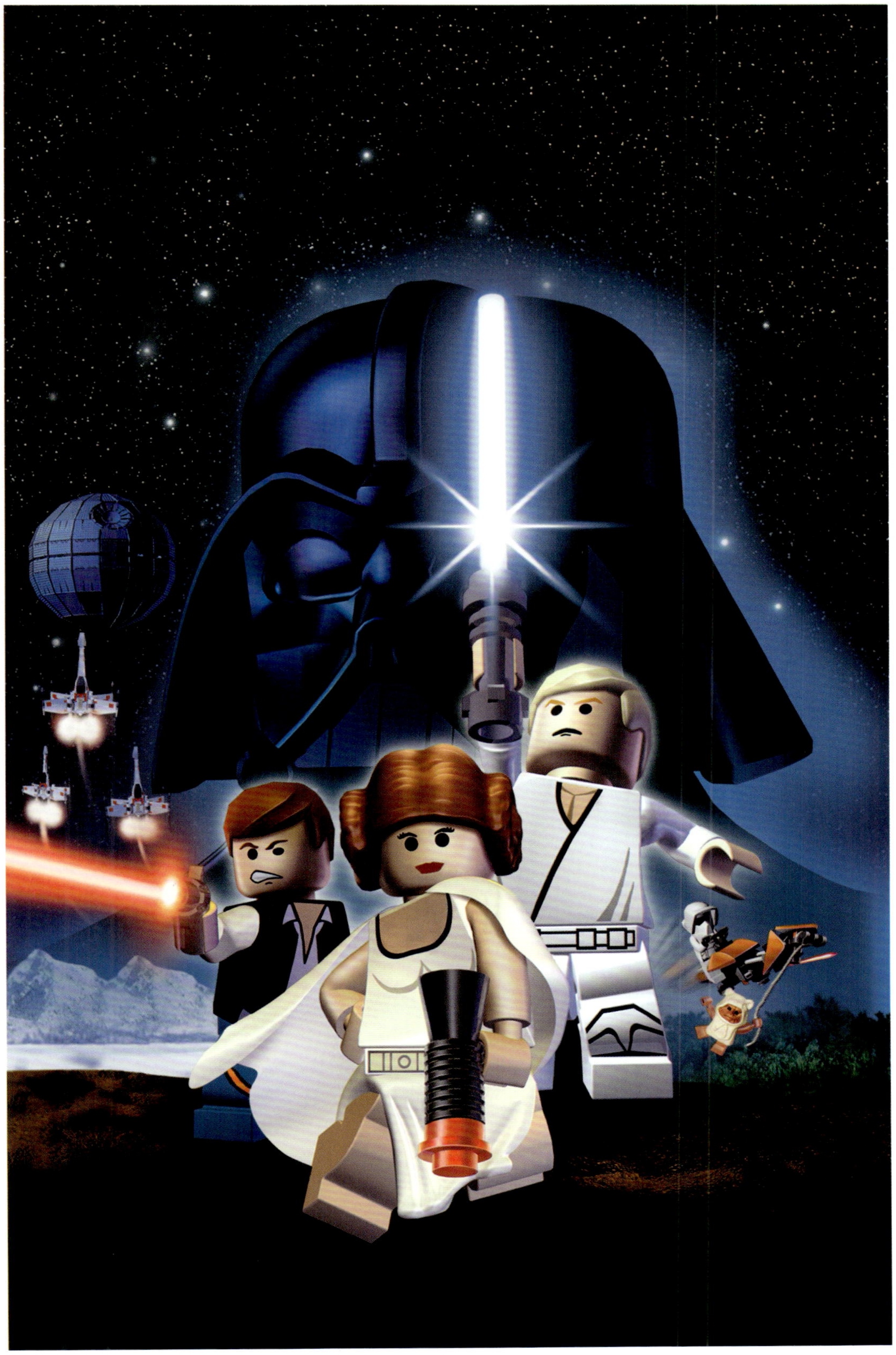

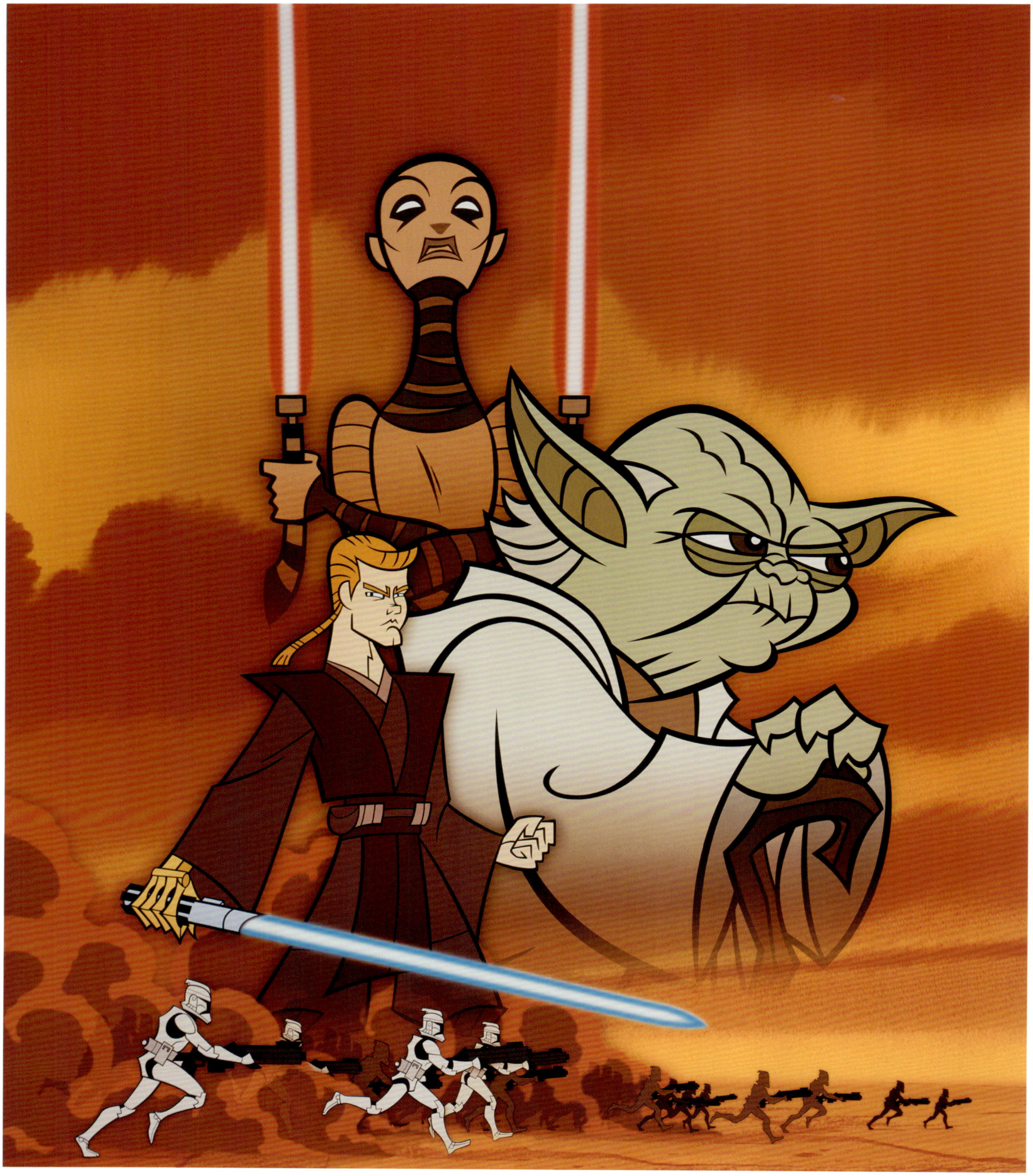

ABOVE

Cartoon Network Studios

Final mixed-media artwork for *Star Wars: Clone Wars* promotional poster, 2003

Promotional poster for *Clone Wars* micro-series Part One

RIGHT

Cartoon Network Studios

Final mixed-media artwork for *Star Wars: Clone Wars* promotional poster, 2003

Exclusive poster distributed via the *Star Wars* Fan Club

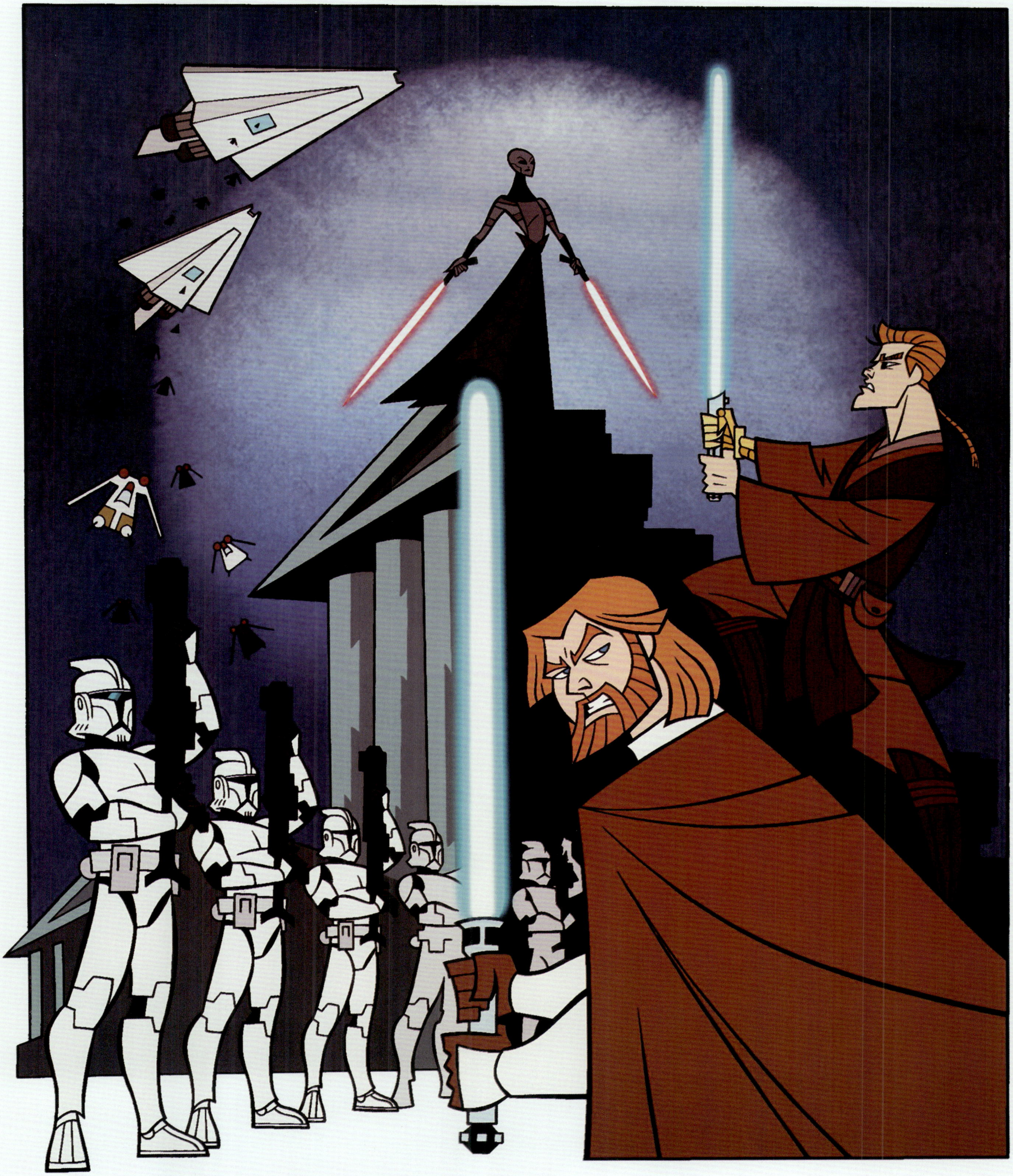

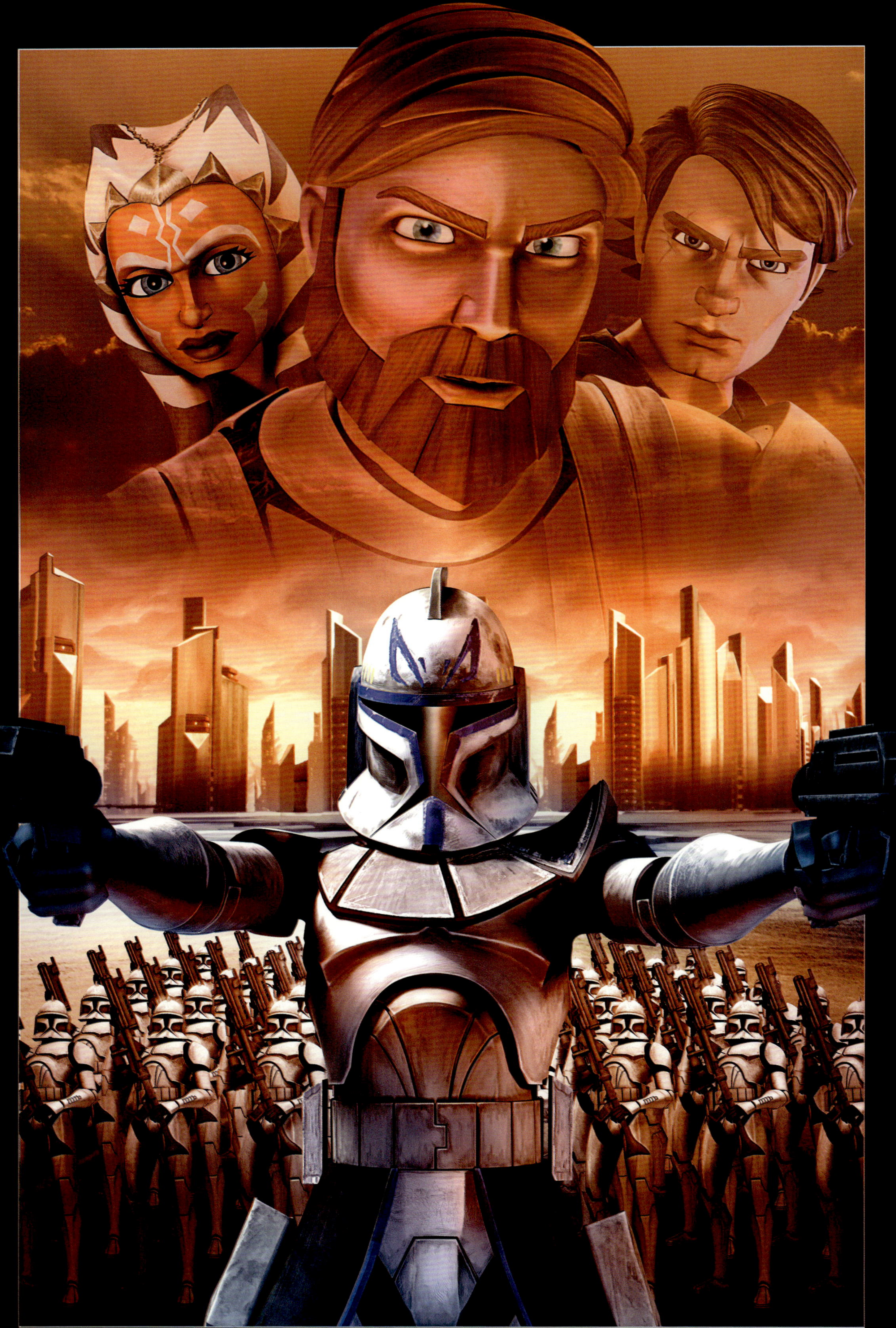

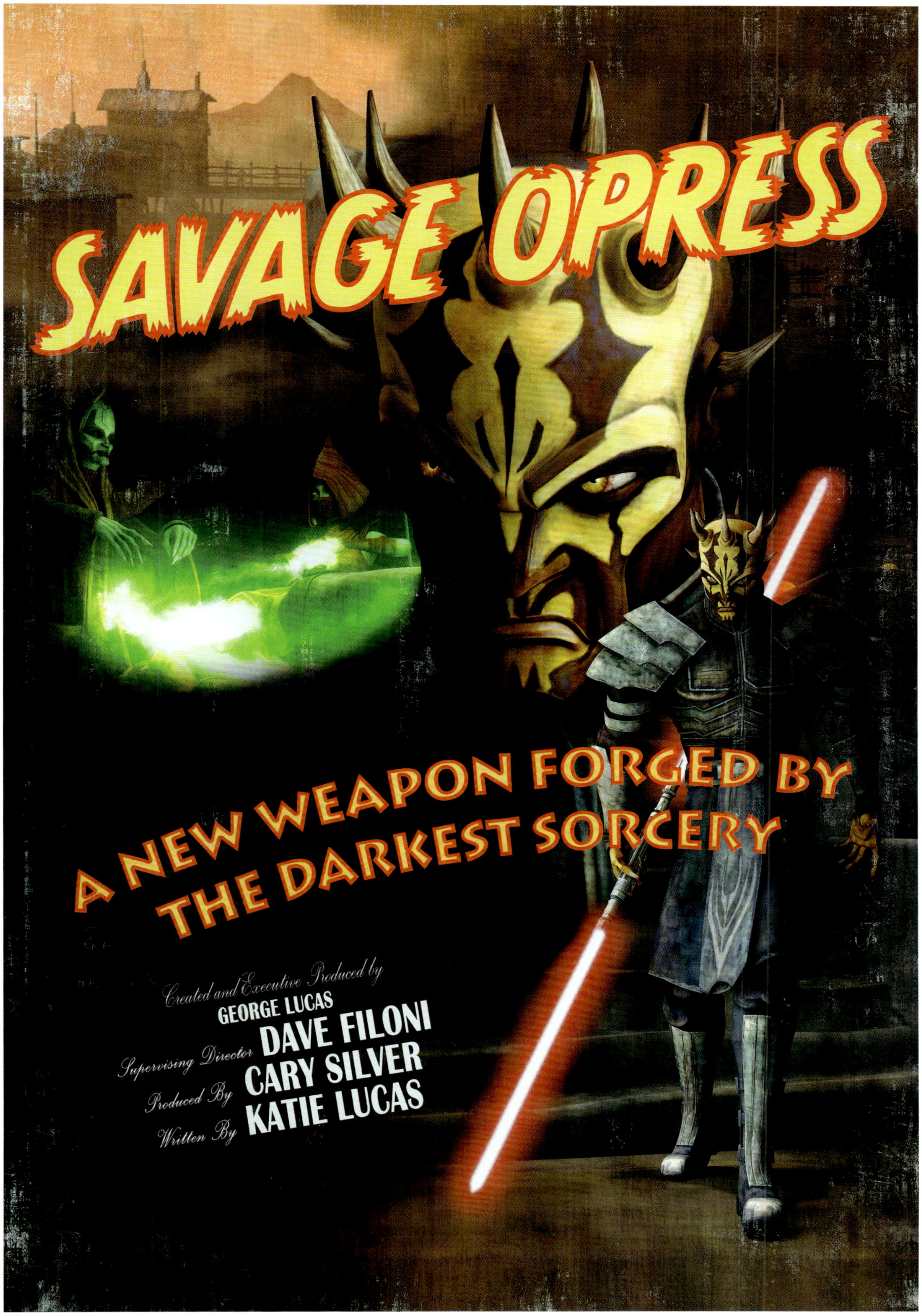

LEFT

John Blas

Republic Forces

Final digital artwork for *Star Wars: The Clone Wars*, 2008

Licensing art produced for season 1 of *Star Wars: The Clone Wars*

RIGHT

Lucasfilm Animation

Final digital artwork for *Star Wars: The Clone Wars* promotional poster, 2010

Produced for theatrical screening of the Nightsisters trilogy arc

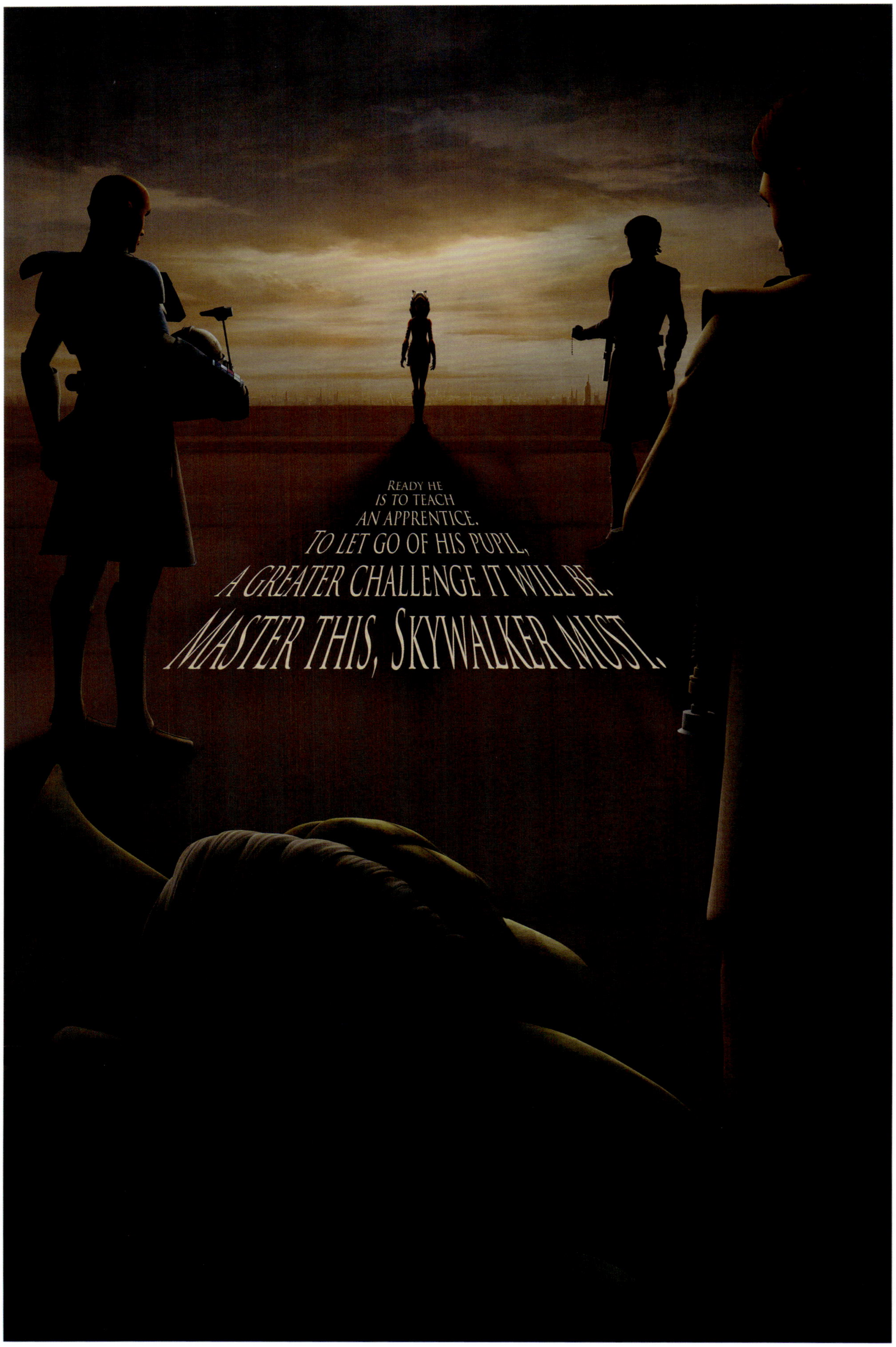

LEFT

Lucasfilm Animation

Lost Apprentice

Final digital artwork for *Star Wars: The Clone Wars*, 2013

Art distributed with DVD box set of *Star Wars: The Clone Wars* season 5

RIGHT

Lucasfilm Animation

Ventress

Final digital artwork for *Star Wars: The Clone Wars*, 2010

Licensing art produced for season 2 of *Star Wars: The Clone Wars*

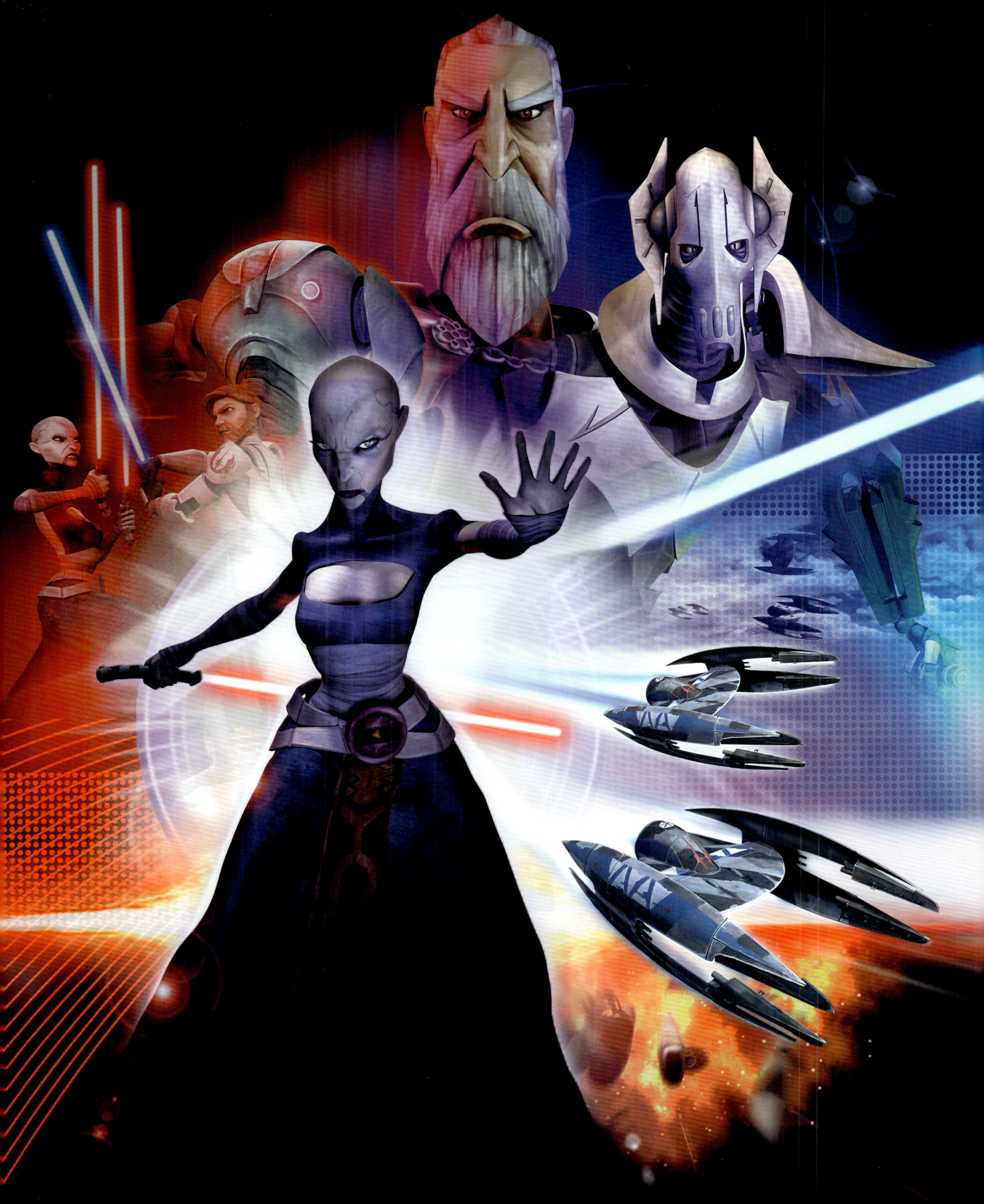

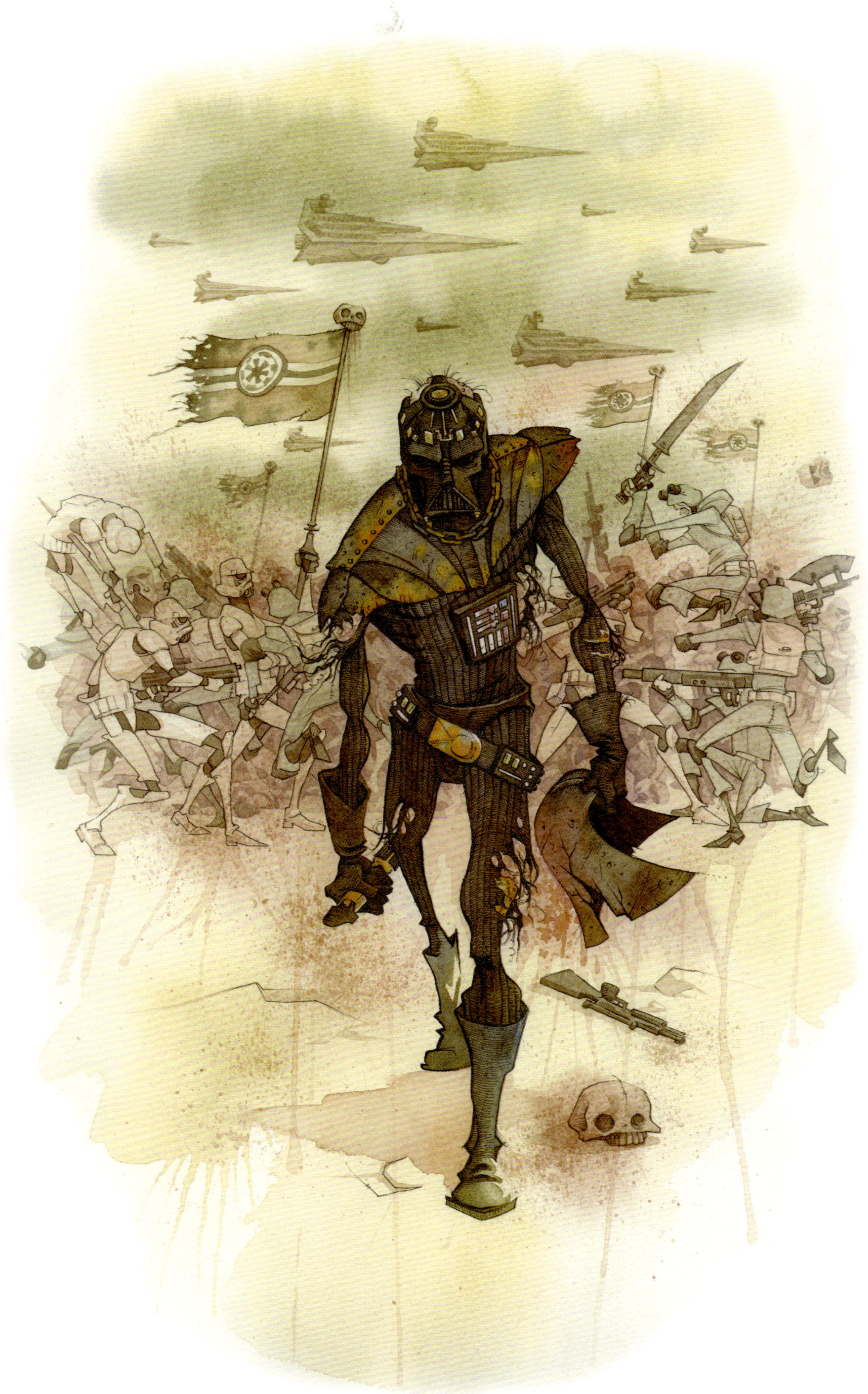

LEFT

Gris Grimly

Vader's Helmet, 2013

Limited-edition giclée print for Acme Archives

RIGHT

Dave Kinsey

Raider, 2010

Limited-edition Mondo screen print

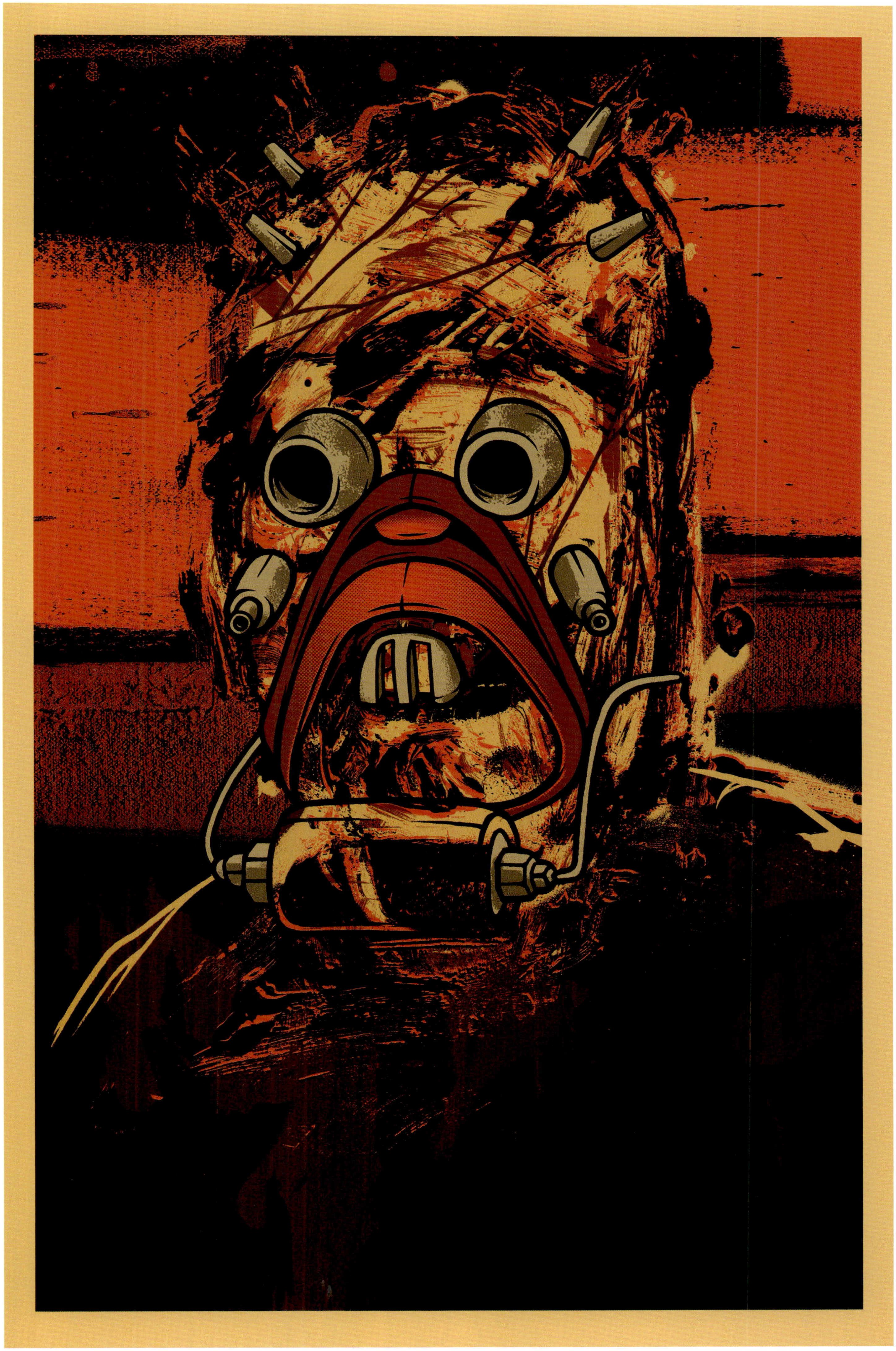

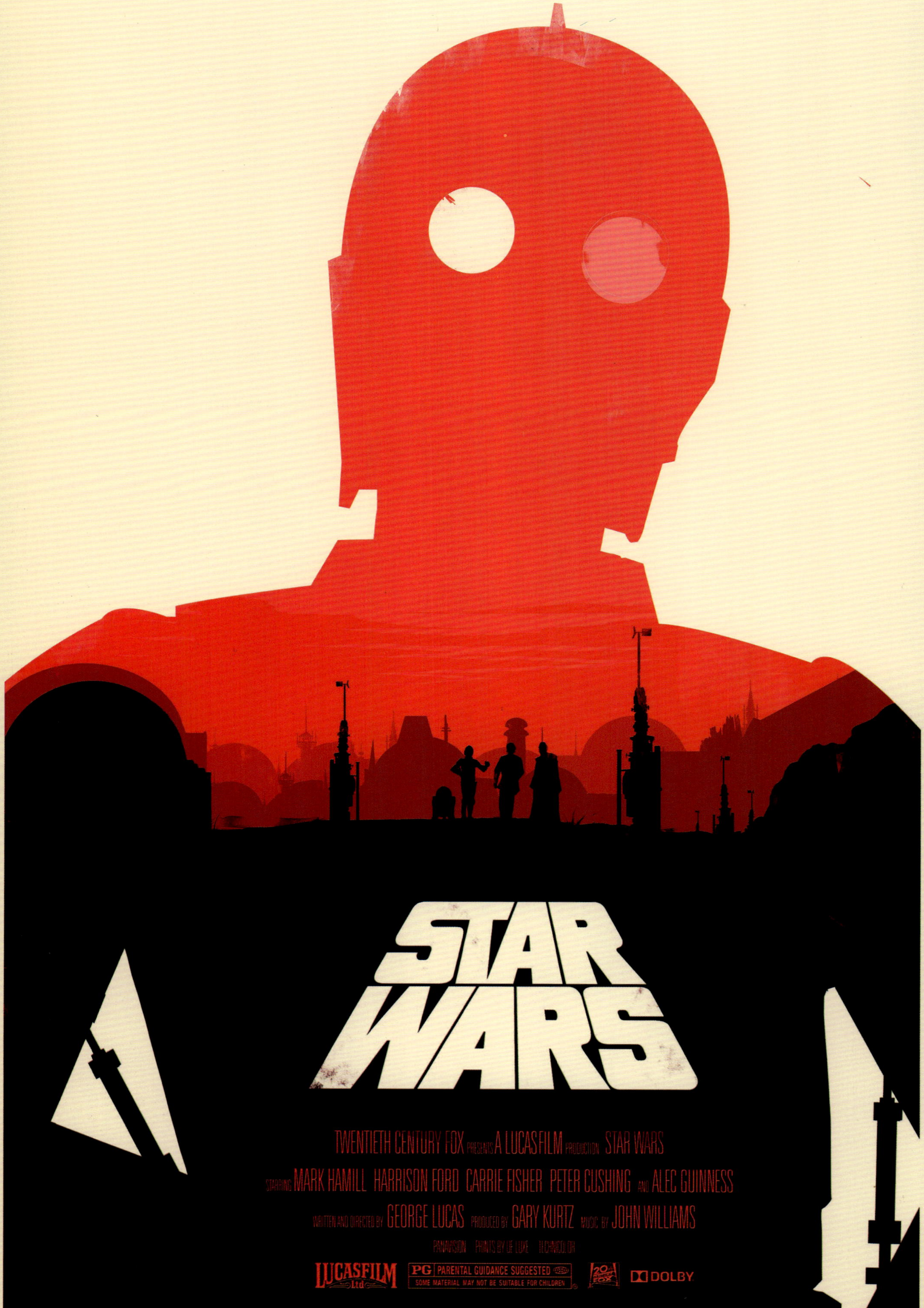
STAR WARS
TWENTIETH CENTURY FOX PRESENTS A LUCASFILM PRODUCTION STAR WARS
STARRING MARK HAMILL HARRISON FORD CARRIE FISHER PETER CUSHING AND ALEC GUINNESS
WRITTEN AND DIRECTED BY GEORGE LUCAS PRODUCED BY GARY KURTZ MUSIC BY JOHN WILLIAMS
PANAVISION PRINTS BY DE LUXE TECHNICOLOR
LUCASFILM Ltd
PG PARENTAL GUIDANCE SUGGESTED
SOME MATERIAL MAY NOT BE SUITABLE FOR CHILDREN
DOLBY

GATEFOLD PANEL ONE

Olly Moss

Star Wars, 2010

Limited-edition Mondo screen print

GATEFOLD PANEL TWO

Olly Moss

The Empire Strikes Back, 2010

Limited-edition Mondo screen print

GATEFOLD PANEL THREE

Olly Moss

Return of the Jedi, 2010

Limited-edition Mondo screen print

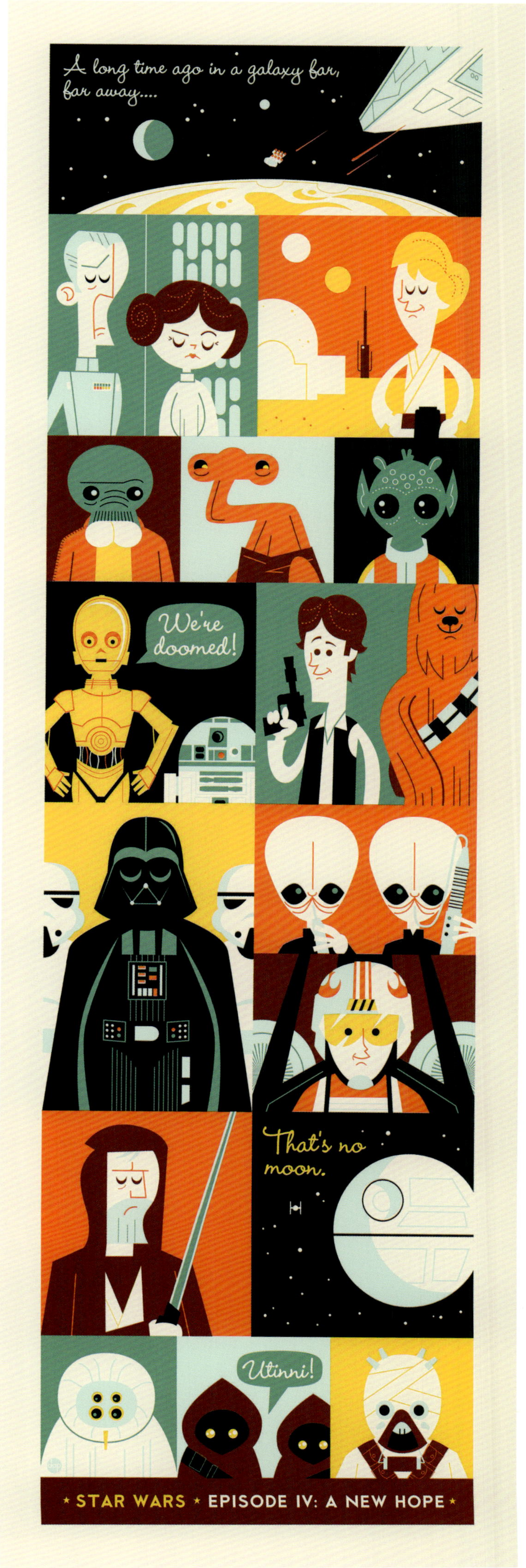

NEAR RIGHT

Dave Perillo

Star Wars: Episode IV *A New Hope*, 2013

Limited-edition screen print for Acme Archives

CENTER RIGHT

Dave Perillo

Star Wars: Episode V *The Empire Strikes Back*, 2013

Limited-edition screen print for Acme Archives

FAR RIGHT

Dave Perillo

Star Wars: Episode VI *Return of the Jedi*, 2013

Limited-edition screen print for Acme Archives

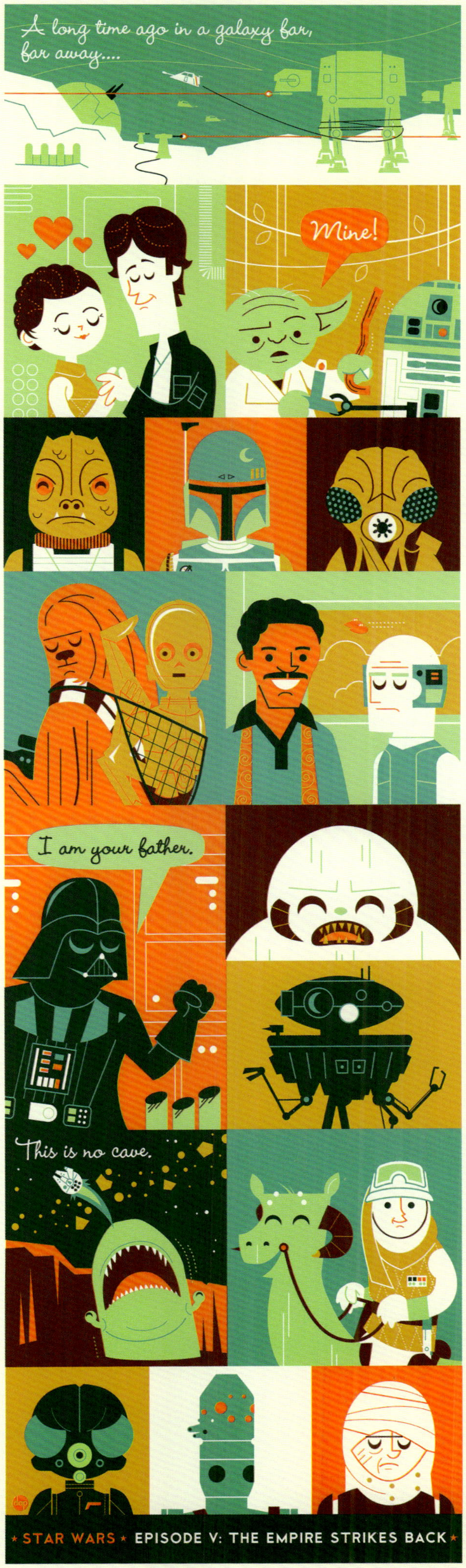
A long time ago in a galaxy far, far away....
Mine!
I am your father.
This is no cave.
★ STAR WARS ★ EPISODE V: THE EMPIRE STRIKES BACK ★

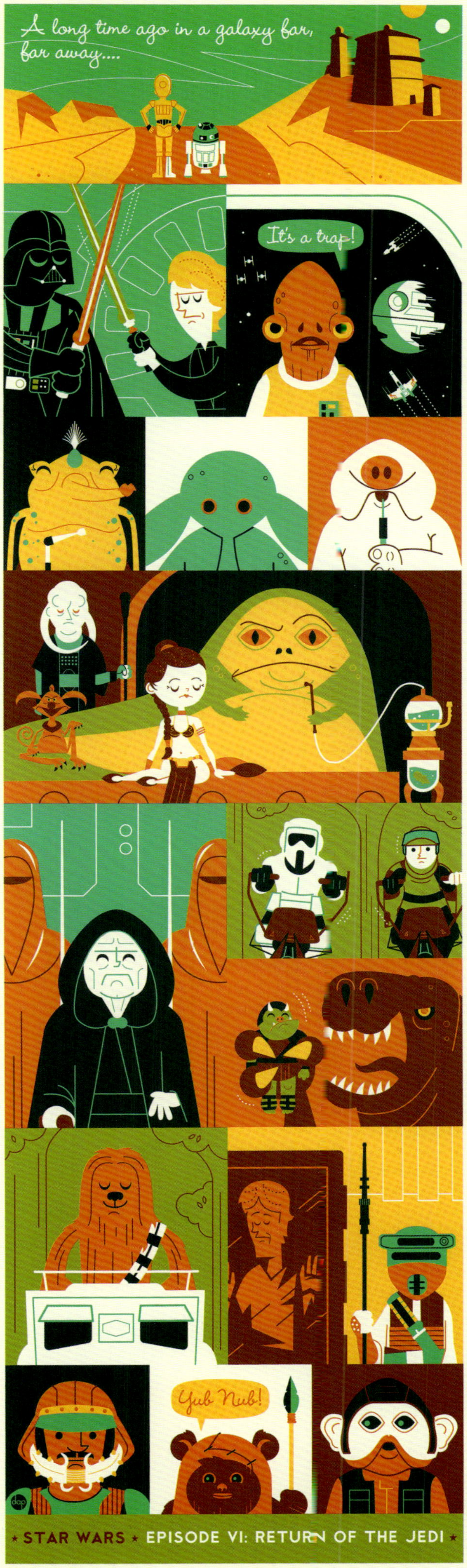
A long time ago in a galaxy far, far away....
It's a trap!
Yub Nub!
★ STAR WARS ★ EPISODE VI: RETURN OF THE JEDI ★

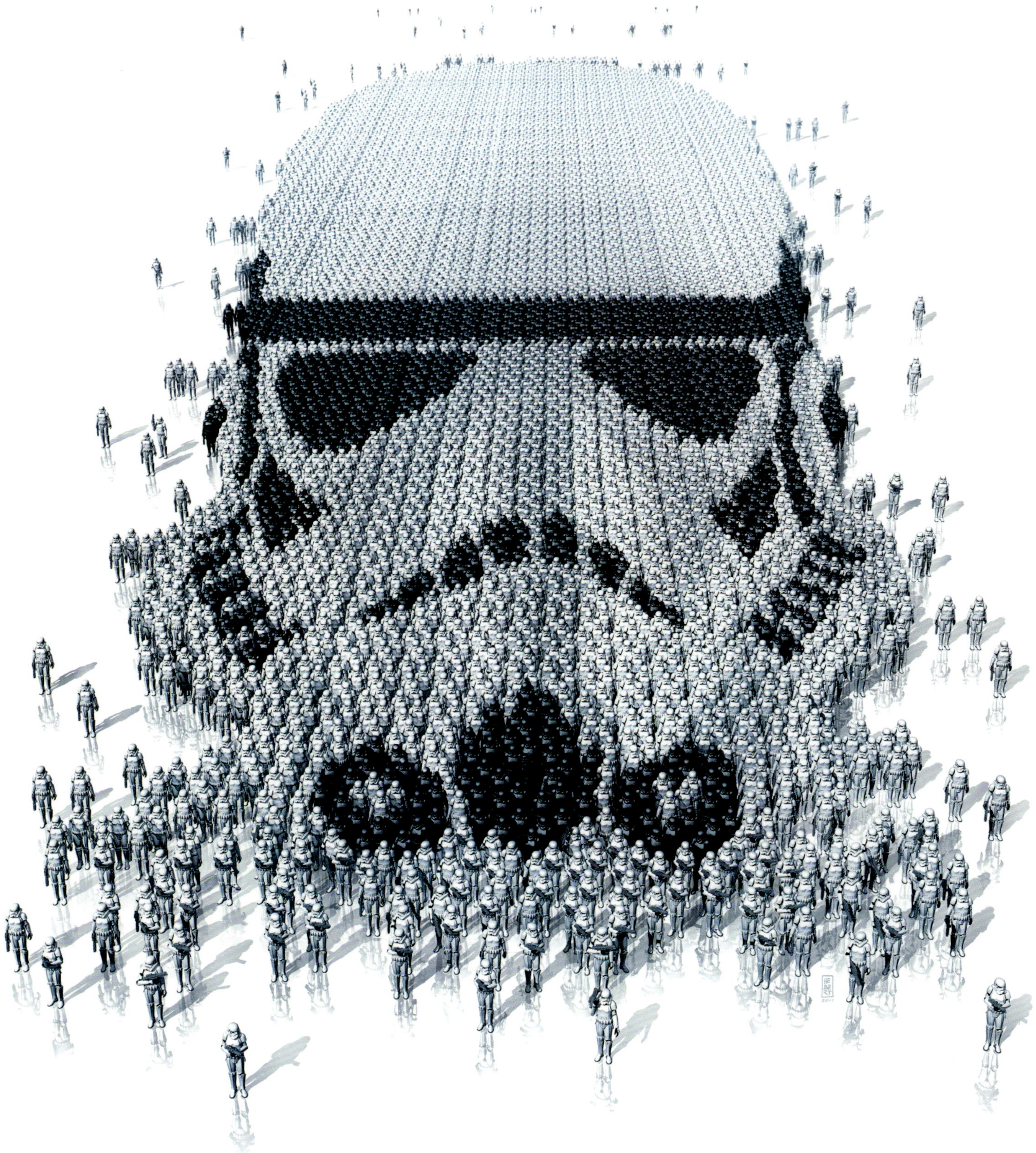

ABOVE

Louis C. Hébert

Final digital artwork for *Star Wars:* Identities poster, 2013

Promotional poster for *Star Wars:* Identities museum exhibition

RIGHT

Louis C. Hébert

Final digital artwork for *Star Wars:* Identities poster, 2013

Promotional poster for *Star Wars:* Identities museum exhibition

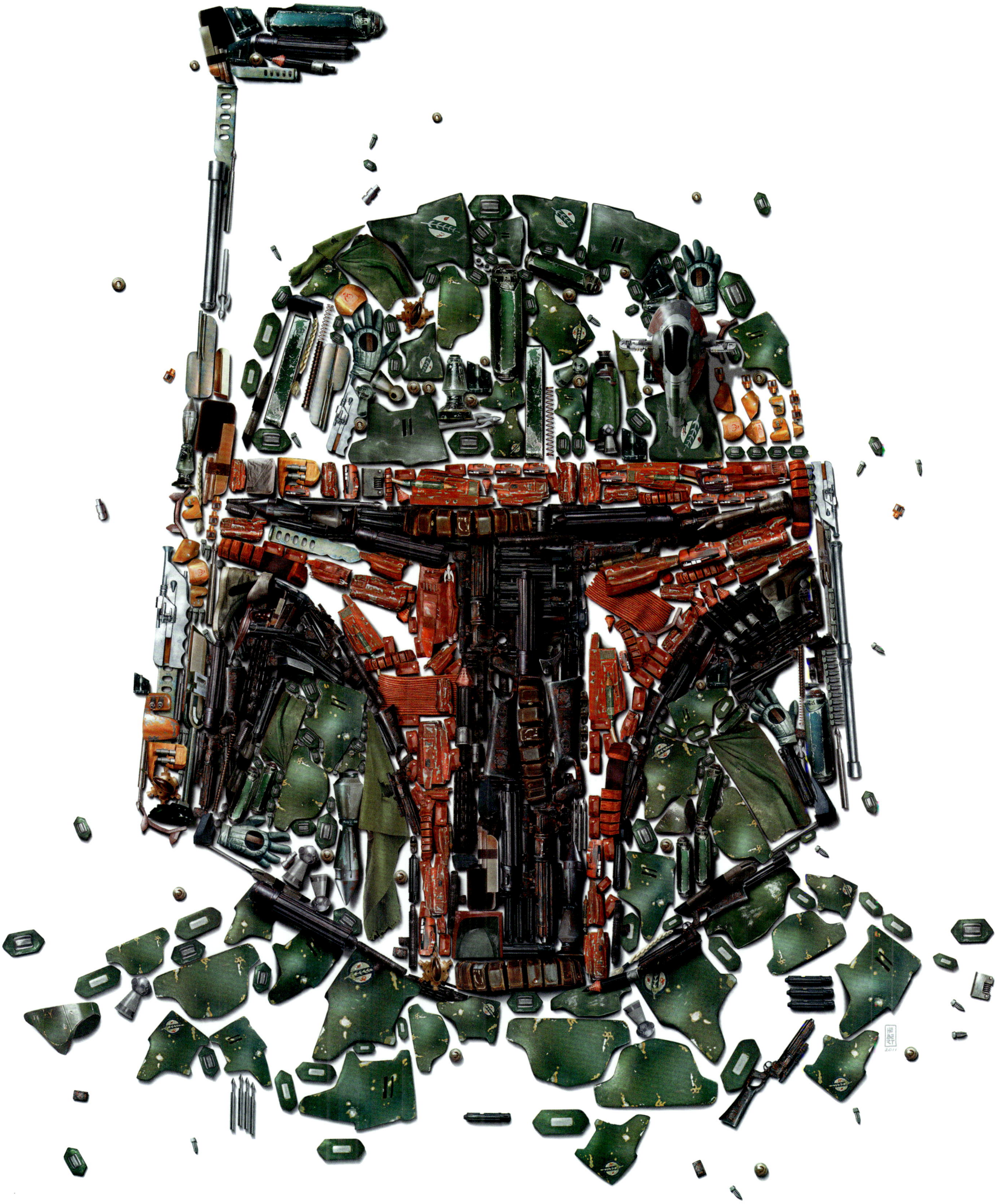

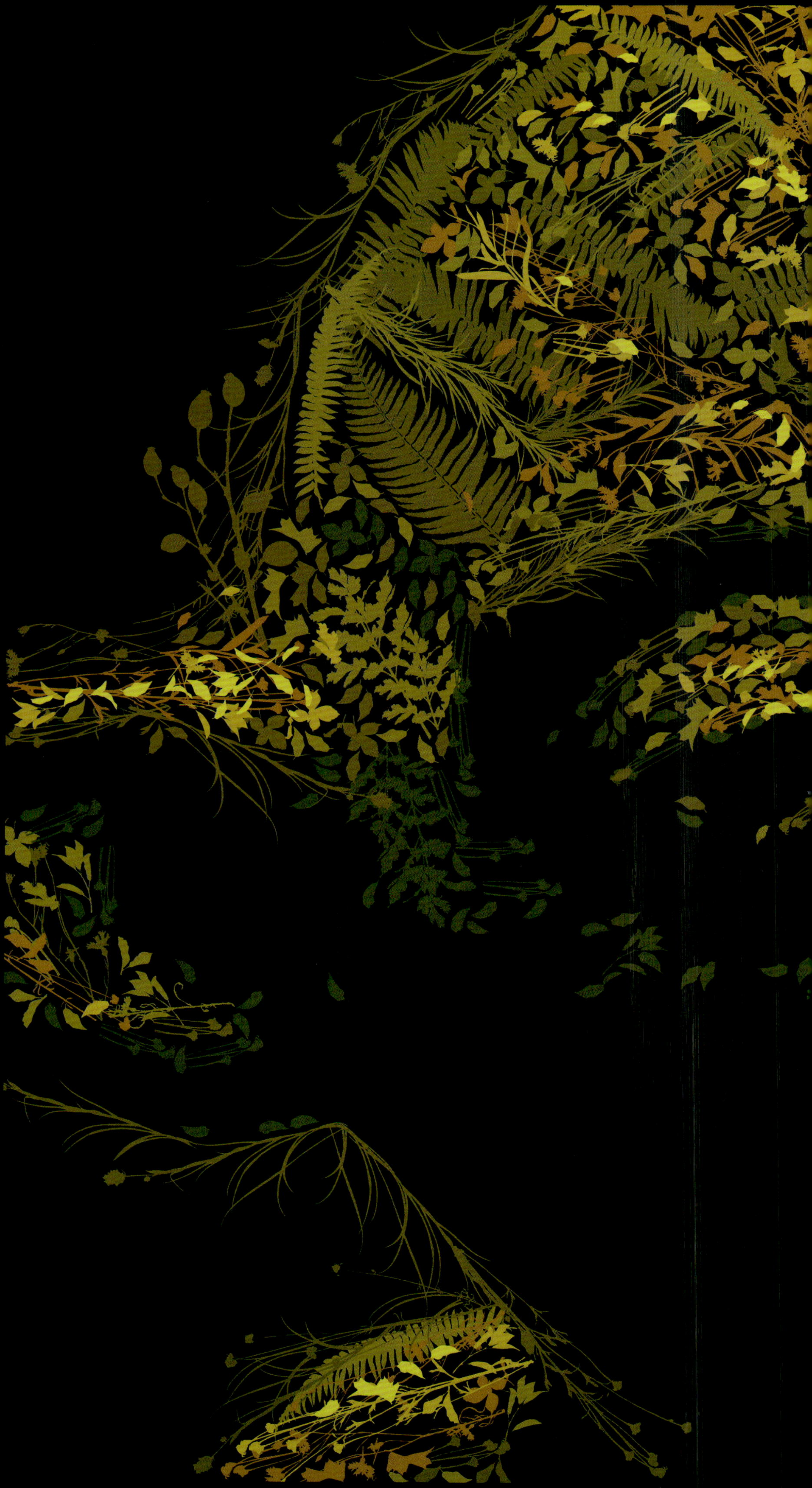

RIGHT

Todd Slater

Great Warrior - Yoda, 2010

Limited-edition Mondo screen print

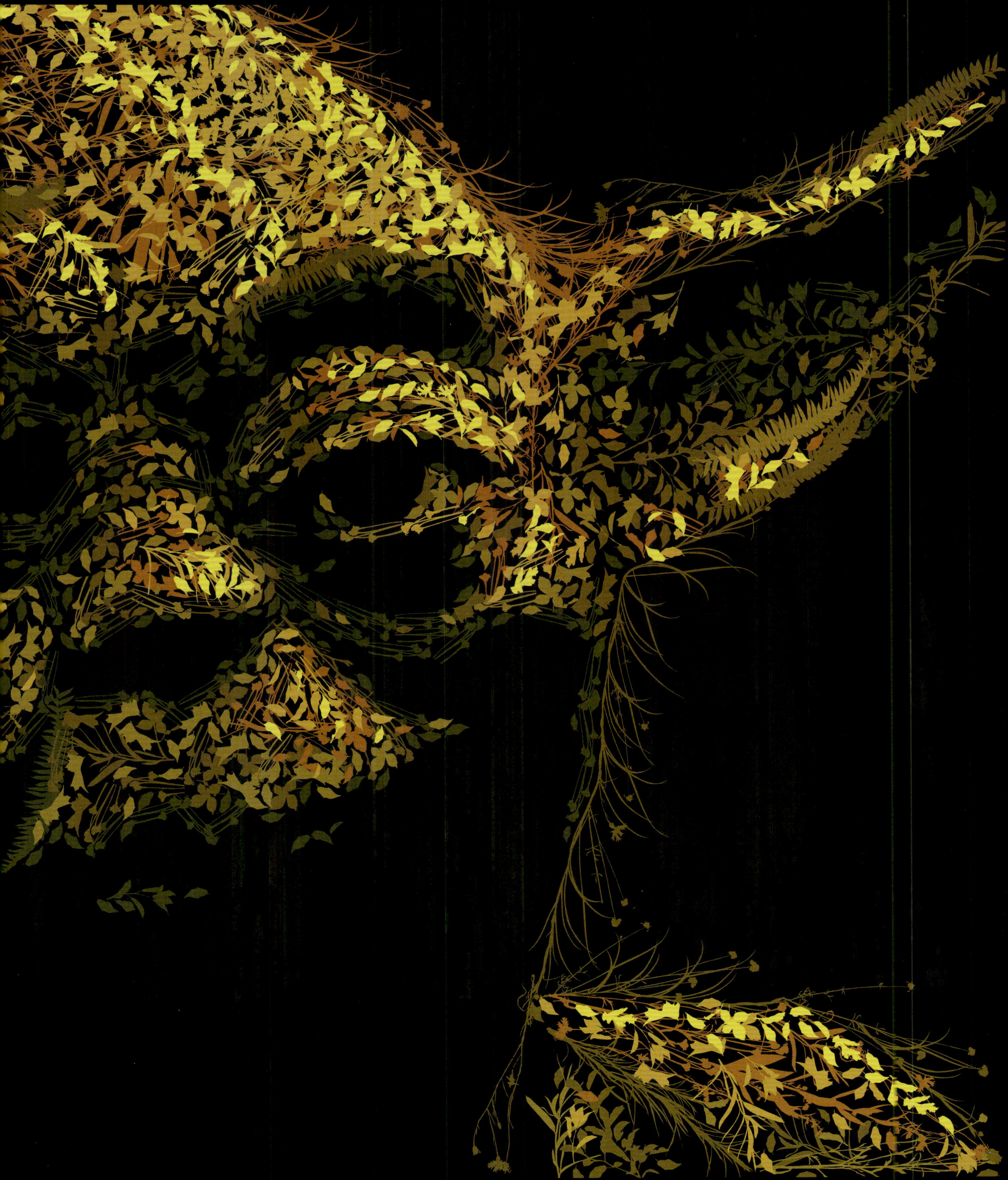

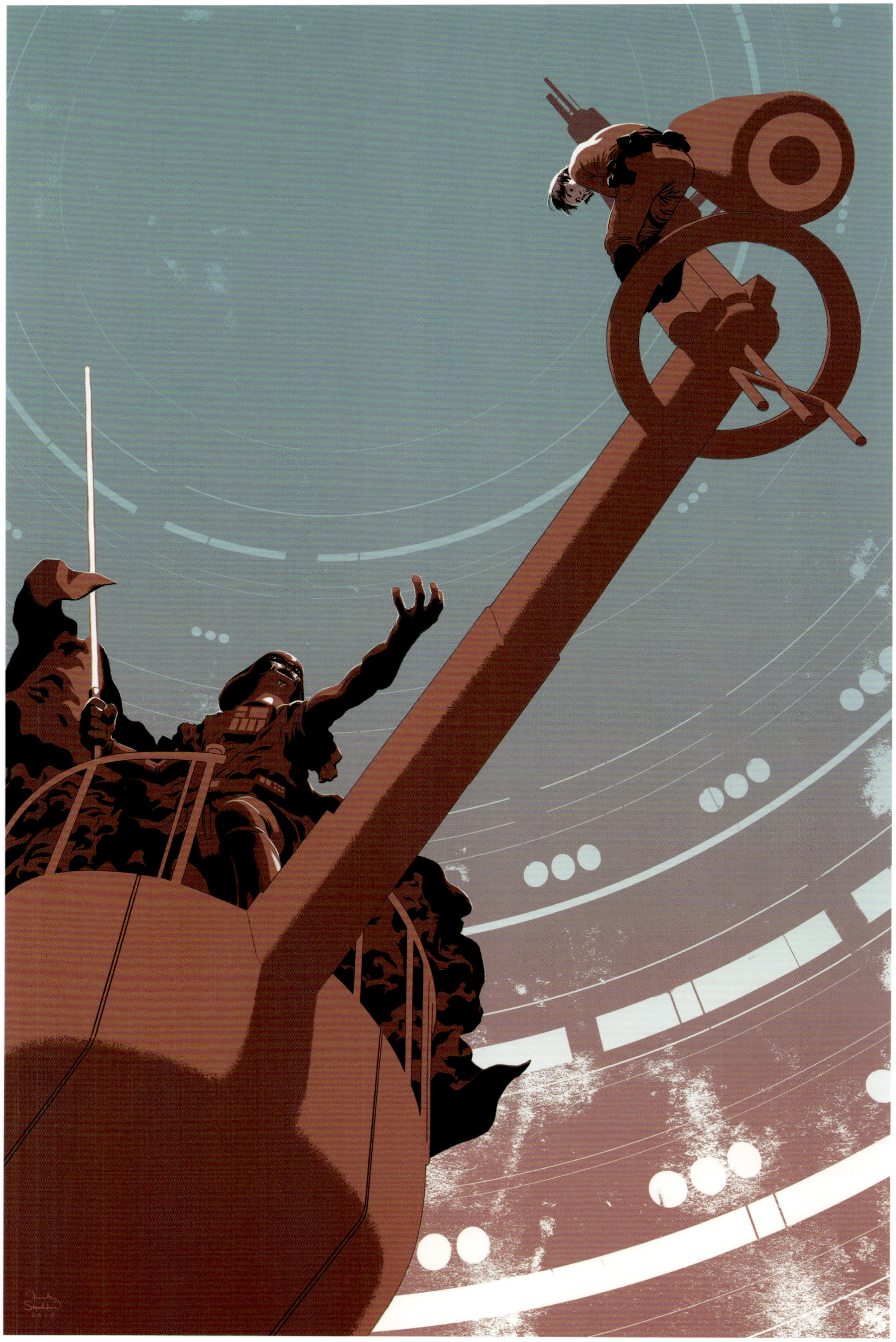

LEFT

Frank Stockton

Luke's Destiny, 2010

Limited-edition Mondo screen print

RIGHT

Rob Jones

King's Lead Hat, 2010

Limited-edition Mondo screen print with metallic inks

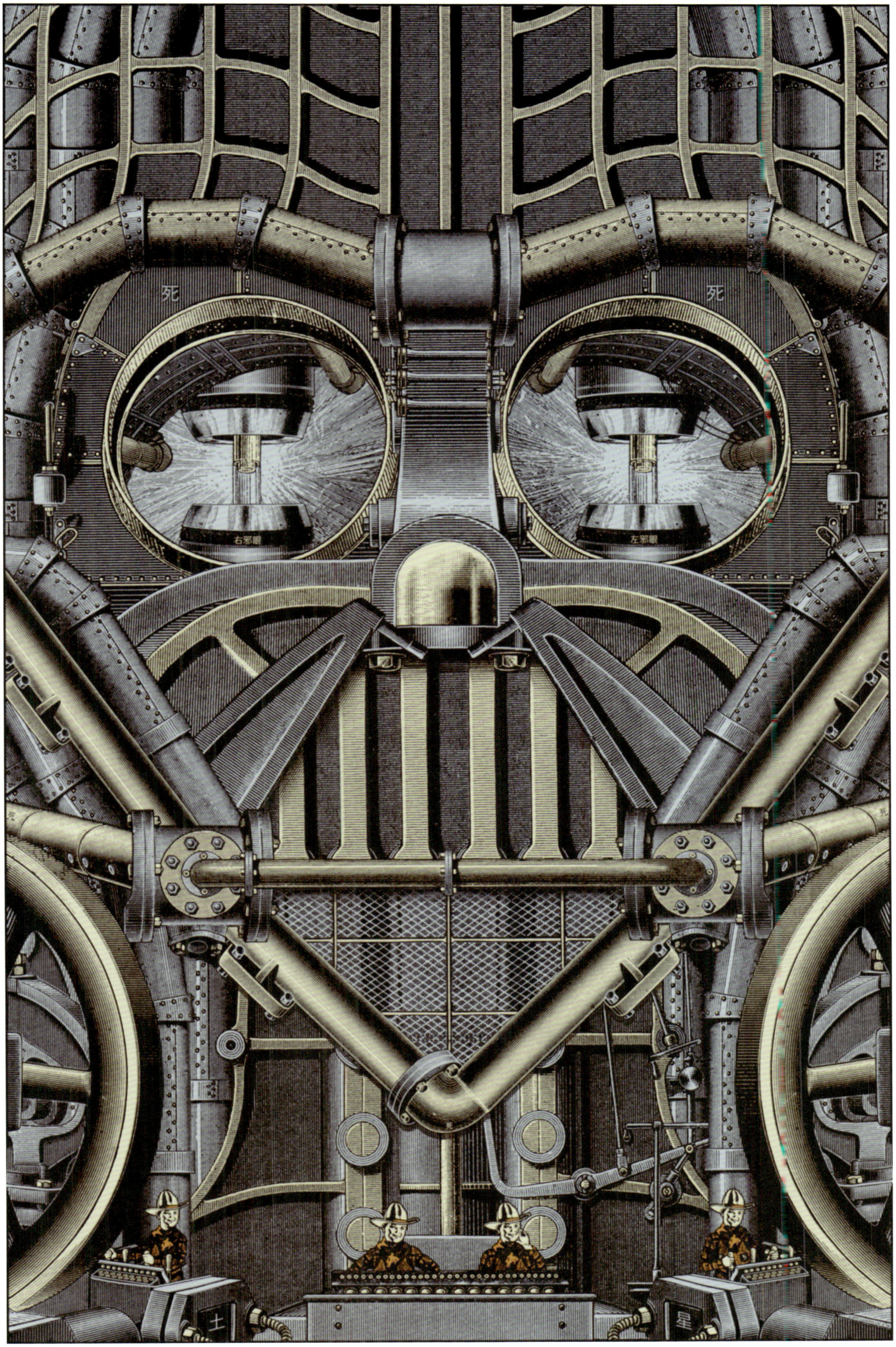
死
死
右邪眼
左邪眼
土
星

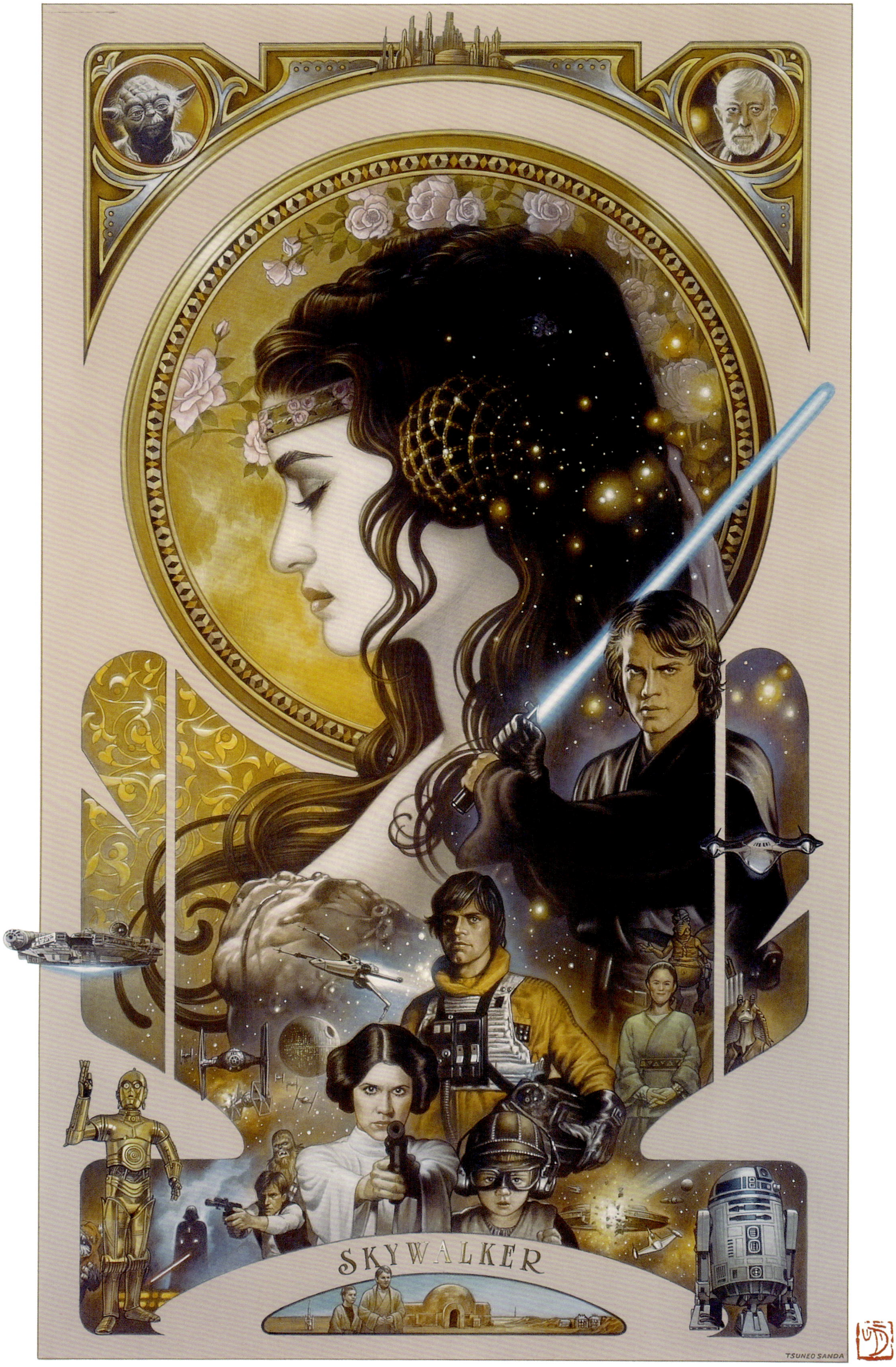
SKYWALKER
TSUNEO SANDA

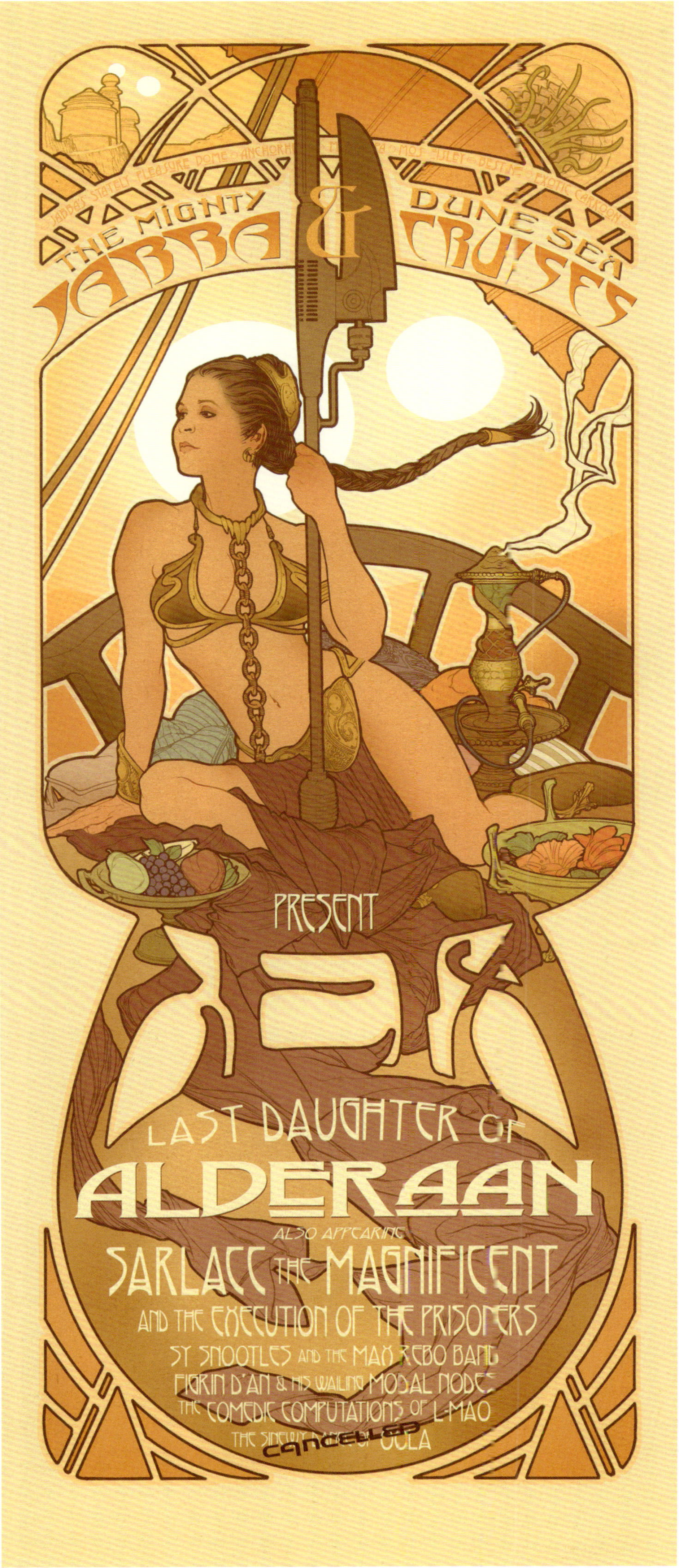

LEFT

Tsuneo Sanda

Skywalker, 2009

RIGHT

Adam Hughes

Last Daughter of Alderaan, 2007

Limited-edition giclée print for *Star Wars* Celebration IV

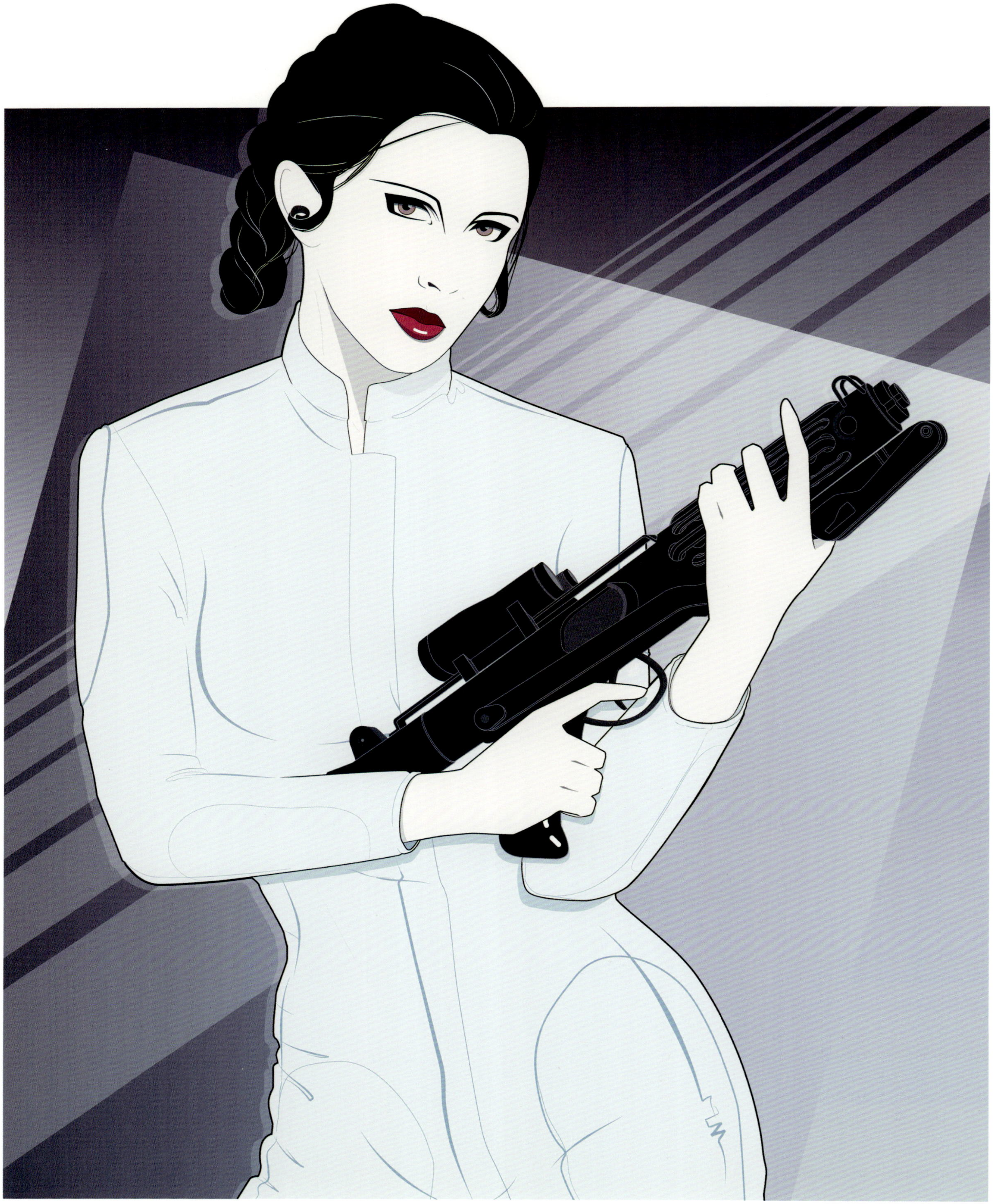

ABOVE

Craig Drake

The Princess, 2008

Limited-edition lithograph

RIGHT

Craig Drake

The General, 2009

Limited-edition lithograph

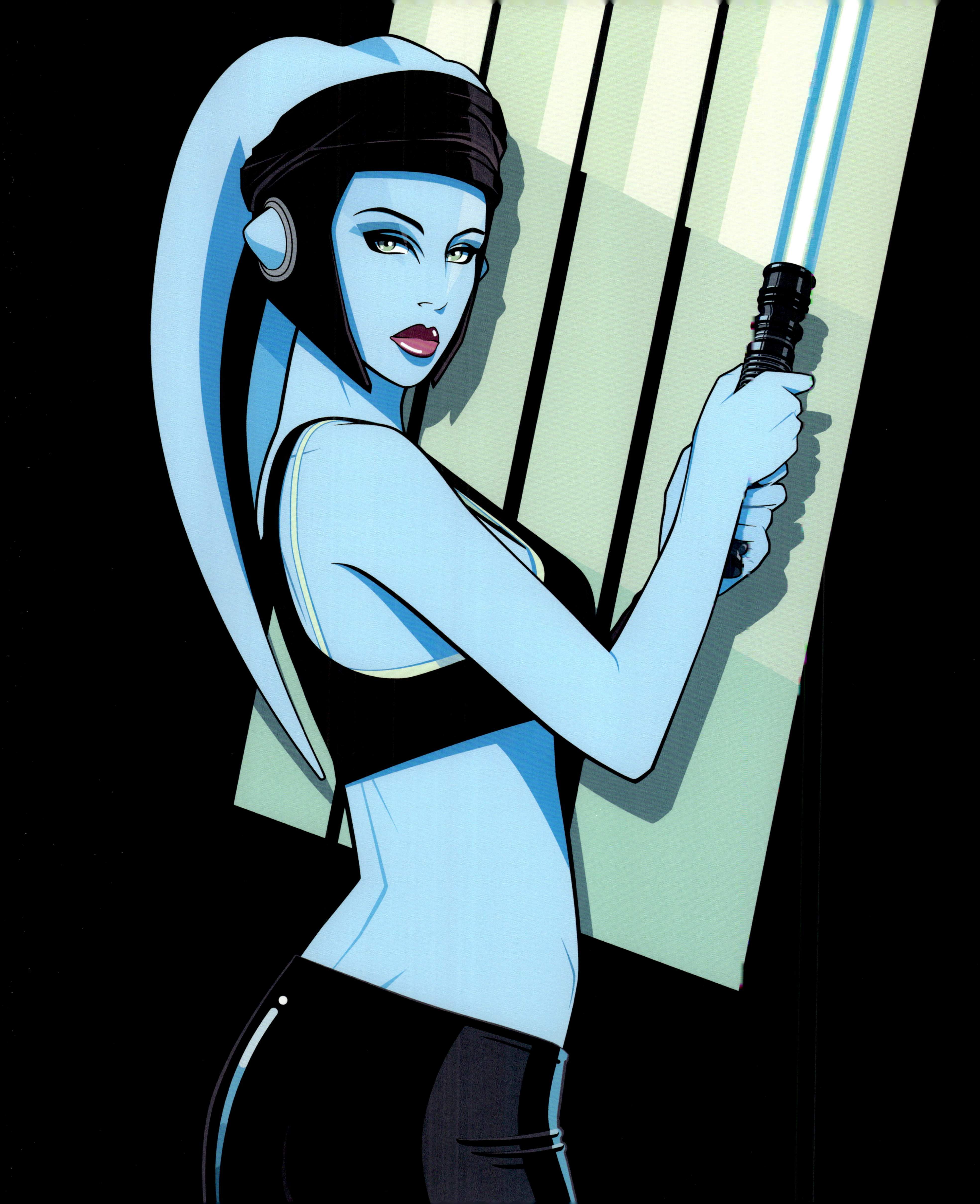

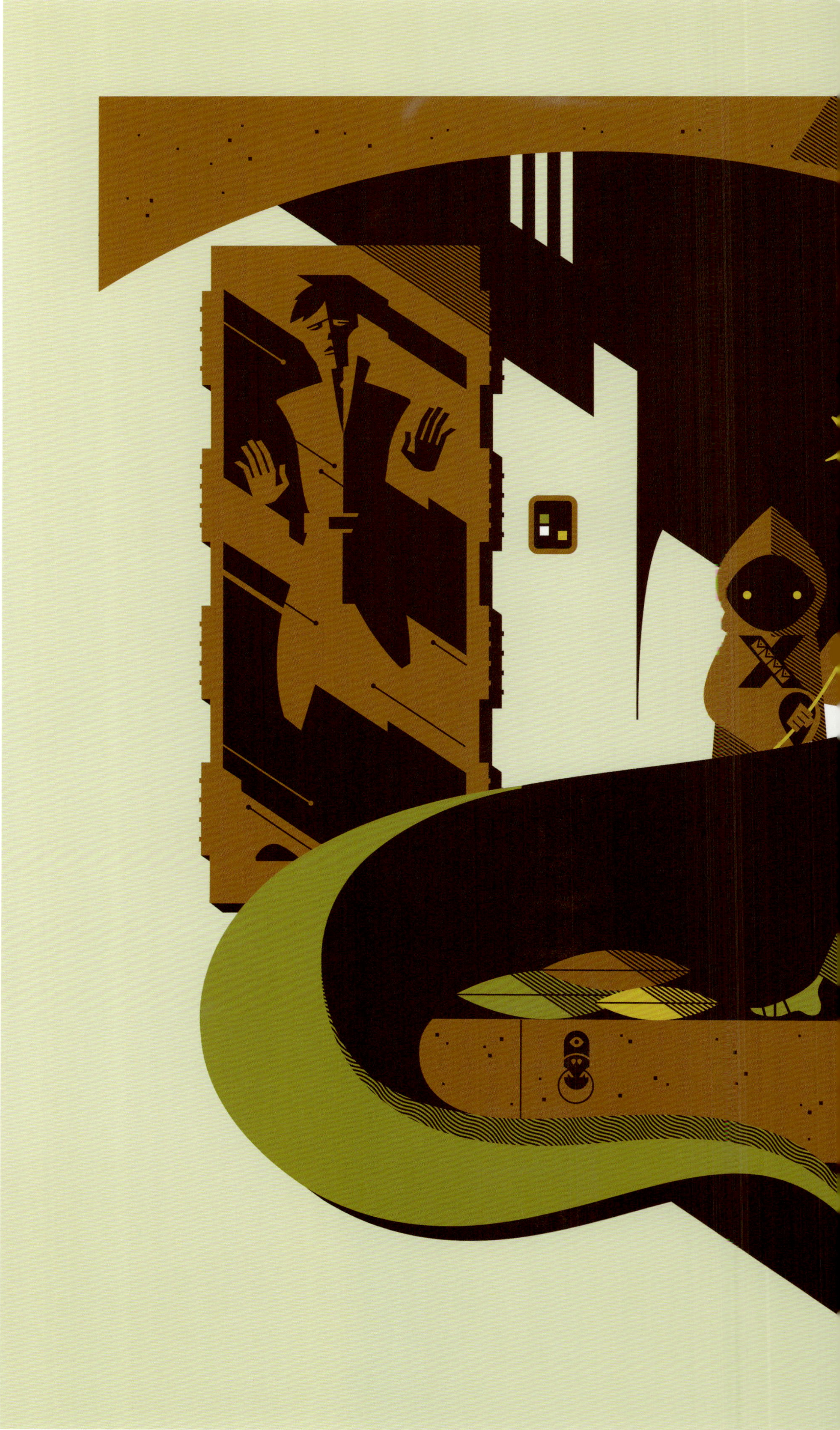

RIGHT

Tom Whalen

Jabba's Palace, 2010

Limited-edition Mondo screen print

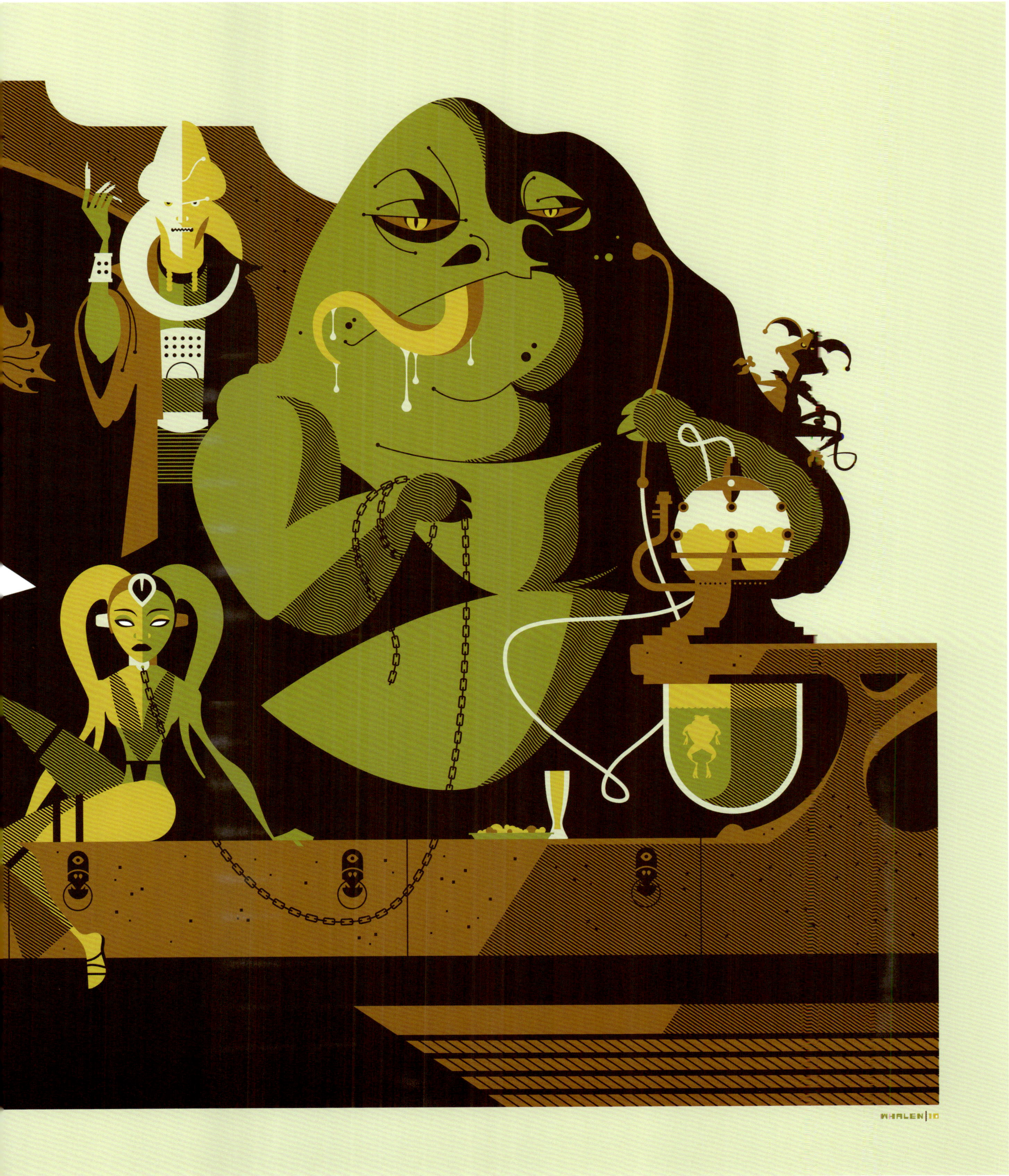
WHALEN|10

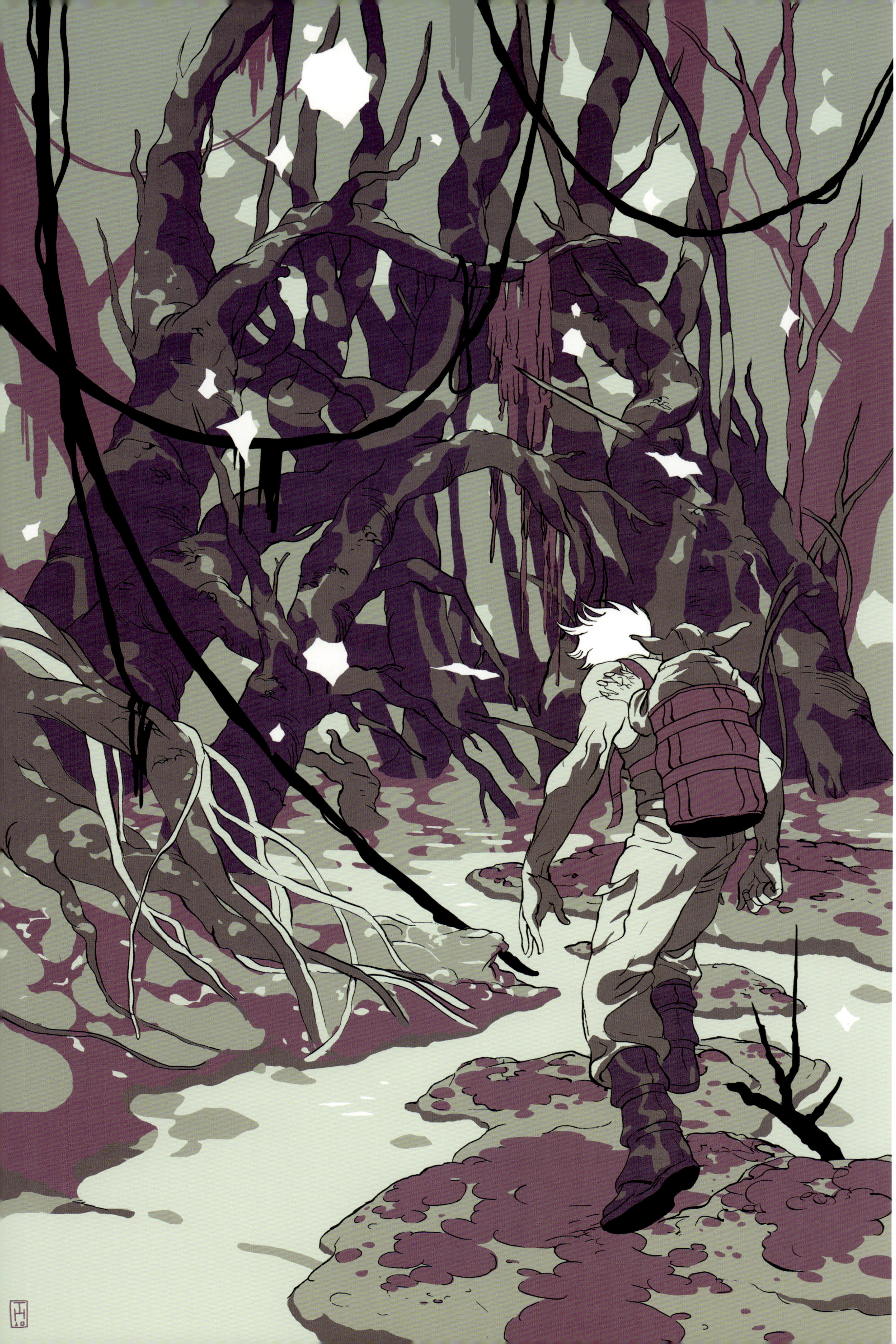

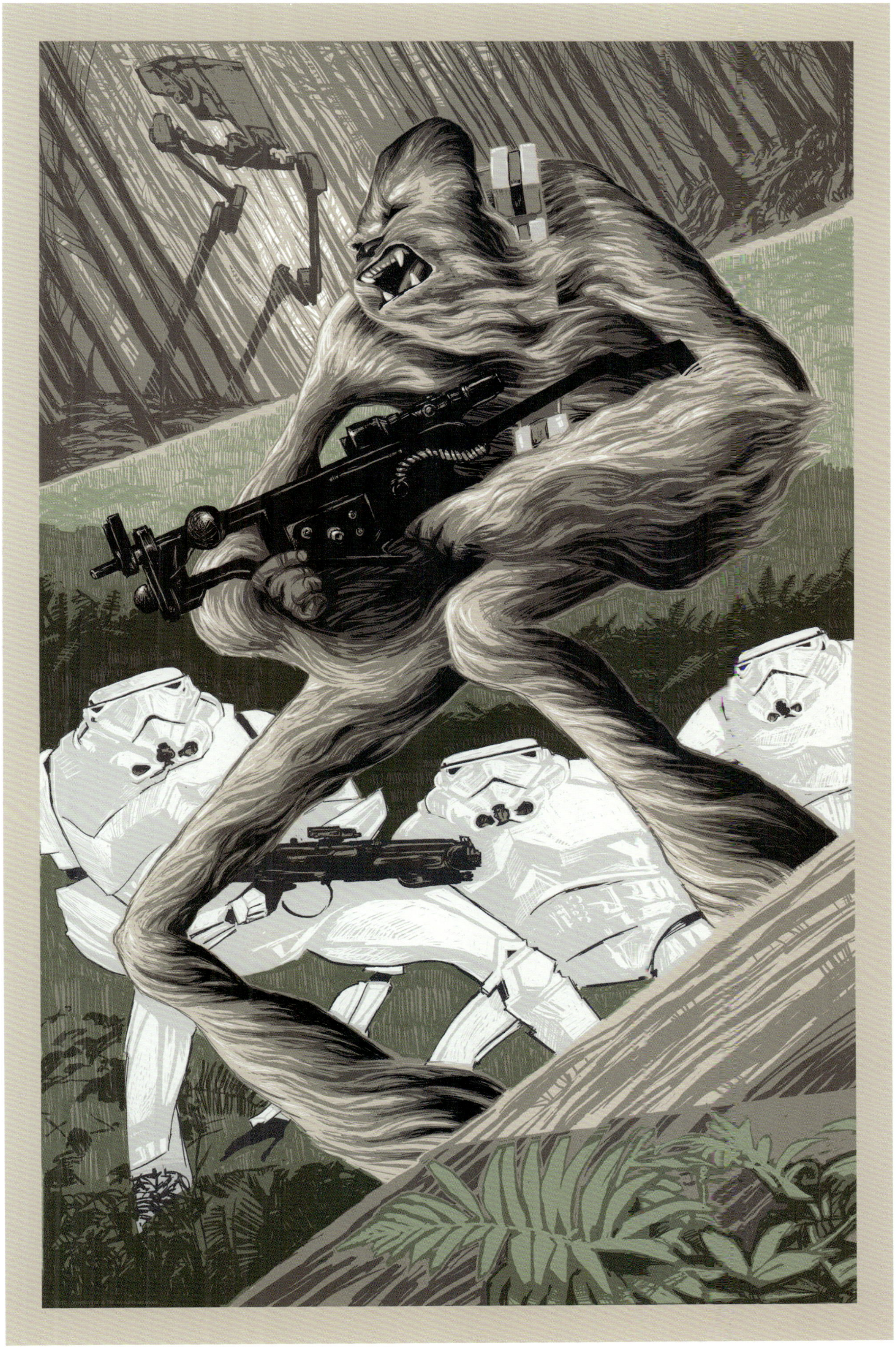

LEFT

Tomer Hanuka

Father: Encounter on Dagobah, 2010

Limited-edition Mondo screen print

RIGHT AND FOLLOWING SPREAD (DETAIL)

Rich Kelly

Attack Position, 2010

Limited-edition Mondo screen print

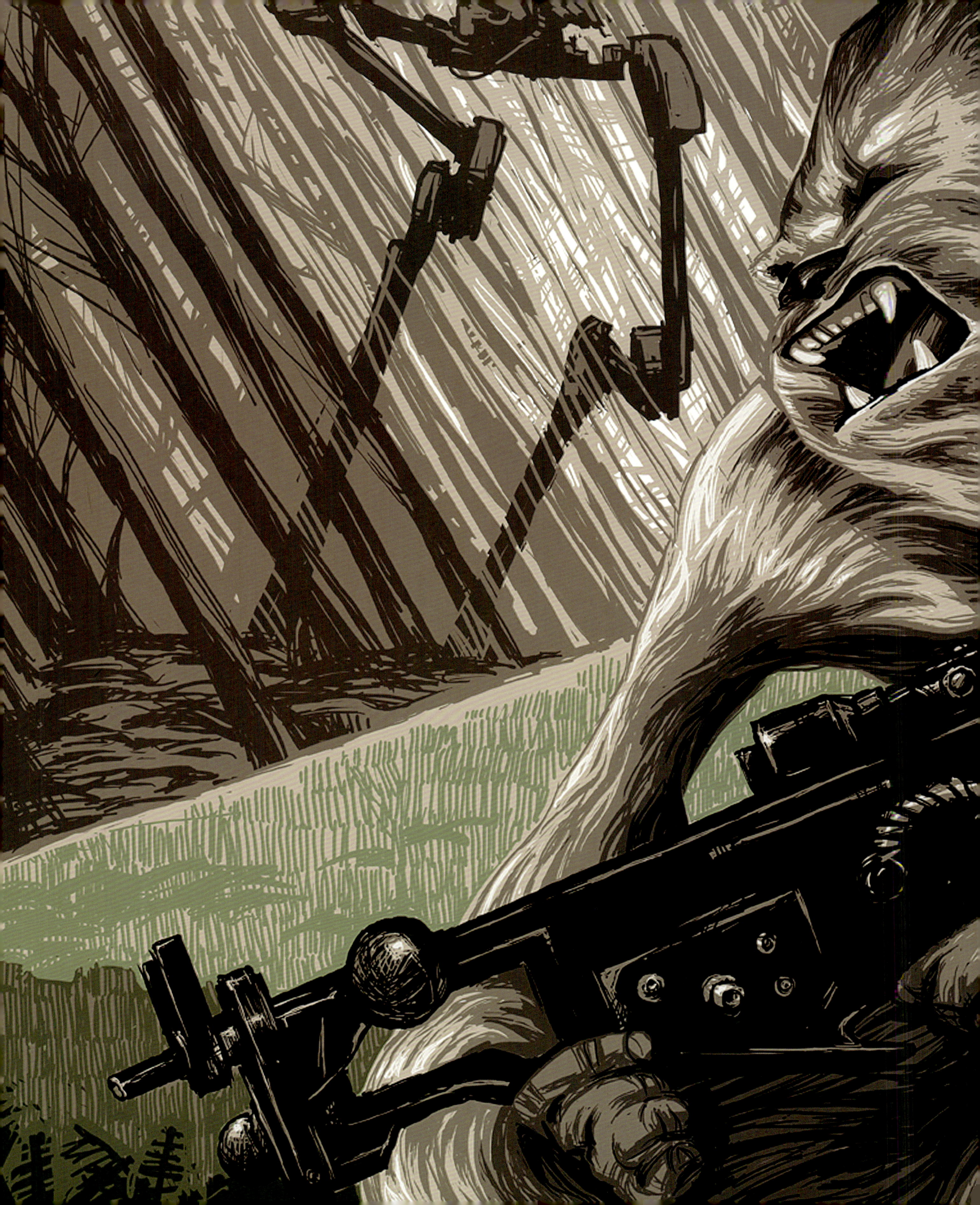

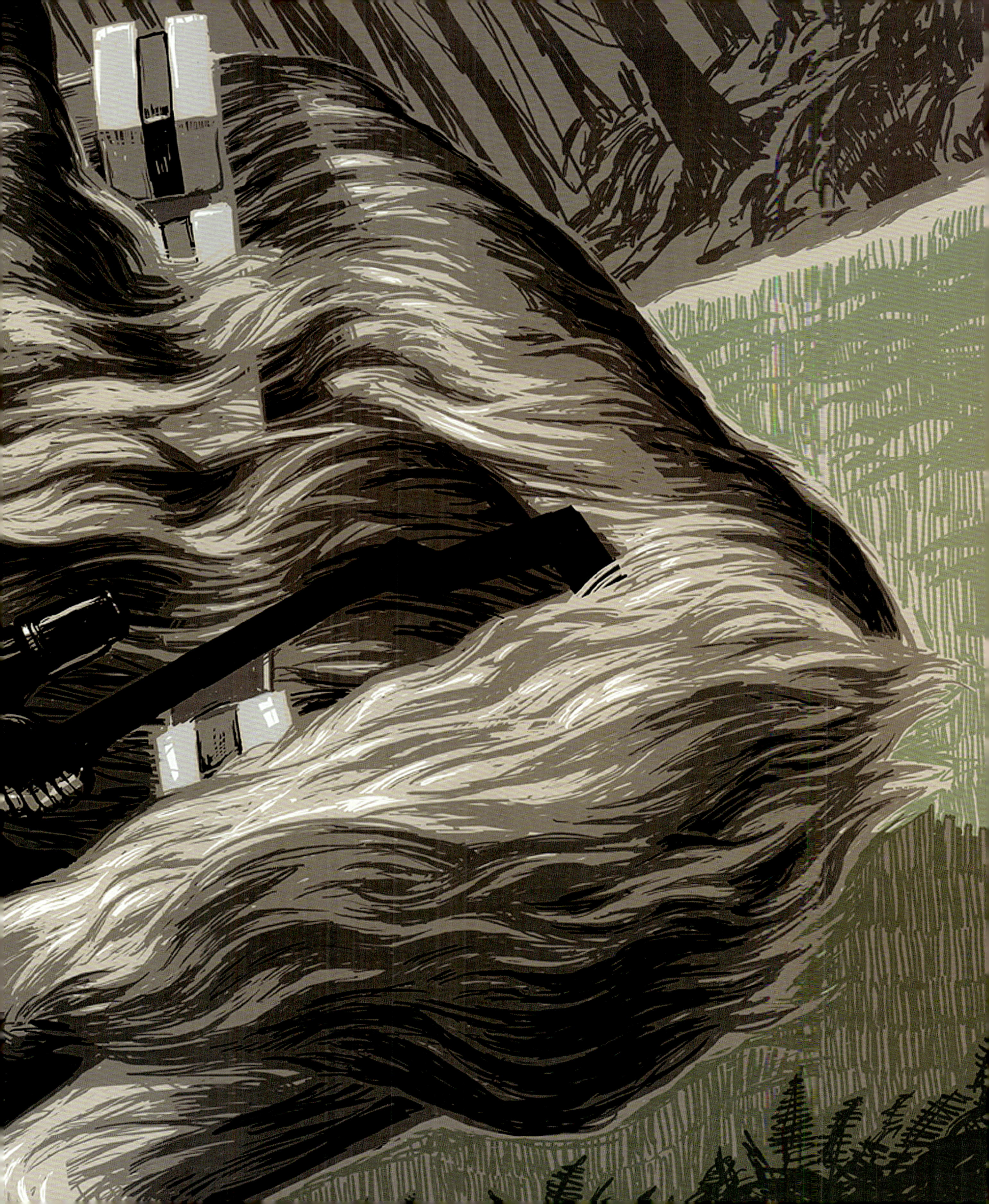

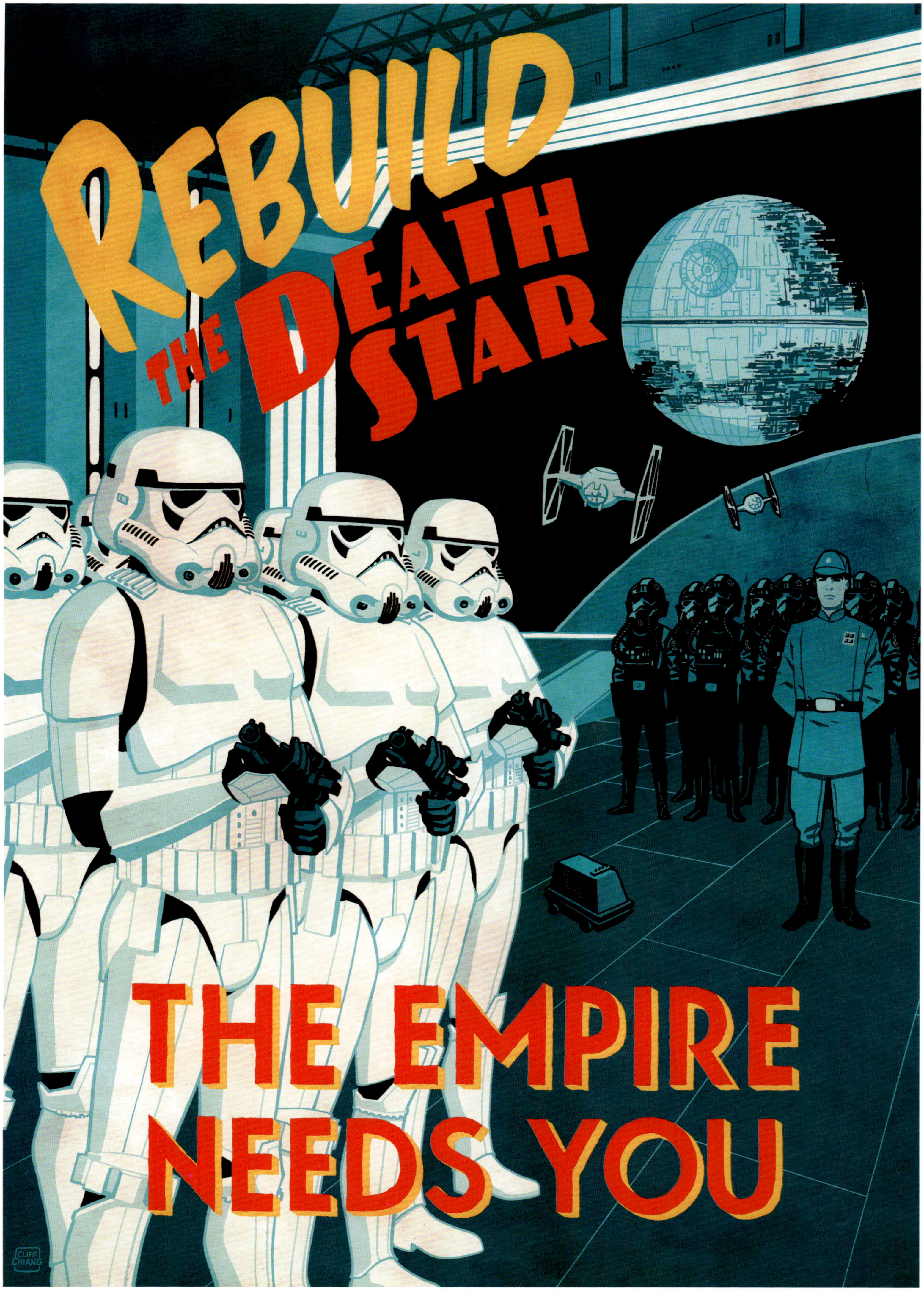
REBUILD
THE DEATH STAR
THE EMPIRE
NEEDS YOU
CLIFF CHIANG

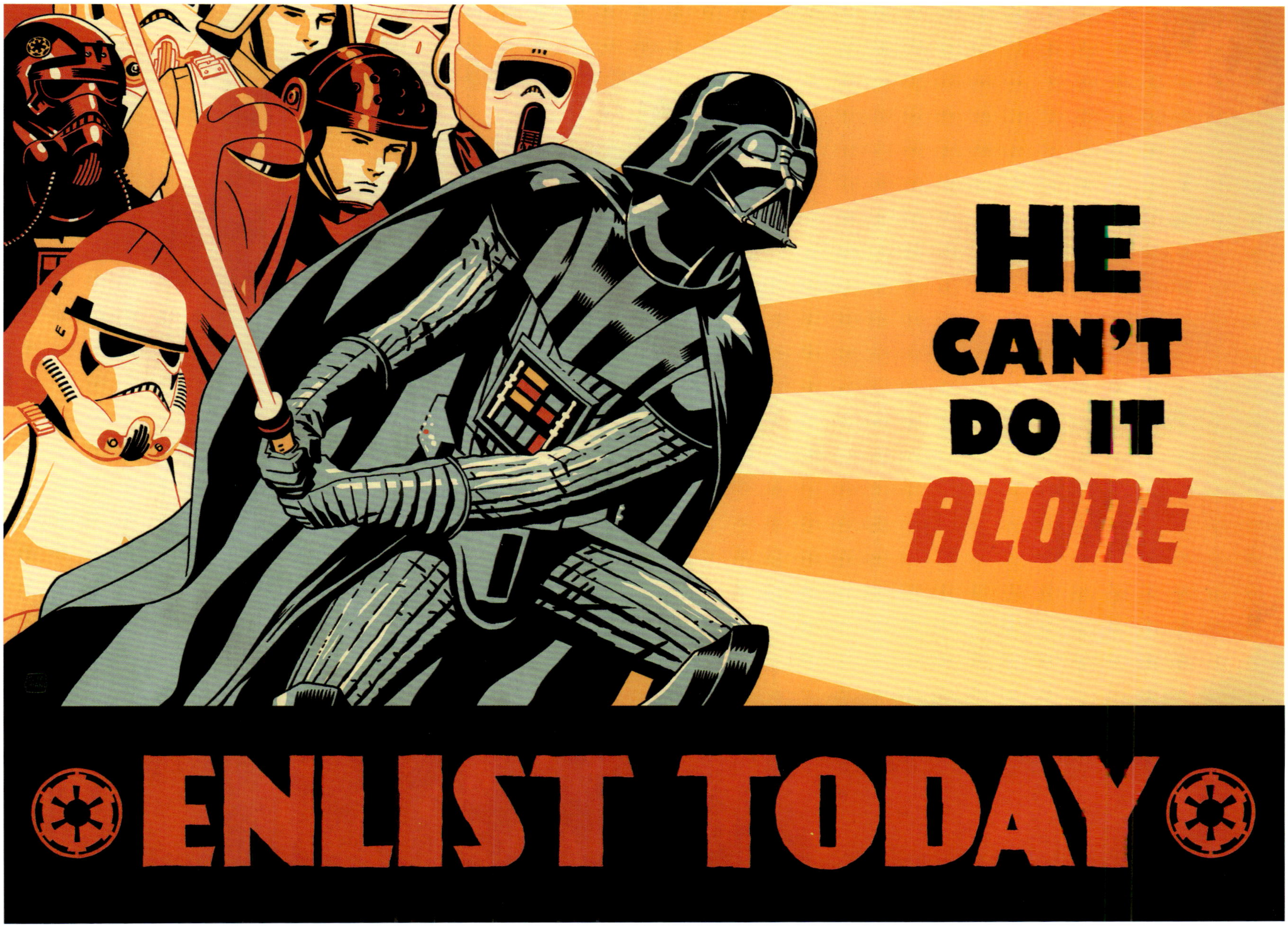

LEFT

Cliff Chiang

Rebuild the Death Star, 2013

Limited-edition giclée print for Acme Archives

ABOVE

Cliff Chiang

Enlist Today, 2013

Limited-edition giclée print for Acme Archives

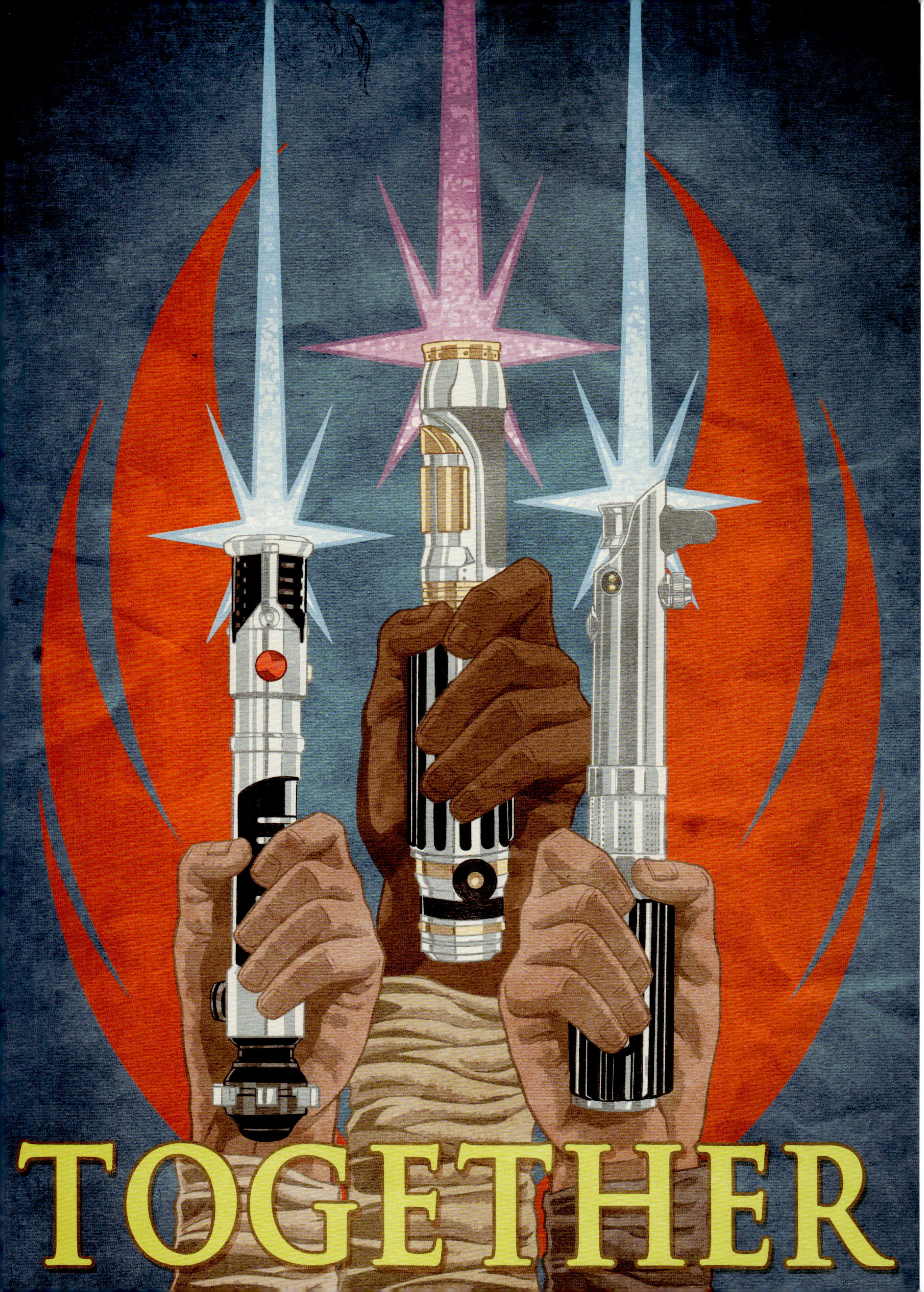
TOGETHER

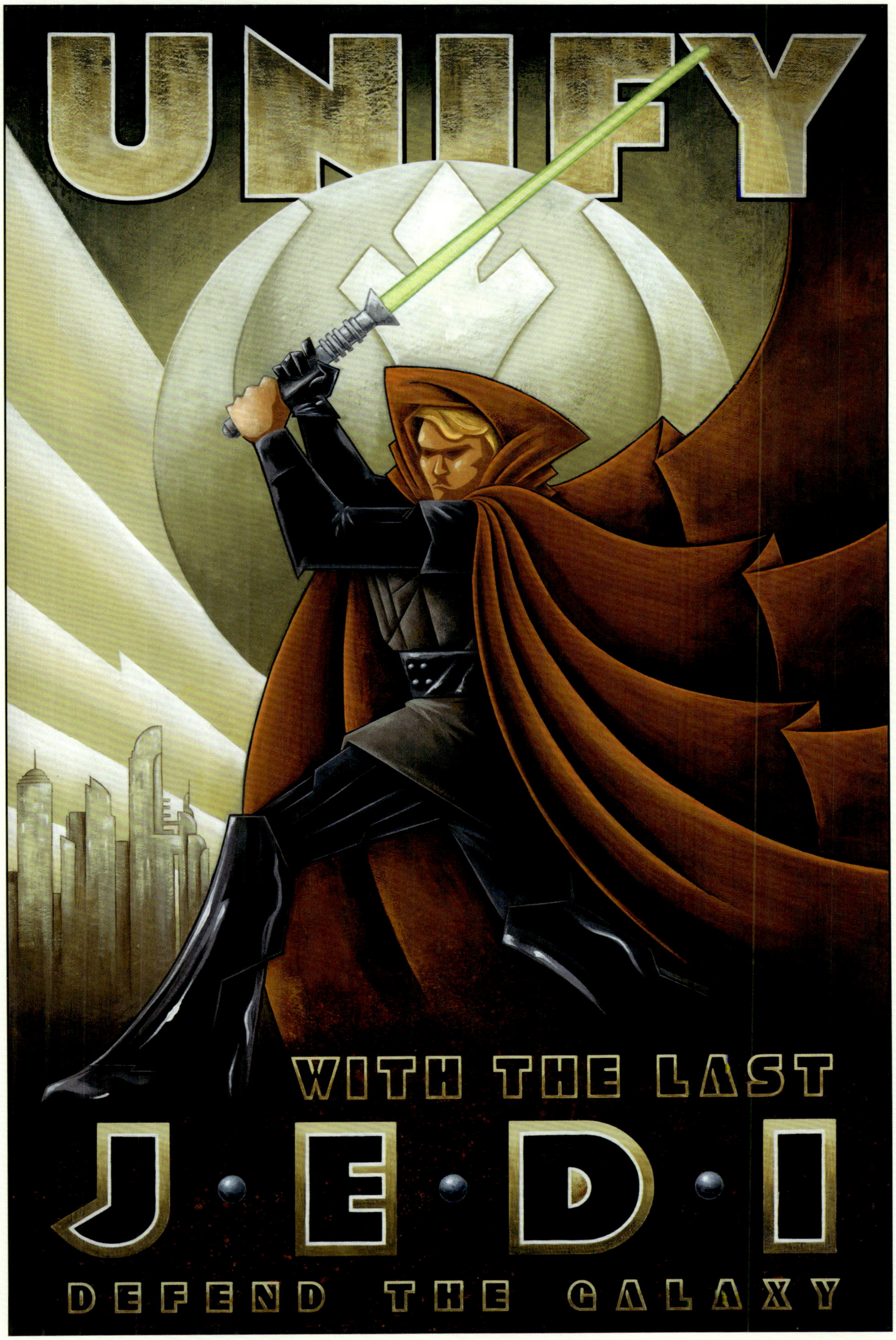

LEFT

Joe Corroney

Together, 2012

Poster-inspired artwork for Topps

RIGHT

Mike Kungl

Unify with the Last Jedi, 2011

Limited-edition giclée print for Acme Archives

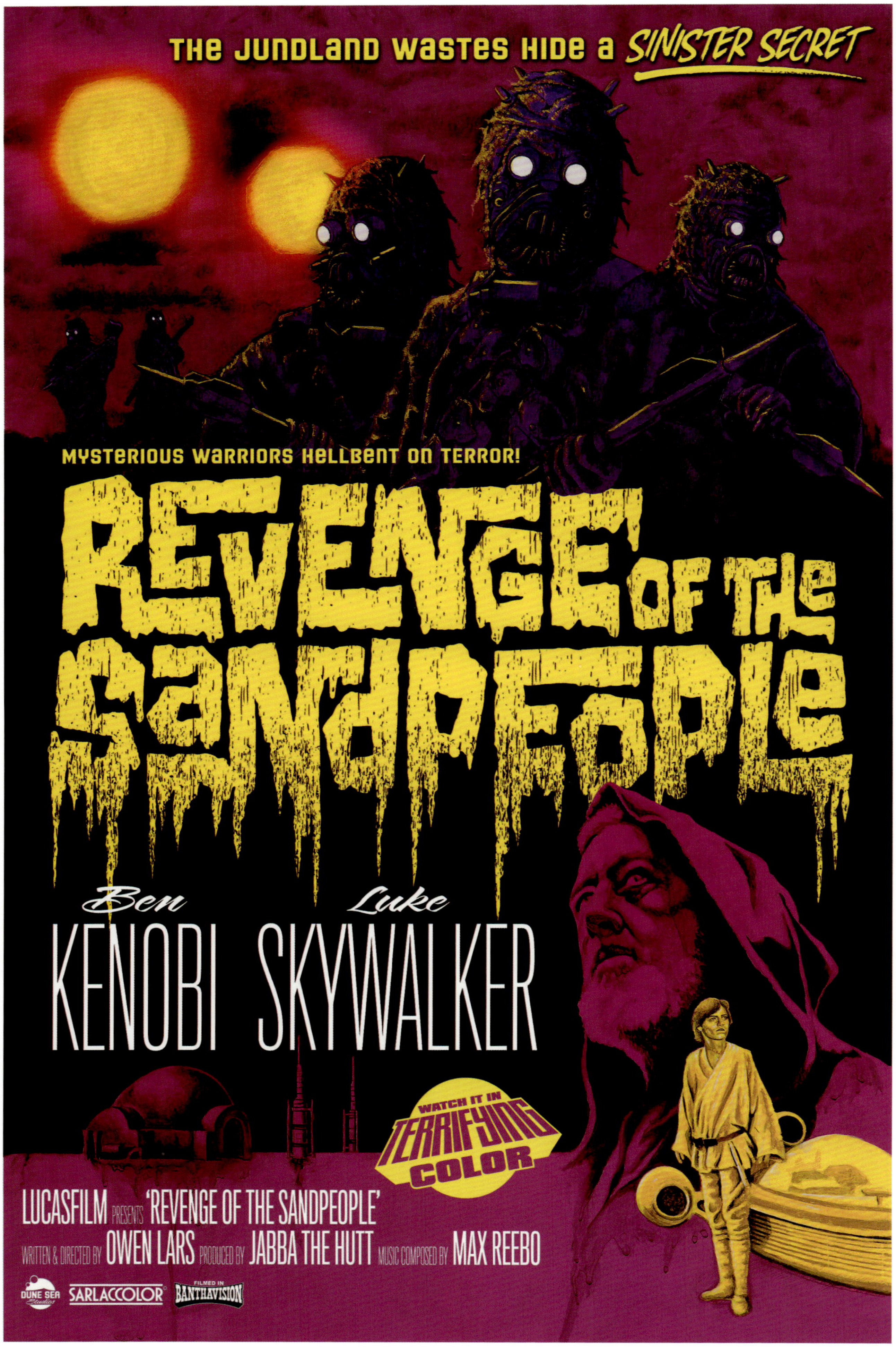

LEFT

Mark Daniels and Mark Steele

Revenge of the Sandpeople, 2012

Limited-edition lithograph for Acme Archives

RIGHT

Mark Daniels and Mark Steele

Lair of the Rancor, 2012

Limited-edition lithograph for Acme Archives

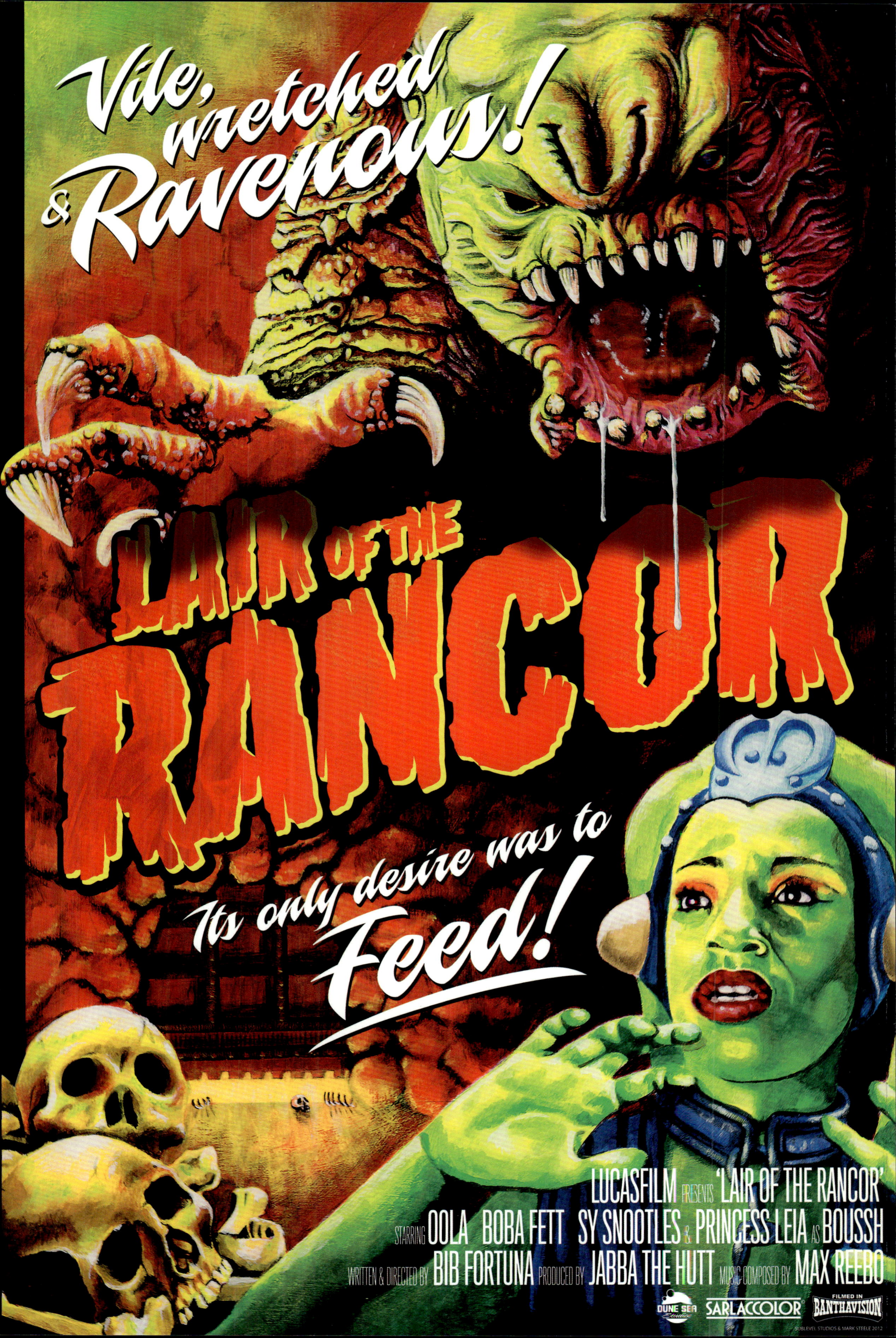

Vile, wretched & Ravenous!
LAIR OF THE RANCOR
Its only desire was to Feed!
LUCASFILM PRESENTS 'LAIR OF THE RANCOR'
STARRING OOLA BOBA FETT SY SNOOTLES & PRINCESS LEIA AS BOUSSH
WRITTEN & DIRECTED BY BIB FORTUNA PRODUCED BY JABBA THE HUTT MUSIC COMPOSED BY MAX REEBO
DUNE SEA Studios
SARLACCOLOR
FILMED IN BANTHAVISION
SUBLEVEL STUDIOS & MARK STEELE 2012

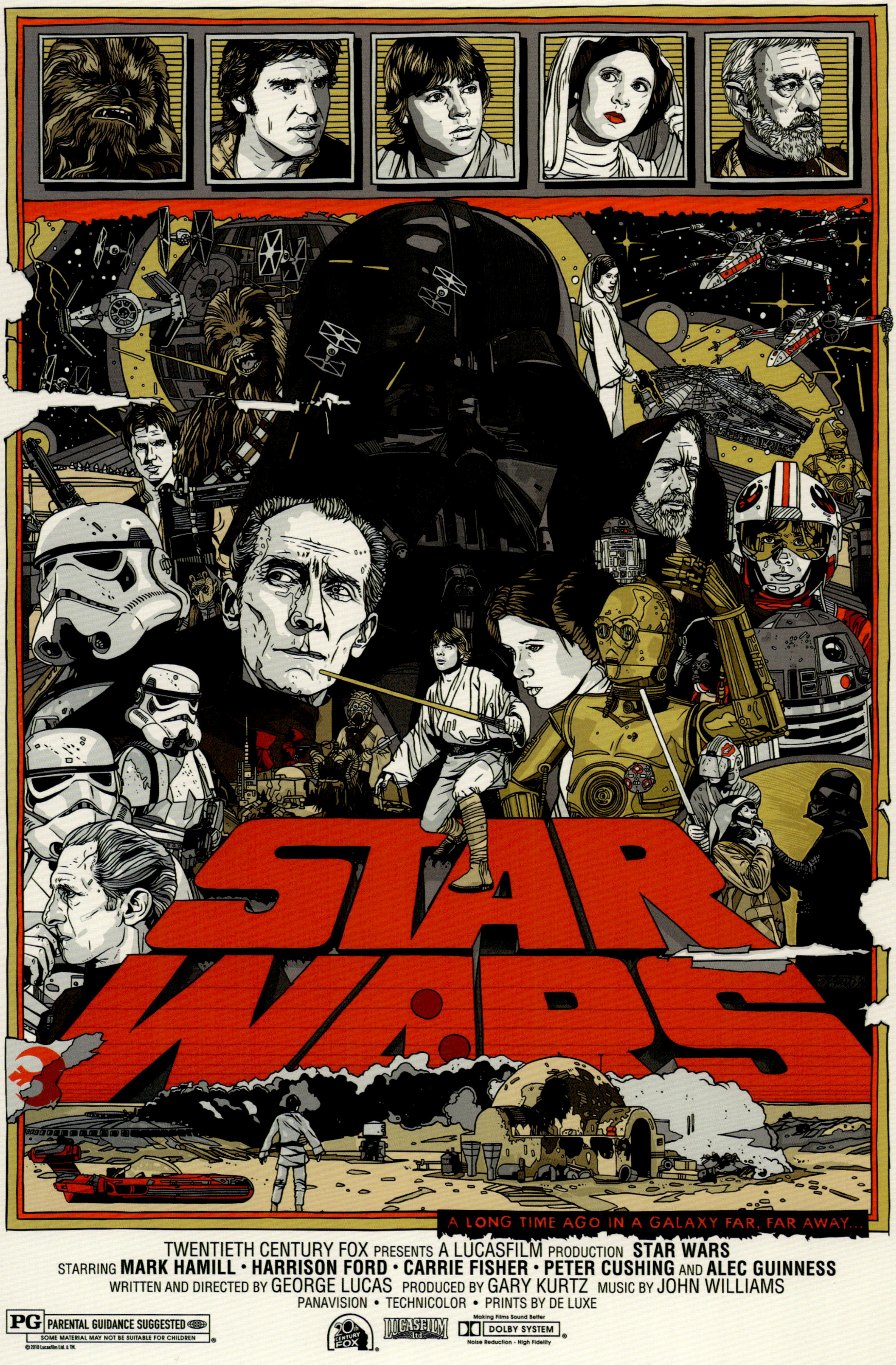
STAR WARS
A LONG TIME AGO IN A GALAXY FAR, FAR AWAY...
TWENTIETH CENTURY FOX PRESENTS A LUCASFILM PRODUCTION STAR WARS
STARRING MARK HAMILL • HARRISON FORD • CARRIE FISHER • PETER CUSHING AND ALEC GUINNESS
WRITTEN AND DIRECTED BY GEORGE LUCAS PRODUCED BY GARY KURTZ MUSIC BY JOHN WILLIAMS
PANAVISION • TECHNICOLOR • PRINTS BY DE LUXE
PG PARENTAL GUIDANCE SUGGESTED
SOME MATERIAL MAY NOT BE SUITABLE FOR CHILDREN
© 2010 Lucasfilm Ltd. & TM.
Making Films Sound Better
DOLBY SYSTEM
Noise Reduction - High Fidelity

GATEFOLD PANEL ONE

Tyler Stout

Star Wars, 2010

Limited-edition Mondo screen print

GATEFOLD PANEL TWO

Tyler Stout

The Empire Strikes Back, 2010

Limited-edition Mondo screen print

GATEFOLD PANEL THREE

Tyler Stout

Return of the Jedi, 2010

Limited-edition Mondo screen print

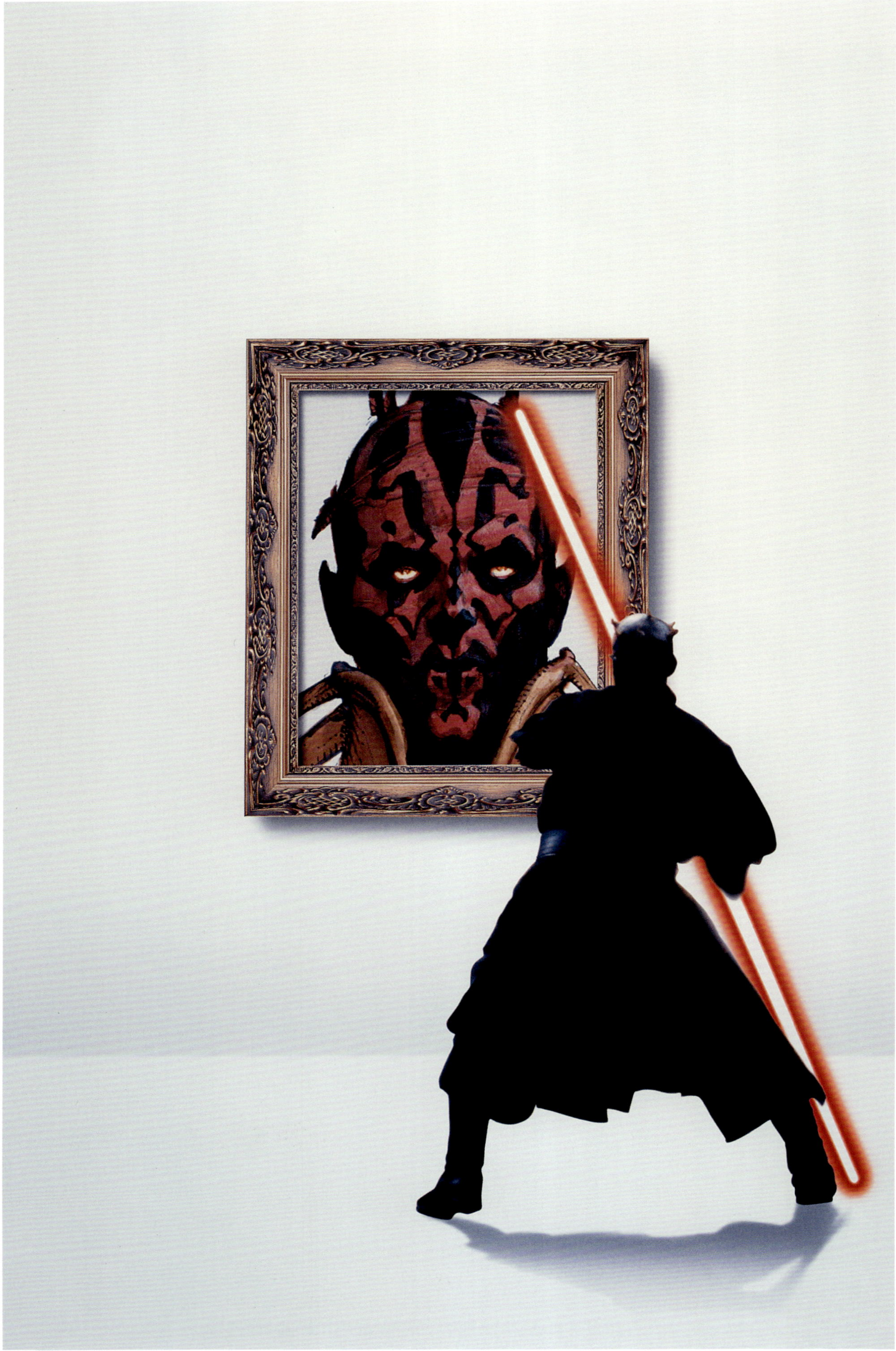

LEFT

Unknown

Final mixed-media/digital artwork for *The Art of Star Wars* poster, 2000

Promotional poster for *The Art of Star Wars* exhibition at Barbican Centre

RIGHT

Unknown

Final mixed-media/digital artwork for *The Art of Star Wars* poster, 2000

Promotional poster for *The Art of Star Wars* exhibition at Barbican Centre

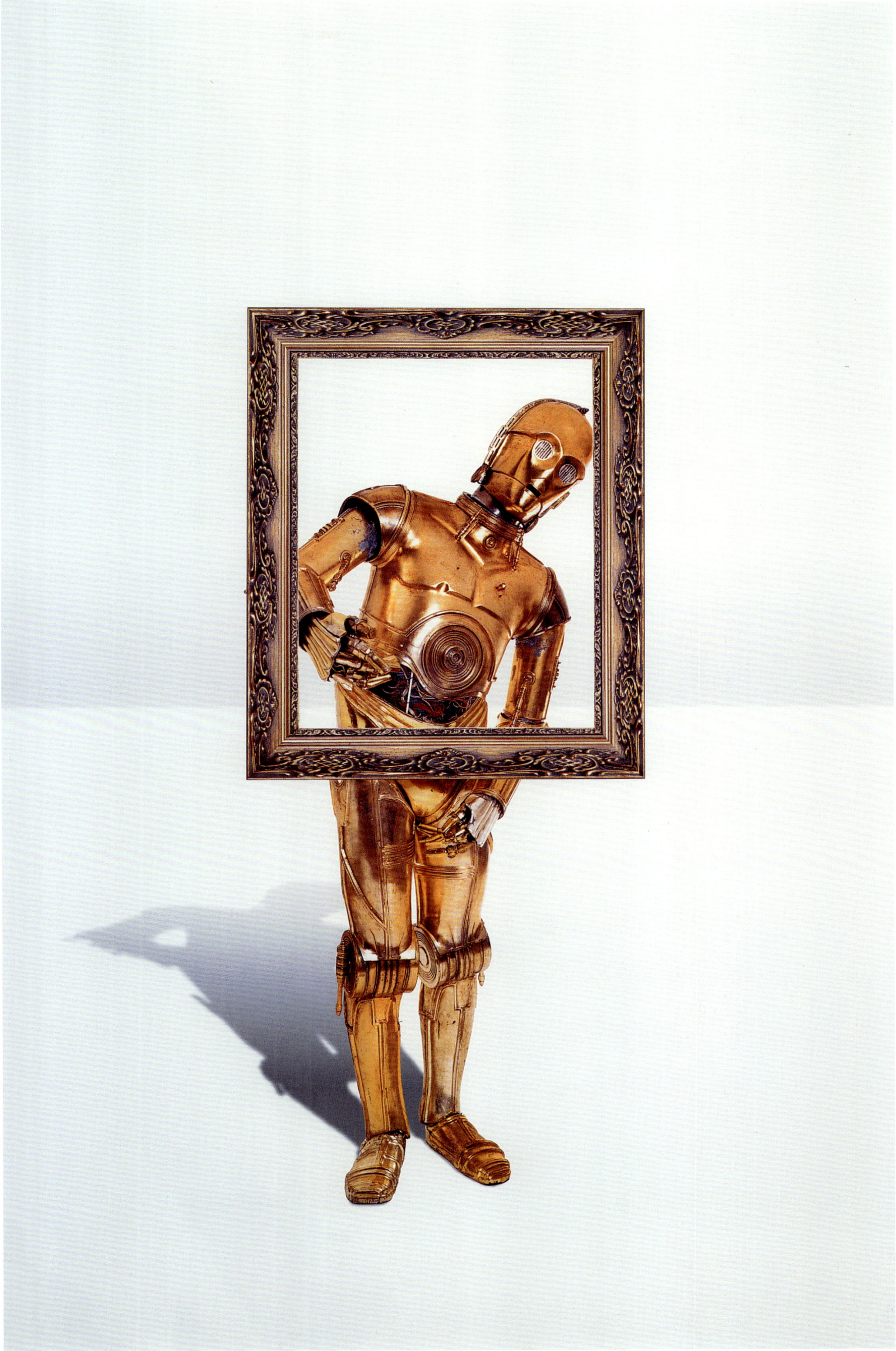

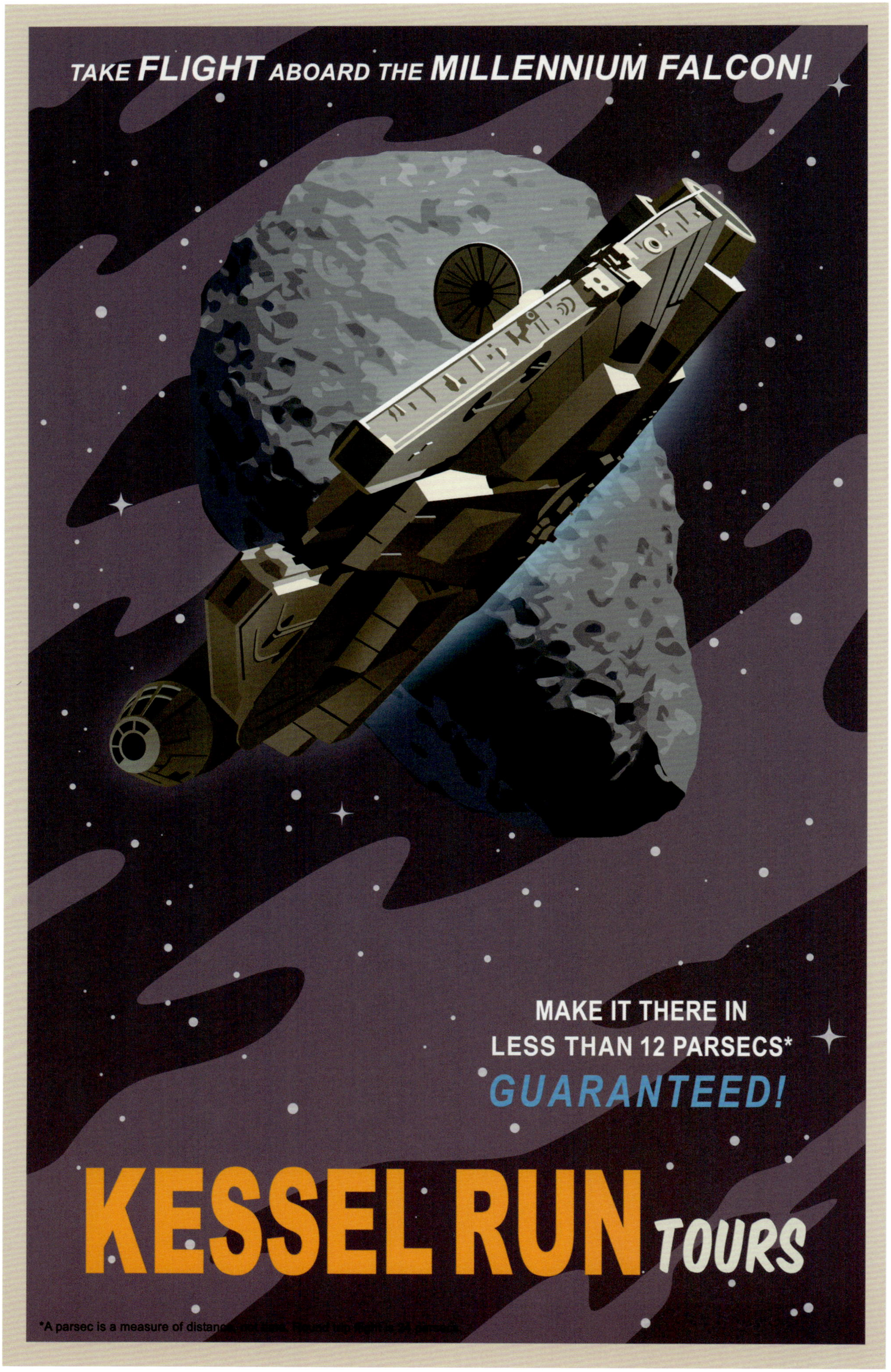

LEFT

Steve Thomas

Kessel Run Tours, 2010

Limited-edition giclée print for Acme Archives

RIGHT

Steve Thomas

Jawa Sandcrawler, 2011

Limited-edition giclée print for Acme Archives

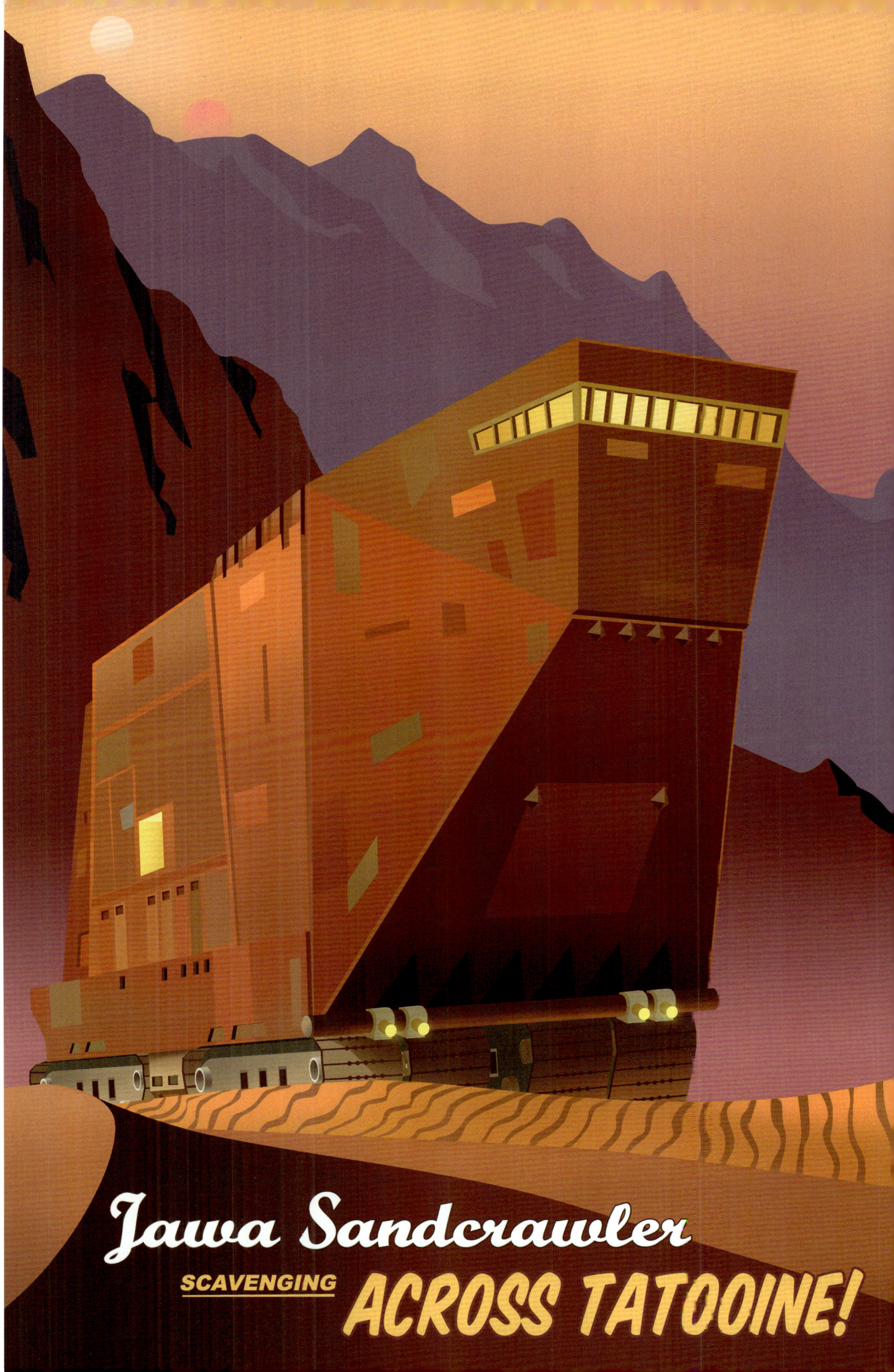
Jawa Sandcrawler
SCAVENGING
ACROSS TATOOINE!

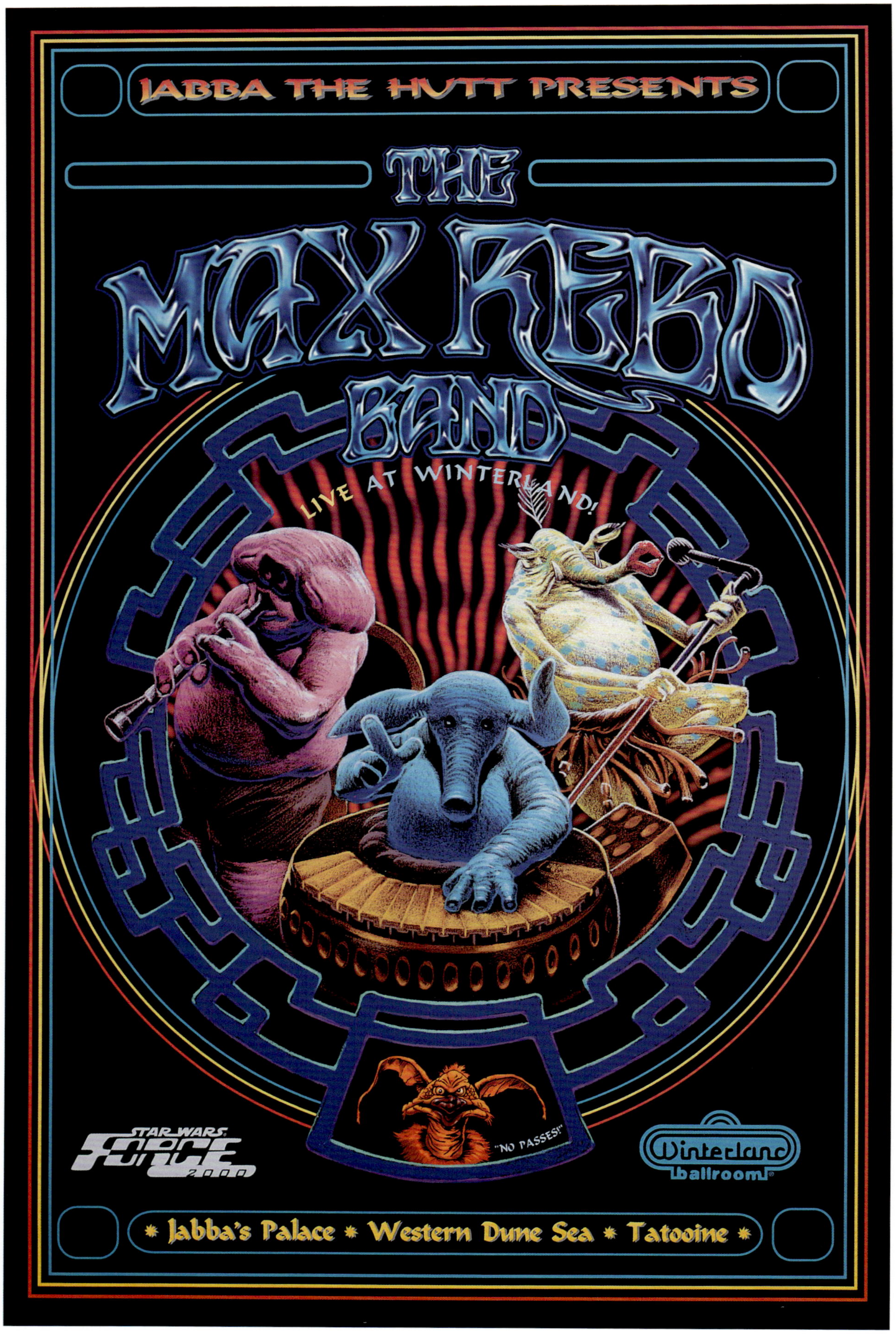

LEFT

William Brent

The Max Rebo Band Live at Winterland Ballroom 1997

Promotional art produced for Western Graphics

RIGHT

Steve Thomas

Cruise the Galaxy, 2011

Limited-edition giclée print for Acme Archives

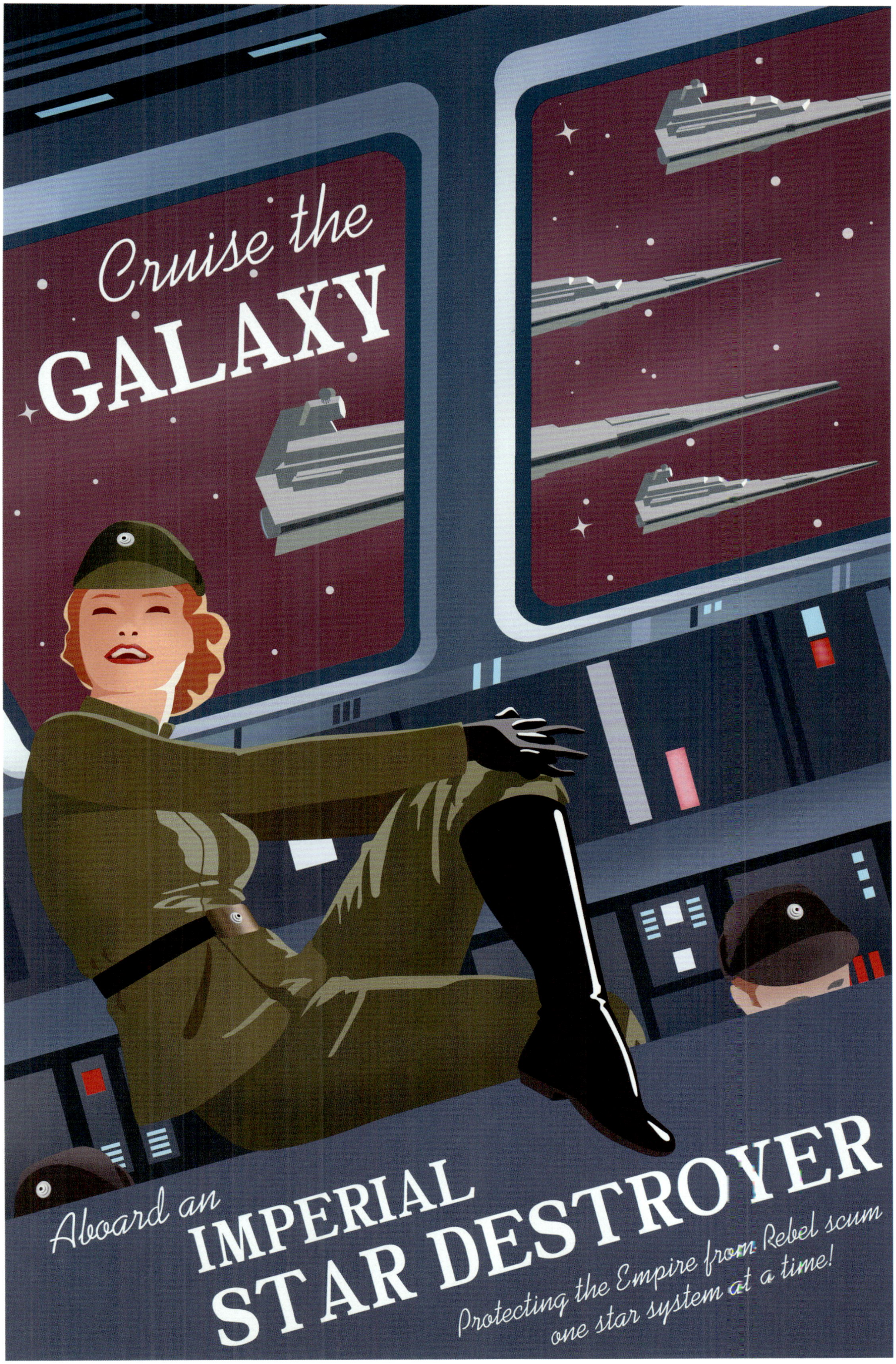
Cruise the
GALAXY
Aboard an
IMPERIAL
STAR DESTROYER
Protecting the Empire from Rebel scum
one star system at a time!

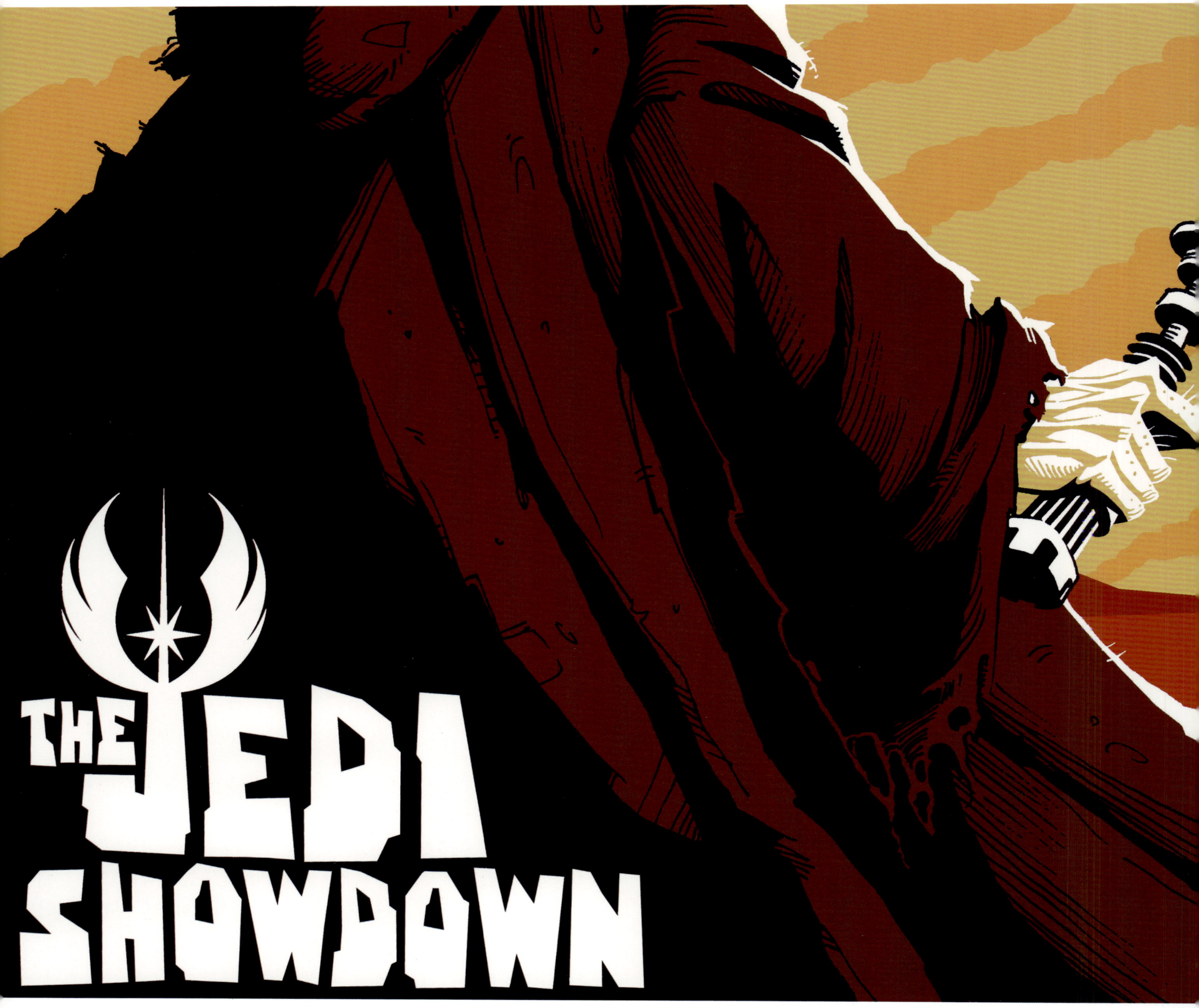

ABOVE

Gris Grimly

The Jedi Showdown, 2013

Limited-edition screen print for Acme Archives

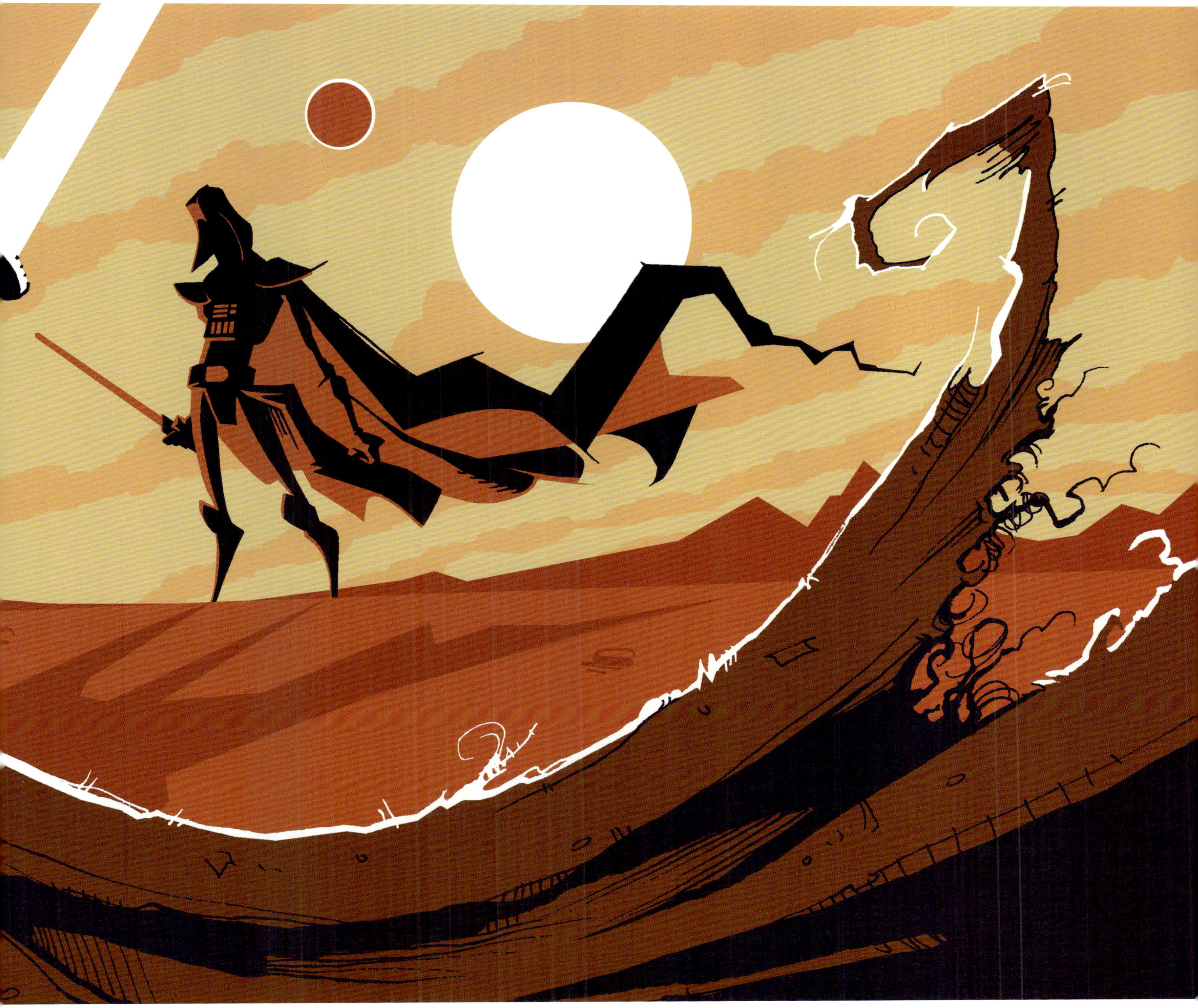

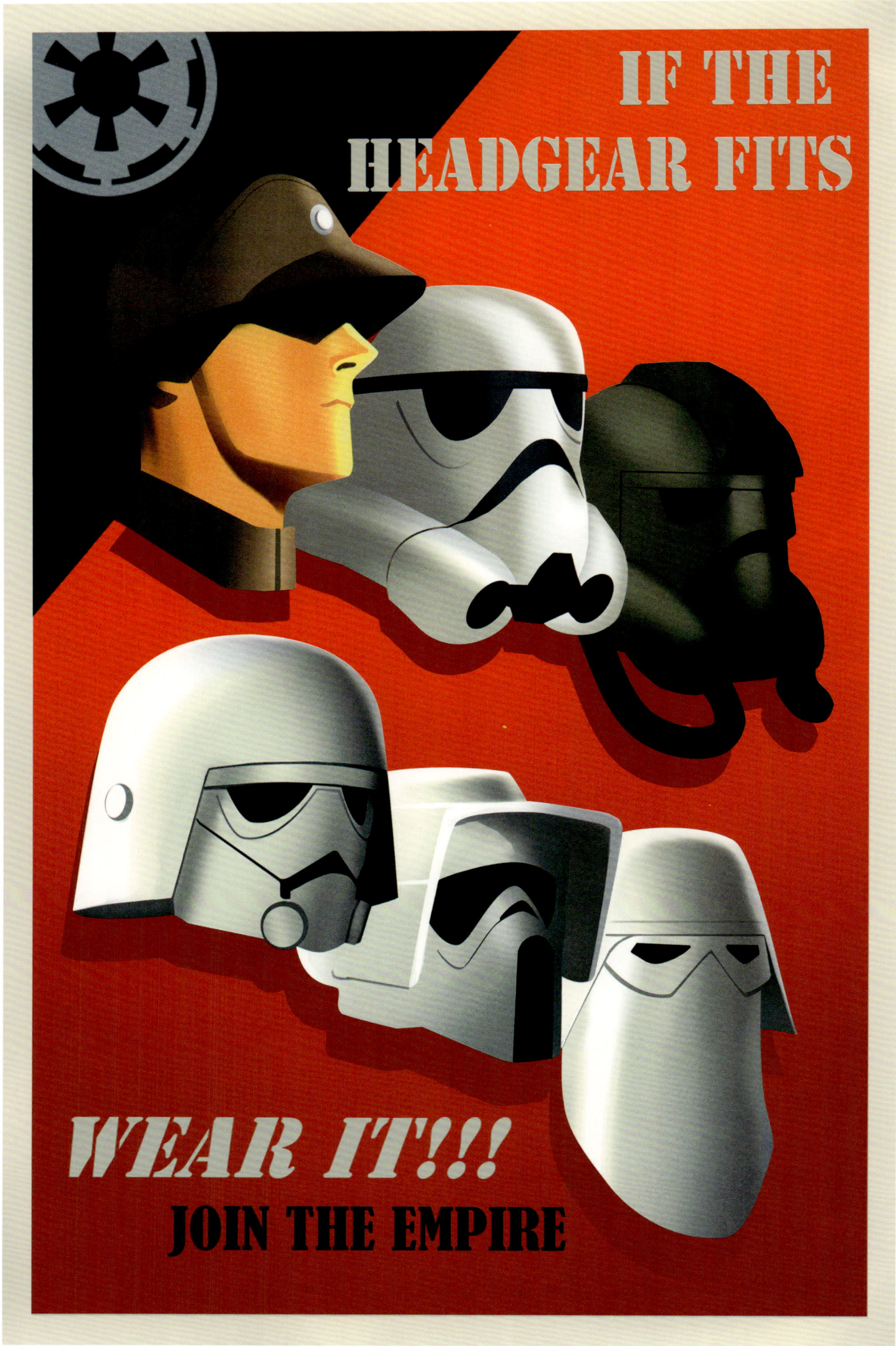

LEFT

Amy Beth Christenson

If the Headgear Fits, 2014

Advance poster-style promotional cards for *Star Wars Rebels*

RIGHT

Amy Beth Christenson

Explore the Galaxy, 2014

Advance poster-style promotional cards for *Star Wars Rebels*

FOLLOWING SPREAD

Brian Rood

Final digital artwork for exclusive *Star Wars* Celebration V poster, 2010

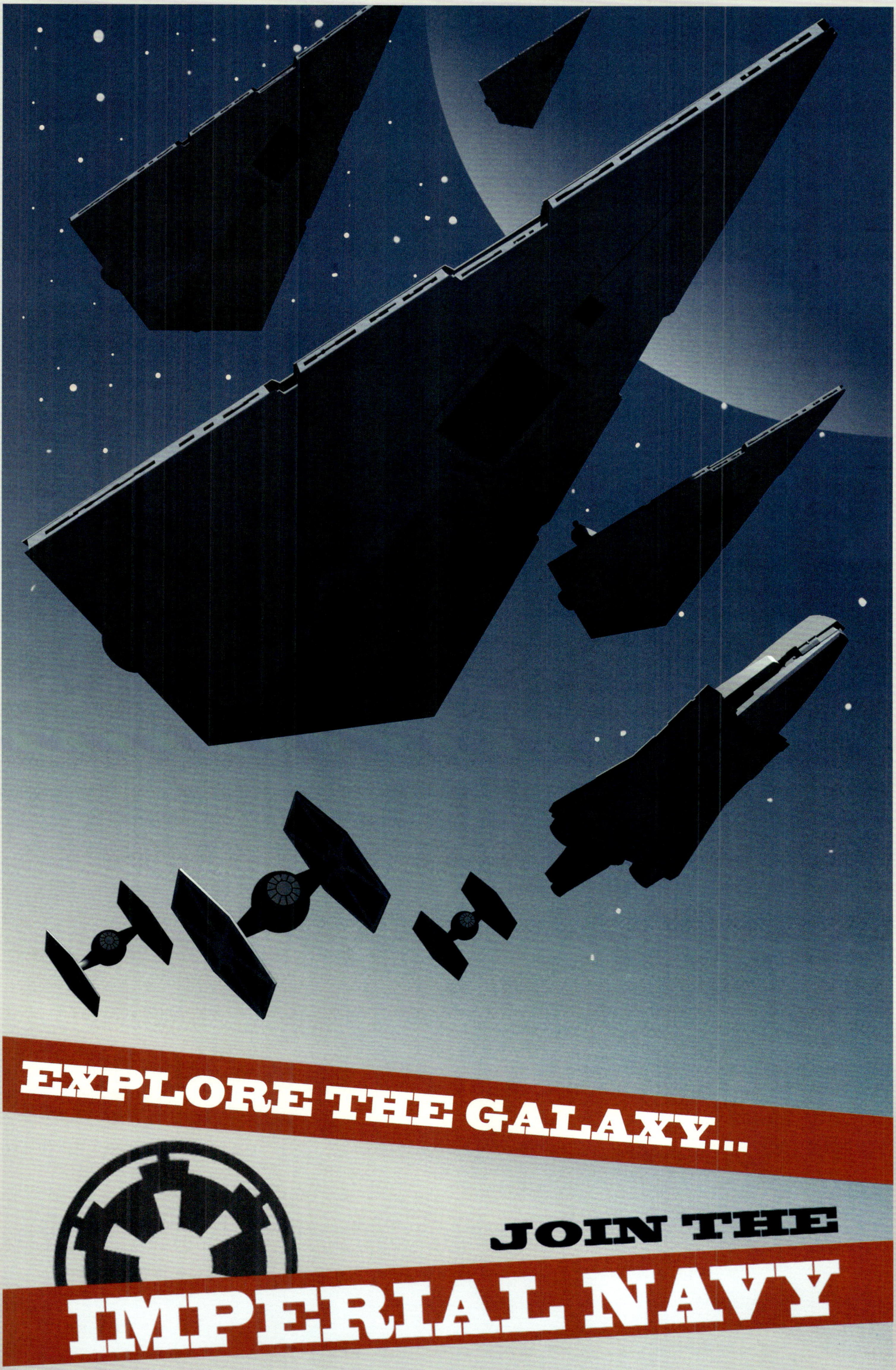
EXPLORE THE GALAXY...
JOIN THE
IMPERIAL NAVY

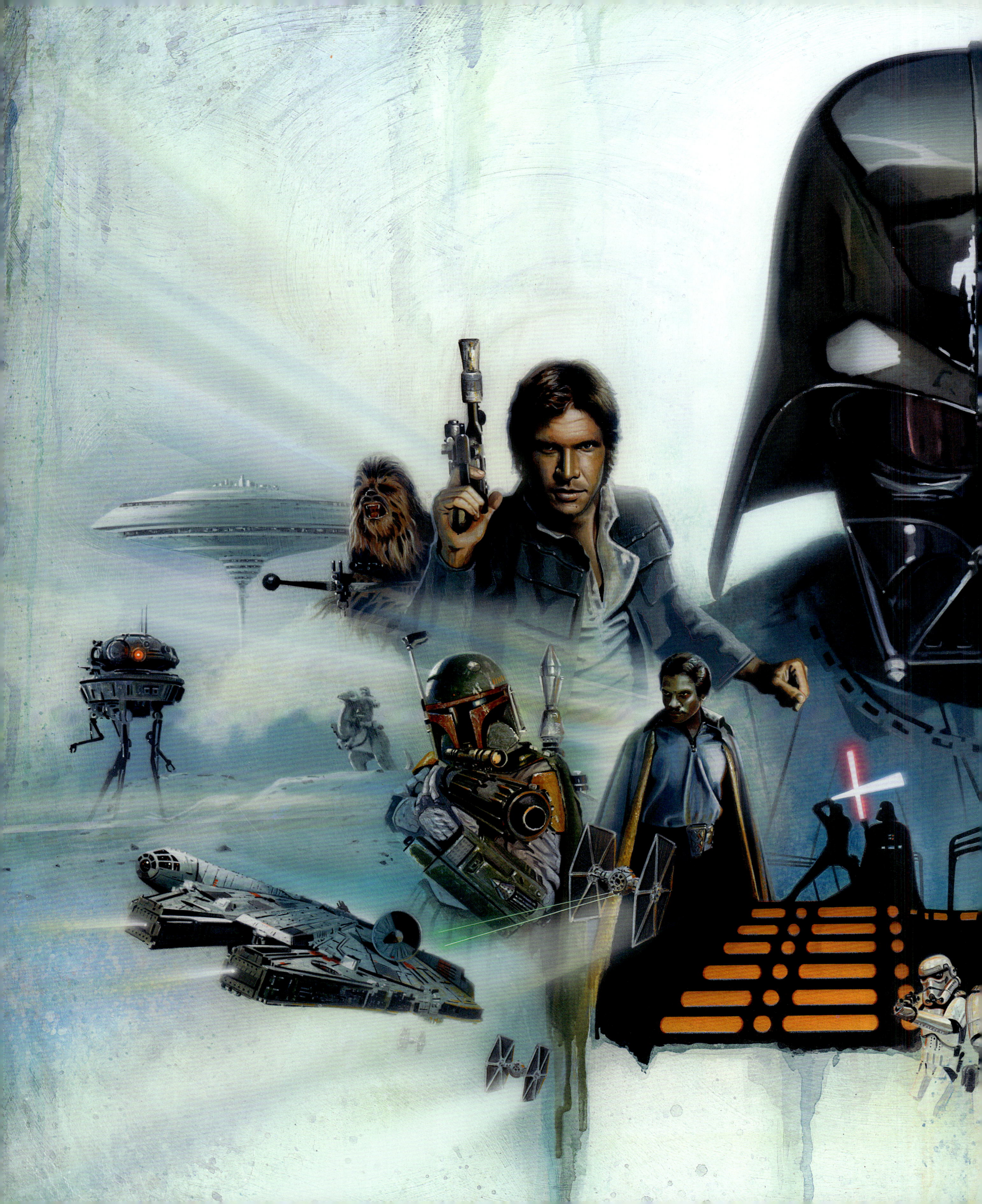

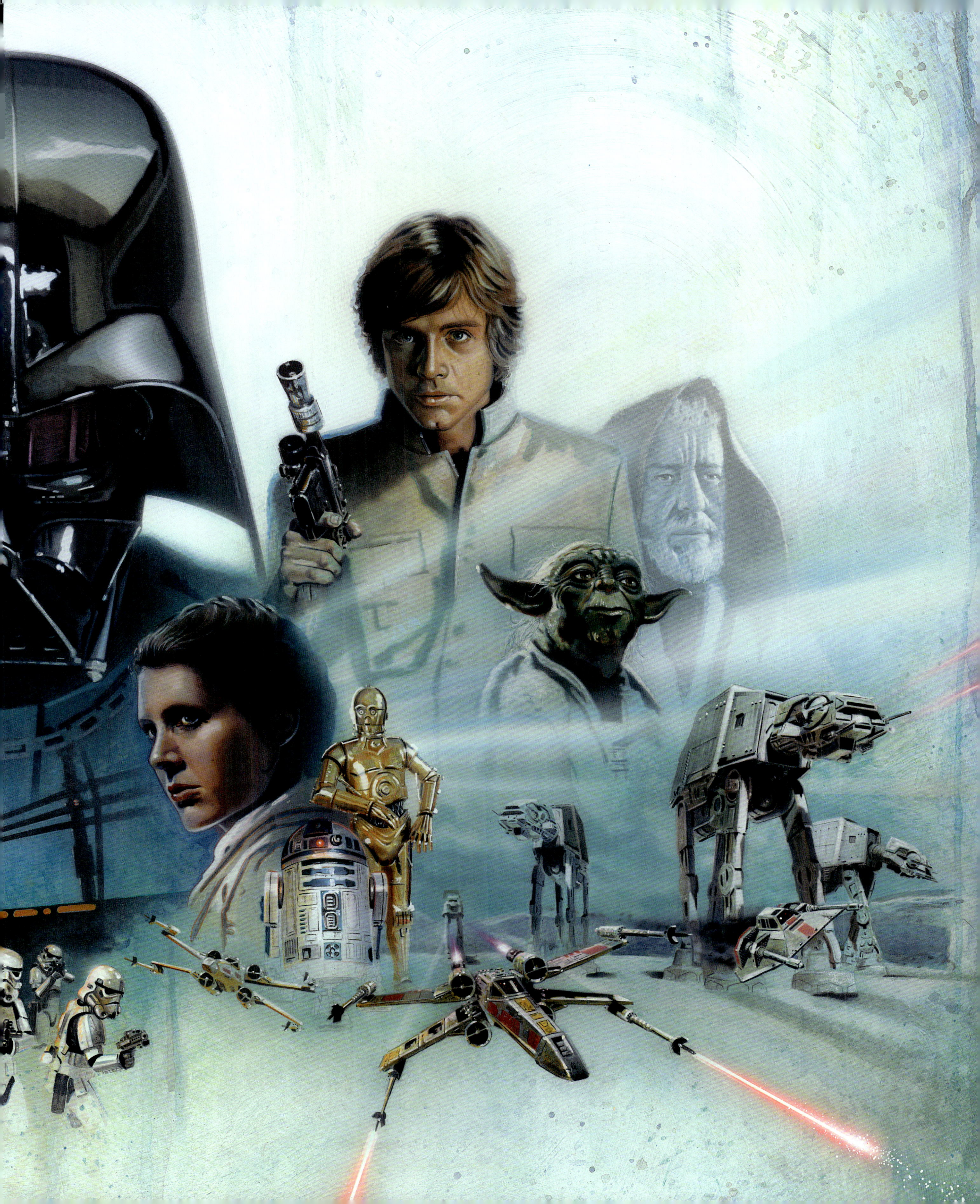

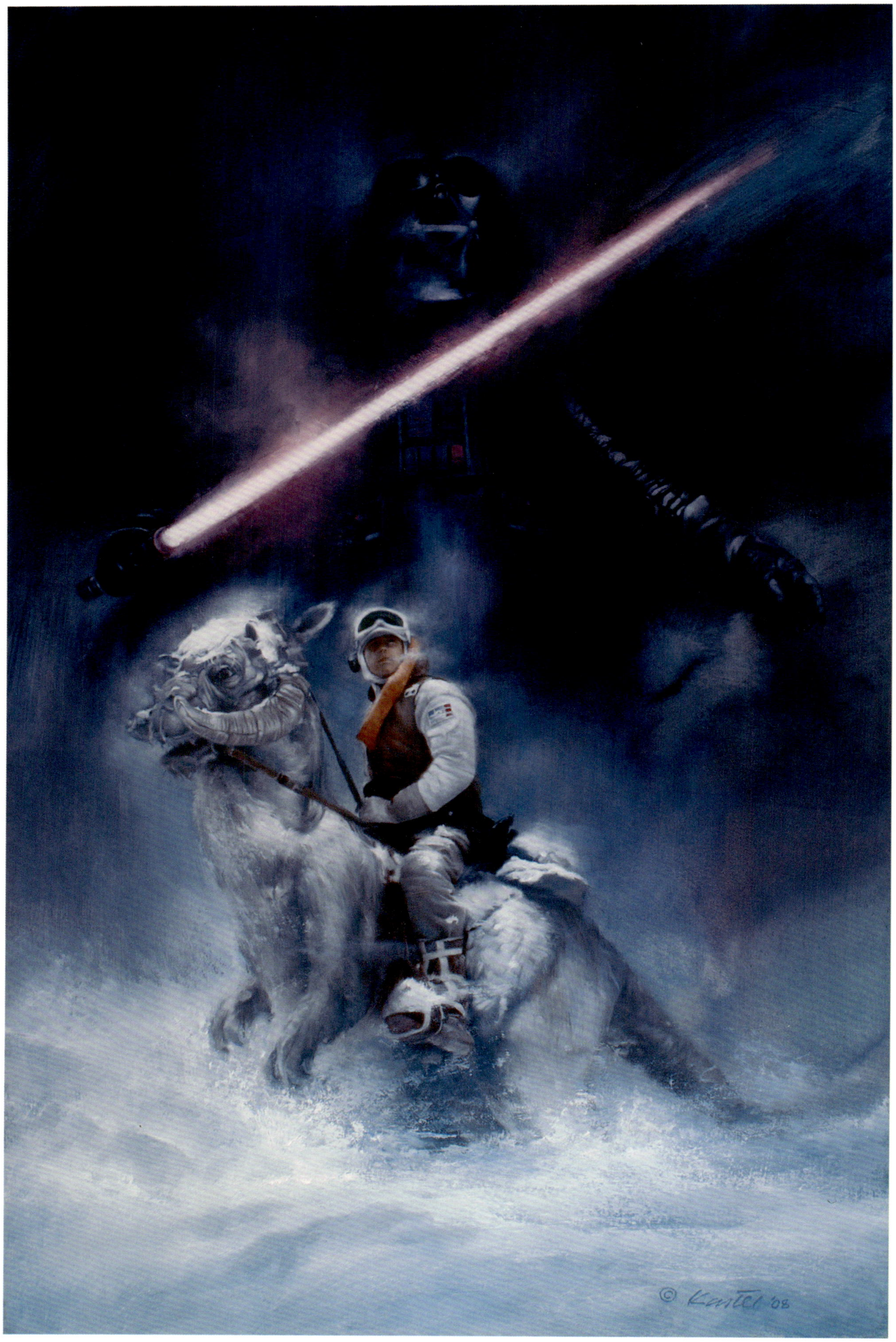

LEFT

Roger Kastel

Final painted artwork for "unofficial" *The Empire Strikes Back* poster, 2008

ARTISTS' BIOGRAPHIES

John Alvin was a master of the illustrative movie poster, having worked on hundreds of movie campaigns with more than 140 finished posters to his credit. Alvin graduated from the Art Center College of Design in Los Angeles in 1971, getting his start in poster art on Mel Brooks's *Blazing Saddles*. The well-received design led to assignments on *Young Frankenstein* and other Mel Brooks films, and soon Alvin was in demand as a top poster artist. His instantly recognizable output included the theatrical posters for *Blade Runner*, *Aladdin*, *Beauty and the Beast*, *The Little Mermaid*, *The Lion King*, *The Color Purple*, and *Gremlins*. For 1982's *E.T. the Extra-Terrestrial*, Alvin designed the iconic image of E.T. touching his finger to the finger of his human friend, Elliott. The creator of numerous pieces for Disney's Fine Art collection, Alvin demonstrated the ability to add emotional weight to his subjects, which became known as "Alvin-izing" among Disney aficionados. He passed away in 2008. *38, 80, 81, 82, 110*

Kia Asamiya, born in 1963, is a manga artist with a career that stretches back three decades. After graduating from the Tokyo Designer School, he made his debut on the series *Shin Seiki Vagrants* in 1986. Under his birth name of Michitaka Kikuchi, he contributed to anime releases, including *Sonic Soldier Borgman* and *Project A-ko*, and he has worked as a model designer for several films in the Godzilla franchise. Asamiya's output is well represented in both Japanese manga and American comics, on such releases as *Corrector Yui*, *Möbius Klein*, and *Junk: Record of the Last Hero*, as well as *Batman: Child of Dreams*, *Hellboy*, and *The Uncanny X-Men* for the overseas market. In 1999, Asamiya illustrated the manga adaptation of *Star Wars*: Episode I *The Phantom Menace*. Among the most popular and widely distributed manga series associated with Asamiya are *Martian Successor Nadesico* and *Silent Möbius*. *114*

John Berkey spent most of his life in a small Minnesota town, but through his illustrations he shared a vision that spanned time, space, and imagination. After an eight-year stint at an advertising agency in St. Paul, Minnesota, during the 1960s, Berkey began a series of commissions illustrating NASA's astronauts and the agency's orbital and moon missions. In the 1970s, Berkey earned recognition for his paintings of huge, detailed spaceships, which adorned Ballantine's science fiction book covers. Berkey's art appeared in magazines, in advertisements, and on movie posters, including *Star Wars*, *The Towering Inferno*, and the 1976 remake of *King Kong*. For the U.S. Postal Service Berkey contributed paintings for postage stamps, including the Santa Claus Christmas stamp in 1983 and 1991, and the "Old Elvis" stamp in 1992. By the time of his induction into the Society of Illustrators Hall of Fame in 2004, Berkey had earned recognition as one of the most innovative and influential futurist painters of his time. He died in 2008. *27, 28, 29, 30–31, 31, 32–33*

Randy Berrett earned fame as an illustrator of book and album covers before becoming an influential member of the Pixar animation team. After graduating from the Academy of Art University in San Francisco, Berrett found regular work in the fantasy genre. Among his most recognizable paintings during this time was the album cover for Dio's *Holy Diver*, released in 1983. After he joined Pixar in 1996, Berrett worked as a character designer, set designer, and matte painter on such films as *Brave*, *Up*, *Ratatouille*, *The Incredibles*, and *Toy Story 2*. Berrett later returned to his alma mater to teach visual development classes at the Academy of Art University. His work has been featured in books including *Art of Monsters University*, *The Art of Toy Story: 100 Collectible Postcards*, and *Pixar: 25 Years of Animation*, released in conjunction with the Oakland Museum of California (OMCA). *97*

John Blas has been working in motion picture marketing and advertising for more than seventeen years. He graduated with a degree in marketing and business administration from the University of Southern California and began his career at Walt Disney Motion Pictures Group to focus on live action and animated films. In 2003, Blas was promoted to senior vice president of worldwide creative advertising for Disney Feature Animation and Pixar. In this role, he spearheaded all ad campaigns and provided strategic creative direction to other divisions, including consumer products, broadcast networks, and theme parks. Blas was instrumental in creating memorable marketing campaigns on such films as *Toy Story*, *Tarzan*, *Finding Nemo*, and *Cars*. He currently provides marketing and creative advertising consulting for a range of entertainment clients, including Lucasfilm, Columbia Pictures, and Lionsgate. *124*

William Brent was born in 1954 and started drawing when he was ten. In his childhood he discovered paperback editions of *Tarzan*, *John Carter*, and other novels by Edgar Rice Burroughs, which featured amazing painted covers by Roy Krenkel and Frank Frazetta. In 1987 he started at Winterland Productions, a rock and roll merchandising company, and remained there for fourteen years. During the rerelease of the *Star Wars* trilogy in the late nineties, Brent produced a faux concert poster in a "Fillmore West" style starring the alien musicians from Jabba the Hutt's palace. Brent has produced concept art and storyboards for animation, texture mapping and matte painting for games, and promotional art for movie studios. Brent is currently working in oils on personal projects, as well as teaching Photoshop and Fantasy Figure Drawing at the Academy of Art University in San Francisco. *166*

Renato Casaro was born in 1935 in Treviso, Italy. In 1951 he began a graphic apprenticeship in Venice and earned his first commissions to produce cinema billboards in his hometown in exchange for free movie tickets. In 1953, at the age of nineteen, Casaro moved to Rome to work at Studio Favalli on movie campaigns. Two years later he opened his own studio, becoming the youngest movie painter in Italy at age twenty-one. In 1966, Casaro scored his first international success with his artwork for the Dino De Laurentiis film *The Bible: In the Beginning*. The following years saw Casaro take on international campaigns for major movie releases, leading to notable poster designs, including 1988's *The Last Emperor* and 1991's *Dances with Wolves*. Beginning in 1985, Casaro made a series of educational trips to the American West to research his "Going West" painting cycle, and followed it up with a journey to the African bush to develop his cycle "African Impressions." *94*

Tom Chantrell enjoyed a career as a commercial artist that spanned half a century and helped define the aesthetic of British film advertising. Born in Manchester in 1916, he won a League of Nations poster competition at age thirteen and briefly attended Manchester Art College. After joining a local advertising agency, Chantrell moved to London and began his focus on movie posters, with his first design being the Edward G. Robinson film *The Amazing Dr. Clitterhouse* in 1938. Chantrell served in the Royal Engineers bomb disposal unit during World War II, and produced movie poster designs for Allardyce Palmer from the end of the war through the 1970s. Among Chantrell's most recognizable posters are his designs for *Star Wars*, *The King and I*, and *One Million Years B.C.* Respected for his technical ability and his unmatched work ethic, Chantrell served as an inspiration for generations of film artists. He died in 2001. *24*

Howard Chaykin was born in Newark, New Jersey, in 1950 and started his comics career as an assistant to the legendary Gil Kane. In the early 1970s, Chaykin drew for *Marvel Spotlight* and DC's *Sword of Sorcery*, and in 1976 he illustrated the first *Star Wars* promotional poster, which was sold at San Diego Comic-Con nearly a year before the movie's release. Chaykin also penciled the comics adaptation of the original *Star Wars* movie with writer Roy Thomas, and worked as both writer and artist for the early issues of Marvel's ongoing *Star Wars* series. In 1983, his original series *American Flagg!* became a hit for First Comics, featuring mature themes and Chaykin's distinctive angular artwork. Bringing his talents to DC, Chaykin revamped *The Shadow* and the 1940s aviator hero *Blackhawk*, and he created the provocative adults-only series *Black Kiss* for Vortex Comics. In the 2000s he returned to DC on the limited series *Guy Gardner: Collateral Damage* and the graphic novel *Mighty Love*. *15, 16–17*

Cliff Chiang graduated from Harvard University with a joint degree in English literature and visual arts. His professional career included an editorial stint at *Disney Adventures* magazine and a staff position at DC Comics' Vertigo imprint. Chiang later made the move into freelance illustration, and his clients have included *GQ* magazine, Lucasfilm, Warner Animation, Dark Horse Comics, Dynamic Forces Entertainment, and the American Civil Liberties Union. Chiang's work as both a writer and artist has appeared in comic book outlets, including *Detective Comics*, *Human Target*, *Red Sonja*, *Wonder Woman*, *Grendel: Red, White, and Black*, and *Dr. Thirteen: Architecture & Mortality*. He lives and works in Brooklyn, New York. *152, 153*

Amy Beth Christenson experienced her first moviegoing moment with the original *Star Wars* film, inspiring her to spend her childhood drawing fantastic characters and creatures. Growing up in a small farm town in Kansas, Christenson pursued art training at the Kansas City Art Institute and the Ringling College of Art and Design, receiving her BFA in illustration in 2000. For the next eleven years, she combined her passions for *Star Wars* and video games as a concept artist for LucasArts. Christenson worked on eight shipped titles during that time, including a role as senior and lead concept designer for the games of *Star Wars*: The Force Unleashed series. In 2011 she became a senior concept designer at Lucasfilm Animation on *Star Wars: The Clone Wars*. Her art has been featured on Acme Archives limited-edition prints and sketch cards for the Topps Star Wars Galaxy series, and she was one of twelve artists chosen to create a limited-edition print for the official *Empire Strikes Back* Thirtieth anniversary celebration. *119, 170, 171*

Joe Corroney first saw *Star Wars* at the age of four, and reading the movie's Marvel Comics adaptation put him on a path to become a comic book illustrator and a destiny to become a *Star Wars* artist. Joe has been providing Lucasfilm with official *Star Wars* artwork for books, games, trading cards, comic books, posters, and magazines since 1997. Other comics in his portfolio include *Star Trek*, *True Blood*, *Farscape*, *G.I. Joe*, *Fallen Angel*, *24*, *Doctor Who*, and *The Phantom*. He instructed at the Comic Book Illustration Course at the Columbus College of Art and Design in Columbus, Ohio, from 1998 to 2008, and has taught the Ohio State University's Comic Book Workshop. Currently, he is developing his creator-owned comic book series *Death Avenger* and continues to create new *Star Wars* artwork for Lucasfilm. *154*

Mark Daniels believes that—after the fall of civilization nearly twenty years ago and the rise of the undead, unwashed, and ill-informed—he somehow retreated to his secret art studio on the outskirts of Stoke-on-Trent, England, with his wife Rachel and their two children, Zac and Amy. *Star Wars* has been part of his DNA since he first saw it in 1978 at the age of five, and though Daniels has had the pleasure of working on other famous sci-fi and fantasy franchises, *Star Wars* remains his first love. His work is largely graphical, combining illustration with typography, and his influences include Ralph McQuarrie, Ron Cobb, Syd Mead, Drew Struzan, Chris Foss, Olly Moss, Jason Edmiston, Tyler Stout, and Aaron Horkey—all of who make him sick with envy for being so hideously talented. *156, 157*

Craig Drake is originally from Detroit, where he earned his BFA in graphic design from Detroit's College for Creative Studies. In 1998 he moved to San Francisco to work in animation and freelance design, putting in time at companies such as Adobe. After gaining experience as a designer at games developer Electronic Arts, Drake began working at Lucasfilm in 2006. His first *Star Wars* parody image followed soon after, capturing Princess Leia posed in a distinctive style inspired by Patrick Nagel and associated with the 1980s. The image was produced as a limited-edition print and earned the attention of Duran Duran's Simon Le Bon, who requested a personal copy. Since then, Drake has produced a line of Nagel-inspired prints of various pop-culture figures, bringing a sleek eighties aesthetic to everyone in his path. *144, 145*

Witold Dybowski was born in 1958 and produced film posters for the cinema market in Poland during his career as a commercial artist. Official publicity material from the United States was not permitted in Poland during the Cold War, requiring all Polish film posters to be handmade and offering the opportunity for illustrators like Dybowski to indulge in experimental creative freedom—one of Dybowski's *Return of the Jedi* designs featured an exploding Darth Vader, and Dybowski did not actually see *Jedi* until three years after its release. Other posters by Dybowski include the Polish promotions for *Airplane!; Paris, Texas; Indiana Jones and the Temple of Doom;* and *Aliens*, as well as a design for the 1988 Polish-made crime comedy *Nowy Jork, czwarta rano*. *93*

Gris Grimly is a storyteller and creator of a madhouse of imagination. For more than a decade, Grimly's distinctive style and wide selection of mediums have captivated fans worldwide. Since the release of his first book, *Monster Museum*, Grimly has illustrated more than twenty books, including *The Dangerous Alphabet*, his *New York Times* bestselling collaboration with author Neil Gaiman. Grimly's own stories have been realized in *Little Jordan Ray's Muddy Spud* and the Wicked Nursery Rhymes series, and his artwork has been recognized by the Edward Gorey House and the Edgar Allan Poe Museum. Grimly served as writer and director of the short film *Cannibal Flesh Riot!* and directed the opening sequence for the syndicated TV show *Elvira's Movie Macabre*. A stop-motion feature film based on Grimly's adaptation of *Pinocchio* has been attached to director Guillermo del Toro. *128, 168–169*

Tomer Hanuka, born in 1974, is an Israeli illustrator and cartoonist based in New York City. After completing three years of mandatory service in the Israeli Army, Hanuka moved to New York at age twenty-two and studied at the School of Visual Arts. Post-graduation, he became a regular contributor to magazines including *Time*, the *New Yorker*, *Spin*, the *New York Times*, and *Rolling Stone*. Hanuka has won multiple medals from the Society of Illustrators and the Society of Publication Designers, as well as from *American Illustration and Print* magazine. With his identical twin brother Asaf, Hanuka created the experimental comic book series *Bipolar* for Alternative Comics, earning nominations for the Eisner, Harvey, and Ignatz awards. Hanuka contributed key frames to the acclaimed 2008 animated documentary *Waltz with Bashir*, and a book collecting his work entitled *Overkill* appeared in 2012. *148*

Louis C. Hébert was born in Montreal in 1959 and inherited his drawing talents from his father, the landscape artist Jean-Louis Hébert. He attended the École des beaux-arts de Montréal and the Cégep du Vieux Montréal before contributing his first editorial illustrations to magazines and newspapers. In 1984, Hébert founded Studio de la montagne (later Hébert Communication), and during the 1990s he illustrated numerous movie posters and video jackets. Hébert's paintings of Formula 1 racing cars have earned widespread acclaim, and some pieces have earned places in the private collection of the Grand Prix de Formule 1 de Montréal. For the *Star Wars*: Identities museum exhibition, Hébert designed a series of promotional posters that depicted characters from Darth Vader to Queen Amidala by using a series of smaller, related images. Hébert is currently exploring the mediums of digital painting and painting on metal. *136, 137*

Tibor Helényi, born in 1946, helped define the imaginative, experimental field of Hungarian poster art through a career that lasted decades. By incorporating elements of twentieth-century popular visual culture, Helényi created striking posters for exhibitions and localized Hungarian theatrical releases. He studied at the University of Fine Arts under József Baska and Sándor Ernyei, and in the mid-1970s he became a member of the Perspektíva-csoport, a group of young and talented poster artists. Helényi worked as a graphic designer for *Interpress Magazin* from 1977 to 1992, and most of his paintings depict highly realistic figures and strong distortions captured from unusual visual angles. Helényi designed Hungarian posters for many of the classic science-fiction movies of the 1970s and 1980s, including *Alien*, *Close Encounters of the Third Kind*, *Robocop*, and the films of the classic *Star Wars* trilogy. *92*

Adam Hughes is one of the best artists working today in the field of "Good Girl Art," rendering superheroines and damsels in distress in the manner of legendary pinup artists Alberto Vargas, George Petty, and Gil Elvgren. A New Jersey native, he started in comics at the age of nineteen on *The Maze Agency* for Comico, followed by Dark Horse's *Ghost* and Image's *Gen[13]*, for which he served as both artist and writer. His career with DC began with *Justice League America* in 1989, but he earned widespread recognition for his four-year run as the cover artist of *Wonder Woman*. Hughes has since become a specialist at covers, and he handles penciling, inking, and coloring while employing a mix of traditional and digital techniques. Hughes designed several characters for the *Star Wars* Roleplaying Game from Wizards of the Coast, and contributed a cover for Dark Horse's *Star Wars Legacy* depicting Luke Skywalker. His covers, including those he produced for DC's *Catwoman*, have been collected in the 2010 book *Cover Run: The DC Comics Art of Adam Hughes*. *143*

Robert Hunt received a bachelor's degree in art history from the University of California and a master's degree in illustration from the Academy of Art in San Francisco. He has created numerous editorial illustrations, book covers, and special design projects in his career, including the famous "boy in the moon" logo for Dreamworks SKG. Hunt has also created advertisements, packaging, motion logos, and documentary projects focused on the Tour de France and the Bay Bridge earthquake reconstruction. Among Hunt's clients are FedEx, the Detroit Pistons, and the American Red Cross, and his work has appeared in *Rolling Stone*, *Scientific American*, and the *Wall Street Journal*. Hunt's art has been featured in the New York Society of Illustrator's exhibits at the Museum of American Illustration and in outlets such as *American Illustration*. As an associate professor at the California College of the Arts, Hunt teaches illustration and painting. *84*

Rob Jones is a designer and graphic artist who got his first big break after sending his unsolicited poster design to the White Stripes. The band, impressed with his work, offered to use Jones's artwork to promote the remainder of their American tour dates. Jones entered into collaboration with Jack White that led to further projects, including posters for White's band The Dead Weather and a series of posters for another White project, The Raconteurs, that resembled the lobby cards from a fictional Japanese movie. Other work by Jones has included posters commissioned for Tarantino Fest and his Darth Vader print "King's Lead Hat" produced in association with Mondo. In 2011, Jones won a Grammy for his work on the White Stripes' box set *Under Great White Northern Lights* and accepted the award while wearing a custom pink leather suit. *141*

Tom Jung grew up in Boston and attended the School of the Museum of Fine Arts until he was drafted by the U.S. Army. After his discharge Jung started as a freelance illustrator working for several New York ad agencies, and eventually broke into the field of movie marketing in 1958. Assigned the job of redesigning posters and press kits of foreign films for American audiences, Jung captured the essences of classics such as Fellini's *La Strada*. After taking a role as an art director with MGM, Jung designed famous film posters for *Doctor Zhivago*, *Ice Station Zebra*, the 1966 rerelease of *Gone with the Wind*, and the infamous sci-fi flick *Plan 9 from Outer Space*. As his career took off Jung produced more classic movie imagery, including the *Star Wars* Style "A" one-sheet and striking posters for *Papillion*, *The Empire Strikes Back*, and the 1978 animated version of *The Lord of the Rings*. *2, 4–5, 19, 22–23, 25, 46–47, 50, 51, 52–53, 54, 62, 63, 64–65, 70, 72, 73, 74, 89, 90*

Roger Kastel is a native of White Plains, New York, who began his art career by studying at the famed Art Students League while still in high school. After serving in the Navy during the Korean War, Kastel became a professional artist for New York studios and ad agencies. Kastel's first illustrated paperback cover appeared in the 1960s, and by the 1970s he hit his full stride as an artist. After working for every major publishing house in New York, he illustrated the paperback cover for Peter Benchley's bestselling book *Jaws*. Kastel painted the style "A" poster for *The Empire Strikes Back* in 1980, and his work has been recognized in the prestigious books *200 Years of American Illustration* and *The Illustrator in America*. A longtime member of the Society of Illustrators, Kastel is also a member of the Artists Fellowship, the Kent Art Association, and the Portrait Society. He is currently active in the field of fine art and portraiture. *9, 57, 58, 59, 60–61, 174*

Rich Kelly is an illustrator and artist in Chicago. Before he started designing band posters, Kelly geared his portfolio toward editorial illustration. His prints examine the subject matter present in his commercial projects, including the historical narratives surrounding explorers and those who have pushed the limits of the human body and scientific understanding. With his editorial roots, Kelly tries to create a narrative for the viewer to interpret whether the subjects are real or fictional. Kelly's print "Attack Position" depicts Chewbacca versus the Empire in a dynamic composition inspired by *Return of the Jedi*. Each of Kelly's paintings begins with a detailed drawing, followed by a painting process he describes as relinquishing some degree of control to let the paint do its job. *149, 150–51*

Dave Kinsey was born in Pittsburgh in 1971 and attended the Art Institute of Pittsburgh and Atlanta. He moved to California in 1994 to pursue a career as a designer and fine artist. Through his art, Kinsey attempts to capture the essence of the human condition through a symbolic portrayal of contemporary life. Using a range of mediums, Kinsey constructs multilayered, textured environments designed around complexity. His art has been shown in galleries and museums worldwide, and has been featured in the *New York Times*, the *Washington Post*, and *Hypebeast*. In 1997 Kinsey founded the design studio BLK/MRKT, attracting clients including Nike, Apple, and DC Shoes. The studio expanded in 2001, adding a fine art gallery and a BLK/MRKT Editions art series, and recently launched its own clothing and lifestyle brand, BLK/MRKT Original. In 2012, Kinsey was selected as the thirty-third annual artist in the esteemed Kenwood Vineyards Artist Series, and earned a spot in an international Absolut artist campaign to design a signature Absolut Vodka bottle. *129*

Mike Kungl completed art and design school to embark on a successful advertising career, spending nearly two decades creating award-winning logos, package designs, and illustrations for companies such as Panasonic, Johnson & Johnson, Toshiba, and Nissan Motors. After choosing to focus on art full-time, the California-based Kungl saw success on one coast spark recognition on another when he was selected to create the official artwork for Miami Beach's twenty-fifth annual Art Deco Weekend. The Miami honor was just one of many, in a succession of developments that highlighted Kungl's growing reputation as a recognized collectible artist. In addition to strong sales of his images in the United States, Kungl's art has risen in popularity throughout Europe, Japan, and Australia. His artworks have been featured in magazine articles, how-to books, and television shows. Kungl currently works in his Southern California studio, creating high-quality gift and home decor products under the M. Kungl Studios name. *155*

Ellen Lee, a veteran of both Pixar Animation Studios and Lucasfilm, studied product design at Stanford University and industrial design at the Pratt Institute. During nearly twelve years as a designer for Pixar, she contributed to productions such as *Finding Nemo*, *The Incredibles*, and *Ratatouille*. Lee also worked as a concept model maker and advertising art director at Lucasfilm. During the prerelease period of *Star Wars*: Episode I, Lee collaborated with Lucasfilm director of marketing Jim Ward and advertising firm New Wave Creative to create the teaser poster campaign for the highly anticipated movie. Her design, "The Shadow of Vader," relied on subtle symbolism and featured Jake Lloyd as young Anakin Skywalker amid the desert landscape of Tatooine. On closer inspection Anakin's shadow casts the ominous and familiar silhouette of Darth Vader's helmet and cape. The poster appeared in theaters on November 10, 1998, ten days before the first trailer welcomed fans back to the galaxy far, far away. *107, 108–09*

David McMacken was born and raised in the Pacific Northwest before moving to Los Angeles. He majored in advertising illustration at the Art Center College of Design and graduated in 1967, gaining a unique perspective on design and commercial iconography. McMacken formed the Institute for Better Vision, an L.A.-based design studio, to specialize in record album design and other projects for the music and entertainment industries. His clients included Capitol Records, Warner Bros., Columbia, Motown, and Bizarre Records. McMacken's painting of the cover for Frank Zappa's album *200 Motels* proved to be a pivotal event in his life, and he continued to illustrate influential album releases, including Zappa's *Over-Nite Sensation*, Weather Report's *Black Market*, AC/DC's *Ballbreaker*, and Kansas's *Leftoverture*. McMacken has also worked in animation for Murakami Wolf Swenson on releases such as *Puff the Magic Dragon* and *The Mouse and His Child*. He lives in Astoria, Oregon. *115*

Ralph McQuarrie, born in Indiana in 1929, was a legend in the field of conceptual illustration. McQuarrie produced concept paintings for *E.T. the Extra-Terrestrial*, the original *Battlestar Galactica* television series, all three films in the classic *Star Wars* trilogy, and the movie *Cocoon*, for which he won an Academy Award for Visual Effects. Prior to his career in film production, McQuarrie worked as a technical illustrator at Boeing. After partnering with young filmmaker George Lucas, he painted scenes from Lucas's script that were impressive enough to convince a skeptical studio to bankroll the film. In doing so he designed some of the most iconic characters in movie history, including C-3PO, R2-D2, and Darth Vader. McQuarrie's paintings have been reproduced as collectible posters and prints, and his original artworks have appeared in museum exhibitions, including the wildly popular touring show *Star Wars: The Magic of Myth*. He passed away in 2012. *13, 14, 44, 45, 78, 79*

Olly Moss, born in 1987, is a London-based artist, graphic designer, and illustrator who graduated from the University of Birmingham in 2008 with a degree in English literature. After earning notice for his striking T-shirt designs for Threadless.com, Moss garnered a reputation as a reinventor of pop-cultural icons through his minimalist interpretations of movie posters such as *The Deer Hunter* and Charlie Chaplin's *The Great Dictator*. Moss was commissioned by Marvel Studios to create a poster for their 2011 release *Thor*, and other memorable projects by Moss include the cover artwork for the video game *Resistance 3* and work for clients including the *New York Times*, *Computer Arts* magazine, Apple, Nike, and Urban Outfitters. In

September 2013, Moss joined with former Telltale Games employees to found the video game studio Campo Santo. *130, 131, 132*

Del Nichols was born in Evansville, Indiana, in 1926. During World War II he served in the U.S. Army Air Force as a B-24 aerial nose gunner in the Pacific theater. After the war Nichols graduated from Nashville's Harris School of Art and Design. As a commercial artist he produced pieces for clients including General Motors and the magazines *Redbook* and *Good Housekeeping*. Contracted to work on a promotional project for Coca-Cola, Nichols designed a series of *Star Wars* posters to be distributed at Burger King restaurants during 1978. The posters became a phenomenon in themselves, and are highly sought after by collectors today. In his later career Nichols turned to fine art and exhibited his works at galleries across the country. He died in 2013 in Marietta, Georgia. *40, 41, 43*

Noriyoshi Ohrai has been producing artwork for films and books for almost fifty years. Born in 1935 in Akashi City Hyogo Prefecture, Ohrai dropped out of Tokyo National University of Fine Arts and Music in 1957. Beginning in 1962, he began illustrating manga and editing newspaper advertisements. In 1973 he set up his own studio in Miyazaki, his wife's hometown. Ohrai's poster for *The Empire Strikes Back* won him the Seiun Best Artist Award at the Japanese SF convention, and in 1981 Ohrai held his first exhibition as an artist at Miyazaki's Aoki Gallery. Following his popular poster for the 1985 release *The Goonies*, Ohrai produced works in a variety of media, including commercial posters, records, game software, and plastic model kits. In 2014 Miyazaki Art Center held an exhibit of more than 1,000 pieces of his work—including 300 original drawings and rough sketches—marking the first time such an extensive display could be viewed in one place. *36–37, 39, 49, 67, 68–69, 71, 91*

Michelangelo Papuzza was an Italian commercial artist who produced some memorable designs for movie posters used in Italian and international releases. For the 1969 rerelease of Clint Eastwood's *A Fistful of Dollars*, Papuzza captured the rough-hewn star in all his Old West glory. For the 1977 Italian release of *Star Wars*, Papuzza captured the cast in a colorful pose that conveyed the feel of paperback pulp novels. Other movie poster designs by Papuzza include *Justine*, the 1969 George Cukor thriller released in Italy under the name *Rapporto a quattro*. *35*

Dave Perillo was born in 1974, the same year Wham-O introduced the Slip 'N Slide—an event he refuses to dismiss as mere coincidence. In the first grade, Perillo created an autobiographical "Me Book," in which he laid down his ambition to become the comic strip character Ziggy when he grew up. He abandoned his dream after realizing Ziggy was not real, was completely bald, and didn't wear pants. Instead, Perillo fell back on his second-choice career path and pursued a career in art. Perillo draws inspiration for his work from a grab bag of resonant pop-cultural sources, including 1950s sci-fi B movies, the animated cartoons of Hanna-Barbera, *The Twilight Zone*, and famous advertising icons, as well as figures such as director Alfred Hitchcock, *Peanuts* cartoonist Charles Schulz, album cover illustrator Jim Flora, special effects pioneer Ray Harryhausen, pop artist Roy Lichtenstein, and puppeteer Jim Henson. Perillo, who currently lives in suburban Philadelphia, believes that bowling is the sport of kings and that a bag of Swedish Fish is a seafood dinner. *134, 135*

Tim Reamer has been a graphic designer and illustrator for San Diego Zoo Global for more than thirty years while simultaneously enjoying a vibrant freelance career. Inspired by his childhood collection of Golden Age comic books, he credits comics and science fiction with inspiring his imagination despite the public perception that they were subjects not worthy of serious discussion. Reamer produced the original style "A" poster for *Return of the Jedi*, an airbrushed illustration showing only Luke Skywalker's hands clasped around the handle of a lightsaber. Among Reamer's other projects is a public sculpture that stands on the sand in the coastal community of Ocean Beach, California. Reamer began attending San Diego Comic-Con in 1972 and has maintained his regular annual attendance ever since. *83*

Brian Rood is a professional illustrator who works in the entertainment, comic, and commercial art fields. He is known for his photo-realistic paintings of Hollywood stars and characters, and his client list includes Lucasfilm, Hasbro, Disney, Paramount Pictures, Sony Pictures, EA Games, Topps, and Marvel Comics. Rood has produced exclusive estate artwork for renowned pop-cultural figures such as Ray Charles, Muhammad Ali, Sammy Davis Jr., Frank Sinatra, Richard Pryor, and other great entertainers of the twentieth century. His *Star Wars* contributions include more than one hundred illustrations for use on Hasbro's toy packaging, as well as a watercolor painting of Yoda selected to appear in the *Star Wars* Blu-ray release. "Working on *Star Wars* is really a dream come true," Rood has said. "There are so many creative avenues you can take, that the ideas for new paintings are nearly endless." *172–73*

Mike Sadd is a freelance designer based in Bristol who specializes in video post-production and motion design. Sadd graduated with a degree in graphic design from University College Falmouth and studied design and illustration at University of the West of England. Formerly a senior designer with Fixel, Sadd gained expertise in storyboarding and animation, working with designers and agencies including BDH, Rubberductions, Swift Films, and HarperCollins. He enjoys fine art illustration and photography. *118*

Tsuneo Sanda was born in Osaka, Japan, and discovered a love of art as a child, when he would draw on the pavement with chalk. He says his early influences include Rembrandt, René Magritte, Paul Davis, and Robert Peak. He spent his early years running his own advertising firm while creating original artwork in his spare time. After winning the top prize in a Japanese science fiction art competition, he came to the attention of *Omni* magazine, which gave him the first of many cover assignments in 1989. He then began concentrating on science fiction themed art, and has produced numerous posters and artworks for *Star Trek* and *Star Wars*. Since 1995, his *Star Wars* work has included book covers, comic book art, and prints for the Celebration conventions and the company's exclusive holiday cards. *142*

Manuel Sanjulián (Manuel Perez Clemente) was born in Barcelona. He studied art at the Belles Arts of San Jordi school. Sanjulián began his work with Selecciones Ilustradas, a prominent European art agency, and his technical abilities and vision made him an instant success in European markets. Sanjulián has worked for the most important publishing houses, advertising agencies, and movie studios in the United States and has won many awards. He has had several shows at the Society of Illustrators. *55*

Kazuhiko Sano was born in 1952 in Tokyo, where he studied oil painting before moving to San Francisco in 1975. He attended the Academy of Art University and majored in illustration, graduating in 1980 with a master of fine arts. Sano's creative output over the subsequent decades ranged from book covers to postage stamps, including scientific illustrations for *National Geographic* and *Scientific American* magazines. His other clients included General Electric, IBM, the American Red Cross, Coca-Cola, United Airlines, and the Walt Disney Company. Sano created *Return of the Jedi*'s style "B" poster, and illustrated the U.S. Postal Service's commemorative Frank Sinatra stamp in 2008. Retrospective shows that toured Japan enabled the publication of his first book, *Retrospective 1980–2000: The Art of Kazuhiko Sano*. Other exhibits of Sano's artworks have been held in 1992 at the Central Museum in Tokyo and in 1996 at the American Museum of Illustration in New York City. In 1986 Sano returned to the Academy of Art University in San Francisco to accept a teaching position, a role he continued to play until his death in 2011. *85, 86–87, 96*

Robert Silvers, born in 1968, is the inventor of the now-iconic Photomosaic process, a technique he developed in 1995 while still a student at MIT. Silvers's ubiquitous Photomosaics portray familiar images throughout history and contemporary culture by offering a unique optical perspective that encourages close viewing. His works have gained acclaim and found their way into art collections held by Coca-Cola, CNN, Disney, IBM, National Geographic, and more. Senator Barry Goldwater and Vice President Al Gore are among those who have commissioned Photomosaic portraits, and *Premiere* magazine named the Photomosaic poster for *The Truman Show* one of the top fifty movie posters of all time. Exhibitions of Silvers's work have been held at London's National Portrait Gallery and in numerous cities worldwide. Silvers lives outside Boston, Massachusetts. *111, 112–13*

Wojtek Siudmak, born in 1942 in Wieluń, Poland, moved to France in 1966. He earned fame as an illustrator of science fiction and fantasy literature, including his work on the covers of the Polish edition of Frank Herbert's *Dune* series. Siudmak's fantastic style incorporates elements of surrealism with imaginary constructions that rely on the power of dreams. His works have been distributed worldwide and have been used on posters to promote movie releases, theater showings, and museum exhibitions. Siudmak's work has also been found at the Cannes Film Festival, the Festival International du Film Fantastique et de Science-Fiction, the Marais Festival in Paris, and the Festival of Films of the World in Montreal. His *Star Wars* poster featured a nearly photo-realistic rendition of Obi-Wan Kenobi, though his Leia proved considerably more statuesque and his Luke substantially more muscular than the actual movie characters. In 1998, a cycle of exhibitions featuring Siudmak's work toured the museums of five major Polish cities and concluded at the National Museum in Warsaw. *34*

Todd Slater operates out of a converted garage studio on the outskirts of Austin, Texas, as prolific as he is piercingly inventive. In less than a decade since graduating from art school, he has created hundreds of dazzling posters featuring the music industry's hottest acts, including the Black Keys, Jack White, the Avett Brothers, and Muse. Slater began making posters in 2003 and by 2004 was in heavy rotation with venues and bands across the country. By 2005 he had exploded onto the poster scene with hits like his designs for Velvet Revolver, Arcade Fire, and Interpol. Slater draws his inspiration directly from each artist's music, translating their sounds into gut graphical instincts, and has an acute sense for the vibes that drive color selection and design schemes. His use of black varnishes and metallic inks is considered one of his specialties. *138–39*

John Solie attended the University of Wisconsin at La Crosse and graduated from the Los Angeles Art Center. In a commercial illustration career spanning more than forty years, he has spent much of his time painting portraits, sculpting famous people, and producing more than 200 movie posters, including those for *Ryan's Daughter* and *Soylent Green*. Solie's work has appeared in magazines such as *Reader's Digest*, *TV Guide*, and *People*, and he has painted more than 175 book covers. Solie's bronze sculpture of Walter Cronkite, commissioned by CBS, is now displayed in the lobby of the CBS building in New York City, and many of his other paintings hang at the Kennedy Space Center and the Johnson Space Center. Solie and his wife relocated to Seal Rock on the Oregon coast, where he painted and sculpted in a three-story barn-shaped studio called "Wind Rush." He later moved to Tucson, Arizona. *18, 20–21*

Mark Steele claims that not many people can be blessed with abundant talent, and therefore neither can he. However, Steele is one of only a handful of people on the planet to have made the transition from lawyer to *Star Wars* artist. Steele's love of portraiture, combined with his passion for 1950s B movies, made him the ideal artist to work on a series of limited-edition prints for Acme Archives, including the vivid "Revenge of the Sandpeople" and "Lair of the Rancor," done in collaboration with artist Mark Daniels. Steele gained inspiration for the lurid art style from the work of Basil Gogos, and set out to replicate the vivid, pulpy feel of the best posters from the heyday of the horror genre. When it comes to *Star Wars*, Steele says, "It's got spaceships, robots, and Princess Leia—what's not to love?" *156, 157*

Frank Stockton hails from Santa Ana, California, and graduated from the Art Center College of Design in Pasadena in 2005. After moving to New York City, he pursued a career in illustration, and since then Stockton's work has appeared in outlets such as *Esquire*, the *New York Times*, and *The New Yorker*, as well as on comic book covers including *Ultimates: Iron Man* and IDW's *The Last Unicorn*. In 2007 he contributed as a featured artist to Ashley Wood's *Swallow* Vol. 3, and 2010 saw him nominated for an Eisner Award in the category of Best Short Story for "Hamburgers for One," which he wrote and illustrated. In 2012, Stockton received a Silver Medal for Editorial Illustration from the Society of Illustrators in New York. The same year, he decided to shift his focus from illustration to painting, and enrolled in UCLA's MFA program. *140*

Tyler Stout hails from Brush Prairie, Washington, and produces screen-printed posters for bands and movies. Often commissioned by the Alamo Drafthouse in Austin, Stout has complete creative freedom and has been able to make posters his primary professional outlet while doing some freelance illustration and design work. Stout produced the theatrical poster for the 2008 movie *Hell Ride*, and has designed for mediums as diverse as shirts and snowboards. His artistic inspirations include painters like Drew Struzan and Reynold Brown, and the iconography of exploitation movies has helped fuel his creative engine. *158, 159, 160*

Drew Struzan has achieved unprecedented success in the hundred-year history of motion picture advertising, with more than thirty-nine years of experience and hundreds of movie posters to his credit. After graduating with honors from the prestigious Art Center College of Design in Pasadena, California, Struzan created graphics for album covers at the Los Angeles design studio Pacific Eye & Ear. But it was his partnership in the film design studio Pencil Pushers Inc. that launched his association with the movies. Struzan started on the cult classics *Killer Force*, *Empire of the Ants*, and *Food of the Gods*, and quickly became a sought-after talent for A-list movie releases, including *Star Wars*, *Back to the Future*, *Hook*, and the Indiana Jones trilogy. His work has been displayed in Japan to standing-room-only crowds, and he was the first and only living artist to have a one-man show at the Norman Rockwell Museum in Stockbridge, Massachusetts. Struzan is the subject of the 2010 documentary *Drew: The Man Behind the Poster*. *6, 26, 88, 95, 99, 100, 101, 102, 103, 104, 105, 116*

Steve Thomas created graphics and illustrations for newspapers for fourteen years before becoming a freelance illustrator. With experience in every section of the newspaper from Life & Entertainment to Sports, Thomas tries to come up with interesting yet familiar illustration ideas. His love for vintage propaganda and product art from the early twentieth century, combined with his interest in retro-futuristic design, has driven many of his most popular designs. As he puts it, "Who doesn't want to travel the solar system, or join the fight against the villains of 1980s arcade games?" Thomas's experience also extends into marketing and advertising art for companies from label expo organizers to architecture firms. Since he began creating limited-edition prints and posters, Thomas has created artworks for licenses including *Star Wars*, Disney, *Star Trek*, Marvel, and the Muppets. *164, 165, 167*

Boris Vallejo was born in Lima, Peru, in 1941 and attended Escuela Nacional de Bellas Artes on an art scholarship. In 1964, with only a few dollars in his wallet and no fluency in English, he put together a portfolio and immigrated to the United States. Vallejo found work as an advertising illustrator in New York until deciding to go freelance, turning out comics pages for Marvel and Warren Publishing as well as painted book covers for various publishing houses. Through these efforts Vallejo earned fame for his mastery of the human form, and soon his vibrant paintings became familiar sights on the covers of *Tarzan*, *Doc Savage*, and *Conan* paperbacks and in the pages of the iconic magazine *Heavy Metal*. Vallejo's movie poster designs include 1968's *Barbarella* and 1983's *National Lampoon's Vacation*. Internationally recognized as a master of fantasy art and erotica, Vallejo has extended into nearly every medium with his paintings of heroic barbarians and bizarre alien creatures on trading cards, in calendars, and realized as three-dimensional sculptures. *75, 76–77*

Tom Whalen was raised by feral robot wolves in the backwoods of northeastern Pennsylvania, nourished on a steady diet of comic books, Arnold Schwarzenegger movies, and Swedish fish. Infatuated with all things giant, Japanese, and city-destroying, Whalen is a confessed monster junkie who cannot wait for the earth to be overrun by zombies or vampires. He fell in love with comic books after encountering them as a child in his grandmother's candy store, studying the artwork in *G.I. Joe*, *The Transformers*, and *The Official Handbook of the Marvel Universe* and trying to reproduce their colorful heroes and villains. His appetite for drawing led him to Kutztown University in Pennsylvania to study illustration, typography, and design. His "modern vintage" style is the product of his passion for pop culture, and he feels blessed to be able to express that passion through illustration. *146–47*

Charles White III was born in Southern California and attended the Art Center College of Design in Los Angeles, and his subsequent career as an illustrator has spanned more than three decades. In 1967, White moved with his family to New York City and began experimenting with a range of artistic mediums, developing an airbrushing technique that changed the face of his art. Returning to L.A. in 1976, White launched a clothing line and took on an array of clients including Levi's, *National Lampoon*, Harley-Davidson, and the Rolling Stones. Among White's movie poster designs are *Nashville*, *Star Wars*, and *The Rocky Horror Picture Show*. Roman Coppola's 2012 film *A Glimpse Inside the Mind of Charles Swan III* featured events based on White's life, with the title role played by Charlie Sheen and sets designed after White's 1970s art. Now based in Venice, California, White is still creating every day. *26*

FOR LUCASFILM LTD.

Executive Editor J. W. Rinzler
Art Director Troy Alders
Image Archives Tina Mills and Stacey Leong
Director of Publishing Carol Roeder

FOR ABRAMS

Editor Eric Klopfer
Project Manager Daniel Wallace
Designer Liam Flanagan
Production Manager True Sims

Library of Congress Control Number: 2014930736
ISBN: 978-1-4197-1400-9

Artwork for Star Wars: Identities posters courtesy of Bleublancrouge for X3 Productions
Artistic Director: Gaetan Namouric with Jean-François Leblanc and Sébastien Maheux

Artworks on pages 2, 15, and 16 courtesy of David Mandel.

CASE FRONT
Tom Jung
Black-and-white concept treatment for *Star Wars* style "A" theatrical one-sheet, 1977

CASE BACK
Robert Hunt
Black-and-white concept treatment for *Return of the Jedi* style "B" theatrical one-sheet, 1982

Printed in China
10 9 8 7 6 5

Abrams books are available at special discounts when purchased in quantity for premiums and promotions as well as fundraising or educational use. Special editions can also be created to specification. For details, contact specialsales@abramsbooks.com or the address below.

ABRAMS
THE ART OF BOOKS SINCE 1949
115 West 18th Street
New York, NY 10011
www.abramsbooks.com

ACKNOWLEDGMENTS
Lucasfilm would like to thank Laela French, Marco Crescenti, Matt Shell, Hez Chorba, Pablo Hidalgo, Chris Argyropoulos, Christopher Holm, Connie Wethington . . . and Mr. George Lucas.

Special thanks to Steve Sansweet and Pete Vilmur. Some information in this book comes from *The Star Wars Poster Book* (Chronicle Books, 2005).